SOJOURNER IN THE PROMISED LAND

*S*ojourner
in the
*P*romised Land

FORTY YEARS AMONG
THE MORMONS

Jan Shipps

University of Illinois Press
Urbana and Chicago

Library of Congress Cataloging-in-Publication Data
Shipps, Jan, 1929–
Sojourner in the promised land : forty years among the Mormons / Jan Shipps.
p.   cm.
Includes bibliographical references and index.
ISBN 0-252-02590-3 (alk. paper)
1. Mormon Church—History.
2. Mormon Church—Study and teaching—History.
3. Shipps, Jan, 1929– .
I. Title.
BX8611.S493   2000
289.3'09—dc21   00-008491

C 5 4 3 2 1

For Stephen, Teri, Lindsay, and Lorin Shipps

CONTENTS

ACKNOWLEDGMENTS

This is not a typical collection of essays, although it started out that way when Liz Dulany, my longtime friend and valued colleague, encouraged me to pull this work together. Like so many historians of Mormonism, I owe a debt of gratitude that can never be fully repaid to this esteemed member of the staff of the University of Illinois Press, who is primarily responsible for the press's exceptional Mormon list. I nevertheless take this opportunity to say that for this—and for much else—I am extremely grateful to Liz for her friendship and her invaluable advice and assistance.

The reference staff at the Indiana University Library in Bloomington has been unfailingly helpful to me for many years as I have gone about my research on Mormonism. Nancy Cridland, during her distinguished career as the university's librarian for history and religion from 1967 to 1998, was especially helpful, seeing to the purchase of virtually everything in print about the Mormons and adding many out-of-print works to the library's existing cache of Mormoniana, a collection that includes a surprising number of volumes purchased in the nineteenth century. As a result, the time I have spent in the university library in Bloomington has been almost as fruitful as the time spent in libraries in the Intermountain West.

When I traveled to Utah in the summer of 1964 to begin research for my doctoral dissertation, I sought advice from Everett L. Cooley, the director of the Utah State Historical Society who, while a visiting professor in the history department at Utah State University during the 1960–61 academic year, introduced me to the study of the Mormon past. Although he was willing to serve as a mentor from long distance while I worked on my M.A. thesis, Dr. Cooley warned me that it would be a mistake to continue trying to write about the Saints from afar. He said I would need to get used to traveling to the libraries and archives where LDS records are held. Keeping that warning in mind, I have made much use of Utah archival resources. For the material in this book, I particularly used the Archives of the Church of Jesus Christ of Latter-day Saints in Salt Lake City and the Special Collections at the Marriott Library at the University of Utah.

It pleases me that I am able to express publicly my gratitude to staff members in the Historical Department Church Library located in the LDS Church Office Building in Salt Lake City. They have all been friendly and courteous to me on the many occasions when I have sought assistance. In particular, Mary Gifford and Veneese Nelson have been consistently obliging in responding to queries of every sort, both on-site and when, stymied by lack of access to information in church publications or in fugitive materials I remembered seeing in the church library, I have called with queries from my office in Indianapolis or my study in Bloomington.

For all that, doing what I have done in the area of Mormon history would have been impossible without the encouragement and support of the LDS History Division and the staff of the Reading Room of the LDS Church Archives. It seems especially appropriate to express here my gratitude to the late Leonard J. Arrington, who, as church historian, was primarily responsible for my being awarded one of the 1974 summer fellowships made available on a competitive basis to scholars who would travel to Salt Lake City to work in the LDS Church Archives. The summer stint of more or less total immersion in the archival sources that this fellowship allowed, plus Arrington's prompting me to examine more closely the beginnings of his faith, led, in time, not only to my interpretation of Mormonism as a new religious tradition but also to much of the work included in this volume, including the "layering" analysis that stands at the heart of "Joseph Smith and the Creation of LDS Theology" and "Difference and Otherness: Mormonism and the American Religious Mainstream."

When Richard E. Turley became managing director of the church's Historical Department, he also extended assistance and support, as have virtually all the longtime members of the Reading Room staff, especially Ron Barney, Randy Dixon, Linda Haslam, Bill Slaughter, Steven R. Sorenson, and Ron Watt. Whenever I have worked in the archives, Gordon Irving, who, from its initial operation, headed up the church's exemplary James Moyle Oral History Program, has always welcomed me and been helpful.

Early on, my work was greatly aided by Dr. Cooley (who became the head of the Special Collections Division at the University of Utah's Marriott Library) and by the members of his staff. More recently, Gregory C. Thompson, head of the Special Collections Division, and Stan Larson, a staff member, have pointed me to important materials and scholars who might be of assistance. By making special arrangements for supervision that made it possible for me to use archival material in the evenings, first Dr. Cooley and afterward Dr. Thompson allowed me to expand my actual research time in Utah. In so doing, they have made it possible for me almost to double what I could accomplish during research trips.

In my study of American perceptions of and attitudes toward the Mormons, I am indebted to many people. The late Eugene Levitt was generous with his time and expertise in helping me with the research design; Thomas G. Alexander was very helpful in participating with me in a pretest of the research protocol; Margaret Loomis assisted with the development of the research sample; Sandra Davidson provided the technical assistance that made possible analysis of data I gathered to use as the basis for a paper presented to the Organization of American Historians; and Edward J. Stephenson did some secondary analysis and redrew the tables for publication here. I am happy to have this opportunity to express my appreciation to all of them.

Many people read and made helpful comments on one or more of the essays or sections of this book, including Douglas D. Alder, Thomas G. Alexander, Philip Amerson, Leonard J. Arrington, Davis Bitton, David J. Bodenhamer, Kathleen Flake, Ralph D. Gray, Klaus J. Hansen, Walter Nugent, Elbert Peck, Amanda Porterfield, Martin Ridge, Mac Rohrbough, Jonathan Sarna, Rowland A. Sherrill, Peggy Fletcher Stack, and John W. Welch. Lavina Fielding Anderson, Philip L. Barlow, and Mark Silk read an early version of the manuscript and made valuable suggestions.

Besides Liz Dulany, I owe special thanks to two members of the staff of the University of Illinois Press: Terry Sears, the managing editor; and Jane Mohraz, an associate editor. Jane, who worked with me to prepare the manuscript, was particularly patient and extremely helpful. My husband, Tony Shipps, read every word. His corrections and suggestions for improvement made this a much better and more readable book. While I owe much to him and to the host of other scholars who have been of assistance during my many years of studying the Latter-day Saints, I alone am responsible for the content and interpretation in this volume.

Much of the material seeing print for the first time in this book was originally written on the state-of-the-art IBM Selectric typewriter my mother gave me to celebrate my appointment to a tenure-track position on a university faculty, a wonderful machine that I nearly wore out before making the change to a desktop computer. In addition to this typewritten material that had to be scanned and adapted to make it readable, several of my articles that have been previously published also needed to be scanned and the resulting texts modified since they appeared in a variety of formats and type styles. Joy Kramer, a longtime friend who is a super support staff person in the School of Liberal Arts' computer lab at Indiana University–Purdue University, Indianapolis, is responsible for creating the digitized text that served as the preliminary manuscript from which I worked to shape this book. Without her help, its various essays would likely still be scattered through my (alas) untidy files. Working with scrupulous care, Joy also turned figures into clip-art that had initially been drawn on graph paper by hand. This facilitated their redrawing with a sophisticated computer program for insertion in the manuscript.

On a more personal note, if this had been a full-scale autobiography, much would have been included in it about our extraordinary son and his wonderful family, to whom this work is dedicated. But except for our year in Logan, where he negotiated second grade, and his playing an unaccompanied Bach violin sonata in the Kirtland Temple during a powerful early morning worship service that brought the 1976 annual meeting of the Mormon History Association to a close, Stephen has only observed my life among the Mormons from afar. As he and the members of his family read these pages, they will doubtless discover much about me and my Zionic sojourn that they have never known.

Finally, appreciation, as always, goes to Tony, my cherished companion of a half-century. He puts up with and rarely complains about a wife whose attention is apportioned among her work, his work, and our life together. For this relief, much thanks.

I have been given permission to use the following materials from copyrighted works: "Currents," from *American History Illustrated* (January 1982), © 1982 the National Historical Society, 2245 Kohn Road, Harrisburg, PA 17110; "Joseph Smith (1805–1844)" and "Mormonism after the Death of Joseph Smith," from *Makers of Christian Theology in America,* edited by Mark Toulouse and James O. Duke, © 1997 by Abingdon Press; "The Scattering of the Gathered and the Gathering of the Scattered," from the Juanita Brooks Lecture Series, © 1991 by Dixie College; "Brigham Young and His Times: A Continuing Force in Mormonism," from *Journal of the West,* © 1984 by Journal of the West, Inc., 1531 Yuma, Manhattan, KS 66505-1009; "Remembering, Recovering and Inventing What Being the People of God Means: Reflections on Method in the Scholarly Writing of Denominational History," from *Reimagining Denominationalism: Interpretive Essays,* edited by Robert Bruce

Mullin and Russell Richey, © 1994 by Oxford University Press, Inc.; "Background Books: The Mormons' Progress," from *Wilson Quarterly* (Spring 1991), © the Woodrow Wilson International Center for Scholars, 370 L'Enfant Promenade S.W. Suite 704, Washington, D.C. 20024; and "Submission in Salt Lake," from *Religion in the News* (Fall 1998) © the Leonard E. Greenberg Center for the Study of Religion in Public Life.

PROLOGUE

"That celebrated Mormon-watcher" is how Dallin H. Oaks, an apostle who sits on his church's Council of the Twelve, identified me when he quoted from one of my articles on Mormonism in an address he gave at Brigham Young University in 1988.[1] The "celebrated" part of his description was surely overstated, even if it is true that for years journalists from all over the United States (and outside it as well) have been calling me to ask for a non-Mormon "take" on what is going on whenever a story about the Latter-day Saints makes its way into the news. But Oaks was entirely correct in calling me a "Mormon-watcher." I have been interested in, doing research on, speaking on, and writing about the Latter-day Saints for four decades, ever since 1960, when I moved with my family to Utah and spent nine months completing my undergraduate education at Utah State University in Logan.

Before we left the Midwest to live in Utah, I was already aware that the area where we were headed was populated mainly by Mormons. To my knowledge, however, before we became residents of the Mormon state, I had never actually met a member of the institution whose official name is the Church of Jesus Christ of Latter-day Saints. Moreover, with the exception of knowing that Brigham Young, who had many wives, led his followers to the Intermountain West in the middle of the nineteenth century, I was unfamiliar with Mormon history and Mormonism. I knew nothing at all about Joseph Smith, the first Mormon prophet, whose revelations gave rise to the LDS Church, the Reorganized Church of Jesus Christ of Latter Day Saints, and many other ecclesiastical organizations—most of them quite small—that are part of this tradition. I did not even know that *Mormon* and *Latter-day Saint* were used as synonyms.

Not long after we settled in Cache Valley, we learned that active members of the LDS Church were called Mormons or Latter-day Saints.[2] We quickly

1

discovered that Mormons who signaled their distance from the church by drinking coffee or failing to keep the Word of Wisdom in some more egregious way, such as using tobacco or alcohol, were known as Jack Mormons.[3] Everyone else was Gentile. Everyone. Protestants, Catholics, and those in the category designated as "none" by pollsters who inquire about religious affiliation. Even Jews were Gentile. Not until the early 1970s would I become acquainted with (or learn much about) the non-Utah Saints who dispensed with the hyphen and used an uppercase *D* in spelling Latter Day.[4]

This Saints-Gentile dichotomy was, for me, an entirely new way of dividing up the world. It seemed if not alien, certainly atypical enough to merit examination. My preliminary probing indicated that many of the surface differences I was noticing betokened far more than novel nomenclature. Gaining some understanding of this tradition would not be an easy task, for back then, even more than now, Mormonism was more than a religion—it was a separate culture, a way of life. Finding answers to one set of questions simply led to the posing of other queries, which, when answered, generated even more inquiries. Almost before I realized it and without fully anticipating where my inquisitiveness would lead, I had embarked on what would become a lifelong study of the people who lived in the "kingdom in the tops of the mountains" and their belief structure and peculiar culture. Although my family and I would live in Utah for only nine months, my curiosity, first about Mormon history and later about the manifold dimensions of this singular tradition, has never been fully satisfied.

Between 1961 and 1965, I was in graduate school at the University of Colorado. During those years, I managed to establish a good foundation for moving into Mormon studies. My master's thesis in 1962 and doctoral dissertation in 1965 both dealt with the way in which Latter-day Saints figured in local, state, and national politics.[5] While still in graduate school, I published my first article, "Second-Class Saints," which dealt with the Mormon practice of denying priesthood ordination to black men, a very hot LDS topic in the sixties.[6] My husband, who—in the beginning anyway—did not exactly encourage my growing interest in Mormonism, said that the best thing about this article was its title. I was affronted by his judgment, but I have long since concluded he was right. Similarly, notwithstanding the respectable amount of worthwhile information in my master's thesis and Ph.D. dissertation, I am aware they were written by a historian who was still very much an apprentice. If the things I wrote during graduate school are by no means conspicuous scholarly contributions, they did turn out to be exceptionally useful exercises for me, providing considerable knowledge of the broad sweep of LDS history.

At the annual meeting of the American Historical Association held in San

Francisco in 1965, the year I completed graduate school, a distinguished group of LDS and RLDS scholars and "at least one prominent non-Mormon historian" founded the Mormon History Association (MHA), which became a major force in the emerging movement in which historians, using the tools of their profession, would write new accounts of the Mormon past.[7] I was not at that organizational meeting, but I joined the MHA soon enough to be classified as a charter member, and I have remained an active participant to this day. By virtue of writing about this particular topic at that particular point in time, I became part of the development of what came to be called the "new Mormon history."[8] In time, my interest in (and writing about) the Saints would extend beyond the boundaries of history to the interdisciplinary field of religious studies. Consequently, simply being a modern practitioner of Clio's art was where I started but not where I ended up.

I have made countless trips to Utah to do research and attend professional meetings and other gatherings during the past four decades. Although I never returned to Utah to live and never became a member of one of the churches founded by the Mormon prophet (I remain a lifelong Methodist), many Latter-day Saints are intimate friends, and Mormonism has remained a focus of my scholarship. In time, I started to live as a sojourner in the place that the Saints, even now, call the promised land. Zion became my home away from home.

In 1971, as a part-time instructor in the history department, I taught my first class at Indiana University–Purdue University, Indianapolis (IUPUI). Two years later, when the IUPUI School of Liberal Arts inaugurated the Religious Studies Program, I was offered a full-time faculty position. I accepted this offer, but only after negotiating for a joint appointment in history and religious studies. Since then, besides publishing articles and reviews, writing *Mormonism: The Story of a New Religious Tradition* (1985), and serving as the senior editor for *The Journals of William McLellin, 1831–1836* (1994), I have worked up scores of lectures and papers on Mormon topics that were presented at professional meetings and symposia. Many of these have never been published. As the years passed and word spread that I, a non-Mormon, was concentrating my scholarly attention on the Latter-day Saints, I received (and responded positively to) many requests to write about Mormonism for publications most scholars of Mormonism do not read. As a result, much of what I have written about the Latter-day Saints either has never seen print or else has appeared in somewhat obscure venues or as chapters in books about American religion.[9]

As emeritus professors so often do, when I retired from teaching at the end of the 1994 calendar year, I started getting my files in order. During this (still ongoing) process, I found this book. This is to say, I rediscovered all the papers I had presented at professional meetings, papers I had put aside thinking I would get them ready for publication when I had time. As my days of preparing lectures, grading papers, advising students, serving on faculty committees, administering an academic center, and, perhaps most important, driving fifty-six miles to school in the mornings and fifty-six miles back each night were at an end, that time had clearly come.

Rereading a variety of lectures and conference papers from the array in my files, I started to think about compiling an anthology for publication. It seemed to me that some of these unpublished essays were sufficiently meaty to become a part of such a volume.[10] A second component could be fashioned from my relatively unknown articles and book chapters, materials that, for the most part, had not made their way into the LDS field of vision.[11]

When Liz Dulany at the University of Illinois Press expressed interest, I began to pull together a collection that I started to think about as a "Mormon Miscellany." But when I started editing and rewriting, creating an introduction, and preparing headnotes, an unanticipated third component of this work manifested itself, a component that pushed me into turning what would have been an ordinary book of collected essays into a much more substantial and coherent work.

Here is what happened. From among the unpublished materials, I selected the following: "Gentiles, Mormons, and the History of the American West"; "From Satyr to Saint: American Perceptions of the Mormons, 1860–1960"; "Surveying the Mormon Image since 1960"; "From Gentile to Non-Mormon: Mormon Perceptions of the Other"; and "Thoughts about the Academic Community's Response to John Brooke's *Refiner's Fire.*" Then, to flesh out the ideas in those papers (as well as to make a book of respectable length and scholarly heft), I added book chapters plus essays and articles, most of which were originally published in places other than the standard Mormon periodicals (*BYU Studies; Dialogue: A Journal of Mormon Thought; Exponent II;* the *Journal of Mormon History; Sunstone;* and *Utah Historical Quarterly*). Having made my selections, I started to prepare them for the press. As I began to revise and sometimes considerably expand things I had written throughout the years, and especially as I organized them into topical sections, I began to reflect on my itinerancy in a world that is not my own.

Hardly realizing what I was undertaking, I started to incorporate those reflections as part of the construction of the manuscript, surrounding my professional writings about the Saints with an ongoing personal description of what, during these past four decades, has been an amazing cognitive encounter with a form of otherness that from beginning to end has, to me, been both familiar and strange. As I did so, I realized that this work I had been thinking about as a typical retrospective collection was turning into something that does not fit into that conventional academic genre.

Instead, I was blurring genres by encircling my articles, essays, and book chapters with the sort of reportage and reminiscence that, in earlier days, might have ended up in one of many books or articles chronicling journalists' and travelers' observations of Mormons and Mormonism.[12] The subtitle of this volume acknowledges this similarity, but a key difference separates my commentary from those of the many journalists and other observers who concentrated on the foreground, on particular Mormon people they met, places they visited where Saints resided, and their interactions with members of the LDS community. In nearly all such writing, Mormonism itself is treated as static, as a panoramic religious background as fixed in structure and belief as most people seem to think medieval Roman Catholicism was. Almost as soon as I began describing my life among the Mormons, I started recognizing the extent to which Mormonism is not now and has never been a fixed tableau. Any proper recounting of what has happened to me during the past forty years necessarily requires a description of what, for the same four decades, has been happening in the Church of Jesus Christ of Latter-day Saints and the dynamic religious system of which it is the main institutional expression.

In describing to myself and others what I was doing (and why this seemingly simple project was taking so long), at first I said I was combining intellectual autobiography with things I had written at various points across several decades. This, I reasoned, might be useful for it would explain to the reader where I stood in the process of becoming acquainted with Mormonism's otherness as I penned the essays and articles that would become chapters in this book. But after I finished—or thought I had finished—I reviewed the entire manuscript and discovered I had been doing something more. The collected essays and articles are tied together with the autobiographical matter to form a rough narrative that recounts Mormonism's movement from one state of affairs to another. As my own experience as a historian of Mormonism is a part of this transition, I was no longer merely an outside observer. The larger story of a dramatic modulation in the corporate experience of the Mormon tradition that I have been observing all these years is reflected in what happened to me and how I wrote about the various dimensions of the Mormon experience.

In much the same manner that my 1985 study of Mormonism dealt with process as I analyzed significant changes in an earlier period of Mormonism, so this book of essays and commentary describes an equally significant developmental process in the life sequence of a lived religious tradition. In its particulars, the history in these pages is unique to Mormonism. But as a history of movement from insularity to universality, which is one of the key things traced in many of these chapters, the process I describe is one the world's other great religions have all experienced in some form or other.

There is one significant difference. For my 1985 book, I had to discover and refine earlier parts of this tradition's story using the traditional tools of history and the interpretive strategies of religious studies. This time, I did not have to retrieve the story in its entirety from the historical record. Much of it occurred before my very eyes.

Since readers would need to be alerted to the presence in these pages of a description of process, I decided to turn what had been a more or less standard introduction to an essay collection into this extended personal prologue. I have also fashioned an epilogue in which I have reviewed my own story and have provided a summary analysis of how Mormonism managed to emerge from the shadows of provinciality to become a universal church.

Before I go on, however, I should point out the difference between what I have done here and what I was doing when I wrote an essay some twenty years ago about my experiences as a non-Mormon student of Mormonism.[13] That first foray into autobiography came when I was elected to the presidency of the Mormon History Association, to the obvious surprise of many both within and outside that organization.[14] One consequence was that the editors of *Dialogue* invited me to write something for what, at the time, was the chief independent "journal of Mormon thought." They asked me to explain who I was and how I came to occupy a place at the head of an organization with a membership that was not just primarily but overwhelmingly Mormon. The resulting essay focused on my experiences. I called it "An 'Inside-Outsider' in Zion," and in it I described as best I could how an amalgam of what I had read and was continuing to read in books and articles, what I was discovering in the archival records, and my association with Mormons of all stripes, from professional historians to Latter-day Saints in the pews, was turning me into something more than a mere observer.

While the personal accouterments interspersed with the chapters of this work necessarily include some of this same autobiographical material written from the perspective of two added decades, here the focus of my own story is not further revelation of what happened to me and how I reacted to what I experienced as I continued with my Mormon studies. Instead, in this work, I am more concerned with what I observed. Disclosing this, I describe:

1. some of the strategies I developed to mine the historical record as well as my findings (especially in part 1, Studies in Perception);

2. my reflections on method and writing about religion (in part 2, History, Historiography, and Writing about Religious History, and in part 3, Putting Religion at the Heart of Mormon History and History at the Heart of Mormonism);

3. how circumstances and my perseverance in this particular research arena, even as I maintained my Methodist standing, combined to make me a virtual extension, at times, of the church's Public Communications Division, (in part 4, Deciphering, Explicating, Clarifying: Exercising an Inside-Outsider's Informal Calling);

4. the ways in which what I have learned and experienced allowed me to address the "Is Mormonism Christian?" question and how personal spiritual experience carried me beyond knowledge to understanding (in part 5, How My Mind Was Changed and My Understanding Amplified).

Of greatest importance, the review in the epilogue of how I became a "Mormon-watcher" is written from a perspective that allows me to indicate how my being in the right place at the right time during the past forty years has permitted me to observe closely, and sometimes quite directly, the process of transformation that has altered this tradition so dramatically.

To put a fine point on it, during four decades I watched Mormon culture reconfigure itself. I have been an observer as LDS community life and worship practice have been modified so much that many of the "Deseret Saints" who grew to adulthood in the intermountain region when Mormonism was still primarily a provincial religious movement seem discomfited, even bewildered, by the change. Looking back from the turn of the century, I return to the inside-outsider issue and argue that while my experiences certainly caused my conceptions of the Saints and how I am related to them to shift dramatically, it was neither who I was (and am) nor how I reacted as I came to know members of the Church of Jesus Christ of Latter-day Saints and the RLDS Church as friends, familiars, and intimates that permitted me to become an inside-outsider.

More than anything else, what made a place for an outsider like me to get so close is that in the years between 1960 and the end of the century, Mormonism experienced a conversion in which it changed from being an institution and a people embedded in a particular culture to being a church, belief system, and worshiping body able to thrive in many cultures. The rocky transition between these two utterly different ways of being a faith community made many of the insiders with whom I have shared these years uncomfortable, but the very fact that the transition was occurring allowed me to stay close enough to behold the transformation. If Mormonism had remained a closed culture, it would not have been as open to an outsider as it has been to me.

Significantly, it was not simply that I remained in close touch with Latter-day Saints but also that I kept doing research on the history of the tradition and spent a lot of time concentrating on what occurred in the past half-century that permitted me, first, to appreciate the change that was occurring and, then, to understand that I was observing a fundamental process through which religions must pass if their message is to be a universal one. Being far enough inside to witness what was going on yet staying outside far enough to recognize and analyze the process, I have come away from my years of association with the Saints realizing that the Mormon message is being universalized and that as I watch this happening, I am able to observe while what it means to be Mormon is being transfigured.

In watching what has been happening in Mormonism, I am now able to discern the outlines of the dislodging of a faith system from the specific cultural context of its origins and its being translated (a religious concept that excites awe) into an adaptive system capable of adjusting to the great variety of conditions in many cultures. Moreover, I am convinced that generalizing from the experience of the Latter-day Saints could turn out to be of great value in the study of what either takes place or fails to take place when religious systems are confronted with altered environments. What my sojourn among the Saints suggests is that in the face of the revolutionary changes taking place in our world, religious systems must also change or they will become encapsulated, reaching and providing meaning to fewer people. Almost inevitably, their theologies will become theologies of withdrawal from the world, leaving the field white to the harvest for faith systems that can fit into and function in a multiplicity of cultures.

The dynamic evolution of contemporary Mormonism is described throughout the essays included here. The genesis of "Gentiles, Mormons, and the History of the American West," an essay that incorporates a part of my story not found elsewhere in the book, was an invitation to present the keynote address for the "Seventy Years of Western History at the University of Colorado" conference held in Boulder in 1995. Perhaps I was selected because this "preconference," which preceded the Western History Association annual meeting in Denver, honored my friend and mentor H. Lee Scamehorn, the professor of history who had served as the chair of my doctoral committee and was retiring from teaching. Invited to attend were all those who had earned graduate degrees in the history department at Colorado. Invited, as well, were graduate students who were then working toward such degrees, especially those concentrating on western history.

My address, expanded for publication, locates me vis-à-vis Mormonism and Mormon history. It is an appropriate place to begin because it permits readers unacquainted with me and my work to "know where I'm coming from." Such information is always an advantage when reading about the Latter-day Saints. Besides that, this address to non-Mormon historians who write about the American West gives pride of place to my "doughnut hypothesis," which proposes an explanation for the neglect of the Latter-day Saints in much of the modern writing about Western history, a neglect that is truly stunning in view of the size of the Mormon community in the West and the contributions Saints have been making to the development of the region since they settled there in 1847.

When Patricia Limerick, a history professor at the University of Colorado and the prime mover behind the "Seventy Years of Western History at the University of Colorado" conference, invited me to present the keynote address, she said that in addition to assessing the place of Mormonism in contemporary writing about the history of the American West, I was to describe how, as a non-Mormon, I managed to become a Mormon history specialist whose work appears to be acceptable to people both inside and outside the LDS community.[15] While this dual charge worked against constructing a smooth narrative, rehearsing the story anew allowed me to see things I had missed when I told my story the first time. Moreover, to be quite frank, the different context (preparing something for an audience of western historians rather than Latter-day Saints) and the lengthened chronological perspective worked together to make me more candid than I had been years earlier.

∽

Since each of the book's five parts is preceded by an introduction, the remainder of this work is sketched out only in brief compass here. Part 1, Studies in Perception, contains two essays in which I have analyzed the content of media coverage of Mormonism across time. It also includes a consideration of the Saints' perceptions of and attitudes toward non-Mormons and an essay describing the media's expectations about how Southern Baptists were likely to be treated in Mormon land.

"From Satyr to Saint: American Perceptions of the Mormons, 1860–1960," the section's lead essay, flowed from my conviction that until the middle of the twentieth century, the print media played a crucial role in shaping the images that, lodged in the minds of the non-Mormon public, kept outsiders and Latter-day Saints at arm's length from, if not at war with, each other. Outlining an elaborate research project in which I adapted survey research methodology to print materials, this essay reports my findings. The depiction of the Mormon image since 1960, found in the second essay in this section, takes into account the radical alteration in the media environment after the advent of radio and television and the ever more deliberate public relations strategies the LDS Church has been using throughout the twentieth century, especially since the 1960s, as it sought to manage information about the church and its members. Reflecting on how information about the Saints was presented in the electronic as well as the print media, this analysis of the public image of the Saints in recent years is at once less systematic and more comprehensive than "From Satyr to Saint."

The third essay, about the Saints' conceptions of outsiders, is primarily focused on nineteenth-century LDS perceptions of people outside the communion of Saints, but it looks forward to what would happen to those perceptions when the church started to grow exponentially in the middle of the twentieth century. The section's last essay, written during the summer of 1998 when the Southern Baptist Convention held its annual meeting in Salt Lake City, was commissioned for *Religion in the News,* a new magazine. It was initially intended as an uncomplicated account of the way in which the print and electronic media reported on a story in which conflict between the LDS community and the Baptists was clearly anticipated by Southern Baptists leaders and most reporters. That conflict failed to materialize, however. As a result, my examination of the media's treatment of the convention ended up as a description of what went on in the Southern Baptist Convention itself, a story that sheds light on the differences between this very conservative evangelical body and the LDS Church.

Part 2, History, Historiography, and Writing about Religious History, is introduced by a description of how I developed my own approach to writing about the Mormon past. The section features two very short pieces: (1) a short discussion of the place of history in connecting past and present that was initially written for a popular historical journal, *American History Illustrated;* and (2) a brief examination of the state of Mormon historiography in the 1980s that accompanied an article about contemporary Mormonism by the English journalist Malise Ruthven in the *Wilson Quarterly.*[16] Following these, as the center of this consideration of writing religious history, I have placed an essay I wrote for *Reimagining Denominationalism.* This extended and systematic reflection on method is followed by an essay, first published in the *Christian Century,* that deals with Mormon women's history. It is included because it shows the power that the story of the past is able to wield in the present. The section closes with reflections about John Brooke's *Refiner's Fire* that propose an explanation for the academic community's embrace of this flawed work and review the Saints' negative response to it.

Part 3, Placing Religion at the Heart of Mormon History and History at the Heart of Mormonism, contains three essays illustrating my conscious effort to incorporate analyses of the impact of the religious perceptions of the human actors involved in the historical dramas into forthright accounts of the past. None of the three is concerned with the story of Joseph Smith and the beginnings of Mormonism, which is where such efforts are usually made in writing LDS history. But in writing about the literal reality as opposed to symbolic verity of Mormonism's understanding itself as the restoration of primitive Christianity, I touch on the experiences of the early Saints and describe why the theological claims they so readily embraced were plausible enough to them to be accepted as fact. The other two essays deal with Brigham Young's leadership of the Mormon movement and the LDS diaspora in the mid-twentieth century. Chronologically traversing LDS history from the earliest years and the pioneer period to the 1940s and 1950s, these three narratives demonstrate that capturing religion's place in the lives of human actors does not always turn standard history into sacred epic but that it does tend to turn the story of ordinary men and women (and their families) into the history of a chosen people.

Part 4, Deciphering, Explicating, Clarifying: Exercising an Inside-Outsider's Informal Calling, focuses on my manner of formulating an explanation of the LDS system of belief intelligible to those who know little or nothing about the tradition. Following the introductory remarks that communicate not only the story of how I became a putative expert on Mormonism but also the responsibility for clarity and fairness this imposes, this section includes two previously published essays, one written for an encyclopedic compendium about theology in the United States and the other for a book about the experience of religious minorities in the United States. Both are organized around a particular way of describing LDS theological structure and Mormon historical development, a scheme of explanation that recognizes the Church of Jesus Christ as the essential core of the Mormon movement and presents the gathering of Israel and the "restoration of all things" as subsequent theological and historical "layers," layers that sometimes so enveloped Mormonism's essential core that the Latter-day Saints' Christian understanding of themselves virtually disappeared from view.

I initially devised this way of explaining Mormonism as a means of assisting the journalists who called on me for help about a whole assortment of news stories connected with the Latter-day Saints, everything from the 1987 "Mormon murders" to the persistence of plural marriage, the construction of new temples, the proxy baptism of Holocaust victims, the difference between Mormons and Southern Baptists, and so on and so forth. This means of explanation was devised for those media people whose knowledge of Mormonism was virtually nil when they received their assignments to cover a Mormon story. As the final essay in this section reveals, however, what started as a sort of "Cliff Notes" summary of the tradition designed to help others turned out to be a great help to me. Looking at Mormonism in this schematic fashion permitted me to see a great deal about the Latter-day Saints' relationship with the American religious mainstream that I had not seen earlier.

Up to this point, while the prologue and section introductions are written in the first person, most of the essays are written in the third person and the dispassionate language of scholarship. Part 5, How My Mind Was Changed and My Understanding Amplified, and the epilogue are more subjective. The two essays in part 5 are reprinted from *BYU Studies* and *Sunstone,* while the single heretofore unpublished essay in the latter includes a portrayal of the difference in the Mormonism I first encountered in 1960 and the Mormonism I would come to know in the final decades of the twentieth century. In all three I describe change. The first is about alterations in my thinking about Mormonism's Christian connection, and the second is about the heightened sensitivity that accompanies movement from erudition (having information at hand) and experiential comprehension.

The final essay also begins as an "Indiana Jan" adventure, a story of what happened to me. But instead of remaining fixed on my forty-year sojourn among the Saints, the ground shifts. The focus is adjusted so that it highlights the inhabitants of the promised land and the religion under whose aegis the land was sanctified and turned into a kingdom in the tops of the mountains. Rather than an account of my journey from place to place, the fabulous story this essay tells is one of Mormonism's moving from there to here.

What happened during this passage will be the subject of the next book I write on Mormonism.[17] The burden of this one is that this movement, this transformation, is well underway and that, as is always the religious case, this transformation is no more likely to alter the tradition's essentials than did the transformation that carried Mormonism from its pioneer years into the twentieth century. Practically everything in this work indicates that, as has happened before, the more Mormonism changes, the more it remains the same in the hearts and minds of the Latter-day Saints.

Notes

1. Oaks was one of the speakers at the LDS Afro-American symposium that was held on June 8, 1988, in the DeJong Concert Hall at Brigham Young University. Sponsored by the Charles Redd Center for Western Studies, this symposium marked the tenth anniversary of the revelation that "all worthy male members of the Church may be ordained to the priesthood without regard for race or color." Oaks quoted from an article I wrote soon after this revelation was announced. See Jan Shipps, "The Mormons: Looking Forward and Outward," *Christian Century* 95 (August 16–23, 1978): 761–66.

2. Today the official "Media Style Guide" of the church warns that the "use of 'Mormon Church' or 'Mormon' by the media in stories mentioning either The Church of Jesus Christ of Latter-day Saints or members of that Church is both incorrect and confusing." In the popular parlance of the 1960s, however, it was not just those outside the church who alluded to church members as Mormons. The Saints, in speaking of their community collectively, often referred to themselves as Mormons. Also, even in material prepared and distributed by the church, the need for clarity generally overrode opposition to the use of the nickname so that, for many years, "the Mormons" was placed in parentheses and printed after the official name of the church when it appeared in print or on television.

3. In the nineteenth century, this appellation usually meant a friendly outsider; however, in the twentieth century, it started to signify a Latter-day Saint who "kicks against the traces." The Word of Wisdom is the health code that revelation directs Latter-day Saints to follow. It is printed as section 89 in the Doctrine and Covenants of the Church of Jesus Christ of Latter-day Saints. In practice, keeping the Word of Wisdom means abstaining from alcohol, tobacco, coffee, tea, and harmful drugs. See Joseph Lynn Lyon, "Word of Wisdom," in *Encyclopedia of Mormonism*, 5 vols., ed. Daniel H. Ludlow (New York: Macmillan, 1992), 4:1584–85.

4. These were members of the institutional form of Mormonism headquartered in Independence, Missouri. Many of them were descendants of the Mormons who remained in the Midwest after the 1844 murder of the Prophet Joseph Smith and his brother Hyrum. Under the leadership of the prophet's son Joseph Smith III, they had "reorganized" the Church of Jesus Christ in 1860, calling it the Reorganized Church of Jesus Christ of Latter Day Saints. Since its members refused to accept the leadership claims of Brigham Young and since they rejected the revelation on eternal marriage (which had been the justification for plural marriage) as well as other doctrines promulgated by the prophet in the final years of his life, these "Josephites" were regarded as apostate Mormons by many Latter-day Saints.

5. Jo Ann Barnett Shipps, "The Mormons in Politics, 1839–1844" (Master's thesis, University of Colorado, 1962); Jo Ann Barnett Shipps, "The Mormons in Politics: The First Hundred Years" (Ph.D. diss., University of Colorado, 1965). Graduate school regulations at the University of Colorado required me to use my legal name, hence the author's name listed on both my thesis and my dissertation is Jo Ann Barnett Shipps. (I adopted Jan as a nickname in 1946, when, as a sixteen-year-old, I entered Alabama College for Women, now Montevallo University. I was housed in Old Main, a dormitory in which at least a dozen other students named Jo Ann were living. My adopted name stuck, and even to members of my own family I have been Jan since

then. Jan is the name on my Social Security card and the IRS also knows me as Jan. But I still get the odd inquiry about who this Jo Ann Shipps might be.)

6. Jan Shipps, "Second-Class Saints," *Colorado Quarterly* 11 (Autumn 1962): 183–90.

7. "Minutes of the Formative Meeting of the Mormon History Association," in Leonard J. Arrington, "Reflections on the Founding and Purposes of the Mormon History Association, 1965–1983," *Journal of Mormon History* 10 (1983): 95–98. The non-Mormon scholar was Merle Wells.

8. My place among the "new Mormon historians" was signaled by the inclusion of one of my early articles, "The Prophet Puzzle: Suggestions Leading toward a More Comprehensive Interpretation of Joseph Smith," in *The New Mormon History: Revisionist Essays on the Past,* ed. D. Michael Quinn (Salt Lake City: Signature Books, 1992), 53–74. This was originally published as the lead article in the first issue of the *Journal of Mormon History* 1 (1973): 3–20.

9. Multiauthored volumes represent an important development in recent scholarship about American religion. At least since the 1950s, one of the strategies that scholars, journalists, and other observers have been using to address the incredible diversity of American religion is the book-length survey containing a series of discrete chapters about different faith communities. At first, works like this usually consisted of summary accounts prepared by a single author, and because they were designed to provide an overview of the nation's religious landscape, besides chapters on Roman Catholic, Judaic, and the larger Protestant bodies, all had obligatory chapters on the so-called American religions: Christian Science, Seventh-day Adventists, Jehovah's Witnesses, and, of course, Mormonism. But the format of the volumes with separate chapters on various institutions, groups, and movements written by a single author changed after the publication in the late 1960s and the 1970s of several magisterial surveys of American religion, particularly those of Edwin Scott Gaustad, Sydney Ahlstrom, and Robert Handy. In the late 1970s and the 1980s, as a consequence of funding from foundations—especially Lilly Endowment, Incorporated, and the Pew Charitable Trusts, both of which have religion divisions—projects addressing important themes in the history of American religion started to appear on the scholarly landscape. Many of these projects started with conferences in which papers addressed the project themes from various institutional and religious perspectives. Typically, the papers were edited with an eye to turning conference proceedings into a coherent book. In several of these projects, the conference papers cum book chapters were written by scholars specializing in the study of the various denominations and movements. Jay P. Dolan regularly contributed the chapters on Roman Catholicism, for instance; Russell E. Richey often wrote about Methodism; Grant Wacker usually wrote about pentecostalism; and, for several of these projects, I wrote the chapters on Mormonism.

10. There is a whole category of unpublished papers in my files that I did not consider for publication in this volume. They are early versions of several chapters of a book-in-progress on Mormonism since the end of World War II that I read at Sunstone symposia or professional meetings. They include "The Impact of the Bureaucratization of the LDS Church on Mormon Culture" (plenary address at the Sunstone West Symposium, Berkeley, Calif., February 1987); "Correlation and the Context of Authority in Twentieth-Century Mormonism" (paper presented at the Sunstone

Symposium, Salt Lake City, August 1987); "The Church Office Building as a Symbol of Success and Growth" (plenary address at the Sunstone Symposium, Salt Lake City, August 1990); "From Peoplehood to Church Membership" (paper read at the annual meeting of the Mormon History Association, Claremont, Calif., June 1991); "Being Mormon: The Latter-day Saints since World War II" (paper read at the annual meeting of the Western History Association, Tulsa, Okla., October 1993); "The Difficult Problem of Maintaining Balance between Center and Periphery in an Expanding Church" (banquet address at the Sunstone Symposium, Salt Lake City, August 1994); "Marketing Mormonism: The LDS Church's Use of Public Relations and Advertising Techniques to Represent Themselves and Sell Their Message to the World" (paper read at the annual meeting of the American Society of Church History, Atlanta, Ga., January 1996). Neither did I consider reprinting "Making Saints in the Early Days and the Latter Days," which was presented as a public lecture at Brigham Young University, Provo, Utah, October 25, 1989, and as a plenary address at the annual meeting of the Society for the Scientific Study of Religion, October 1989, before being published in *Contemporary Mormonism: Social Science Perspectives,* ed. Marie Cornwall, Tim B. Heaton, and Lawrence A. Young (Urbana: University of Illinois Press, 1994), 64–83. None of this material is included here. When revised, these papers will become part of *Being Mormon: The Latter-day Saints since 1945,* which is under contract with Indiana University Press.

11. The essays I selected from books are "The Reality of the Restoration in LDS Theology and Mormon Experience," in *The American Quest for the Primitive Church,* ed. Richard Hughes (Urbana: University of Illinois Press, 1987), 181–95; "Remembering, Recovering, and Inventing What Being a People of God Means: Reflections on Method in the Scholarly Writing of Religious History," in *Reimagining Denominationalism: Interpretive Essays,* ed. Robert Bruce Mullin and Russell E. Richey (New York: Oxford University Press, 1994), 177–97; "Joseph Smith (1805–1844)" and "Mormonism after the Death of Joseph Smith" in *Makers of Christian Theology in America,* ed. Mark Toulouse and James O. Duke (Nashville: Abingdon, 1997), 210–17, 373–78; and "Difference and Otherness: Mormonism and the American Religious Mainstream," in *Minority Faiths and Mainstream American Protestantism,* ed. Jonathan D. Sarna (Urbana: University of Illinois Press, 1998), 81–109. All of these have been edited for style. In addition, in some of them I have made substantial changes—additions, corrections, and so on.

12. Such works are legion. In the nineteenth century, "among the Mormons" was often part of the title. See, for example, Phil Robinson, *Sinners and Saints: A Tour across the States and Round Them with Three Months among the Mormons* (Boston: Roberts Brothers, 1883); and Fitz Hugh Ludlow, "Among the Mormons," *Atlantic Monthly* 13 (April 1864): 479–95. In 1958, William Mulder and Russell E. Mortensen selected enough from among the plentiful supply of such material to fill a volume, which they shaped and edited into a handsome and valuable book that made its way into libraries all across the nation: *Among the Mormons* (New York: Alfred A. Knopf, 1958). In the twentieth century, the titles are more descriptive: "Those Amazing Mormons," or "Mormons, Inc.," and so on. See Andrew Hamilton, "Those Amazing Mormons," *Coronet* 31 (April 1952): 26–30; and "Mormons, Inc." *Time,* August 4, 1997, 50–57.

13. Jan Shipps, "An Inside-Outsider in Zion," *Dialogue* 15 (Spring 1982): 138–61.

14. It was not as surprising as some might have thought. Counted among the members of the Mormon History Association at that time were historians who were very active members of the Church of Jesus Christ of Latter-day Saints and very active members of the Reorganized Church of Jesus Christ of Latter Day Saints, as well as scholars who were less active but were part of the LDS and RLDS communities. A substantial contingent of people not engaged in writing Mormon history but simply interested in it were also members. A small group of scholars whose interest in Mormon history was connected to proving that Mormonism is not true were also members. Nevertheless, apart from Mario De Pillis, Lawrence (Larry) Foster, Mark Leone, and me, precious few non-Mormons were actively engaged in writing the history of the Latter-day Saints.

15. This could have reflected a certain personal curiosity on Limerick's part. When she presented the annual Tanner lecture to the Mormon History Association in 1994, she stunned the audience with the information that although she had not remained in the church much past childhood, she had been reared as a Latter-day Saint.

16. Malise Ruthven, who is the author of several books on Islam, wrote *The Divine Supermarket: Shopping for God in America* (New York: William Morrow, 1989), which includes several chapters on the Mormons.

17. Before I can turn to that, I am committed to the completion of a book on religion in midsize American cities that I have been working on for several years.

Gentiles, Mormons, and the History of the American West

For several decades, the postal service has been issuing stamps of various denominations that acknowledge and champion national icons. Although the primary reason for this program is to appeal to stamp collectors, other reasons are unmistakable. Familiarizing the visually oriented citizenry of the United States with images of civic heroes and heroines; military, scientific, literary, and artistic figures; and stars of stage and screen is important. But designers of these celebratory emblems are also using sheets of stamps with a related theme as a mechanism for imparting information about the nation's past. When a new offering becomes available, the postal service supplies local post offices with huge four-color posters of the new stamps to use as wall decorations, posters that provide history lessons to those who wait in line to have letters stamped and packages weighed. The particular subjects selected in recent years suggest that inculcating diversity as a communal value is also a significant goal of the postal service's stamp program.

In 1994, a sheet of 29-cent stamps labeled "Legends of the American West" was made available to stamp collectors and the general public. Advertising this "classic collection," posters appeared on post office walls all across the country showing blow-ups of colorful portraits of sixteen historic personages (Buffalo Bill, Jim Bridger, Annie Oakley, Chief Joseph, Bill Pickett, Bat Masterson, John Frémont, Wyatt Earp, Nellie Cashman, Charles Goodnight, Geronimo, Kit Carson, Wild Bill Hickok, Jim Beckworth, Bill Tilghman, and Sacagawea), plus generic representations of a cowboy, an Indian (here called Native American), an overland mail carrier, and a picture of western wildlife (buffalo, grizzly bear, mountain goat, bobcat, and bald eagle). Taken together, the images on this sheet of stamps served up (and continue to dole out) current understandings of the western story. Against such backdrops as plains, mountains, blue skies, a canyon, a pioneer town, a range filled with longhorn cattle as far as the eye can see, the "Legends of the West" collection describes a region populated by explorers, peaceful and warlike Native Americans, soldiers, law enforcers, ranchers, cowhands, pony express riders, and residents of frontier towns, including such show people as Buffalo Bill and Annie Oakley and the gunfighter Wild Bill Hickok. Besides popularizing conventional perceptions of the history of the West, the disparate personages portrayed on this sheet of twenty stamps also dispense a now familiar message of western diversity that includes nonhumans as well as humans (one entire stamp is devoted to animals, and several animals are pictured on other stamps); women (three stamps) and men (sixteen stamps); Native Americans (four stamps), African Americans (two stamps), and Anglo-Saxons (ten stamps).

That certain significant legendary westerners were not included in this postal assembly is not surprising. In such collections, as in historical museums and other display venues, space is at such a premium that some consequential emblematic figures are inevitably absent. Still, the question of why no gold miner and no one connected with western railroads is pictured is interesting, as is the absence of the Latinos and Hispanics, Chinese, and other Asians who settled in the West. An oversight that is more astonishing—indeed notorious—is the absence of Brigham Young and the Mormons.

The stamps included in this collection were clearly intended to set forth legends of the "Old West," not rehearse western history from start to finish. That might explain the absence of California and the Southwest—home to miners, Latinos, the Union Pacific, and Asian laborers, but this does not explain why the Latter-day Saints are not there.

After all, the Mormons were part of the Old West. Settlers traversed the Mormon trail and the Oregon trail at about the same time, and, in petitioning for the entrance of the State of Deseret into the union, the Saints claimed a huge portion of the western land mass. Moreover, with their plural marriage, temple building, block voting, and economic communalism, they were as legendary as almost any other western type. Nineteenth-century accounts of western history nearly always included extensive accounts of the LDS kingdom and its inhabitants, and hundreds, possibly thousands, of books and articles about the Saints circulated throughout the nineteenth century and early part of the twentieth. The Mormons are not missing from the government's pictorial précis because their story is only now being recovered and recorded in historical monographs. The Mormon story is conveniently available; it was simply ignored.

That this occurred is by no means exceptional. In print as well as pictorial overviews of the American West, the story of the Latter-day Saints is frequently neglected or altogether overlooked, and this is more likely nowadays than it once was. Why this is the case is the burden of this essay.

While the place of Mormon history in the history of the American West is my topic, the presentation of my bona fides is the best place to start because my being an outsider, a person with only a tourist visa to Mormon land, goes such a long way toward explaining how and why I am able to see what many others miss. Although it could well have turned out otherwise—in unfamiliar realms many auslanders become embittered rather than empathetic—my sojourner status is also responsible for my being as bothered as any Latter-day Saint would be when the legitimate Mormon claim to a place in the history of the American West is slighted or entirely overlooked.

No doubt what accounts for this is that despite being "Gentile," I managed to be accepted enough to become what the eminent LDS historian Leonard Arrington once described as "the den mother of Mormon history." Since it was so often used during the time I served as the first woman president of the Mormon History Association, this nickname stuck. So did the reality it described, providing me with a place to stand, a perspective from which to pose and suggest answers to the question of why the story of the Latter-day Saints is so often slighted in popular formulations of western history and also why it is now almost routinely neglected by historians of the American West.

My particular experience as an observer of the Latter-day Saints and historian of Mormonism and the convergence of Mormon and western history are two separate stories. The hinge connecting them here is my long and active participation in the Western History Association and western history generally.

Members of the Western History Association (WHA), convening outside the West for the first time since the association was organized, assembled in 1972 in New Haven, Connecticut, for what turned out to be a memorable rendezvous. Prompted by Howard Lamar, the eastern dean of western history, Yale University proved to be a splendid host. An opening Wednesday evening soiree, in which western history colleagues greeted one another around and through the bones of a massive dinosaur, was followed by dinner down at Mory's (complete with Whiffenpoof serenade). During the next two days, visits to the Co-Op and the Beineke Library (still new enough for its translucent marble exterior to be a novelty) and excursions to Mystic Seaport and Sturbridge Village were interspersed among the association's regular array of sessions. The weather was fine, a large attendance at a meeting so far from the West was exciting, and the western camaraderie was expansive enough to make even novice meeting attenders—of which I was one—feel comfortable.

This veritable festival of western history reached its high point on Friday night with a sumptuous banquet, whose entree was accompanied by bottles of red and white wine in the center of each of the round tables filling every inch of space in a great hall. A palpable enthusiasm and heightened level of general satisfaction were present as this meal drew to a close and the banquet program began. After the university had been thanked and toasts had been drunk to all who had helped with the meeting and the cause of western history generally, the members of the association and their guests settled down to listen to an address delivered by one of the stars of Yale's history team, John Morton Blum. (This was the John Blum who edited the Morgenthau diaries and wrote biographies of Teddy Roosevelt, Woodrow Wilson, and Franklin D. Roosevelt, not the John Porter Bloom of Territorial Papers fame, who was president of the WHA that year.) The announced topic of the dinner speech was "Henry A. Wallace as a Western Man."

Unfortunately, the speaker had misjudged the occasion. Instead of using revealing quotes and telling anecdotes to convince his audience of sated and slightly tipsy scholars of the American West that the sectional orientation of the 1948 Progressive candidate for president was western, he read a thought-provoking scholarly treatise. As I recall, the argument went something like this: the U.S. vice president from 1941 to 1945 was an old-line Progressive; he was born in Iowa, which, despite its location east of the Missouri River, was actually a western state in the days of Wallace's youth; as for Progressivism, notwithstanding its having been taken up by the man from Oyster Bay (who incidentally was also a western man at heart), the movement was a thoroughly western phenomenon; therefore, Wallace must be understood as quintessentially western. I cannot say for sure whether I have reconstructed correctly that argument from more than a quarter-century ago. I can say that despite its merits, the argument was not stated so concisely. Blum's several propositions were made and supported at such length and in such detail that the enthusiasm that had characterized the conference to that point started to fizzle out in much the same way air escapes from a tire with a slow leak. It is not unusual for a banquet speech at the end of a conference to be somewhat anticlimactic. But as the quarter-hours passed, many of the men and women (not so many women back then) who had traveled so far to the East to talk about studying the West probably started thinking less about whether

Wallace was a western man than about how tired they were and how long it would take to return to the part of the West from whence they came.

In reconstructing the process by which I became an inside-outsider in the community of Mormon historians and considering the question of neglect of Mormon history by so many western historians, especially in recent years, that long-ago WHA banquet address kept intruding on my thoughts. The task of making a case that the story of the Latter-day Saints is an integral part of the western saga resembles the task Blum set himself twenty-three years ago. The eminent banquet speaker had to take a topic that was not western on its face and make it western. In a certain sense, I must do the same. Considering how often Mormonism is given shallow coverage, consigned to the western history ghetto that capsule accounts imply, or even left out entirely, it seems obvious that the Mormon story must somehow seem un-Western to many who study, theorize, and write about the history of the American West.

My intention here is to raise neglect of the Mormon West to consciousness and suggest some reasons why many, if not most, historians of the West shape the western story like a doughnut, circling all around the Great Basin, taking into account and telling nearly every western story except the Mormon one. (I used my doughnut metaphor to describe this peculiar phenomenon to the distinguished western historian Martin Ridge. He thought about it for a bit and agreed with me. Then, said he, "And you're the one who writes about the hole!") Before I make my case for including the Latter-day Saints in the western story and truly including those who write about the Mormons in the western history-writing guild, my own connection to Mormonism and Mormon history needs to be clarified. To do that, I need to go back to that speech in New Haven and indicate how it—and the entire meeting—changed me and the way I would subsequently write about Mormonism.

First, some background. Because so much of my published work has dealt with the Latter-day Saints, it is not uncommon for people to conclude that I must be a Saint. I am not. I have never been a Mormon or, for that matter, a saint in the usual meaning of the term. As far as I can determine, I first met Mormons in 1960, when our family (my husband, Tony, and son, Stephen, then eight years old) moved to Utah so that Tony, who had a doctorate in English and a newly minted library degree, could accept an appointment to a position in the library at Utah State University in Logan. I knew so little about Mormonism that I remember thinking that it must be some distinctive form of Protestantism, perhaps a bit like the Nazarenes or the "no-music" Christians. Or possibly a Mormon was akin to a Lutheran; I am pretty sure that at the time I had never met anyone I knew to be Lutheran.

Of course, I was wrong, probably on all these counts. Yet it took years for me to discover how very wrong I was, not about whether Mormonism is Christian but about its being some idiosyncratic form of Protestantism. Learning about the distinctiveness of Mormon culture did not take nearly so long. Neither, as it turned out, did learning about Mormon history.

What had initially attracted my husband and me to Logan was that it was a small town. After a decade of suburban and city life in the Chicago area and in Detroit, we were ready for the remembered neighborliness and tranquility of the small towns in which we grew up. Although I did not immediately plunge into community activities as I might have done had I not decided to return to school that year to complete my bachelor's degree, I first thought that Logan was a more or less typical small town. It was such a friendly place that we were soon drawn into its communal life. Yet as that happened, I began to sense that we had somehow wandered into a "twilight zone," that without realizing it we had become actors in one of Rod Sterling's oft-used plots: a traveler has car trouble and is towed into what appears to be an ordinary small town for help that, inevitably, is long delayed, and, as time passes, the traveler begins to realize things in this particular small town are "ever so slightly different."

Conspicuous differences in Logan included periodic visits from LDS home teachers—they were probably stake missionaries, but the effect was the same—and gentle yet persistent pressure on our eight-year-old son to participate in Primary, the LDS after-school program for children in the elementary grades. More gradually, we discovered that Logan had a social order based on categories we did not fully comprehend, categories reflecting people's standing in or attitudes toward the LDS Church and Mormonism generally. The director of the library—whose wife, he said, divorced him when he stopped wearing his ritual temple garment—described himself as a Jack Mormon. Several library staff members also called themselves Jack Mormons. The four-person history department included three active Mormons and a "Gentile," who was a pillar of the Presbyterian church (Logan's only Protestant church). The political science department was a hotbed of "inactives," and so on. Not knowing the code, we were at sea.

Seeking reassurance that life as we had known it had not disappeared, we started to frequent the public library, only to find a book subtitled *The True Story of Short Creek, Arizona* shelved with the fiction. (Short Creek was the name of a town on the Arizona strip where modern polygamists lived; they still live there, but it is now called Colorado City.) Multiple copies of Leonard Arrington's *Great Basin Kingdom,* which came out not long before we arrived in Logan, were prominently displayed in the library and everywhere else in town.[1] But Fawn Brodie's biography of the Mormon prophet, *No Man Knows My History,* and Juanita Brooks's *Mountain Meadows Massacre* were locked up behind the desk, along with the so-called Kinsey Reports and other "dirty" books.[2]

As for my experience at the university, I had been a music major at the Alabama College for Women in the mid-1940s, but I had been away from music for eleven years and was never very gifted anyway. Consequently, when I entered the baccalaureate program at Utah State, I changed my major to history. As a southerner and a Protestant, perhaps I was seeking familiar contexts when, in my second quarter there, I signed up for the Civil War and Reconstruction course and a course on the Renaissance and Reformation. Imagine my surprise when both turned out to be Mormon history.

The instructor for the Civil War course—fresh out of graduate school that semester—lost control of the class by following the interests of his students. While we read (and were tested on) the entire Randall and Donald Civil War and Reconstruction survey, much of the class discussion centered on the causes of the war, making a place for extended treatment of the Utah War, a topic on which we spent many—and I must say interesting—class sessions. A fair amount of attention was also directed to Reconstruction. Both students and the professor constantly compared what the federal government did to the South after the war with the "occupation" of the mountain West by U.S. marshals during the antipolygamy raids.

The second of these courses dealt with the story of the Latter-day Saints from a different perspective. As taught by the Presbyterian professor, the history of the Reformation became a battle between Catholics (the bad guys) and Protestants (the good guys). The instructor tried in every possible way to connect it to something his students knew. Consequently, when he presented an account of the pope or members of the College of Cardinals trying to exercise cultural control or when Catholicism appeared in a particularly bad light, the class would hear the familiar refrain, "just like the Mormons." He would then go into an unsympathetic description of some episode in the LDS past, usually followed by an argument with certain of his LDS students.

Before moving on—and, incidentally, moving on from Utah to Colorado was what the Shipps family did as soon as the academic year closed—I hasten to add that Utah State University now has a fine history department in which courses are taught as advertised, a department in which, as I understand it, even western history courses are not filled to the brim with the story of the Latter-day Saints.

The nine months we lived in Logan seemed a very brief interval to me, but the culture shock that accompanied the experience of living among the Saints set my curiosity on fire. Consequently, when I entered the master's program at the University of Colorado the next year, I told the department chair that I wanted to write a thesis on the Mormons. His reaction to this prefigured what I have since discovered: at the University of Colorado, as elsewhere in western universities, Mormon and western history appear not to have been in the same ballpark. Rather than send me to Robert Athearn, the department's specialist in western history, the chair decided that my mentor should be Hal Bridges, the department's specialist on American society and thought. As a result, although both my thesis and my dissertation dealt with Mormonism, my course work did not include a survey of the history of the American West. I wrote several papers on the Mormons, including one in a seminar directed by Professor Athearn, but the lack of that survey could well be one of the reasons that all I ever do is write about the (doughnut) holes.

Be that as it may, I did conduct research and write about the Mormons while I was a graduate student, and much of my research was done in Utah archives, but not in the archives of the Church of Jesus Christ of Latter-day Saints, which, back then, were still located at 47 East South Temple in Salt Lake City. In those early years, most of my research had to be carried out in the collections of the Utah State Historical Society and the State Archives, the most complete collections then open to "Gentile" scholars, in other words, all those who failed to fit in any of the various Mormon categories. Perhaps that is one reason that even a cursory examination of my master's thesis and doctoral dissertation and other things that I wrote in the 1960s makes it clear that I was truly a Gentile, a Gentile student of Mormon history.

As is well known, *Gentile* is a signifier of outsiderhood, of not being of the blood of Abraham. Historically, this was an expression that referred to people who are not Jewish. But in a fascinating turn of events, the followers of Joseph Smith started using Gentile to mean those who refused to come into the fold—people who were not Mormon. Many know this, but most fail to realize that this usage was not present at the beginning of the movement. In Mormonism's earliest years, the Prophet Joseph Smith's adherents understood that as members of the Church of Jesus Christ, they had been "adopted into Israel." In this, they were following the claims put forth in the Gospels, especially Luke and John, which is standard Christian dogma, accepted by Catholics and Protestants alike. But when they moved to Kirtland, Ohio, in 1831, where the Mormon prophet was able to gather his followers about him as a hen gathers her chickens under her wing—the metaphor comes from Matthew 23—Smith announced a series of revelations that introduced a more direct Hebraic dimension into Mormonism. By revelation, he called his own father to be the patriarch of the church, and Father Smith instituted the practice of giving individual Saints spiritual messages called patriarchal blessings. Among much else, these blessings informed Mormons of their Hebrew tribal heritage, that is, through which of his progeny they were related to Father Abraham. From this, a concept of "believing blood" developed, and a powerful symbol system gradually grew up to support the notion that people who responded positively when they read the Book of Mormon or heard LDS gospel claims already had the blood of Abraham flowing in their veins. No longer was it simply that those who had ears to hear, heard; by the time the Saints had become western men and women, those who had the opportunity to hear and refused to do so were, ipso facto, Gentile.[3]

For more than a century, this "believing blood" concept was extremely important. In the wake of the explosion in LDS Church membership that followed World War II, however, less has been heard of it. Even the importance of the patriarchy as a connection to Israel appears to be decreasing. Still, for almost a hundred years, *Gentile* had a particular meaning in the Mormon world. Salt Lake City really was the only place on the planet where a Jew could go and be a Gentile.

For Mormons, this divided the world between them and us. For those who stood outside, it made the Mormons other. As a result, the Saints were not so amenable to study and analysis as, say, Methodists in San Francisco, Baptists in East Texas, Presbyterians in the Willamette Valley, and so on. Even if the Mormons were ranchers, cowboys, miners, or, for that matter, industrialists, politicians, or historians, there was something about their otherness that set them so far apart that all too often they simply did not make it into histories of the West. A few notable exceptions notwithstanding, even writing about the secular side of Mormon culture was (and is) largely left to the Saints themselves.

I started working on Mormon history near the end of the hundred years in which not to be Mormon was to be Gentile. This meant that I was clearly Gentile, an outsider. As friendly and helpful to me as many Mormon scholars were, I was an observer. Not only the Saints I discovered in the documents but also the LDS scholars themselves were the observed. This distinction between observer and observed was maintained throughout the 1960s and early 1970s, as I conducted research in the documentary record and reported my findings. When I attended and presented papers in meetings of the Utah State Historical Society or the Mormon History Association, what I read was heard and understood as an observer's reflections on an observed phenomenon. As such, my work was often praised for reporting things that insiders had failed to see, but it was just as frequently criticized for failing to place what happened in proper context. Translated, that means I still did not know the code; I could not speak the language.

Then in 1972, in possession of my first postgraduate research grant to support what I described in the proposal as a "posthumous public opinion study," I went off to New Haven to do research in the Beineke and Sterling libraries on perceptions of Mormonism revealed in accounts published in American periodicals between 1860 and 1960. While there, I attended the meeting of the Western History Association, where I was able to consult with some of the leading scholars of Mormonism. Aside from meetings of the Utah State Historical Society, the Mormon History Association, and the John Whitmer Historical Association (the historical association of the Reorganized Church of Jesus Christ of Latter Day Saints), all of which were Mormon to the core, this was the first professional meeting I had attended. It turned out to be a revelation.

◦

According to several Western History Association regulars with whom I have talked in the years since, one of the things that made that first WHA meeting in New Haven so special was the presence of an unusually large contingent of LDS scholars. Their attendance in such numbers reflected an unprecedented development in the writing of Mormon history, for their presence at the meeting was a part of the opening act of what people who know the field describe as "Camelot," a glorious decade in which the writing of Mormon history flourished and, for a time, appeared to be entering the historiographical mainstream.

This development came about when, in 1972, instead of following the traditional LDS pattern of selecting a member of the ecclesiastical hierarchy to assume the role of the church historian, the LDS First Presidency and Council of the Twelve appointed the well-known economic historian Leonard Arrington to head the Historical Department.[4] Soon after he assumed his new post, the incredibly rich records that constituted the LDS Church Archives were moved into a special wing of the brand-new, twenty-six-story Church Office Building, a structure built to house the rapidly expanding church bureaucracy that accompanied the post–World War II growth in LDS Church membership.

Arrington did not technically preside over the church's documentary holdings, but his title was church historian, a title long held by a member of the church's Council of the Twelve. It is therefore not surprising that a steadily expanding corps of professionally trained historians writing about Mormonism read Arrington's appointment as a signal that, for LDS history, things were beginning to change. Moreover, the influence of the new head of the Historian's Division (often called the History Division) was understood to mean that access to long-restricted documents would permit a fuller and more well-rounded description of the Mormon past.

In keeping with the Camelot legend, this did seem to happen, at least for a while.[5] The church allowed Arrington to put together a division staff that at one time included almost a dozen professionally trained historians who worked full-time. Arrington chose two academic historians to be his assistants: Davis Bitton from the University of Utah and James B. Allen from Brigham Young University (BYU). They kept their positions in their respective history departments while working half-time for the Historical Department of the church.

A sixteen-volume history of the church to be under the general editorship of the church historian was commissioned by the Deseret Book Company, while Allen and Glen M. Leonard set to work preparing a one-volume history of the church for use in the Church Educational System (CES) as well as for new converts and long-standing church members. At the same time, Arrington and Bitton started work on a trade book, also a one-volume history, to be published by Alfred A. Knopf. Before Camelot's final act, these last two works were finished and published, but the multivolume history was abandoned as an official church project.[6]

Arrington's ambitious program included supporting outlets for articles on the history of the Saints that were independent of church control. He did this by encouraging historians in the employ of the church—those teaching at BYU in the history department and the school of religion, those working in the Church Educational System as teachers in or directors of the church's seminaries and institutes, and the staff of the library and the curatorial division of the Historical Department of the church, as well as his own staff—to pursue research that would lead to publication in the *Journal of Mormon History, Dialogue,* and *Sunstone.* In his positions as church historian and as director of the Charles Redd Center for Western Studies, Arrington, who had served as the first editor of the *Western Historical Quarterly* and as president of WHA, also encouraged the integration of Mormon history into the history of the West and the nation. All this made the early 1970s an exciting time to pursue Mormon topics. It was almost like being in the center of a newly awakening universe. These developments also explain why such a substantial group of LDS historians attended the New Haven meeting of the Western Historical Association.

Although the Saints were welcomed with open arms, their presence did not immediately break down the boundaries between the Gentile membership of the WHA and the Saints who were writing LDS history. Notwithstanding the professional meeting setting, LDS historians tended to cluster together, creating a Mormon gathering within the larger western history gathering. Arriving together late to the Westerners' breakfast, they were hailed with enthusiasm, but in that very salute, they were set apart, identified as Mormon rather than as full-fledged western historians.

Note, however, that what I am describing here was not something done to the Mormons; it was a two-way street. What was happening in the world of Mormon history was so exciting, even exhilarating, that it kept Mormon historians talking among themselves. Moreover, although appropriate because the meeting was being held in New England, the WHA session devoted to Mormon history was far more interesting to Latter-day Saints than to western historians because the papers presented on the program dealt with the beginnings of the faith, not with Mormons in the West.

As indicated, one of my reasons for going to New Haven was to consult with Mormon scholars, and consult I did, spending the days of the meeting talking with those who knew Mormonism best. I had long talks with Saints who had been writing LDS history for years; I went with Mormon historians to examine the holdings in the Beineke; and I went with them to breakfasts, lunches, and dinners. In so doing, I became aware of something I had not theretofore recognized. At that WHA meeting—and I would venture to say at practically every WHA meeting since—despite goodwill on both sides, the distinction between them and us has held firm. Only in New Haven, I was a part of "them," so much so that until that fateful dinner, it appeared to me and perhaps to friends who knew me well, that I might cross over. Even if I remained Methodist, I might well become "other."

Remember, however, that one of the many amenities at the Yale meeting was that the banquet tables all had bottles of wine in the center. Every table also had a pot of coffee on it, and cups and saucers were set at every place. Their adherence to the Mormon Word of Wisdom, which forbids consumption of alcohol and hot drinks, meant that my LDS friends could consume neither. As the only Gentile seated at one of those round dinner tables, I started the meal as a proto-insider. But by the time the toasts had been drunk and the coffee poured, that situation started to change.

When a banquet speech goes long and the hour becomes late, I always reach for my glass or cup to stay awake. This time I was seated at a table with seven Latter-day Saints, and, of course, I was the only one who was drinking the coffee and wine. Again and again my cup and glass were filled by my chivalrous table mates, with the result that at the conclusion of Blum's lengthy and sustained argument, I would have agreed with the devil himself that Henry Wallace was a western man. Actually, if memory serves me well, I was only slightly inebriated, not truly intoxicated. But I was happy enough to take a proffered Mormon arm as we strolled back to the hotel.

It was not that night or even that fall that I realized the impact this WHA meeting would have on the way I would henceforth do Mormon history. All that year, I worked away on my study of American perceptions of the Mormons. As I did so, I started to realize that my perception of Gentile perceptions of the Saints was more Mormon than Gentile. Fortuitous circumstances had worked to usher me into what is best described as liminal status, into between-ness.

In the next several months, this status would be made operational in several ways. We had moved to Indiana in 1967. In our first five years there, I had kept my hand in LDS history by doing book reviews and a little writing, but I had made no effort to establish any contact with Mormons in Bloomington. After I returned from New Haven, a Saint I had met at the WHA meeting who knew a Bloomington Saint arranged an invitation for me to speak at the LDS Institute at Indiana University. At the close of this talk, the local stake president—a history buff—came up to me and said, "I'm so glad to meet you. I have enjoyed what you've written, but I thought you were a pseudonym!" Subsequently, perhaps because of the stake president's stamp of approval of my work, I developed an acquaintanceship with Mormonism in the area where I live that allowed me to stay aware of how what was going on in Salt Lake City affected people in the provinces, or, as they called it then, the mission field.

Equally important was what happened the following spring when I went to the annual meeting of the Organization of American Historians, which, that year, was held in Chicago.[7] While I was there, James B. Allen informed me that the members of the Mormon History Association had elected me to membership on the MHA Council. Somewhat taken aback, I was reminded of a phrase the Mormon pioneer Hosea Stout used in reporting that he had been made a member of the legislature of the State of Deseret. "By what means I know not," he had said. How the decision had been made to elect me to the council of the Mormon History Association, I knew not. But I accepted and served for three years on the association's administrative board.

Since I was the first woman to serve on the council, I have been asked many times whether I was selected because I happened to be the right gender. The answer is no. That I was not a token woman but a historian whose Gentile status had given way to something less distanced from the Saints was signaled to me in the first official communication I received; its salutation was "Dear Brother." After completing my service on the council, I spent a year as vice president, and then, in 1980, Mormonism's sesquicentennial year, I became president of the Mormon History Association. This lent a sort of quasi-official cachet to my liminal status, at least as far as the press was concerned.

In the late 1970s, I was invited by Indiana University Press to write a book on Mormonism in the twentieth century. I did a lot of research and started to write, only to discover that it was impossible for me to begin the Mormon story in the middle. I kept trying to drop another book into the footnotes. Finally, I gave up and wrote *Mormonism: The Story of a New Religious Tradition,* on which much of my reputation is based.[8] The decision to do so reflected not only my need to understand Mormon beginnings but also my appointment to the faculty of Indiana University–Purdue University, Indianapolis, which carried with it a half-time appointment in the religious studies department. In any event, I spent much of the 1970s and the early 1980s working on a volume that, in using Mormonism as a case study, allowed me to analyze the process by which religions come into being. This turned my attention away from the Mormonism of the West to Mormonism in the years before the Saints fled to the Great Basin following the death of Joseph Smith.

With that done, however, I have been working off and on in the years since to write a book that will tell the story of the Latter-day Saints since World War II, an event that I regard as a true watershed in Mormon history. Why? Because *Being Mormon,* as I plan to call this opus, is the story of dramatic change. Before 1945, the Mormon faithful were concentrated in the Intermountain West and, in a reprise of the original State of Deseret, in southern California. Mormonism was such an enclave culture that being born Mormon in the 1940s was analogous to being born Jewish. Now, although still centered in Salt Lake City, Mormonism has gone in the past half-century from being primarily western to being a worldwide faith. In the same fifty years, Mormonism has gone from peoplehood to church membership, and Latter-day Saints have gone from simply being Mormon to being Mormon Christians.

In the course of extended research for this book, I have had occasion to reflect at length on what happened in the Mormon history arena in the years after Leonard Arrington became the church historian, the first scholar with professional training to occupy this traditionally influential post. To summarize, following his designation as church historian in 1972, Arrington was presented to the church in its general conference, and, as others in positions of LDS Church leadership regularly are, he was "sustained" in his new position. Since his assistants, James B. Allen and Davis Bitton, were likewise sustained at the same time, this ritual accreditation was interpreted not only by Arrington but also by members of the historical community as an endorsement of the new church historian's plans to revamp and modernize the gathering and preservation of the LDS historical record while at the same time professionalizing the research and writing of Mormon history. The new church historian and his colleagues quickly learned, however, that this endorsement was by no means unqualified. In a "clarification" of enormous significance for LDS scholarship, Arrington was reminded that, unlike the earlier Saints who had occupied the church historian's office, he held a place in the church bureaucracy parallel to that of the heads of the Archives and Library divisions. This reminder foreshadowed what would eventually be made clear. When he was offered the position as church historian, he was not being called to a priesthood office. Notwithstanding his high rank, he would be a part of the LDS Church bureaucracy. The considerable confusion about this issue, not only in Arrington's own mind but also in the minds of historians of Mormonism, is understandable since—as a unit functioning in Weberian terms within the larger institution—the bureaucracy of the Church of Jesus Christ of Latter-day Saints came into being only in the 1970s.[9]

One of the first auguries of exactly how unqualified official endorsement of the new church historian's plans might be came in a letter written by Boyd C. Packer, a member of the Council of the Twelve, to the president of the church and his two counselors (the First Presidency) only two years after Arrington's appointment. This letter was impelled by the appearance of *Letters of Brigham Young to His Sons,* a documentary collection edited by Dean C. Jessee and published in 1974 by the Deseret Book Company "in collaboration" with the LDS Church's Historical Department; it expressed serious concern about "the orientation toward scholarly work" in the church's Historical Department.[10]

Packer's letter gave the new church historian pause. As Arrington's memoirs make clear, he firmly believed that, ultimately, the whole of Mormon history was faith promoting, even when the historical record revealed that in their very real humanity, Latter-day Saints were not always saintly. That their foibles did not prevent them from being faithful had always seemed to him to send an important message to Saints who were struggling to be faithful in the latter days. Consequently, he was convinced that doing scholarly history was a service to the church, and he was sometimes impatient with histories that cleaned the story up so much that all the early Mormons appeared to be perfect.

Now, however, he made a distinction between accounts that, in placing such great emphasis on spiritual experience, divine inspiration, and so on, tended to place the Mormons outside history and accounts that set the Saints down inside the ongoingness of human experience. In response to Packer's concerns, he and his colleagues concluded that the historians on the Historical Department staff ought to increase their preparation of articles that fit into the first category and, thus, would be appropriate for publication in the *Ensign* and the *New Era,* the church's official magazines. At the same time, Arrington decided the members of his staff ought to limit their submission of articles to *Dialogue, Exponent II,* and *Sunstone,* three Mormon periodicals (established respectively in 1966, 1974, and 1976) that were not sanctioned by and had no connection with the church.

The balanced approach of these independent publications gave them enough appeal to Mormon intellectuals to keep them afloat (if sometimes barely), and Arrington was certainly a Mormon intellectual. Nevertheless, even as he personally supported them and what they stood for with public expressions of admiration for what they were doing and with financial contributions, Arrington recognized that too much publishing in these new journals by members of the staff of his department would surely be mistakenly interpreted by the church's ecclesiastical leaders, who were already concerned about the professionalization of Mormon history, as evidence of a secularized historical staff.[11] Yet, as the church historian said in his memoirs, he made a decision that his department should "carry on as usual in a guarded manner."[12]

Guarded they might be, but to no avail. The historical sensibilities of the ecclesiastical leaders of the LDS Church had been shaped by Joseph Fielding Smith's *Essentials in Church History* and other accounts of the Mormon past in which divine and human actors shared equal billing.[13] Thus it was in the very nature of things that many of them would encounter the output of the well-trained historical professionals ensconced in the LDS Church's Historical Department as secular history. The extent to which this was the perception of a substantial portion of the Council of the Twelve became obvious in 1976 when *The Story of the Latter-day Saints,* a fine one-volume narrative history written by James B. Allen and Glen M. Leonard, was published—just as the *Letters of Brigham Young to His Sons* had been—by Deseret Book Company, as it proclaimed on the title page "in collaboration" with the Historical Department.

From the sales standpoint, *The Story of the Latter-day Saints* was an instant success; 10,000 copies were sold in the first four weeks after it appeared, and 5,000 more were ordered by Church Public Communications for placement in U.S. libraries. But it soon became clear that Arrington, the volume's authors, and the historians on the Historical Department staff had little reason to be sanguine about the long-term prospect of writing and publishing Mormon history under the aegis of the church. The distress of several apostles—Ezra Taft Benson, Mark E. Peterson, Boyd K. Packer, and others—was so great that it looked for a time as if the church hierarchy would direct the Deseret Press Company to stop distributing the new history, despite its appeal to the LDS community.

Although this did not happen, the publication of this survey of LDS history, plus the subsequent appearance of *Building the City of God,* a study of various communal experiments and efforts at economic cooperation among the Mormons that Deseret Book Company also published in 1976, put the church leadership on guard. As a result, in whatever format it was published, history written by members of the Historical Department of the LDS Church was thereafter subjected to close hierarchical scrutiny. Arrington was allowed to continue to hold the title of church historian until 1982, but by discontinuing the practice of having him sustained in his position in the church's general conferences, the LDS hierarchy started signaling the difference between a church historian who holds a staff position and a church historian who receives a priesthood "calling" to serve in this capacity.

In the years that followed, the History Division was gradually downsized. Then, in 1980, the division's remaining professional historians were assigned to a newly created Joseph Fielding Smith Institute of Church History at BYU. Arrington was made director of this new administrative unit of the church university and, by private letter, released from his assignment as church historian.

⌥

What transpired in Mormon history during the Camelot period (1972–82) and in the years immediately following is a wonderful tale, complete—when the story is told from the Mormon vantage point—with heroes, heroines, believers, and those accused of unbelief, plagiarism, and even murder. Although not as sensational, the story of what has been happening in Mormon history is also interesting from the perspective of its place in the larger story of the American West. Patricia Nelson Limerick included a chapter on the LDS experience in her survey of western history that emphasized actors, on the one hand, and the acted-upon, on the other, placing the Saints in the latter category.[14] But Richard White was much closer to the mark when he observed in his essay "Trashing the Trails" that the "New Western Historians" have more or less decided to skip Utah.[15]

Although older practitioners of Clio's art were not as delinquent in their coverage of the Saints, the question of where and how the Mormons fit into the history of the West remains. Why is the writing of western history so often doughnut shaped, and why are the Mormons so often missing or else play such a negligible role in historiographical arguments about the West as process (whether Turnerian or not) as opposed to the West as place? Similarly, why—despite Don Worster's appreciation of the work of Leonard Arrington, James B. Allen, and other Latter-day Saints[16]—is Mormonism so often missing from theoretical work on the impact of the West on environmental policy and on the role of capitalism in the presence or absence of agency in the lives of people who live in the West? It "doesn't compute." By virtue of the Saints' location in the center of the American West, the environment and the capitalist system are of critical importance to the history of the Latter-day Saints.

First, with regard to process, however else Frederick Jackson Turner has been read, there is one way of reading his famous essay "The Significance of the Frontier in American History" that allows for a fruitful comparison between the Mormons and the others who traveled to the West.[17] For Turner, the frontier experience operated like a Skinner Box, a controlled environment into which toddlers were placed and—if the experiment worked as the behavioral psychologist B. F. Skinner anticipated—emerged some four or five years later as civilized human beings. The frontier experience worked that way, Turner said. You put a European in at one end, and at the other you get an American committed to individualism, democracy, and the American way. When certain Europeans entered at the eastern end and later came out in the West, perhaps it sometimes worked in this manner, but for the Mormons the frontier experience had an entirely different outcome. In traveling to Zion, Brigham Young's followers experienced the same hardships of the trail and—being first in many areas—had the same opportunities as all the others who traveled to the West to take advantage of nature and Native Americans. Yet something quite different came to pass. The trail was where Saints were made.[18] Whether Mormon converts were from the American Northeast, Midwest, or South or from England, Denmark, or elsewhere, they emerged in the Great Basin not as individualists committed to the capitalistic ethos but as communally oriented Latter-day Saints ready to give what was necessary to build up Zion.[19]

The Mormon saga demonstrates as perhaps nothing else can that the frontier experience certainly could be and often was a transforming process.

In combination with the symbolic sense of being a chosen people, Mormons experienced the frontier as going through the wilderness and living in Zion, God's kingdom in the tops of the mountains. The end result was the creation of a group that took on ethnic characteristics nearly as distinctive and important as the ethnic characteristics of Chicanos, Asians, and Native American groups. Consequently, Mormons may be studied as other ethnic groups are studied, which, in itself, ought to make Mormon history a subject of great interest to new western historians. At the same time, paying attention to what the frontier experience meant to the Saints can advance the project of pointing to the temporariness of the frontier.

But, and this is a big qualifier, the LDS experience is also instructive in the way it reveals that ethnicity is not destiny. The history of the Saints in the past half-century is a clear indication of the way in which ethnicity becomes a matter of choice.[20] In the early years, Saints had to "choose to be chosen" in order to become a part of the chosen people. After that, there was a long period—almost a century—in which being born Mormon automatically provided a person with an ethnic heritage. Now those who would be Mormon must again make a conscious effort to do so, once again choosing to be chosen. The difference between the frontier process according to Turner and the process Brigham Young described reveals the arbitrariness of what was once thought to be universal. The LDS historical panorama thus reveals the variable and transitory nature of the products of process.

Another reason that Mormon and western history so rarely converge, or so it seems to me, is that historians of the West tend to be a secular lot. They may be religious in their personal lives, but in explaining what happened in the past, they shy away from religion. And well they should if what is meant by dealing with religion is making an effort to explain historical events in supernatural terms. Mormon history again provides a perfect example. When historians include accounts of revelation in Mormonism, whether it is the coming forth of the Book of Mormon, the decision to end plural marriage, or the granting of Mormon priesthood to blacks, they often attempt to explain—or explain away—the procedure by which revelation made its way into history. Such a task, I have learned long since, is one for theologians and phenomenologists, not historians. But the *impact* of revelation is quite a different thing.

For example, look at the Great Basin experience from the perspective of region, bringing the legacy of conquest into the mix. A secular historian who sets out to describe how the Saints built a kingdom in Utah will certainly emphasize the fact that the Saints took the land from the native settlers (just as the Hebrews took their promised land from the Philistines). Conquest involves violence; therefore such historians will make much, for instance, of the massacre at Mountain Meadows in which Mormons murdered virtually an entire party of Gentiles who were emigrating to California. They are also likely to characterize the Mormon program of placing Indian children in LDS homes in the twentieth century as an effort to rob them of their ethnic heritage.

Notwithstanding that terrible massacre, which is a significant part of the LDS story, and despite the way certain Saints have worked at turning Native American children in the LDS placement program into ethnic Mormons, there is another side to the story of Mormon conquest. This is an environmental conquest, the way in which the Saints made a barren and arid land "blossom like a rose." Including an account of Mormon conquest of the desert and an explanation of how the Saints interpreted this as fulfillment of prophecy permits historians to preserve the religious dimension of the LDS story without moving into the realm of the supernatural.

Consider as well what happened to Mormonism at the end of the nineteenth century. In an interesting and useful Marxist interpretation of the Mormon story, the anthropologist Mark Leone concluded that the fact that the Mormons were forced to dispense with plural marriage was the coup de grace that turned Utah and the Mormon world into a "client state," to be a kingdom nevermore.[21] Surely he is correct at the secular level. But if the Manifesto, the revelation that was put forward as a press release, is not called into question as revelation and its impact is measured instead, a very different interpretation is possible. The revelation that called for the end of plural marriage was ultimately beneficial for Mormonism.[22] Had plural marriage been allowed to flourish, Mormons would probably have the same sort of status in the nation and the world that the Amish have. They would be a people apart, dependent entirely on what the Great Basin and their own industry could produce.

Revealing how uncomfortable they are in describing modern revelation, non-Mormon historians have described both the Manifesto and the revelation that extended the Mormon priesthood to blacks as acts of cultural accommodation. While such explanations "make secular sense," taking the impact of revelation into account allows historians, whether LDS or non-Mormon, to deal with the transcendent without explaining away all the mystery. Mormon faith and Mormon perception are not required to make the point that had there been no revelation ending plural marriage and no revelation extending the priesthood to all worthy males, Mormonism could never have become a universal faith whose message is as welcome in Africa as in other parts of the world. An analysis such as this does not ask historians to abandon the canons of professional history, but it adds the much-neglected dimension of religion to the human story.

A much more complicated matter needs to be addressed in pondering how the Mormons fit in the historiography of the American West. Comparison of old and new western history reveals a real generational difference. Speculating about the reasons Ray Allen Billington and a number of other practitioners of what some have called "old-style western history" were not as likely to neglect the story of the Latter-day Saints as have western historians in recent years is fascinating. Perhaps the new western historians' shift in emphases is enough to account for this variation. But I suspect that Mormon discontinuity is more consequential than differences, say, in the approaches of Martin Ridge and Patricia Limerick or Richard White.

ᙿ

After more than a century of existing almost entirely as what might be called a minority regional faith, the Church of Jesus Christ of Latter-day Saints has grown in the past fifty years from around 900,000 to more than 10 million members. In the United States alone, there are now more Mormons than members of any one of the following churches: Presbyterian, the United Church of Christ (Congregationalist), Disciples of Christ, or Episcopalian, all ecclesiastical bodies that were once the core of the so-called American mainstream. A number of dramatic changes have accompanied this rapid expansion in church membership, most notably, geographical shifts in where Mormons live and alterations in LDS doctrinal emphasis. Nearly 70 percent of this nation's Latter-day Saints still reside in the intermountain region, plus Arizona, New Mexico, and the states bordering the Pacific Ocean, in other words, in the western United States. But U.S. Mormons now constitute less than half the total number of Saints worldwide. Moreover, although the overall rate of growth in the membership of the church appears to be slowing slightly, in the past decade South America has exceeded the United States in the church's rate of growth and number of new members. This means that while 1.0 out of every 1.3 persons in Utah is Mormon, the archetypal regional enclave of gathered Saints has become an exception to a new LDS living pattern. In the so-called Mormon culture region, people continue to live in LDS communities where Mormon ethnicity, although often attenuated, is alive and well.

Elsewhere in the nation and the world, however, what was once Mormon ethnicity has turned into distinctive practice, which is a very different thing. In accordance with a consolidated meeting schedule instituted by the church

in response to accelerating geographical dispersion, today's Mormons—
many of whom are converts who never lived in the West—gather for a three-
hour block of Sunday meetings. Afterward they return to homes scattered
throughout cities, suburbs, or countryside, as the case may be. Outside the
intermountain region, Latter-day Saints are therefore not a gathered people.
Only belief and practice—including an astonishing proportion of members
who pay tithes—set them apart.

If alteration in LDS living patterns represents a truly remarkable modification in how the members of the church are Mormon, and it does, an accompanying shift in doctrinal emphasis that is equally striking and much
more profound has occurred in recent decades. Mormonism is a faith rooted in both the Old Testament and the New Testament; the LDS gospel is both
the gospel of the God of Abraham and the gospel of Jesus Christ. But during the part of the LDS past most likely to be covered by historians, the Hebraic dimensions of Mormonism were much more noticeable than they are
now. Regardless of whether one was Mormon, the temporal aspects of the
Hebraicism of the Great Basin kingdom were apparent. For one thing, Latter-day Saints lived in a political and economic theocracy. For another, no
secret was made of plural marriage, a form of matrimony that the Saints
accepted as the restoration of a practice in which the Old Testament patriarchs had once engaged. In addition, visitors to nineteenth-century Utah
marveled at the impressive temples in Manti, Logan, St. George, and Salt Lake
City, stunningly beautiful structures whose rituals were described as ancient
ordinances in LDS Church doctrine. Moreover, even though few outsiders
recognized the significance of the church's patriarch (an official whose calling was handed down from one generation to the next), he stood alongside
the church's prophet-president and his two counselors in the First Presidency,
members of the Council of the Twelve, and other general authorities who
presided over the whole church.

But plural marriage was proscribed in 1890, and although the Saints'
peculiar marriage custom was not terminated immediately, it was no longer
accorded ecclesiastical approval after 1904, and the public practice of polygamy among members of the LDS Church gradually disappeared from the
scene.[23] As this was happening, the political and economic kingdom that had
been actualized in the Intermountain West was gradually transformed into
symbol. Much more recently, the office of the church patriarch was elimi-
nated.[24] Instead, each Mormon stake (a geographical subdivision resembling
a diocese) has its own patriarch who dispenses patriarchal blessings locally.
Although this continues the ritual practice, the disappearance of the church

patriarch from the list of Mormon general authorities is particularly significant from the standpoint of Hebraic symbolism.

Today's most visible emblem of the Hebraic aspects of Mormonism is a
proliferation of LDS temples around the world. Yet the ceremonies performed
in them are sacred and are therefore not open to any except worthy Saints.
One consequence of the resulting privacy in this critically important part of
Mormon ritual life is that, while retaining much of its peculiarity (as in
church members' perceptions of themselves as a peculiar people), the public face of the religion of the Latter-day Saints is now so unequivocally Christian that historical Mormonism often appears to have stolen silently away.
Their possession of a work of modern scripture supplementing the Bible,
their rituals of proxy baptisms for the dead, their self-proclaimed identity as
a temple-going people, and other distinctives notwithstanding, Latter-day
Saints now emphasize the fact that theirs is a Christian faith.

For almost two decades, in such church publications as the *Ensign* and the
Church News, handsomely illustrated articles about the life of Christ and the
history of the early Christian church have supplanted articles and illustrations
highlighting LDS prophets and faith-promoting events from Mormon history.
Now, instead of beginning the Mormon story with the Prophet Joseph Smith
as formerly was the practice, LDS missionaries start with the story of Jesus as
they teach potential converts about Mormonism. In 1982, the Book of Mormon was officially subtitled "Another Testament of Jesus Christ." Then, in
December 1995, indicating the importance of its original name (the Church
of Jesus Christ), the LDS Church changed its logo. For many years the key
words (*Church, Jesus Christ, Latter-day Saints*) in the four-line LDS typograph-
ical emblem were all printed in the same size type (see figure 1). The new logo
is composed of three lines: in small print the first line reads "The Church of";
the second, in print almost three times as large, says "Jesus Christ"; and the
third, again in small print, reads "of Latter-day Saints" (see figure 2).

This renewed emphasis on Christ is generating a linguistic shift. While
members of the LDS Church once found the noun *Mormon* quite sufficient
to describe themselves, many—possibly a majority of Latter-day Saints—now
refer to themselves as Mormon Christians or simply Christians. This linguistic modification is having a marked impact on Mormon ethnicity, an impact
that is particularly evident outside the West. The manner in which change is
most readily apparent, however, is not so much in the way the Saints articulate their perceptions of themselves as in the way they express themselves in
speaking of outsiders. Where once those who refused to hear the message
were Gentile, increasingly this is no longer the case. At the behest of their

THE CHURCH OF JESUS CHRIST OF LATTER-DAY SAINTS

Figure 1

THE CHURCH OF
JESUS CHRIST
OF LATTER-DAY SAINTS

Figure 2

leaders, the Saints started in the early 1980s to refer to those who stood out-side the faith as non-Mormons. Within a decade, that designation had been changed to nonmember, and in recent years even that restrictive designation is sometimes questioned because it seems too exclusive.

Mine is an illustrative case. Successive linguistic change means that I start-ed out nearly forty years ago as a *Gentile* historian who studied Mormons; then without changing my religious status in the slightest, I became a *non-Mormon* historian who studies Latter-day Saints. Almost before I had got-ten used to the non-Mormon designation, it was outdated, and I was turned into a historian of LDS history who happened to be a *nonmember*. Now, more often than not, Latter-day Saints seem to think of me as a Methodist histo-rian who studies Mormon Christianity.

Although this last descriptive formulation of the faith (Mormonism as Christianity) was by no means entirely absent from nineteenth-century dis-course, I have not seen Mormonism depicted in this manner in a general textbook or a historical monograph dealing with the American West. Nor have I seen much substantive reference in such works to "the scattering of the Mormon gathering." Instead, most graduate and practically all under-graduate history courses—western and otherwise—continue to put the Saints down in the Great Basin and leave them there.

An outcome of such static treatment of LDS history is that disorienta-tion—even cognitive dissonance—is apt to result when those who learned about the Saints in western history courses come face-to-face with today's Mormonism. To turn a familiar but hackneyed adage on its head, what you see in history books is not what you get when you meet modern Mormonism. Yet along with other undergraduates and graduate students, future western historians are likely to gain their knowledge of this extraordinary faith and fascinating people from books that do not take the changes of the past four decades into account. The transformation of Mormonism from regional faith to worldwide church makes it so difficult to get here from there, from the familiar Mormonism of western history to contemporary Mormon Christianity, that what has been occurring in the past few decades may be the principal reason why today's historians of the American West so often neglect the region's geographical center.

∾

My long sojourn in Zion has not made me one of the West's peculiar people, yet it has situated me in a place peculiar enough to permit me to argue that the existing neglect of the Saints should come to an end. Notwithstanding the recent Mormon metamorphosis, the historical experience of the Latter-day Saints that made the LDS Church what it is today occurred in the Intermountain West, and it occurred at the very time the West was being shaped as a region. In the past half-century, what it means to be a Saint has gone from peoplehood to church membership; as this has occurred, the West itself has likewise undergone change. If not so dramatic as the Mormon transformation, the changing character of the western experience guarantees that western history and the way it will be written is bound to be altered.

The world is carrying the American West with it as it moves into the new millennium. What better time to restore Mormonism—which has been preparing for a new millennium for well over a century and a half—to its proper place in western history? The region's historians who make an effort to integrate the fullness of the story of the Latter-day Saints into the western saga will receive their reward: an amplified and enriched history of both Mormonism and the American West in the nineteenth and twentieth centuries.

Notes

1. Leonard J. Arrington, *Great Basin Kingdom: An Economic History of the Latter-day Saints, 1830–1900* (Cambridge, Mass.: Harvard University Press, 1958; reprint, Salt Lake City: University of Utah Press, 1993).

2. Fawn McKay Brodie, *No Man Knows My History: The Life of Joseph Smith, the Mormon Prophet* (1945; 2d ed., rev. and enl., New York: Alfred A. Knopf, 1976); Jua-

nita Brooks, *The Mountain Meadows Massacre* (Stanford, Calif.: Stanford University Press, 1950; new ed., Norman: University of Oklahoma Press, 1962; reprint, with foreword and afterword by Jan Shipps, Norman: University of Oklahoma Press, 1991).

3. Gentile entry into the kingdom was not automatically proscribed. The Prophet Joseph Smith and his successor Brigham Young both believed that Gentiles could become Mormon but that doing so required a blood exchange. During baptism, the blood of Gentile converts would be replaced by the blood of Abraham. This exchange not only brought them into the literal family of Abraham but also brought their offspring into Abraham's family. This contributed to the Saints' understanding of themselves as an ethnic group.

4. At the same time, Arrington, who had been on the Utah State University faculty, was appointed to a newly funded chair (the Charles Redd Chair in Western History) and as the director of the newly organized Charles Redd Center for Western Studies at BYU. Thomas G. Alexander, a member of the history department at Brigham Young University, was appointed assistant director of the new center.

5. A wonderful description of this important period in the writing of Mormon history is found in Leonard Arrington, *Adventures of a Church Historian* (Urbana: University of Illinois Press, 1998), chapters 5–14. See also Davis Bitton, "Ten Years in Camelot: A Personal Memoir," *Dialogue* 16 (Fall 1983): 9–20.

6. Two in the multivolume history have been published by the University of Illinois Press: Richard L. Bushman, *Joseph Smith and the Beginnings of Mormonism* (1984); and Thomas G. Alexander, *Mormonism in Transition, 1890–1930* (1986). A paperback edition of the latter, with a foreword written by Stephen J. Stein, appeared in 1996. Others include Milton V. Backman Jr., *The Heavens Resound: A History of the Latter-day Saints in Ohio, 1830–1838* (Salt Lake City: Deseret Book, 1983); Richard P. Cowan, *The Church in the Twentieth Century* (Salt Lake City: Deseret Book, 1985); R. Lanier Britsch, *Unto the Islands of the Sea: A History of the Latter-day Saints in the Pacific* (Salt Lake City: Deseret Book, 1986); and F. LaMond Tullis, *Mormons in Mexico: The Dynamics of Faith and Culture* (Logan: Utah State University Press, 1987). Eugene E. Campbell, Bruce Campbell, and Gary Bergera, *Establishing Zion: The Mormon Church in the American West* (Salt Lake City: Signature Books, 1988), is the volume in the sixteen-volume history that Eugene E. Campbell left unfinished at the time of his death. It was completed by his son Bruce with the help of Gary Bergera, publisher of Signature Books.

7. At this meeting, I read a paper, "From Satyr to Saint: American Attitudes toward the Mormons" (see the second essay in this volume for an expansion of this paper).

8. Jan Shipps, *Mormonism: The Story of a New Religious Tradition* (Urbana: University of Illinois Press, 1985).

9. In the first extended private conversation I had with Arrington after he became church historian, he told me the following story. In one of his early meetings with Nathan Eldon Tanner, the member of the LDS First Presidency during the administration of Joseph Fielding Smith, the church president who handled the negotiations that led to his being named church historian, Arrington asked Tanner whether he was being offered a job or given a calling. Tanner answered that this would be up to Arrington himself, but that answer turned out to be both ambiguous and wrong. Even though Arrington was initially sustained in his position, which happens when persons are called to positions in the church hierarchy, subsequent events made it very

clear that Arrington had been offered and had accepted a job. While this might appear duplicitous on Tanner's part, it was not. Arrington's appointment as church historian was a part of a process that was much larger and more complicated than can be seen when the focus remains on what happened in the Historical Department. His being brought into the church administrative structure was a part of the creation of an elaborate church bureaucracy, which, as indicated, came into existence during the first half of the 1970s.

10. The Deseret Book Company, although not directly owned by the LDS Church, is the church's press. As long as the hierarchy approves of the actions taken by the executive staff, it operates independently, but the press always responds to the clearly articulated wishes of the LDS First Presidency and Council of the Twelve.

11. Arrington, *Adventures of a Church Historian*, 120. Arrington made no effort to keep his strong moral support for *Dialogue, Sunstone*, and *Exponent II* secret. His public expressions of admiration for the work being done by their editors and the people who wrote for these independent publications were fervent and animated. Still, in several different conversations with me when I was in Utah on research trips or at professional meetings, he expressed his fears about how publication in these independent periodicals might be interpreted. He also told me about his own financial contributions to these independent periodicals.

12. Arrington, *Adventures of a Church Historian*, 120.

13. Joseph Fielding Smith, *Essentials in Church History: A History of the Church from the Birth of Joseph Smith to the Present Time, with Introductory Chapters on the Antiquity of the Gospel and the "Falling Away"* (Salt Lake City: Deseret News, 1922), was originally prepared as a priesthood manual, but it became the standard one-volume history of the church. As such, it was used (and is still being used) in the LDS Church Educational System's seminary and institute classes, as well as by generations of LDS Sunday School teachers.

14. Patricia Nelson Limerick, *The Legacy of Conquest: The Unbroken Past of the American West* (New York: W. W. Norton, 1987).

15. Richard White, "Trashing the Trails," in *Trails: Toward a New Western History*, ed. Patricia Nelson Limerick, Clyde A. Milner II, and Charles E. Rankin (Lawrence: University of Kansas Press, 1991), 29.

16. Don Worster, *Rivers of Empire: Water, Aridity and the Growth of the American West* (New York: Pantheon Books, 1985), 74–84.

17. Arguably the most important essay ever written on the settlement of the American West, Frederick Jackson Turner's often reprinted essay "The Significance of the Frontier in American History" was first published in the *Annual Report of the American Historical Association* (Washington, D.C.: Government Printing Office, 1893), 199–227.

18. This process is described at some length in Shipps, *Mormonism*, chapter 3. See also Dean L. May, "Thoughts on Faith and History," *Sunstone* 3 (September 1978): 35–37.

19. For the best description of the difference between Mormons and non-Mormons on this point, see Dean L. May, *Three Frontiers: Family, Land, and Society in the American West, 1850–1900* (New York: Cambridge University Press, 1994).

20. That ethnicity is not fixed in American culture is the argument of Werner Sollors, *Beyond Ethnicity: Consent and Descent in American Culture* (New York: Oxford

University Press, 1986). The argument is supported and expanded in Werner Sollors, ed., *The Invention of Ethnicity* (New York: Oxford University Press, 1989), especially the editor's introduction, ix–xx.

21. Mark P. Leone, *Roots of Modern Mormonism* (Cambridge, Mass.: Harvard University Press, 1979), especially chapters 6 and 7.

22. Mormon fundamentalists, who have always believed that God would never change his mind about anything so important as the principle of plural marriage, would disagree with this statement.

23. Large numbers (perhaps 20,000 to 30,000) of schismatic Saints who continue to practice plural marriage reside in the Mormon culture region. The LDS Church does not recognize them as Latter-day Saints and has a policy of excommunicating members who marry into polygamy or even talk of doing so. In a curious turn of the historical screw, the LDS Church now holds that persons who practice plural marriage are outlaws, which is virtually identical to the federal government's position on nineteenth-century Latter-day Saints.

24. For a history of the church patriarchy, see Irene M. Bates and E. Gary Smith, *Lost Legacy: The Mormon Office of Presiding Patriarch* (Urbana: University of Illinois Press, 1996).

PART 1

STUDIES IN PERCEPTION

A half-dozen years elapsed between my earning a doctorate in 1965 and securing a teaching position close enough to our home to avoid the long-distance commuting marriage that is the fate of so many academic couples. During that time, I did what many history "post-docs" do. As a part-time instructor, I taught survey courses at the University of Colorado's Denver Center while we still lived in Boulder and at Indiana University–Purdue University, Indianapolis, after we moved to Indiana, and I worked on a "soft money" project at a university research institute.

The research institute I worked for was the Institute for Sex Research at Indiana University in Bloomington. This is the famed Kinsey Institute, which in 1969 had a grant from the National Institute for Mental Health for a nationwide random sample survey of sexual attitudes and behavior. Despite my abysmal lack of knowledge of sociological method generally and survey research in particular, I was hired as the coordinator for this project. Since the person I replaced performed mainly secretarial duties, this position might well have turned into little more than a glorified secretary's post if I had been a skilled typist. But since I was not much of a typist back then, I set about finding ways to facilitate the research effort I had been assigned to coordinate, an effort that started with constructing and pretesting a questionnaire. After successful pretesting of the questionnaire's elaborate schedule of questions (in which respondents were asked their opinions about pre- and extra-marital sex, homosexuality, and so on), the research plan called for a revised questionnaire to be administered to a sample of respondents carefully chosen to represent the U.S. population. The sampling and the interviewing were to be done by the staff of the National Opinion Research Center at the University of Chicago. From the resulting data, a portrait of public attitudes about homosexuality and other forms of sexual behavior would eventually be developed.

The project was already behind schedule when I came on board, and only the pretesting and gathering of data occurred during the two years I worked on the project.[1] My involvement was therefore limited to the construction of the questionnaire, the rigorous pretesting of this instrument, and analysis of the pretest data.[2] Yet I learned more in the process than I had ever expected to know, not so much about sex as about sociological method, the principles of questionnaire construction, pretesting, and data analysis.

As my detour into the strange world of sex research—and it is a strange world indeed—drew to a close, it occurred to me that I might apply the principles of survey research to a Mormon history project. For almost two years, I had been working with a project staff to develop a means of assessing contemporary public opinion about sexual behavior, surely a topic as sensitive as religion. What if I modified the research approach to assess attitudes about folks with iconoclastic religious beliefs?

Most of the populations whose opinions I would need to track were no longer living. Notwithstanding that stumbling block, I reasoned that if I could find a means of accessing the sources of information from which perceptions would have to have been fashioned, there would be no reason why I could not make use of survey research methods to examine the history of American perceptions of the Mormons across time. If that proved feasible, perhaps I could also examine Mormon perceptions of those who were not Mormon.

Since the great majority of Mormons lived in the Intermountain West from the time the members of the Church of Jesus Christ of Latter-day Saints settled in the valley of the Great Salt Lake in the middle of the nineteenth century until the close of the World War II, I concluded that the portion of the American population coming into direct contact with Latter-day Saints during that century was likely very small. In the days before radio and television, opinions of the Mormons must therefore have been shaped by what people read about the Saints and by hearsay—hearsay informed by the written word. Consequently, what I needed to do to figure out the climate of opinion was to somehow "marry" content analysis to survey research techniques. The resulting data, it seemed to me, would provide information that would be more precise than the general impressions of what people thought about the Mormons and Mormonism that rested on impressionistic studies of American public opinion about the Saints.

Moving ahead, I embarked on the project described in the first essay in this section, a project whose outcome is summarized in its title, "From Satyr to Saint: American Perceptions of the Mormons, 1860–1960." Historians have long known that there was a dramatic shift in the way Americans imagined the Saints in the middle of the nineteenth century and how people constructed the Mormon image a century later.[3] But exactly how their perceptions were altered, what the nature of the alterations were, and when and how they occurred have never been quite clear. The systematic method of assessing the content of articles written about the Mormons that I used in this analysis permits more precision about change across time.

By 1960, however, Americans no longer constructed the Mormon image primarily from what was written in newspapers, books, and periodicals. In addition to deriving their ideas about members of the LDS Church from the print and electronic media, Americans often got their notions from LDS missionaries and from neighbors who happened to be Latter-day Saints. This new situation made using a method that depended on analyses of the content of the printed page impractical as a means of surveying what has happened to the Mormon image since 1960. As a result, I used a different analytic strategy and a more traditional narrative analysis for my study of the LDS image in the past forty years. The results reported in the essay on what happened during this period may not be so precise as the results of my study of perceptions of the Mormons between 1860 and 1960, but this essay addresses a number of different issues, not the least of which is how modern perceptions of the Saints are likely to alter what the LDS Church can expect in future media coverage.

"From Gentile to Non-Mormon: Mormon Perceptions of the Other" is far less successful than my study of what non-Mormons thought about the Saints. I knew that a marked shift in Latter-day Saints' attitudes and perceptions toward non-Mormons had also occurred over the years, and in an effort to describe the nature of the shift and when it occurred, I adapted the methodology I used in my study of American perceptions of the Mormons to LDS materials. I discovered, however, that it was not a change that can be adequately represented along a positive-negative continuum. Perhaps this explains why I regard the outcome of this study as an inadequate indicator of what actually occurred. A more likely explanation for what I regard as a less than successful research project is that the production of full-text versions of many sources of LDS history (and the extraordinary indexing this has made possible) had not even started when I did this study. As a result, I used far too few sources in this analysis.

Although I regard what I was able to come up with as flawed or, at the very least, incomplete, I have decided to include the revision of a paper I wrote reporting some of my results. I do so because I think the question is an important one, and I want to challenge future scholars to do better than I did in fashioning a picture of Latter-day Saints' ideas about non-Mormons at different points in time.

As indicated in the prologue, the last essay in this section is a study of the news blitz that focused so much attention on the annual meeting of the Southern Baptist Convention held in Salt Lake City in the summer of 1998. It rounds out this section not because I analyzed media coverage of this event to discover how the Saints were being perceived by the American public at this time but because I decided it would be useful to see how such a story would play out in the national media. A by-product of the study is that it serves as a useful reminder that the Church of Jesus Christ of Latter-day Saints is not the only religious body with an administrative arm whose business is public communication. In fact, my research revealed that the material distributed by the Southern Baptists, although more muted than earlier Southern Baptist accusations that Mormonism is a particularly dangerous heresy, was much more negative than anything I have ever seen distributed by the LDS Public Communications Department.

A much-abbreviated version of the essay that leads off this section was presented to an annual meeting of the Organization of American Historians in April 1973, so long ago that it is almost hard to remember.[4] The subtitle of that presentation was "American Attitudes toward the Mormons." Neither the version presented there nor the version included here has ever been published, but since a longer version of the paper than the one I read in Chicago was deposited in the LDS Church Archives in 1973, it has been available to researchers for many years. Working from that manuscript copy with my permission, William Smart, the *Deseret News* editor, described the study and included a line graph summarizing the overall results in an issue of the *Church News* published at the time of the LDS Church's sesquicentennial.[5] Moreover, Robert Swierenga, editor of the *Journal of Social History,* used the same paper for twenty years in his methodology courses for history graduate students at Kent State University. Over a quarter-century, I have also responded to countless requests for copies of this paper. This means that there are so many copies of "From Satyr to Saint" in circulation that inquirers are often surprised to discover that it has never been published.

The first essay in this section was prepared earlier than any other essay in the book, but the second essay in the section was, as it were, written yesterday. Prepared during the summer of 1998, it was presented at the 1998 Sunstone Symposium in Salt Lake City. The last two selections in this section might likewise be paired as virtual brackets around the other essays in this book. "From Gentile to Non-Mormon: Mormons Perceptions of the Other," reports the outcome of a research project I undertook in the 1970s, while "Media Coverage of the Southern Baptist Convention in Salt Lake City" was being written as this book was taking shape. "From Gentile to Non-Mormon" was prepared for the annual meeting of the American Society of Church History in 1978. The Southern Baptist Convention study was undertaken to allow me to write an article for *Religion in the News,* a new periodical published by the Center for the Study of Religion and the Public at Trinity College in Hartford, Connecticut. A much truncated version of the essay was published in that periodical in November 1998.[6]

∞

In addition to these four selections, I have written other essays and made a number of presentations that draw on my perception studies. When the Mormon History Association convened in Provo in 1984, I presented a paper entitled "Point Counterpoint: Non-Mormon Perceptions of Mormons and Mormon Perceptions of Non-Mormons" in the opening plenary session. For the most part, this paper combined some of the results reported in "From Satyr to Saint" and "From Gentile to Non-Mormon." For that reason, it is not included here. I also decided not to include the essay reporting the results of a study I made of public opinion about the Mormon apostle Reed Smoot during his senatorial career because it was published in the *Utah Historical Quarterly,*[7] a periodical usually conveniently available to those interested in Mormonism and LDS history.

Notes

1. Mainly because of disagreement between the project's codirectors about how the survey results should be written up (as well as a quarrel about who should be the senior author), the results were not reported in print until 1989, almost two decades after completion of the survey. Eventually a third author had to be brought in to complete the manuscript. See Albert D. Klassen, Colin J. Williams, and Eugene E. Levitt, *Sex and Morality in the U.S.: An Empirical Inquiry under the Auspices of the Kinsey Institute* (Middletown, Conn.: Wesleyan University Press, 1989). Roy Porter noted the publication delay in his devastating review of the book in the [London] *Times Literary Supplement,* February 16–20, 1990. He called the work "an instant antique."

2. When I examined the volume reporting the survey results, I was astonished to discover that two documents I had written ("Training the NORC Field Supervisors" and "Pretesting the Interview") were included as appendices. I was given no opportunity to edit or proofread these reports, which had been composed for internal consumption.

For the record, I should add that in addition to the work I was hired to do on the attitudes project, the Kinsey Institute's senior sociologist, Martin S. Weinberg, and senior psychologist, Alan P. Bell, asked me to serve as the project director for a second institute project, an annotated bibliography of works about homosexuality. In this capacity, I was responsible for overseeing the work of graduate students assigned to annotate books and articles. I also took responsibility for the book's organization and designed a cross-referencing system that made the work more useful than it might otherwise have been. In addition, I was responsible for seeing to the preparation of the final manuscript that was submitted to the press, a far more difficult task in the days before computer software made the organization of complex projects a reasonably simple endeavor. See Martin S. Weinberg and Alan P. Bell, eds., *Homosexuality: An Annotated Bibliography* (New York: Harper and Row, 1972).

3. As used in the title of the second essay in this section and throughout this section, the word *image* refers to what is probably best described as a stereotype deriving from generalized perceptions of Latter-day Saints. Here, as elsewhere in this work, *Mormons* and *Latter-day Saints* are synonymous nouns referring to people connected by birth or baptism to the Church of Jesus Christ of Latter-day Saints.

4. This meeting was held in Chicago. At the time, I was teaching American history survey courses in the history department at IUPUI as a part-time adjunct faculty member. A surprisingly positive reaction to this paper, both on the part of the commentators and those in the audience, led to my being offered a tenure-track position on the faculty of the Religious Studies Program in IUPUI's School of Liberal Arts. I accepted this offer, but only after some negotiations that turned the position into a joint appointment (50 percent in the history department and 50 percent in the Religious Studies Program).

5. William B. Smart, "Changing Attitudes Alter Media Reports," *Church News*, January 5, 1980, 22, 28.

6. Jan Shipps, "Submission in Salt Lake," *Religion in the News* 1 (Fall 1998): 6–8, 23.

7. Jan Shipps, "The Public Image of Sen. Reed Smoot, 1902–32," *Utah Historical Quarterly* 45 (Fall 1977): 380–400.

2

From Satyr to Saint: American Perceptions of
the Mormons, 1860–1960

The accounts left by the early followers of Joseph Smith Jr. persuasively discount the notion that the prophet's charisma is a sufficient explanation for this new religious movement. Smith was a significant figure, but something more than the magnetic force of his personality explains the Mormon movement and the organization of the church that would become the Church of Jesus Christ of Latter-day Saints. That those who gathered around the prophet had a leader who, they were certain, had prophetic gifts was important. But they were seekers; they wanted certainty and evidence of truth. They found these in the restoration claims for church and priesthood that set their new ecclesiastical organization apart from all other churches of the day and in the Book of Mormon, which was, for them, a sign of the approaching return of Christ and the end of time.

From the outside, however, Mormonism appeared to be nothing more than the lengthened shadow of the prophet from Palmyra, a man who was often ridiculed and regarded with contempt. When negative perceptions of the former "glass looker" broadened to include his followers, as they regularly did, a hostile climate of public opinion materialized and surrounded the Mormon community. This charged atmosphere became fertile ground for belligerent actions against the Saints; it also led Smith's followers to interpret both derogatory speech and the sticks and stones that broke their bones as religious persecution.

But just as charisma by no means entirely explains Mormonism, the skepticism and derisiveness of their neighbors does not fully account for the calamities the Mormons encountered in Kirtland, Ohio; Independence and Far West, Missouri; and Nauvoo, Illinois. Divisions within the LDS community paved the way for disaster in both Kirtland and Nauvoo. In Missouri, the Saints were so certain that divine mandate had made this land their inheritance that they uttered words and took actions that undoubtedly added to the old Missouri settlers' grievances against the Saints.[1] For all that, negative perceptions of the Saints held by the non-Mormons who lived in surrounding areas surely nourished the incendiary atmosphere that led their enemies to drive the main body of the Mormons from Kirtland, wage war against them in Missouri, murder their prophet in Nauvoo, and push many of them away from the settled portions of the United States.

Forced to sell their homes for a pittance and leave Nauvoo, their "Jerusalem on the Mississippi," substantial numbers of Saints either returned to the East or established homes in the Midwest. The largest group of Latter-day Saints fled across Iowa and, under the leadership of Brigham Young and the Council of the Twelve, moved in a body to the Great Salt Lake Valley. There, within five years, they built up a kingdom in the Great Basin, which they called the State of Deseret. This was a wondrous feat that the Saints looked upon with justifiable pride but one that generated consternation on the part of the nation—both leaders and the rank and file—because of Deseret's theocratic character. After 1852, when the Saints announced to the world that plural marriage was part of the social fabric of Mormon society, this consternation gradually turned into extremely negative public opinion, which, in turn, generated fierce political, religious, and cultural opposition to Mormonism.

The frenzied disquiet with which many members of the American public regarded the Saints was not of short duration, as alarms about various groups sometimes have been when they were based mainly on second- and third-hand information subsequently countered by direct experience with members of the group. In this case, however, the Saints were separated from the nation by a "mountain curtain" after they settled in the Great Basin. The peaks of the Rockies kept the United States (U.S., "us") and "them" apart. The result was a situation that may be compared with the descent of the iron curtain that kept the United States and the Soviet Union apart for so long. But in this earlier instance, the danger was not an "evil empire" created by a godless political system; it was a religion whose adherents created an earthly kingdom of God. In all our nation's history, there is no comparable example of a situation in which a strained relationship between a religious group and the public lasted so long or was of greater import. Certainly there is no comparable example in which the position of a religion in the United States vis-à-vis the larger American community remained so crucial for so long.

∽

The relationship between Mormonism and the outside world passed through three main stages. First, there was a period of intense antagonism that repeatedly led to violence and finally resulted in the murder of the Mormon prophet and the expulsion of the Saints from civilized American society. Second, there was a less violent period in which, with the exception of the Mormon War of 1857–58 (a hot war), the intense antagonism was expressed through a struggle for economic and political mastery (a cold war). The heights were not dismantled to bring down the mountain curtain, but that curtain became more transparent with the cessation of polygamy and the transformation of the Mormon kingdom from the political to the spiritual realm. Third, a period of accommodation gradually brought this religion and the American public—Zion and Babylon, as the Saints sometimes put it—to terms, terms so mutually acceptable that the harmony between the two has sometimes seemed downright dangerous, especially to those who remained convinced that the LDS Church continued to oversee a corporate empire and those who continued to charge that Mormonism is a Christian heresy.

As critically important as the relationship with the outside world has been in the religious and institutional development of the Mormon faith, so many questions about it remain unanswered that historians have found it impossible to describe the relationship satisfactorily. It is not even clear that the opposition and antagonism to the Mormons and the LDS Church was as intense and sustained in reality as it appeared to be to those whose early lives had been lived out under "clouds of persecution" and to the historians who accept the accounts of those Saints at face value.[2] It is also not totally clear how long the hostility to the Mormons persisted after they renounced polygamy and abandoned the possibility of establishing a political kingdom and whether the hostility was replaced by grudging toleration or by open acceptance and admiration.[3]

There is, moreover, widespread disagreement about just exactly what it was in Mormonism that called up such strenuous objection. Some say that people were opposed to the religion itself, but they do not make it clear whether the objection was theological and the opposition aimed at the extirpation of heresy or whether the intention of the opposition was a more pragmatic desire to destroy a religion that held a one true church position and in many ways failed to fit into the prevailing Protestant pattern in the United States.[4] Others say the problem was not religion; it was polygamy, or politics, or economics, or the way in which the church leaders exercised rigorous social control over the Latter-day Saint community.

Each of these explanations, in turn, raises further questions. Was the opposition to polygamy, for example, primarily opposition to a system of sexual debauchery, to "immorality cloaked under the name of religion," or was it more often opposition to a system in which happiness was defined as "forty feet on a [fireplace] fender," a system that "debased the men, degraded the women, brutalized the children," and generally threatened the "purity of the American Home and the honor of American womanhood?"[5] And how about politics? Were the non-Mormons mainly concerned about the allegiance the Saints swore to a "secret society" in which they were bound, as Ruth Everett and many other hostile journalists charged, "to obey the laws of the Mormon Church in preference to those of the United States?"[6] Or were they more interested in the fact that the Mormons dominated the domestic politics of any area where large numbers of Latter-day Saints resided? Similarly, if the problem was economics, was the objection theoretical or practical—was the fear of Mormon acceptance of the communitarian ideals of the "Order of Enoch" greater than a fear of local Mormon economic power? If it was the control church leaders exercised over the Mormon community, were Mormonism's opponents chiefly worried about the individual freedom of the Mormons themselves—worried because the church organization was so powerful that as one author said, a Mormon woman "could not darn her husband's stockings without Brigham Young's consent?"[7] Or was there just as much concern about the way such complete social control impinged on the freedom of non-Mormon citizens who lived in the Mormon community?

Much greater agreement exists on the reasons non-Mormons now admire the Mormons. Anyone who reads the *Reader's Digest* knows they are all trustworthy, loyal, helpful, friendly, courteous, kind, obedient, cheerful, thrifty, brave, clean, and reverent. Besides that, they do not drink—even coffee—they do not smoke, and they take care of their own. But the situation changed so imperceptibly that it is not clear just exactly when they gained all these virtues.

Finding a way to explain what happened is complicated by the fact that Mormonism, over the years, somehow managed to hold in suspension a great deal of internal inconsistency. Consequently, the Mormon experience has been so incredibly diverse and complex that historians can look at the record and find enough evidence to make almost any theory seem plausible. Since American public reaction over the years reflected the diversity and complexity of Mormonism, the historians who have studied it have come away with such an astonishing variety of explanations, suggested motives, and basic themes that it has proved nearly impossible to make all of them fit into a meaningful overall pattern.

In more instances than not, the path through a maze of conflicting interpretations is paved with knowledge about the religious, emotional, or philosophical commitment of the historian. On the matter of negative or positive public opinion, however, the absence of consensus about its impact is probably as much a function of the lack of an effective method that can be used to describe the attitudes of an earlier day as it is of a particular religious or pragmatic turn of the historical mind.

The rigorous study whose results are reported here was undertaken as an effort to fashion an approach to the available sources that could remedy this rudimentary information deficit by providing a means of measuring attitudes toward and perceptions of Mormons and Mormonism on a negative-positive continuum, while discovering with some precision exactly what it was about the Saints that was abhorred or admired. To do this, I took advantage of two facts: (1) in the days before radio and television, printed sources were vitally important in the formation of perceptions and attitudes, especially perceptions and attitudes about people and things with which the public had little or no direct contact; and (2) over the years, a great deal has been written about Mormonism.

From its beginnings in upstate New York in 1830 to the present day, this indigenous religious movement—now rapidly becoming a worldwide faith—has been potentially newsworthy. In recent years, nearly every newspaper in the country has, at one time or other, printed what can best be described as Mormon human interest stories, and many periodicals have done the same.[8] Besides that, certain events (for instance, the death of a church president or the point at which the balance shifted so that there are now more Latter-day Saints outside than inside the United States) are seen by reporters as hard news, propelling the Saints into the national spotlight. Nowadays, for the most part, such stories about Mormonism are basically respectful, even complimentary, but this represents a 180-degree turn from the press coverage of Mormonism a little over a century ago. Equally or even more newsworthy back then, stories about the Church of Jesus Christ of Latter-day Saints, its leaders, and its members tended toward derision, disdain, and disrespect.

This study, which is clearly a methodological experiment, is a new effort to define the relationship between the Mormons and the public by attacking the problem from a different direction. The same questions that historians have been asking all along have been asked once again, but in this instance they have been asked in such a way that the answers seem to furnish a more coherent description of the American public's reaction to the Mormons than we have had heretofore.

The description derived from this study is in no way complete. It is limited, first of all, to the years between 1861 and 1960 and therefore does not cover the early years, a period of intense antagonism and open violence. In addition, the description is limited to the study of the attitudes expressed in American periodicals that were important enough to be indexed in *Poole's Index* and the *Readers' Guide*. As a result, it can provide only a tentative outline of the total picture of American attitudes toward the Mormons. Similar studies of perceptions and attitudes expressed in books, newspaper articles, pamphlets, encyclopedia entries, and public speeches are needed before the picture, even of the century after 1860, can be considered definitive and final—as definitive and final as a picture based on the printed sources can ever be.

The extent to which printed sources can ever truly reflect public attitudes and opinions is an important question, one to which a definitive answer is not forthcoming. Some years ago, Sigmund Diamond made a study of the reputation of American businessmen by examining their obituaries in the public press. When he presented the results of his study, he prefaced them with a warning that a one-to-one correspondence between public opinion and the content of mass communications must not be assumed.[9] Diamond's caveat is exceedingly important and must be kept in mind as we examine the results of this study.

Nevertheless, it is also important to remember that for three-quarters of the period under study, it was extremely unlikely that an average American would have much opportunity to form an independent opinion based on personal contact with a real live Latter-day Saint. Today, American attitudes are undoubtedly influenced by the Mormon image projected on radio and television, the ubiquitous presence of the recordings of the Mormon Tabernacle Choir in our modern electronic culture, Mormon friends and neighbors, and all those young, neatly dressed, clean-cut Mormon missionaries we see going from door to door. This was not always the case. Before 1930, radio was not a significant factor in the formation of public opinion, and television did not become important until twenty years after that. Moreover, as table 1 suggests, ordinary association between Mormons and non-Mormons was statistically unlikely. Being approached by an LDS missionary would have been a reasonably novel experience.[10]

Accordingly, it stands to reason that the perceptions of Latter-day Saints and opinions about them were primarily shaped by information obtained from printed sources, either directly or secondhand. The main exception to this means of gaining information about the Mormons was hearing about

Table 1. Saints Living inside and outside Utah and LDS Missionaries
Compared with Total U.S. Population

Years	Total LDS Population	Total LDS Population Outside Utah	Missionaries Assigned to U.S. (est.)	Total U.S. Population
1901–10	215,796	64,764	800	84,317,985
1911–20	403,388	145,669	900	102,370,018
1921–30	542,194	164,994	900	118,107,855
1931–40	678,217	342,033	800	138,439,069

them from Protestant ministers who served as "home missionaries," a phrase that, for all practical purposes, came to mean "missionaries to the Mormons" in the second half of the nineteenth century. But so many of their reports were published in church publications that hearing such a presentation was comparable to gaining information from printed sources secondhand.

RESEARCH METHODOLOGY

The form in which I have cast the results of my study may suggest that I have carried out some incredibly complicated process—or that I have had access to a series of reports from the members of some brotherhood scattered back through time. As a matter of fact, the research plan for my project was not especially complicated. Taking a page from the opinion pollster's book, this plan simply called for a careful and complete study of a representative sample of the sources on which American attitudes were based, with the results recorded in a historical data questionnaire (a precoded research instrument) that would allow the resulting data to be analyzed in a manner designed to approximate a posthumous public opinion poll as closely as possible. This meant, of course, that the data could be turned into numbers, allowing them to be analyzed in much the same manner that contemporary survey research data are analyzed.

The decision to test the research plan by studying the articles about the Mormons published in American periodicals was dictated by the fact that these articles are conveniently indexed in *Poole's Index* and the *Readers' Guide* and by the fact that while the periodical press was certainly not the only scene of conflict, it was one of the most important arenas in which the struggle for and against Mormonism was played out in the American mind. A similar research plan could be followed to investigate the attitudes expressed in books, newspaper articles, and other printed sources. Sampling procedures would have to be worked out for each type of source, but the analytic scheme is flexible enough to be used almost without change—a happy circumstance since it would allow valid across-genre comparisons.

The representative sample for the periodical study was drawn in the following manner. More than a thousand entries in *Poole's Index* and the *Readers' Guide* refer to articles about the Mormons, Utah, and polygamy published between 1861 and 1960 (see appendix A). With the exception of articles on Utah antiquities, each of these was placed on a separate index card; duplicate entries were identified and one of the cards pulled; cards with references to articles in English magazines or in books were set aside; then every one of the 738 articles that was left were examined, and the cards referring to articles having no significant mention of the Mormons were removed.[11]

The number of words in the remaining articles were counted and recorded on the cards so that the length of the articles could be taken into account, and they were weighted by circulation to make it more likely that the outcome of the analysis of this material would reflect public opinion. Then the cards were placed in strict chronological order and divided into five-year segments. The number and length of the articles in each time segment were used to indicate how important the so called Mormon question was at different points in time. A sample of two hundred articles was drawn by starting with the first card in each five-year segment and selecting every third card thereafter (see appendix B). Drawing this chronologically stratified sample was tedious and time-consuming, but it was basically a routine procedure. Only meticulous attention to detail was required for its successful execution.

Developing an analytic scheme that would adequately encompass such a complex topic over a time period as extended as this one and pretesting it to make sure it would yield valid and reliable data were much more difficult. I once prepared an exhaustive research-in-progress report containing a technical play-by-play account of the development of the analytic scheme used for this study. Copies are still in my files, but since it is the final version that is important for an appreciation of the study's substantive results, I will summarize by reporting that the development of the research instrument involved a great deal of trial and error. During the process, I mercilessly exploited the technical expertise of my former colleagues at the Institute for Sex Research, the late sociologist Albert D. Klassen Jr. and the late psychologist Eugene E. Levitt. I consulted at length with Donald L. Kinzer, whose work on the history of the American Protective Association gave him special knowledge of negative Catholic stereotypes.[12] By means of a formal survey, I asked for advice from a large contingent of Mormon historians and received helpful suggestions from Thomas G. Alexander, James B. Allen, Fawn M. Brodie, Richard L. Bushman, Everett L. Cooley, Richard O. Cowan, Mario S. De Pillis, Paul

M. Edwards, S. George Ellsworth, Robert B. Flanders, Klaus J. Hansen, John James, Gustave O. Larson, T. Edgar Lyon, D. Michael Quinn, Melvin T. Smith, Jean B. White, and Henry J. Wolfinger. When the research instrument was almost in its final form, a pretest in which Thomas Alexander from the history department at Brigham Young University and I both analyzed a chronologically stratified sample of thirty-seven articles was conducted to establish the validity and reliability of the analytic scheme (and to make sure that the results are something more than my idea of what people thought about the Mormons).[13] A general appraisal is that the research instrument (described below) proved to be an extraordinarily flexible and useful research instrument.

The research instrument (see appendix C) gathers information in three main categories: general descriptive information about the periodical, the article, and the author; specific information about the contents of the article (i.e., content analysis); and information that allows a precise measurement of attitude along a negative-neutral-positive continuum. The first category called for facts; the second for informed opinion; and the last for value judgments. (See figure 3.)

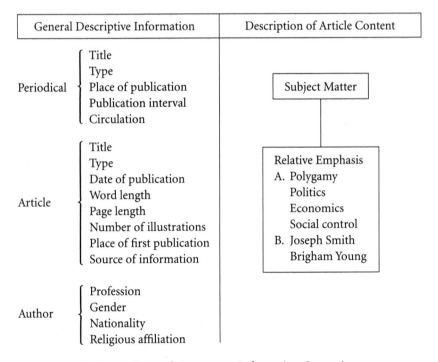

Figure 3. Research Instrument Information Categories

The necessary facts about the periodicals were mainly derived from Frank Luther Mott's *History of American Magazines.*[14] Circulation figures were derived from George P. Rowell's *American Newspaper Directory* and N. W. Ayer and Son's *Directory of Newspapers and Periodicals.*[15] There were instances in which the source of the information in the article was not specified, but for the most part the facts needed for the general description of the article—type, publication date, length, number of illustrations, et cetera—were available in the article itself. Information about authors was obtained from such a variety of reference works that a general statement about the source of that information is impossible.

The section of the research instrument designed to provide a description of the contents of each article called for a primary subject matter designation and a ranking of the relative emphasis on polygamy, politics, economics, and social control and on Joseph Smith and Brigham Young as Mormon leaders along a four-point scale from "major emphasis" to "no emphasis."[16] Another section called for a ranking of the attitudes toward Mormon theological claims, and toward Mormonism as it affected citizenship, family life, and morality/immorality on a series of five-point attitude scales. The section devoted to the measuring of attitudes included a content analysis subsection, in which all references to the Mormons and Mormonism that could definitely be identified as negative or positive were coded according to fifteen negative concept categories and fifteen positive concept categories.[17] The final attitude measurement item required an overall ranking of the article as very negative, somewhat negative, neutral, somewhat positive, or very positive.

In many ways, this precise measurement of attitudes is the key to the study. It is important to remember, however, that this particular part of the analytic scheme is also the most experimental aspect of the entire project. This is not to suggest that the research strategies used to measure attitudes are totally new to historical investigation. The use of attitude scaling does seem to be pretty rare, but an excursion through the research-in-progress reports in the *Historical Methods Newsletter* revealed that content analysis had become fairly standard before I started this research project. Moreover, the work of Richard L. Merritt, who studied the emergence of American nationalism by counting the number of collective self-referent symbols appearing in certain colonial newspapers, and the work of Louis Galambos, who analyzed the contents of selected farm journals to delineate the "agrarian image of the large corporation," demonstrate that the use of this technique to study attitudes has promising possibilities.[18] As important as those studies are, however, they do not constitute any clear-cut precedent for this analytic scheme employing these two research strategies in combination.

For this study, the attitudinal measurement data were summarized in the following manner: the content analysis count of negative references was subtracted from the positive reference count to get a positive or negative score; this raw score was adjusted by article length by computing the score per thousand words; the result was combined with the attitude and overall effect scale rankings to provide an attitudinal index score ranging from -60 to +60, with zero as a neutral midpoint.

After the data were collected, the first step in the analysis was the assignment of an index score to each article in the sample. Because it is not tied to the subject matter of the articles or to the time in which they were written, this score makes precise across-time comparisons possible. It is, furthermore, a continuous rather than a ranked variable, and as an exact measure, it may be used to check for long- and short-term trends and to draw trend lines if significant trends exist. Rounded to a single digit, the index scores may be displayed in contingency tables so that the connection between the attitudes summarized by this gross index and such independent variables as periodical type, word length, profession or religious affiliation of the author, and subject matter may be examined. Scores can also be used as the dependent variable in multiple regressions to identify the independent variables that are the most important indicators of attitude. All in all, the attitudinal index proved to be a valuable analytic tool. The makeup of the index score is depicted in figure 4.

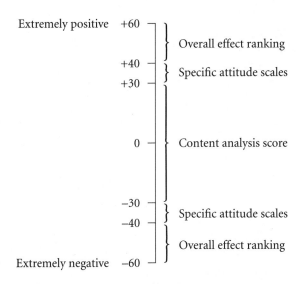

Figure 4. Attitude Measurement Scheme

As indicated, the century was divided into five-year segments for the purpose of drawing the sample. The same division was retained for some of the analysis, but for most of the analysis the data were divided into three major time periods, 1861–95, 1896–1920, and 1921–60. These were determined not by the data but by the circumstances of Mormon and American history.

SURVEY RESULTS, 1860–95

Not very long after the 1857–58 Utah War had ended on its curiously incon- clusive note, American attention was diverted away from the West by the war that began with the rebellion of South Carolina. By then, most people knew the Mormons were carrying on some pretty strange marital maneuvers out there in their mountain kingdom, but slavery, the new Republican party's other "twin relic of barbarism," held the stage in 1861 as the first of these time periods opened. When it closed thirty-five years later, the Utah territorial period was about to end. In the intervening years, so the conventional wis- dom held, public sentiment, primarily mobilized by the mainline Protestant clergy, was so opposed to polygamy that Congress was forced to pass legisla- tion stringent enough to compel the Saints to suspend its practice.[19]

Whether this interpretation is too simple is one of the issues historians of Mormonism argued about during the second half of the twentieth cen- tury. Conceding that public opinion could well have forced Congress to act, some historians agreed with Klaus J. Hansen that the true target of the anti- polygamy campaign was not polygamy so much as it was the temporal (so- cial, economic, and political) power of the Mormon church hierarchy. This was the position I took in my dissertation on the Mormons in politics, but that was before I did this study.

Perhaps polygamy was not as important as some observers thought; per- haps it really was just a serviceable weapon, a "convenient excuse," as Han- sen put it, "to strike at the . . . influence of the Mormon hierarchy."[20] Perhaps, but it was ultimately the violent opposition to polygamy of the various Prot- estant home missionary societies and the Salt Lake City Ministerial Associ- ation that was a main impetus for the campaign to inform the nation about the corruption—read that as sexual debauchery—in Mormon land. More- over, despite their Gentile status, the members of the Utah non-Mormon business and political community were far more willing than the non-Mor- mon religious community to work toward statehood for Utah. In addition, in an important monograph published in 1986, Edward Leo Lyman chal- lenged Hansen's conclusion, saying that his own research in the records of the U.S. Congress (which was prodigious) convinced him that "the practice of plural marriage was the foremost obstacle to admission of Utah as a state."[21] The substantive results of this modest historical record survey cannot settle this historiographical disagreement, but they do shed light on this practical question, as well as on the more theoretical questions posed earlier in this essay.

A summary graph indicating the results of the study for the years between 1860 and 1895 is provided below (see figure 5). Across the base, a time line divides each time period into five-year segments. The mean attitudinal index score for each five-year period was entered, and these were connected by lines illustrating the fluctuations from one five-year period to the next. Dashed lines illustrate the extent to which the picture changed when the data were weighted to take the circulation of each periodical into account. The dotted lines are curvilinear trend lines drawn from a three-degree polynomial regression equation. As in all the summary graphs for the study, a horizontal center line represents neutral, nonjudgmental, attitudes. All the points below that line represent negative attitudes; the ones above it, positive attitudes. The lower the point, the more negative and hostile the attitude; the higher the point, the more positive and favorable.[22]

Attitudinal index scores reveal negative attitudes throughout the period from 1861 through 1895,[23] but they were not uniformly extremely negative.

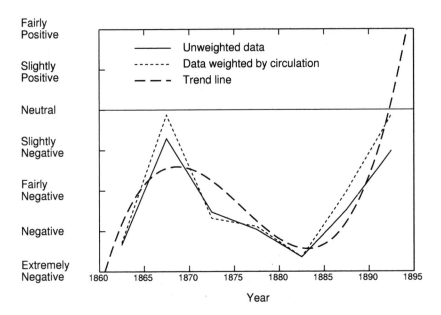

Figure 5. Summary Graph, 1860–95

The scores clearly moved upward toward slightly neutral between 1865 and 1870, only to plunge to extremely negative, the nadir for the entire century, in the period between 1880 and 1885. Between 1885 and 1895, the scores again moved upward. Although there were fluctuations, it is important to remember that the total picture was a negative one. The polynomial regression reflects the changed attitudes after 1890 and describes a trend that moved above the neutral midpoint. This was what many confidently expected. But the mean index scores themselves, regardless of whether the data are weighted by circulation, always remained below the neutral line—and as the summary graph for the period from 1895 through 1920 reveals, the upward trend did not materialize for another thirty-five years.

It is possible that the relatively favorable mean score for the second time segment in the first time period (1865–70) may be somewhat exaggerated, but there was a definite hiatus in the hostility toward the Mormons during these years—a hiatus that can partially be explained by the Mormon support of the Union during the Civil War and by the fact that they—along with so many other Americans—were actively involved in that most popular of all projects in the United States between 1866 and 1870, the building of the transcontinental railroad and the opening of the West.

The mean scores for all the other five-year segments in this first time period conform to the model used by those who posit public opinion as a primary cause and effect agent in Mormon history, especially since the lowest point in negative attitudes for the entire century occurred (according to these data) between 1881 and 1885, just prior to the passage of the Edmunds-Tucker Act, legislation that proved to be, as Leonard Arrington stated, the "dragon" that slew the Mormon temporal kingdom.[24] Quite possibly, American optimism about legislation's efficacy in solving problems and righting wrongs had an immediate effect on the attitudes expressed in the periodical press after the passage of that legislation. But it was much more likely that the Mormon public relations efforts in 1887 and 1888 were reflected in the attitudinal index scores for the period between 1885 and 1890. In any event, there can be no doubt that the climate of opinion, as characterized by the articles published in the five years after 1885, moved rapidly away from the earlier extremely hostile position. Articles published in the last five-year segment in the first time period (1891–95), while still negative, moved upward, echoing the initial satisfaction of non-Mormons that, with the 1890 Woodruff Manifesto, the Saints had surrendered the practice of plural marriage.

Although the number of articles in the initial time period sample (fifty-four) was smaller than the number in the subsequent time periods, the total number of words was greater in this period than in any other. This means that the articles were very long; over three-fourths had more than 2,500 words, and only one had less than 1,000 words. Less than 10 percent had illustrations. Eighty-five percent were scored as negative, and of that 85 percent, three-fourths scored in the extremely negative category. Just how negative the press was during the years between 1860 and 1920 becomes clearer when keeping in mind that, for the purpose of this analysis, articles in the first two time periods with neutral index scores were regarded as basically positive. If it was published before 1920, any article innocuous enough to receive a neutral classification would have to be considered essentially favorable to the Mormons.

Almost half the articles in the first time period sample were essays, not news articles, book reviews, editorials, and the like; and over half were published in monthly periodicals, but of such a variety of types that no useful generalization can be made. About half were published in New York. The average circulation was somewhere between five and ten thousand. The proportion of negative articles in this time period was so great that in the analysis of the general description items, it was hard to distinguish a negative type and a positive type. Except in the matter of the author: ten of the articles, almost one-fifth, were written by non-Mormon public figures (mainly persons involved in politics); one was neutral and the remainder negative—most of them extremely so. Eight of the articles, almost 15 percent, were written by non-Mormon religious leaders; all were negative—six of them extremely so.

As for the content of the articles, it was somewhat easier to distinguish between negative and positive articles, at least as far as emphasis on polygamy and politics is concerned. In the first time period sample, exactly the same percentage of articles were coded as being mainly about politics and polygamy, and exactly the same percentage were coded as having major emphasis on these two themes. But of the total number of extremely negative articles, a few more had major emphasis on politics than on polygamy.

Half of the articles placed either major or great emphasis on politics; 65 percent placed major or great emphasis on polygamy; 74 percent at least mentioned politics; 87 percent at least mentioned polygamy. On average, one negative reference to Mormonism as a political threat or to the church hierarchy's political control of the Mormon community was made for every 325 words; one negative reference was made to polygamy for every 270 words. All in all, the results of this painstaking study add up to the inescapable fact that polygamy was the primary concern of those who wrote about the Mormons between 1861 and 1895.

Perhaps—probably—almost certainly the practice of polygamy was used as a bludgeon to destroy the temporal power of the church. Nevertheless, if what these data tell us is taken as an indication of American attitudes toward the Saints, Americans could deal with political power but not a society in which men had more than one wife. As far as the public was concerned, it is very clear that to most Americans, the central Mormon issue was not politics, but polygamy.

SURVEY RESULTS, 1896–1920

In his survey of Utah/Mormon history, S. George Ellsworth described the years between 1896 and 1920 as years of transition from the pioneer to the modern world. He recognized that the antagonism of the territorial period died slowly but concluded that "Utah and her new ways of life" were pretty well accepted by the people of the nation by the end of World War I.[25] Ellsworth may have been right; the old Mormon/non-Mormon hostility does seem to have disappeared or at least to have changed character in Utah. If it faded away in the larger community, however, its disappearance was not announced in the periodical press, where negative and hostile attitudes continued to dominate (see figure 6).

The most surprising feature revealed by the results of analysis of the data from this second time period (1895–1920) is that, here again, the mean atti-

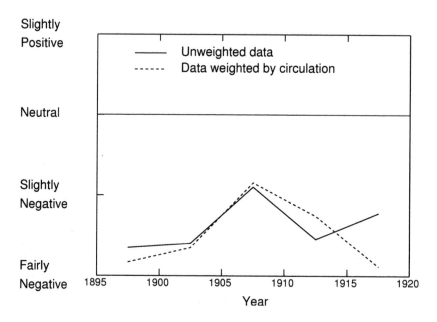

Figure 6. Summary Graph, 1895–1920

tudinal index score is negative throughout this twenty-five year period. This time, however, despite all the writing about Mormonism that accompanied the U.S. Senate investigation of the question of whether Reed Smoot, a member of the Council of the Twelve, should be allowed to keep the seat to which he had been elected in 1902 and subsequent writing about the Saints and the church by the muckrakers, the five-year averages are closer to neutral, ranging from fairly negative to slightly negative. Beyond this, the picture is so muddled that even defining its outlines is difficult for this middle period. While the summary graph in figure 6 shows that the upward, more positive trend that occurred after the Mormons formally abandoned polygamy in 1890 did not continue, this does not necessarily mean that the new trend was negative. In this transitional period, no matter how sophisticated or elegant the analysis, no significant trend line could be established.

Even though a trend cannot be established, a basic shift in emphasis can. Because a distinction is made in this study between generalized references to Mormonism as a threat to the American way of life and Mormonism as a practical political threat, it is possible to see that there was much more emphasis on Mormonism as a dangerous religio-cultural system in the second time period than in the first. The detailed analysis of the data shows that now it was not the Mormons but Mormonism that was the problem. "Utah and the common Mormon people [had] great possibilities of good," it was said, but the Mormon system was "Satanic." Since it was composed of a "hierarch" and "human units [who] move[d] instantly and unquestionably at command," it was "un-American" as well.[26] Of course, this was not a new idea; as David Brion Davis pointed out many years ago, it was there all along.[27] But the distinction made between the people and the system in these years is striking.

Although references to politics did not disappear, the number of those references was considerably reduced—down to one for every 550 words as opposed to one for every 325 words in the first time period. This reduction came in spite of the violent political maneuvering among Mormons, non-Mormons, and anti-Mormons so common during this quarter-century. Even more surprising, however, is that in spite of the gradual disappearance of the practice of plural marriage, references to it were even more numerous in the second time period than in the first—up from one for every 270 words to one for every 204 words. Whatever the situation before 1890, there can be little doubt that in the first two decades of the twentieth century, polygamy really was a convenient excuse to strike not merely at the influence of Mormon leaders but also at Mormonism as a religious system. An anti-Mormon propaganda campaign conducted by American Protestant missionaries and disgruntled politicians can also be documented in the second time period data, but a countercampaign mounted by the church during this period came too late to be reflected here.

The negative climate of opinion persisted through the Mormon centennial in 1930, an occasion that called forth several uncomplimentary historical accounts. (This was in sharp contrast to the next jubilee year—the 1980 sesquicentennial—which turned into a public relations bonanza for the Saints.) The negativity level gave way during the Great Depression, when articles about the self-sufficiency of the Saints led to the mistaken perception that the Church Welfare Plan kept the entire LDS population off all governmental public assistance programs.[28]

Word pictures of the Saints as good citizens doing ordinary things—in such articles as "Recreation for Young People in the Church" (*Playground*, August 1925), "Covered Wagon Days" (*Christian Century*, August 5, 1931), and "Stake No. 118" (*Time*, December 7, 1936)—moved the average attitudinal index above neutral for the first time in the entire century. The trend, especially when circulation impact is considered, moved sharply upward after that—disturbed only by breaks reflecting the news value of the decision of the Arizona authorities in 1944 to eradicate the cache of polygamists living in Short Creek, Arizona, by arresting all the polygamous men living in the isolated town and many of the women as well (see figure 7).

With regard to that journalistic genre popularly known as the exposé, whereas 46.3 percent of the articles in the sample that were published between 1861 and 1895 were coded as exposés and 32.4 percent of the articles published between 1896 and 1920 were similarly coded, of those published between 1921 and 1960, only 7.7 percent were coded as exposés. Of those, most were about the "new polygamists" who lived in Short Creek. Moreover, emphases in the various periodical articles shifted fairly dramatically away from the traditional charges against the church and its leaders during these years. Almost two-thirds (59.5 percent) of the articles placed little or no emphasis on polygamy; 69.0 percent placed little or no emphasis on the LDS Church's control of Utah politics; 80.5 percent placed little or no emphasis on the church's control of the economic life of the area; and 79 percent placed little or no emphasis on the way in which the church hierarchy (known to the Saints as general authorities) exercised social control over the LDS community.

The positive trend that started in the mid-thirties rapidly accelerated with the publication of such extremely positive articles as "They Take Care of Their

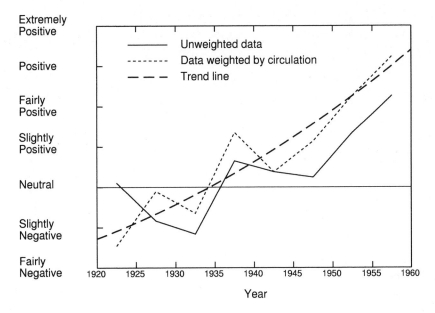

Figure 7. Summary Graph, 1920–60

"Own" in the *Reader's Digest* (March 1949) and "Those Amazing Mormons" in *Coronet* (April 1952). Six years later, "The Mormons: A Complete Way of Life" by Hartzell Spence was also published in the *Reader's Digest,* a periodical that had a huge circulation (over 16,000,000) in the 1940s and 1950s and consequently operated as a powerful influence in shaping public opinion in middle America.[29]

SURVEY RESULTS, SUMMARY

A century-long time line showing the sweep of changed perceptions captures the movement from negative to positive in the popular mind that reflects the transformation of the Mormons from being a population of dangerous and alien people to being 100 percent patriotic Americans (see figure 8).

The sample itself suggests how this radical change occurred. A steadily decreasing percentage of the articles in the sample were published in religious periodicals.[30] This is extremely significant because an article was five times as likely to be negative if it was published in a religious magazine or written by a non-Mormon religious leader. If the author could definitely be identified as Protestant, whether religious leader or not, the article was seven times more likely to be negative. As might be expected, an article was five times as likely

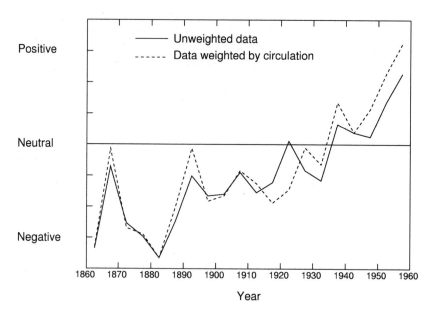

Figure 8. Attitudes Measured by Attitude Measurement Scale, 1860–1960

to be positive if it was written by an LDS Church official or other prominent Latter-day Saint, but most such articles appeared only in the third period. Naturally, there was a strong relationship between the description of
the author—including the author's profession and religious affiliation—and
the attitude expressed in the article written by that author (x^2 significant at
the .01 level). But the correlation between the description of the author and
the length of the article was even stronger (x^2 significant at the .001 level).

Very little difference in attitude was expressed in short articles, but the
longer an article was, the more likely it was to be negative. (A correlation
significant at the .005 level existed between these two variables.) If the article was an essay, it was seven times more likely to be negative; if it was an
editorial, it was four times more likely to be negative; and if it was a scholarly study, it was three times more likely to be neutral.

Historians generally answer questions about what accounts for attitudes
expressed in something that is published on the basis of informed opinions
and knowledgeable impressions. When the data are in the form of statistics,
however, a stepwise regression can answer the question exactly by identifying the items that were the best predictors of attitude. In this study, you can
know most about the attitudes in one of the articles in the sample if you know

whether it was written by a religious leader; after that you can tell more if you know the length of the article, then the type of periodical in which it was published, and finally if it was written by a journalist.

As for the answers this study provides to the general and theoretical questions posed at the outset, keep in mind that these answers come entirely from a study of periodical articles and that while these articles were a carefully chosen representative sample, these answers must in no way be taken as definitive and final. Still, it is helpful to know what in Mormonism accounts for the intensity and persistence of the negative attitudes toward the Mormons described in the time-line graphs. The answers to what caused the strenuous objection to the LDS Church, the Mormon belief system, and the Saints themselves are found in the results of the content analysis of negative concepts. In order of importance (determined by the total number of negative references), the problems Americans identified with Mormonism were (1) polygamy; (2) Mormon political activities and the LDS Church's control of politics within the Mormon community; (3) the Mormon theological system; (4) the LDS Church's control of the economy in Utah and surrounding regions; and (5) the social control that the Mormon leaders exercised over the LDS community.

Of particular significance was the finding that of the total number of references to polygamy, only about 10 percent were references to sexual debauchery or other overt sexual concepts. This seems to indicate that the "gross sensuality" aspect of plurality was not nearly as important as the way it seemed to threaten the institution of marriage and the nuclear family. The findings on politics provide a more complex picture. In the first and last time periods, the total number of references to politics were almost evenly divided between references to Mormonism as a definite practical political threat (as in the ability to control particular elections by instructing members of the church to vote for particular candidates) and to Mormonism as a generalized threat to the American political system and way of life, but in the second time period, no doubt reflecting the importance of the Reed Smoot hearings, the references were overwhelmingly (three to one) to Mormonism as a danger to the American political system and way of life.

These results tell us that there were more objections to polygamy and the church's political activities and control than to Mormon theology. Since no information truly bears on motive, it is not clear how much of the theological opposition was aimed at the extirpation of heresy. The only thing that can be said for sure is that in this sample there were almost twice as many negative references to Joseph Smith, the golden plates, and the origins of

Mormonism as there were references to Mormonism as heresy and that even though the total number of negative theological references diminished, the pattern itself remained consistent across the century.

The number of references to economics and social control was so small that any attempt to differentiate further would be misleading, especially since the economic practices of the Mormons ceased being the source of negative references about 1930 and became the source of a large portion of the positive references made in articles published since then.

Altogether the study data are so rich in explanatory detail that generalization is difficult. Nevertheless, it is accurate to characterize American attitudes toward the Mormons between 1860 and 1960 in three stages. At first everything was subject to criticism. The religion was "one of the most monstrous systems of imposture ever born of Satanic cunning, or accepted by credulous man," as one commentator put it.[31] The Mormon leaders were cruel, unethical, ambitious, greedy, and immoral; the people were crude, coarse, illiterate, dishonest, and sensual; and the system was totally foreign to the United States.

The demise of polygamy and the arrival of Utah statehood made little difference in the way the Mormon religion was described; it was still ridiculous, and if anything, even more un-Christian than it had been in the past. However, there was a definite change in other areas. The leaders were even more ambitious, greedy, unethical, and immoral, but now they were invariably able, efficient, and effective as well. The people were inherently good but, as the victims of the temporal ambitions of their leaders, still a part of an un-American system. At the same time this picture was most fully developed, the sub-rosa suspicion repeatedly appeared that somehow the Mormons were managing to solve the problems facing the United States better than their non-Mormon counterparts.

Between 1935 and 1960, there was almost no emphasis on Mormonism's origin or how Mormonism differs from Christianity. At this point, the important thing was not what the Mormons believed but the fact that they believed it sincerely. With the increasing emphasis on self-reliance, the people were no longer seen as the victims of their leaders, who were—in any case—gentle, thoughtful, and kind people of the highest ethical and moral character presiding over an extraordinarily American society and culture.[32]

To put it another way, the early descriptions of Salt Lake City are much like the witty Irishman's reply when he was asked if Port Said was the wickedest spot on earth. "Oh, my dear," he said, "it's really a great deal wickeder than that." Descriptions of the city that stood at Mormondom's center in the years following the transformation of the Mormon image in the 1930s were foreshadowed by a description of Utah written in 1912: "If ever the typically American qualities, the dauntless enterprise of the pioneers, their fierce courage, their ingenuity, adaptability and foresight, left a monument for posterity, that monument is the new Zion overlooking the Great Salt Lake."[33]

༄

It is now possible to see that, from the perspective of methodology, I extended this study a few years beyond the point where periodical articles can be regarded as a rough but fairly accurate index of the Mormon image. But from the perspective of what happened to perceptions of the Mormons during the "sixties" decade (which actually extended well into the 1970s), 1960 was a perfect stopping point for this study.

The Vietnam War years propelled a new negative to the fore in the United States. This was the time of the "hippie generation," of long hair, short skirts, bare feet, marijuana, and not LDS but LSD. Whereas a century earlier, Mormons had been the very epitome of being un-American, they became more American than the Americans in the 1960s. They looked the way most people, at least in the older generation, thought Americans ought to look and acted the way Americans ought to act. With rampant sexual permissiveness, young people living together without benefit of marriage—some of them living in communes with who knows how many sexual partners—it seemed to many of the nation's citizens that Mormons were exemplary figures. As the mountain curtain turned into a scrim, observers were able to see that the Saints were truly saints; the satyrs were in the world outside.

Appendix A: Articles Included in Poole's Index and Reader's Guide under
"Mormons and Mormonism," "Utah," and "Polygamy," 1860–1960

Journal Title	Number of Journal Articles	Date of First Article	Date of Last Article	Number of Articles in Sample
American	2	Nov. 12, 1881	Nov. 19, 1881	1
American Antiquarian	1	Nov. 1892		0
American Catholic Quarterly	5	Oct. 1879	July 1895	2
American City	1	Sept. 1949		0
American Forest	1	Apr. 1958		0
American Heritage	1	Oct. 1956		0
American Historical Association Report	1	1917		1
American Historical Review	3	Apr. 1939	July 1952	1
American Journal of Science	4	Mar. 1872	June 1878	0
American Journal of Sociology	4	Mar. 1903	Jan. 1948	0
American Magazine	5	May 1908	June 1953	2
American Mercury	11	Mar. 1926	May 1954	6

Journal Title	Number of Journal Articles	Date of First Article	Date of Last Article	Number of Articles in Sample
American Naturalist	7	Jan. 1875	June 1877	0
American Review	1	Feb. 1935		1
Andover Review	6	July 1884	Sept. 1888	1
Annals of the American Academy of Political Science	1	Jan. 1902		0
Arena	13	Feb. 1899	Nov. 1906	7
Arizona Highways	2	Apr. 1955	June 1957	0
Atlantic/Atlantic Monthly	14	Apr. 1864	Nov. 1942	2
Baptist Quarterly Review	1	Apr. 1888		1
Bay State Monthly	1	Oct. 1885		1
Better Homes and Gardens	2	Feb. 1954	Oct. 1956	0
Bibliotheca Sacra	5	Jan. 1885	Jan. 1903	2
Bookman	1	Sept. 1904		0
Brush and Pencil	1	June 1899		0
Business Week	6	Mar. 15, 1941	Feb. 27, 1960	1
California Magazine	2	Feb. 1893	June 1893	0
Catholic World	2	Nov. 1877	June 1952	0
Century	7	Jan. 1882	Jan. 1916	2
Chautauquan	2	May 1900	May 1900	1
Christian Century	7	Mar. 26, 1930	Mar. 19, 1958	3
Collier's	12	Nov. 6, 1909	July 6, 1956	4
Commonweal	4	Sept. 3, 1937	Jan. 19, 1951	0
Coronet	3	Jan. 1951	Apr. 1959	2
Cosmopolitan	4	Sept. 1895	May 1911	1
Country Life	2	June 1927	Mar. 1938	1
Current Literature	6	June 1900	Nov. 1911	4
Current Opinion	5	Feb. 1913	Mar. 1917	1
Dance Magazine	3	Feb. 1953	Mar. 1960	0
DeBow's Commercial Review	1	Feb. 1861		1
Delineator	3	Sept. 1911	Nov. 1911	0
Dial	1	Jan. 1, 1903		0
Eclectic Magazine	1	Dec. 1881		0
Education for Victory	1	Feb. 3, 1945		0
Educational Review	1	May 1915		0
Era	1	June 1903		1
Every Saturday	2	Sept. 23, 1871	Dec. 2, 1871	0
Everybody's Magazine	10	Dec. 1910	Sept. 1911	4
Flying	1	May 1953		0
Forum	10	Nov. 1887	Oct. 1926	1
Galaxy	9	Oct. 1, 1866	Dec. 1875	3
Gunton's	2	Feb. 1900	June 1900	0
Hampton's Magazine	1	Jan. 1910		1
Harper's Magazine (monthly)	14	Sept. 1871	Oct. 1960	4
Harper's Weekly	6	Feb. 2, 1890	Oct. 16, 1915	2
[Dawson's] Historical Magazine	2	Aug. 1869	May 1870	1
Hobbies	3	Sept. 1945	Sept. 1953	2
Holiday	1	Mar. 1959		0
Hours at Home	1	May 1865		0
House Beautiful	1	June 1950		0
Independent	15	Feb. 9, 1893	May 23, 1925	5
Industrial Arts and Vocational Education	2	Mar. 1942	Apr. 1952	0
Industrial Arts Magazine	1	Mar. 1921		0

Journal Title	Number of Journal Articles	Date of First Article	Date of Last Article	Number of Articles in Sample
International Review	2	Sept. 1881	Feb. 1882	2
Journal of Geology	1	Nov. 1912		0
Journal of Home Economics	1	Dec. 1945		0
Ladies' Home Journal	7	Dec. 1924	June 1925	1
Lakeside Monthly	2	May 1869	Jan. 1871	2
Land of Sunshine	2	June 1901	Oct. 1901	1
Library Journal	5	Sept. 1, 1931	May 1, 1941	0
Life	10	Apr. 13, 1944	May 2, 1960	4
Lippincott's Magazine	10	July 1870	June 1900	4
Literary Digest	17	May 23, 1914	Jan. 15, 1938	6
Literary World	5	June 16, 1883	Oct. 27, 1888	1
Littell's Living Age	2	Dec. 1861	July 18, 1863	1
Look	2	Oct. 5, 1854	Jan. 21, 1858	2
Lutheran Quarterly	1	Apr. 1900		1
Magazine of American History	3	Apr. 1884	Nov. 1889	3
Magazine of Art	2	Mar. 1937	Apr. 1942	1
Magazine of Western History	6	Apr. 1886	Apr. 1891	2
McCall's	2	Nov. 1955	Dec. 1955	1
McClure's Magazine	3	Jan. 1911	Feb. 1911	1
Methodist Quarterly Review	1	Apr. 1882		1
Methodist Review	4	Sept. 1896	Jan. 1905	1
Midland Monthly	2	Oct. 1897	Mar. 1899	0
Missionary Review of the World	35	Jan. 1901	Apr. 1932	9
Monthly Labor Review	3	Nov. 1925	Aug. 1941	0
Munsey's Magazine	1	June 1900		0
Musical America	3	Jan. 1, 1958	Apr. 1959	0
Nation	26	Feb. 23, 1882	Oct. 22, 1955	10
National Education Association Journal	15	1920	Oct. 1960	0
National Geographic	8	Mar. 1907	Apr. 1957	2
National Magazine (Boston)	3	Jan. 1900	Aug. 1902	0
National Quarterly Review	1	July 1879		1
National Republic	1	Sept. 1931		0
Nation's Business	1	June 1944		0
Natural History	2	Dec. 1954	June 1956	0
Nature Magazine	1	Jan. 1940		0
New England Magazine, n.s.	1	Apr. 1906		1
New Princeton Review	1	Sept. 1886		0
New Republic	3	Oct. 16, 1915	May 13, 1946	0
Newsweek	27	Jan. 5, 1935	Nov. 21, 1955	5
New Yorker	1	May 23, 1942		0
New York Times Magazine	4	July 20, 1947	Apr. 24, 1960	0
North American Review	13	July 1862	Jan. 1908	4
Occupations	1	Apr. 1951		0
Old and New	3	May 1870	Oct. 1870	1
Our Day	13	Jan. 1888	May 1894	4
Outing	2	Feb. 1911	Apr. 1911	1
Outlook	26	June 6, 1896	July 2, 1924	11
Out West	2	Apr. 1903	Sept. 1905	0
Overland Monthly	10	Sept. 1870	Oct. 1911	2
Penn Monthly	1	Mar. 1871		0
Playground	1	Aug. 1925		1
Political Science Quarterly	2	June 1903	Mar. 1942	0

Journal Title	Number of Journal Articles	Date of First Article	Date of Last Article	Number of Articles in Sample
Popular Mechanics	1	Mar. 1947		0
Popular Science Monthly	2	Aug. 1876	Dec. 1876	2
Potter's American Monthly	1	Oct. 1881		0
Presbyterian Review	2	Apr. 1881	Apr. 1886	1
Princeton Review, n.s.	1	Mar. 1883		0
Public Opinion	8	June 19, 1886	Dec. 28, 1893	1
Publisher's Weekly	1	June 8, 1940		0
Quarterly Journal of Economics	2	May 1917	Nov. 1922	1
Reader's Digest	7	June 1937	Apr. 1958	4
Recreation	3	Oct. 1941	Aug. 1949	1
Review of Reviews	4	Mar. 1893	Sept. 1929	0
Saint Nicholas	2	Nov. 1913	Oct. 1919	0
Saturday Evening Post	9	Dec. 9, 1922	Sept. 17, 1960	2
Saturday Review	6	Aug. 26, 1939	Dec. 28, 1957	2
School and Society	17	Mar. 27, 1915	Dec. 16, 1950	3
School Arts	1	Oct. 1947		0
School Review	2	May 1915	Feb. 1945	0
Science	15	Apr. 30, 1915	Jan. 22, 1954	0
Science Digest	1	Feb. 1946		0
Science Newsletter	3	June 5, 1937	Jan. 21, 1956	1
Scientific American	5	Sept. 12, 1903	July 1956	1
Scientific Monthly	1	May 1928		0
Scribner's Monthly	6	Feb. 1872	Jan. 1904	2
Senior Scholastic	4	Oct. 4, 1943	Nov. 17, 1954	1
Southern Review, n.s.	1	Oct. 1876		0
Spirit of Missions	1	Feb. 1909		0
State and Local Taxation	3	1907	1912	0
Sunset: The Magazine of Western Living	3	June 1953	Oct. 1960	1
Sunset: The Pacific Monthly	7	Oct. 1912	Mar. 1929	2
Survey	2	May 8, 1915	July 1936	0
System	1	May 1917		0
Technical World	2	Dec. 1912	Dec. 1912	0
Theatre Arts	3	Apr. 1949	Dec. 1958	0
Time	25	June 8, 1936	Nov. 28, 1960	8
Travel	10	Apr. 1934	Aug. 1959	0
Unitarian Review	1	Feb. 1885		1
United Service	10	July 1890	Apr. 1891	3
U.S. News & World Report	1	Oct. 14, 1955		0
Vogue	1	Feb. 1, 1958		0
Wilson Library Bulletin	1	May 1956		1
Woman's Home Companion	1	Sept. 1940		0
Woman's Journal	1	July 20, 1929		0
World's Work	4	Dec. 1902	Mar. 1916	1
World Today	4	Feb. 1905	Jan. 1909	1

Appendix B: A Chronological Listing of the Articles in the Sample

A bracket containing the overall ranking assigned to the article and the weighting factor used when the data were analyzed to take impact into account follows each citation.

February 1861. Cartwright, Samuel A. et al. "Hereditary Descent; or, Depravity of the Offspring of Polygamy among the Mormons." *DeBow's Commercial Review* 30:206–16. [Negative, 1]

July 18, 1863. "Mormonism in Wales." *Living Age* 78:124–27. [Negative, 1]

October 1, 1866. Tullidge, E. M. "Views of Mormondom." *Galaxy* 2:209–14. [Slightly positive, 3]

May 1869. Waite, C. B. "Utah." *Lakeside Monthly* 1:290–93. [Slightly negative, 1]

May 1870. Lapham, Fayette. "The Mormons: Interview with the Father of Joseph Smith, the Mormon Prophet." [Dawson's] *Historical Magazine* 7:305–9. [Slightly negative, 1]

September 1870. Brigham, William T. "The Church of Latter-Day Saints: Part I." *Old and New* 2:320–26. [Neutral, 1]

January 1871. Chamberlin, Everett. "My Christmas at Salt Lake." *Lakeside Monthly* 5:57–68. [Negative, 1]

September 1871. Fitch, [Mrs.] Thomas. "The Mahomet of the West." *Overland Monthly* 7:235–41. [Fairly negative, 1]

February 1872. Seeley, R. H. "The Mormons and Their Religion." *Scribner's Monthly* 3:396–408. [Fairly negative, 1]

November 1872. "Saved from the Mormons." *Galaxy* 14:677–85. [Negative, 1]

October 1875. Codman, John. "Through Utah." *Galaxy* 20:487–96. [Slightly negative, 1]

August 1876. Beadle, J. H. "Social Experiments in Utah." *Popular Science Monthly* 9:479–90. [Negative, 1]

December 1876. Medderburn, Daniel. "Mormonism from a Mormon Point of View." *Popular Science Monthly* 10:156–73. [Neutral, 1]

July 1879. Onderdonk, James L. "The Present Phase of the Mormon Problem." *National Quarterly Review* 39:89–94. [Extremely negative, 1]

August 1880. Mather, Frederic G. "The Early Days of Mormonism." *Lippincott's Magazine* 26:198–211. [Negative, 1]

March 1881. Goodwin, C. C. "The Political Attitude of the Mormons." *North American Review* 132:276–86. [Extremely negative, 1]

September 1881. Codman, John. "Mormonism." *International Review* 11:221–34. [Fairly negative, 1]

November 12, 1881. Thompson, Ralph E. "Mormon Solution of the Mormon Problem." *American* 3:68–69. [Negative, 1]

January 1882. Edmunds, George F. "Political Aspects of Mormonism." *Harper's New Monthly Magazine* 64:285–88. [Negative, 1]

February 1882. McBride, John R. "Utah and Mormonism." *International Review* 12:181–96. [Extremely negative, 1]

April 1882. Hanson, Andrew J. "Utah and the Mormon Problem." *Methodist Quarterly Review* 64:205–26. [Extremely negative, 1]

July 14, 1883. Paddock, Cornelia. "'Sinners and Saints': Paddock vs. Robinson." *Literary World* 14:225–27. [Negative, 1]

December 20, 1883. "A Radical Remedy for Polygamy." *Nation* 37:502–3. [Negative, 1]

January 1884. Murray, Eli H. "[Answer to] John Taylor's 'Ecclesiastical Control in Utah.'" *North American Review* 138:13–23. [Negative, 11]

April 1884. Robinson, John C. "The Utah Expedition." *Magazine of American History* 11: 335–41. [Fairly negative, 1]

September 1884. Beatty, William A. "A Practical Consideration of the Mormon Question." *Overland Monthly,* n.s. 4:296–303. [Fairly negative, 1]

February 1885. Bartol, C. A. "The Puritan and the Mormon." *Unitarian Review* 23:155–63. [Fairly negative, 1]

October 1885. Reed, Victoria. "The Mormon Church." *Bay State Monthly* 3:348–56. [Extremely negative, 1]

April 1886. "Memorial to Congress in 1844 [plus editorial comment]." *Magazine of Western History* 3:727–35. [Fairly positive, 1]

April 1886. Eells, James. "The Mormon Question." *Presbyterian Review* 7:358–63. [Negative, 1]

July 1886. Wood, William A. "An Old Mormon City in Missouri." *Magazine of American History* 16:98–99. [Fairly negative, 1]

January 13, 1887. Leonard, D. L. "Decline of the Mormon Theocracy." *Nation* 44:29. [Fairly negative, 1]

August 18, 1887. "Progress in Utah." *Nation* 45:133. [Negative, 1]

December 31, 1887. "The Question of Statehood for Utah." *Public Opinion* 4:269–72. [Negative, 1]

January 1888. McNiece, R. G. "Shall Utah Be Made a Mormon State?" *Our Day* 4:4–10. [Extremely negative, 1]

April 1888. McKay, Stanley A. "Two American Religions: I. Mormonism." *Baptist Quarterly Review* 10:172–87. [Negative, 1]

September 1888. Hazard, Caroline. "'Early Days of Mormonism, Palmyra, Kirtland, and Nauvoo.' By J. H. Kennedy." *Andover Review* 10:321–27. [Extremely negative, 1]

November 1889. Bancroft, Hubert Howe. "A Chapter from the History of Utah." *Magazine of American History* 22:358–70. [Slightly positive, 1]

January 1890. "Forty Years in the American Wilderness." *American Catholic Quarterly Review* 15:123–50. [Extremely negative, 1]

February 27, 1890. [Cox, J. D.]. "Bancroft's Utah: I." *Nation* 50:179–80. [Fairly negative, 1]

March 1890. Gates, Susa Young. "Family Life among the Mormons." *North American Review* 150:339–50. [Positive, 1]

April 1890. "When Brigham Young Was King." *American Catholic Quarterly Review* 15:284–301. [Negative, 1]

September 25, 1890. Wright, G. Frederick. "The Mormon Question in Idaho." *Nation* 51:243–44. [Fairly negative, 1]

October 30, 1890. Wright, G. Frederick. "The Mormon Muddle in Utah." *Nation* 51:338–39. [Fairly negative, 1]

November 1890. Hamilton, W. R. "History of the Mormon Rebellion of 1856–57 [chapter 7]." *United Service* 4:446–59. [Negative, 1]

December 1890. McNiece, R. G. "The Mormon Manifesto against Polygamy." *Our Day* 6:413–23. [Extremely negative, 1]

January 1891. Hamilton, W. R. "History of the Mormon Rebellion of 1856–57 [chapter 9]." *United Service* 5:65–71. [Slightly negative, 1]

February 1891. Hamilton, W. R. "History of the Mormon Rebellion of 1856–57 [chapter 10]." *United Service* 5:148–61. [Slightly negative, 1]

April 1891. Kennedy, James Harrison. "Miracles in the Mormon Church." *Magazine of Western History* 13:761–67. [Fairly negative, 1]

January 1893. Cook, Joseph. "New Conspiracies of Mormonism." *Our Day* 11:39–42. [Negative, 1]

February 16, 1893. "Utah and Statehood: Additional Opinions." *Independent* n.v. 6–7. [Slightly negative, 1]

April 8, 1893. Ralph, Julian. "A Week with the Mormons." *Harper's Weekly* 37:324–27, 330. [Fairly positive, 1]

May–June 1894. [Cook, Joseph]. "Utah at the Door of Congress." *Our Day* 13:231–34. [Negative, 1]

September 1895. Cockerill, John A. "Brigham Young and Modern Utah." *Cosmopolitan* 19:501–12. [Positive, 1]

June 6, 1896. Young, Eugene. "Self-Government by the Mormons." *Outlook* 53:1067–69. [Slightly negative, 1]

September 1897. Larned, William Trowbridge. "The Rocky Mountain Prophets." *Lippincott's Monthly Magazine (McBride's)* 60:382–93. [Neutral, 1]

February 1899. Everett, Ruth. "Woman's Life in Utah." *Arena* 21:183–92. [Extremely negative, 1]

June 1899. Curtis, Theodore W. "A Word for the Mormons." *Arena* 21:715–36. [Fairly positive, 1]

December 16, 1899. "Mr. Roberts's Appeal." *Outlook* 63:896–98. [Fairly negative, 1]

January 27, 1900. "The Roberts Case." *Outlook* 64:201–2. [Fairly negative, 1]

February 1, 1900. "The Exclusion of Roberts." *Independent* 52:327–28. [Negative, 1]

February 24, 1900. Nutting, John D. "The Mormons: A Reply [An Answer to C. B. Spahr's 'The Mormons,' with Editorial Commentary]." *Outlook* 64:467–70. [Extremely negative, 1]

February 1900. Hartt, Rollin Lynde. "The Mormons." *Atlantic* 85:261–72. [Extremely negative, 1]

March 1900. Hudson, Mrs. J. K. "The Grandmother's Story: A Mormon Episode." *Lippincott's Monthly Magazine* 65:450–63. [Negative, 1]

April 1900. Anstadt, P. "Mormonism, Its History, Doctrines, Strength, Methods and Aims." *Lutheran Quarterly* 30:228–43. [Extremely negative, 1]

May 1900. Sparks, Edwin Erle. "The Expansion of the American People [Discussion of Mormons in American Reforms and Reformers' Section]." *Chautauquan* 31:165–67. [Fairly positive, 1]

June 1900. Hudson, Mrs. J. K. "One of the Lord's People." *Lippincott's Monthly Magazine* 65:944–55. [Slightly positive, 1]

October 1900. Smythe, William E. "Mormon Land Tenure." *Current Literature* 29:426–27. [Fairly positive, 1]

February 9, 1901. Smythe, William E. "The Secret of Mormon Success." *Harper's Weekly* 45:164–65. [Slightly positive, 1]

June 1901. Bicknell, Ralph E. "The Modern Zion." *Land of Sunshine* [*Out West*] 14:449–62. [Neutral, 1]

February 1902. Shoemaker, Joel. "A Co-operative Commonwealth." *Arena* 27:164–73. [Slightly positive, 1]

April 17, 1902. Nutting, John D. "A Study of the Present Mormon Problem." *Independent* 54:924–30. [Negative, 1]

July 1902. Lunn, George R. "A Study of Mormonism: Part II: Social and Political Character." *Bibliotheca Sacra* 59:434–50. [Fairly negative, 1]

August 1902. Smith, Joseph [III]. "Origin of American Polygamy." *Arena* 28:160–67. [Slightly negative, 1]

November 1902. Smith, Joseph F. "Real Origin of American Polygamy: A Reply." *Arena* 28:490–98. [Slightly positive, 1]

January 1903. Bosworth, L. A. M. "Mormonism the Same Yesterday, Today, and Forever." *Bibliotheca Sacra* 60:171–76. [Extremely negative, 1]

March 1903. Forman, S. M. "Recent Observations in a Mormon Town." *Missionary Review of the World* 26:209–10. [Extremely negative, 1]

May 1903. Smith, Joseph F. "The Mormonism of Today." *Arena* 29:449–56. [Fairly positive, 1]

June 1903. Halsey, James Diddle. "Mormonism as It Is To-day." *Era* 11:511–22. [Negative, 1]

January 1904. Dellenbaugh, F. S. "A New Valley of Wonders." *Scribner's Magazine* 35:1–18. [Slightly positive, 1]

April 1904. Dailey, George. "Mormonism and How to Meet It." *Missionary Review of the World* 27:251–61. [Extremely negative, 1]

June 1904. Baker, Ray Stannard. "The Vitality of Mormonism." *Century Magazine* 68:163–77. [Slightly negative, 1]

December 1904. "Scientific Aspects of Mormonism [book review]." *Missionary Review of the World* 27:942–43. [Fairly negative, 1]

January–February 1905. Spencer, E. B. T. "Notes on the Book of Mormon." *Methodist Review* 65:31–43. [Negative, 1]

May 1905. Ewing, William C. "The Golden Bible and Mormonism." *Current Literature* 38:428–32. [Slightly negative, 1]

September 1905. Cullom, Shelby M. "The Menace of Mormonism." *North American Review* 181:379–85. [Negative, 1]

October 1905. Brigham, Johnson. "The Original Manuscript of the Book of Mormon." *World Today* 9:1101–6. [Slightly negative, 1]

January 6, 1906. Irving, G. A. "Some Aspects of Mormonism." *Outlook* 82:32–35. [Slightly negative, 1]

April 1906. Johnson, Clifton. "The Trail of the Mormon." *New England Magazine* 34:131–39. [Slightly negative, 1]

November 1906. Schroeder, Theodore. "Polygamy and the Constitution." *Arena* 36:492–97. [Negative, 1]

December 29, 1906. Irving, G. A. "The Ways of Mormons." *Outlook* 84:1064–68. [Fairly negative, 1]

March 2, 1907. Borah, W. E. "Mormonism in Idaho." *Outlook* 85:530. [Slightly negative, 1]

October 17, 1907. Smoot, Reed. "Utah in Politics." *Independent* 63:926–30. [Positive, 1]

May 1908. Doty, Madeleine Zabriskie. "Mormon Women and What They Think of Polygamy." *American Magazine* 66:41–47. [Slightly positive, 1]

November 6, 1909. Comstock, Sarah. "The Mormon Woman." *Collier's* 44:16–17. [Slightly negative, 1]

January 1910. Welliver, Judson C. "The Mormon Church and the Sugar Trust." *Hampton's Magazine* 24:82–93. [Fairly negative, 3]

July 1910. Harvey, Charles M. "The Story of the Salt Lake Trail." *Atlantic* 106:112–22. [Neutral, 1]

January 1911. Hendrick, Burton J. "The Mormon Revival of Polygamy." *McClure's Magazine* 36:245–61. [Extremely negative, 2]

February 1911. Wallace, Dillon. "Saddle and Camp in the Rockies: In the Land of Zion." *Outing Magazine* 57:578–90. [Neutral, 1]

March 1911. "The Mormon Revival of Polygamy." *Current Literature* 50:289–92. [Extremely negative, 1]

April 15, 1911. Russell, Isaac. "Mr. Roosevelt to the Mormons." *Collier's* 47:28, 36. [Slightly positive, 3]

May 1911. Cannon, Frank J., and Harvey J. O'Higgins. "Under the Prophet in Utah" [6th installment]. *Everybody's Magazine* 24:652–64. [Negative, 3]

June 1911. Cannon, Frank J., and Harvey J. O'Higgins. "Under the Prophet in Utah" [7th installment]. *Everybody's Magazine* 24:825–35. [Extremely negative, 3]

July 1911. Cannon, Frank J., and Harvey J. O'Higgins. "Under the Prophet in Utah" [8th installment]. *Everybody's Magazine* 25:94–107. [Extremely negative, 3]

September 1911. Smith, Joseph [III]. "Mormons Who Are Not Polygamists." *Everybody's Magazine* 25:427–28. [Slightly negative, 3]

October 7, 1911. "The Mormonism of To-day." *Outlook* 99:310–11. [Fairly positive, 1]

November 1911. "A Methodist Minister's Defense of Mormonism." *Current Literature* 51:536–37. [Slightly positive, 1]

October 1912. Woehlke, Walter V. "The Garden of Utah." *Sunset: The Pacific Monthly* 29:355–68. [Slightly positive, 1]

April 1913. "Mormonism's Reply to Its Latest Critics." *Current Opinion* 54:310–11. [Slightly negative, 1]

November 1913. Paddock, [Mrs.] John, and Elizabeth Vermilye. "Facts on Mormonism." *Missionary Review of the World* 36:855–56. [Extremely negative, 1]

May 23, 1914. "The Christian Attitude toward the Mormon." *Literary Digest* 48:1257–58. [Neutral, 1]

March 27, 1915. "Conditions at the University of Utah." *School and Society* 1:456–59. [Slightly negative, 1]

April 7, 1915. "The University of Utah." *Outlook* 109:800–801. [Fairly negative, 1]

May 22, 1915. Kingsbury, J. T. "Dean Holman's Criticism of the Administration of the University of Utah." *School and Society* 1:745–47. [Slightly negative, 1]

June 12, 1915. "Preliminary Summary of Findings of the Committee of Inquiry of the American Association of University Professors on Conditions at the University of Utah." *School and Society* 1:861–64. [Slightly negative, 1]

August 1915. Whitney, Orson F. "The 'Mormon' President." *Sunset: The Pacific Monthly* 35:356–58. [Positive, 1]

January 1916. "Liberty in Utah." *Century* 91:475. [Extremely negative, 1]

March 1916. "The Mormons of Mexico." *World's Work* 31:484. [Extremely negative, 2]

December 20, 1916. Davenport, Frederick M. "The Junction of Jew and Mormon." *Outlook* 114:863–65. [Fairly positive, 1]

1917. Daines, Franklin D. "Separatism in Utah, 1847–1870." *American Historical Association Report,* 331–43. [Slightly positive, 1]

December 7, 1918. "Changing Heads of the Mormon Church." *Literary Digest* 59:32–33. [Neutral, 3]

November 1919. LaRue, William E. "Mormons of Today and How to Win Them." *Missionary Review of the World* 42:866–69. [Negative, 1]

January 1921. Roundy, Rodney W. "Mormonism of Today and How to Meet It." *Missionary Review of the World* 44:21–24. [Slightly negative, 1]

November 1922. Gardner, Hamilton. "Communism among the Mormons." *Quarterly Journal of Economics* 37:134–74. [Neutral, 1]

August 1923. [Moore, Frank L.] "Mormonism." *Missionary Review of the World* 56:650–52. [Slightly negative, 1]

July 2, 1924. Hagedorn, Hermann. "My Mormon." *Outlook* 137:358–59. [Slightly negative, 1]

February 1925. Werner, Milton R. "Brigham Young." *Ladies' Home Journal* 42:23, 99–100, 103. [Fairly negative, 10]

May 23, 1925. "Salt Lake City: Zion of the Mormons." *Independent* 114:579–82. [Slightly positive, 1]

August 1925. Kirkham, Oscar A. "Recreation for Young People in the Church." *Playground* 19:253–54. [Extremely positive, 1]

March 1926. De Voto, Bernard. "Utah." *American Mercury* 7:317–23. [Fairly negative, 1]

October 1926. Smoot, Reed. "Why I Am a Mormon." *Forum* 76:562–69. [Positive, 1]

February 25, 1928. "When Michigan Groaned under a Mormon King." *Literary Digest* 96:46–50. [Neutral, 6]

November 17, 1928. "A Mormon Utopia." *Literary Digest* 99:31–32. [Slightly positive, 6]

January 1930. De Voto, Bernard. "The Centennial of Mormonism." *American Mercury* 19:1–13. [Negative, 1]

March 26, 1930. "The Second Hundred Years Will Be the Hardest." *Christian Century* 47:388. [Fairly negative, 1]

April 1930. Rice, Claton S. "Mormonism and the Way Out." *Missionary Review of the World* 53:273–78. [Fairly negative, 1]

August 5, 1931. Hutchinson, Paul. "Covered Wagon Days." *Christian Century* 48:991–92. [Fairly positive, 1]

November 1931. La Rue, William E. "Why Give the Gospel to the Mormons?" *Missionary Review of the World* 54:844–46. [Fairly negative, 1]

August 1933. Larsen, Louis W. "Childhood in a Mormon House." *American Mercury* 29:480–87. [Fairly negative, 1]

February 1934. Brooks, Juanita. "A Close-up of Polygamy." *Harper's Magazine* 168:299–307. [Slightly positive, 1]

July 1934. Markey, Morris. "Kingdom in the Desert." *American Magazine* 118:64–65, 134–35. [Neutral, 6]

February 1935. Burgess, R. L. "This Is the Place: The Mormons and the Land." *American Review* 4:410–22. [Fairly negative, 1]

December 21, 1935. "Polygamy: Court Says Religious Freedom Includes but One Wife." *Newsweek* 6:12. [Extremely negative, 1]

May 1936. Borah, Leo A. "Utah, Carved by Wind and Waters." *National Geographic Magazine* 69:577–623. [Fairly positive, 3]

June 6, 1936. "No More Mormons on the Dole." *Literary Digest* 121:55. [Fairly positive, 2]

December 7, 1936. "Stake No. 118." *Time* 28:52–53. [Slightly negative, 2]

June 30, 1937. W[illett], H. L. "Question Box." *Christian Century* 54:841. [Negative, 1]

August 7, 1937. "Those Queer Mormons." *Literary Digest* 124:25–26. [Positive, 2]

October 4, 1937. "Mormons, Money, Missions." *Time* 30:43. [Positive, 2]

March 1938. Sheldon, H. P. "Guns and Game." *Country Life* 73:24, 115. [Slightly positive, 1]

October 1938. De Voto, Bernard. "The Easy Chair: Vacation." *Harper's Magazine* 177:557–60. [Slightly negative, 1]

March 1939. Russell, Oland D. "King James I of Michigan." *American Mercury* 46:273–81. [Slightly negative, 1]

August 26, 1939. De Voto, Bernard. "Millennial Millions: The Story of the Mormons." *Saturday Review of Literature* 20:3–4, 14. [Fairly negative, 1]

February 1940. Wells, Anna Mary. "Mrs. Brigham Young." *American Mercury* 49:194–200. [Slightly positive, 1]

May 1940. Fisher, Vardis. "A Condensation of *Children of God.*" *Reader's Digest* 36:144–88. [Fairly positive, 12]

August 12, 1940. "Cumorah's Pageant." *Time* 36:42–43. [Slightly negative, 2]

March 15, 1941. "Utah Steps Out." *Business Week* n.v. 24, 26. [Neutral, 1]

October 1941. Waspe, Ileen A. "Their Silver Jubilee." *Recreation* 35:457, 470–71. [Fairly positive, 1]

April 1942. Hobbs, Gladys. "Art in the Marketplace." *Magazine of Art* 35:138–39. [Neutral, 1]

June 6, 1942. Marshall, Margaret. "Notes by the Way [review of *Desert Saints* by Nels Anderson]." *Nation* 154:658. [Fairly positive, 1]

December 12, 1942. English, Richard. "The Mormons Move Over." *Collier's* 110:86–87, 101. [Slightly negative, 8]

March 20, 1944. "Fundamentalists." *Time* 43:55. [Fairly negative, 3]

July 3, 1944. "Polygamy: Utah Jails 15 Fundamentalists." *Life* 17:22–23. [Slightly positive, 12]

April 23, 1945. Stegner, Wallace. "Mormon Trees." *Senior Scholastic* 46:18. [Fairly positive, 1]

September 1, 1945. "Joseph Smith and the Mormons." *Hobbies* 50:19. [Fairly negative, 1]

January 26, 1946. McWilliams, Carey. "Memo on the Mormons." *Nation* 162:97–98. [Slightly positive, 1]

July 1946. Wayne, John Lakmord. "Solomon Spaulding's Manuscript." *Hobbies* 51:78–79, 82. [Negative, 1]

April 1947. Cannon, M. Hamlin. "Migration of English Mormons to America." *American Historical Review* 52:436–55. [Slightly positive, 1]

July 28, 1947. "This Is the Place." *Newsweek* 30:72–73. [Slightly positive, 2]

October 27, 1947. "Mormon Family Has a Reunion." *Life* 23:59–60. [Fairly negative, 12]

May 15, 1948. Baum, Arthur W. "Utah's Big Baby." *Saturday Evening Post* 220:38–39, 154, 156, 158, 160–61. [Neutral, 10]

March 1949. Best, Katharine, and Katharine Hillyer, "They Take Care of Their Own." *Reader's Digest* 54:73–76. [Extremely positive, 23]

November 21, 1949. "U. of U." *Newsweek* 34:87. [Slightly positive, 2]

May 1, 1950. Williams, Richard L. "Politician without a Future." *Life* 28:109–10, 113–16. [Neutral, 14]

June 3, 1950. Cerf, Bennett. "Trade Winds." *Saturday Review of Literature* 33:4–5. [Slightly positive, 1]

January 1951. Lang, Kurt. "Destiny on Wings." *Coronet* 29:137. [Extremely positive, 5]

August 20, 1951. "Witness for Christ." *Newsweek* 38:70–79. [Neutral, 2]

April 1952. Hamilton, Andrew. "Those Amazing Mormons." *Coronet* 31:26–30. [Extremely positive, 5]

June 1952. Breed, Jack. "Roaming the West's Fantastic Four Corners." *National Geographic Magazine* 101:705–42. [Neutral, 5]

August 16, 1952. Doxey, Roy W. "The Mormons and the Negro." *Nation* 175:inside front cover. [Positive, 1]

January 3, 1953. Taylor, Margie. "Is Salt Lake City like Atlanta, Georgia?" *Nation* 176:20. [Negative, 1]

July 13, 1953. "Budget for Living." *Newsweek* 42:56. [Slightly positive, 2]

August 1953. "Utah's Fabled Color Country." *Sunset: The Magazine of Western Living* 111:34–39. [Slightly positive, 1]

November 13, 1953. Jessop, Edson, and Maurine Whipple. "Why I Have Five Wives." *Collier's* 132:27–30. [Slightly positive, 7]

May 1954. Cary, James. "Untold Story of Short Creek." *American Mercury* 78:119–23. [Fairly negative, 1]

October 5, 1954. Evans, Richard L. "What Is a Mormon?" *Look* 18:67–68, 70, 71–72. [Positive, 8]

June 1955. Evans, Richard L. "What Is a Mormon?" *Reader's Digest* 66:143–46. [Positive, 23]

December 1955. Fitzgerald, John Dennis. "Papa Married a Mormon." *McCall's* 83:50–51, 123, 125, 127–29, 133–35, 137, 139–40, 143–44. [Fairly positive, 11]

January 21, 1956. "Texans Are Different." *Science News Letter* 69:38. [Fairly positive, 1]

May 1956. Kirkpatrick, L. H. "Culture on Commercial Channels." *Wilson Library Bulletin* 30:697–99, 701. [Neutral, 1]

July 1956. Vogt, Evon Z., and John M. Roberts. "A Study of Values." *Scientific American* 195:25–31. [Slightly positive, 1]

May 1957. "Community of Saints." *Harper's Magazine* 214:82, 84. [Positive, 1]

January 21, 1958. Spence, Hartzell. "The Mormons." *Look* 22:56–64, 66–69. [Extremely positive, 10]

April 1958. Spence, Hartzell. "The Mormon Church: A Complete Way of Life." *Reader's Digest* 72:184–86, 188, 190. [Extremely positive, 24]

September 15, 1958. "London's Mormon Temple." *Time* 72:53. [Fairly positive, 5]

October 11, 1958. Taylor, Frank J. "The Saints Roll Up Their Sleeves." *Saturday Evening Post* 231:34–35, 88–90. [Extremely positive, 3]

April 13, 1959. "Mormons and Civil Rights." *Time* 73:96. [Negative, 5]

June 22, 1959. "Dancingest Denomination." *Time* 123:47. [Slightly positive, 5]

May 2, 1960. "The Joseph Smith Saints." *Life* 48:63–66. [Fairly positive, 13]

November 28, 1960. "The Senior Apostle." *Time* 76:77–78. [Fairly positive, 5]

Appendix C: Shipps Historical Data Questionnaire

Appendix C: Shipps Historical Data Questionnaire

1. Reference from Poole's Index or Readers' Guide:

2. Article Number _____

3. Periodical Number _____

              Day   Month   Year

4. Date of article   _____/_____/_____

5. Word length:

    A.   Approximate number of words _____

    B.   Word length category

0 - 0-499 words	5 - 2,500-2,999 words
1 - 500-999 words	6 - 3,000-3,999 words
2 - 1,000-1,499 words	7 - 4,000-4,999 words
3 - 1,500-1,999 words	8 - 5,000-7,499 words
4 - 2,000-2,499 words	9 - 8,000+ words

6. Exact page length _____

    (If entire article is on a single page =0l; if portions are on two pages = 02; always count both first and last pages, e.g. "pp. 38-44" = 07)

7.   Type of article

0- general essay	5 - description and travel
1 - feature article	6 - book review
2 - contemporary news article	7 - biography/autobiography/ memoir
3 - scholarly study	8 - fiction
4 - editorial	9 - other, write in description

                                    _____

8. Type of periodical

  0 - general quality editorial/opinion/literary magazine

  1 - general popular editorial/opinion/pictorial/literary magazine

  2 - general magazine on specialized subject; write in subject in space below

  3 - national and world affairs magazine

  4 - men's/women's magazine

  5 - quarterly, literary, and "little" magazines (except scholarly journals)

  6 - scholarly journals, write in subject in space below

  7 - religious magazines, write in denomination in space below

  8 - region and travel magazines

  9 - other; write in type _____

9. Information about periodical

  A. Publication interval

    0 - once a week or more (weekly)

    1 - more than once a month, but not weekly

    2- once a month (monthly)

    3 - every two months (bi-monthly)

    4 - quarterly

    5 - irregularly

    6 - other, write in

    9 - information not available (NA)

  B. Circulation

00 - 499 or less	11 - 75,000-99,999
01 - 500-999	12 - 100,000-199,999
02 - 1,000-1,499	13 - 200,000-399,999
03 - 1,500-1,999	14 - 400,000-699,999
04 - 2,000-4,999	15 - 700,000-999,999
05 - 5,000-9,999	16 - 1,000,000-1,999,999
06 - 10,000-14,999	17 - 2,000,000-2,999,999
07 - 15,000-19,999	18 - 3,000,000-3,999,999
08 - 20,000-29,999	19 - 4,000,000-4,999,999
09 - 30,000-49,999	20 - 5,000,000+
10 - 50,000-74,999	99 - statistics unavailable

C. Place of publication

New England
    01 - Maine
    02 - New Hampshire
    03 - Vermont
    04 - Massachusetts (except Boston)
    05 - Rhode Island
    06 - Connecticut
    07 - Boston
Mid-Atlantic
    11 - New York (except New York City)
    12 - New Jersey
    13 - Pennsylvania (except Philadelphia)
    14 - New York City
    15 - Philadelphia
Midwest
    21 - Ohio
    22 - Indiana
    23 - Illinois
    24 - Michigan
    25 - Wisconsin
West North Central
    31 - Minnesota
    32 - Iowa
    33 - Missouri
    34 - North Dakota
    35 - South Dakota
    36 - Nebraska
    37 - Kansas
South Atlantic
    41 - Delaware
    42 - Maryland
    43 - District of Columbia
    44 - Virginia
    45 - West Virginia
    46 - North Carolina
    47 - South Carolina
    48 - Georgia
    49 - Florida
East South Central
    51 - Kentucky
    52 - Tennessee
    53 - Alabama
    54 - Mississippi
West South Central
    61 - Arkansas
    62 - Louisiana
    63 - Oklahoma
    64 - Texas

Far West
    71 - Montana
    72 - Idaho

    73 - Wyoming
    74 - Colorado
    75 - New Mexico
    76 - Arizona
    77 - Utah
    78 - Nevada
Pacific
    81 - Washington
    82 - Oregon
    83 - California
    84 - Alaska
    85 - Hawaii
    99 - Information unavailable (NA)

10. Subject matter of article (CHOOSE CLOSEST CATEGORY)

General

00 - general essay or feature article on Mormonism which covers historical background as well as contemporary Utah situation
01 - general discussion of Mormon/Utah society and culture focusing primarily on contemporary Utah situation (most works of the "life among the Mormons" genre and most travel accounts will fall in this category)
02 - historical surveys of Mormonism which place little or no emphasis on the contemporary Utah situation
03 - articles which cover more than one specific aspect of Mormonism but do not fit in the general categories 00, 01, or 02 above

Theological and religious concerns, intra-church programs and activities

10 - general description of Mormon theology, Mormonism as a religion, what Mormons believe, et cetera
11- articles on individual church leaders as religious leaders
12 - general character of church hierarchy, organizational structure of the church hierarchy, changes in personnel in church hierarchy
13 - church buildings, building programs, Mormon temples
14 - missionary activity, growth of the church
15 - Mormonism as a religious movement in other nations
16 - Church youth program
17 - Church welfare program

Specific LDS doctrines (except polygamy)

20 - the Word of Wisdom
21 - endowments, temple work, genealogy
22 - Mormonism and the Black race
23 - articles on any other specific LDS doctrine except polygamy, write in subject_____
24 - articles on general theological subjects not covered in categories from 10 through 23 above, write in subject _____

Polygamy

30 - general article covering all aspects of polygamy
31 - theological justification of polygamy
32 - background (i.e., history) of practice of LDS polygamy
33 - the practice of polygamy in Utah prior to 1890
34 - effect of polygamy on wives and family
35 - the end of polygamy, the Manifesto
36 - continuation of polygamous relationships after the Manifesto
37 - latter-day revivals of polygamy
38 - articles on polygamy which do not fit squarely in the categories from 30 to 37

Mormonism and Politics

40 -   general church control of political affairs within LDS community
41 -   Mormonism and Utah politics
42 -   Mormonism and state politics in states other than Utah
43 -   Mormonism and national politics
44 -   individual Mormon/Utah political leaders
45 -   articles on politics which do not fit squarely in categories 40 to 44

Mormonism and Finance/ Economy

50 -   general church control of economic affairs within LDS community
51 -   Mormon communitarian movements
52 -   Mormon/Gentile business relationships
53 -   Church investments and business interests (not implying control)
54 -   articles on tithing and church income in general
55 -   articles on economic practices which do not fit squarely in categories 50 to 54

Articles of Limited Scope

60 -   limited aspects of Mormonism/Mormon culture other than polygamy, politics, economics
        theology (e.g., Mormon coins, immigration)
61 -   Mormons in a specific geographical area (e.g., Mexico, Idaho)
62 -   individual Mormons (general treatment, not as political or religious leaders)
63 -   Joseph Smith
64 -   Brigham Young
65 -   articles on non-Utah LDS churches and splinter groups

Articles Focused on "Utah" as Opposed to "Mormonism"

70 -   general articles on the state of Utah
71 -   geographical descriptions of all or portions of Utah
72 -   Utah education, educational system
73 -   non-Mormons in Utah
74 -   Utah industries and resources

Miscellaneous

80 -   Other, i.e., articles on subjects other than those listed above, write in
        subject_____

11. Source of article

0 - apparently written originally for this periodical
1 - reprint of article published in another journal (not newspaper)
2 - condensation of longer article or book published elsewhere
3 - chapter from a book
4 - reprint or portions or entire newspaper articles
5 - reprint of government document
6 - reprint of pamphlet or broadside
7 - a combination of two or more of the above
8 - not sure about source. If exact source known, write in _____

12. Source of information in article

    0 - personal observation (traveler, visitor to Utah, Utah resident)
    1 - interviews with Utah residents
    2 - books and articles mainly written by non-Mormons, non-Mormon newspapers
    3 - books and articles mainly written by Mormons
    4 - government documents
    5 - source of information is uncertain

13. Illustrations

    A. 1.   Number of illustrations or other visual material   _____

    B. Type of illustration (CIRCLE ALL THAT APPLY)

        0 - there are no illustrations, maps, charts, et cetera
        1 - photograph
        2 - idealized artistic rendering (painting, drawing, etching) of subject
        3 - artistic rendering of subject intended to correspond with reality
        4 - cartoon or caricature
        5 - map
        6 - charts, graphs, statistical tables

C. What proportion of the article is devoted to illustrations and other visual materials?

        0 - none   4 - about half
        1 - less than one-tenth   5 - more than half, but not three-fourths
        2 - about one-fourth   6 - three-fourths or more
        3 - about one-third

D. Subject matter of illustration (CIRCLE ALL THAT APPLY)

        0 - no illustrations   5 - Utah business or industry
        1 - portrait of single individual   6 - Utah scenery (mountains, canyons
           or posed group portrait   Great Salt Lake, city or town street scenes)
        2 - portrayal of Mormon women   7 - Utah/Mormon architecture (except
           or polygamous families   church edifices)
        3 - Mormons en route to Utah,   8 - church edifices; if not LDS
           Utah/Mormon pioneer life   write in denomination _____
        4 - activities of Danites,   9 - other, write in subject:
           "avenging angels," et cetera   _____

E. General impact or illustrations

        0 - no illustrations
        1 - does not specifically concern Mormons
        2 - concerns Mormons, shows them in an unfavorable light
        3 - concerns Mormons, but impact neutral
        4 - concerns Mormons, shows then in a favorable light
        5 - concerns Mormons, but impossible to make judgment about impact

14. Information about the author

    A. Description

        0 - journalist, professional writer
        1 - non-Mormon public figure
        2 - Mormon church official or Mormon prominent in secular affairs
        3 - non-Mormon religious leader
        4 - Mormon apostate or some other variety of "professional" anti-Mormons
        5 - scholar (legitimate Ph.D. or other person with academic connection)
        6 - article signed, but no information about author available
        7 - article is unsigned
        8 - pseudonym used or author is anonymous
        9 - multiple authors (write in) _____

    B. Gender

        0 - male
        1 - female
        2 - author not identified in any way
        9 - multiple authors (write in genders)_____

    C. Nationality

        0 - American
        1 - British
        2 - other
        3 - no information about author's nationality available
        4 - author not identified in any way
        9 - multiple authors (write in nationalities)_____

    D. Religious affiliation
        0 - objective evidence indicates that author is Mormon
        1 - internal evidence indicates that author is Mormon
        2 - objective evidence indicates that author is Protestant
        3 - objective evidence indicates that author is Roman Catholic or Jewish
        4 - objective evidence indicates that author is RLDS or other splinter group Mormon
        5 - either objective or internal evidence indicates that author is unspecified variety of
            non-Mormon
        6 - either objective or internal evidence indicates author is an apostate, or at least is an ex-Mormon
        7 - no information about author's religious affiliation is available
        8 - author not identified in any way
        9 - multiple authors (write in religious affiliations)_____

15. Relative emphasis in article on polygamy, politics, economics, and social control: (DO NOT SELECT A MAJOR EMPHASIS IF THERE IS NONE, OR IF MAJOR EMPHASIS IS NOT ONE OF THESE FOUR SUBJECTS. ONLY ONE OF THE FOUR SUBJECTS SHOULD BE CODED "0")

	Major emphasis	Great emphasis	Some emphasis	No emphasis
A. polygamy	0	1	2	3
B. politics	0	1	2	3
C. economics	0	1	2	3
D. social control	0	1	2	3

16. Relative emphasis on Joseph Smith and Brigham Young as Mormon leaders

   0 - only Joseph Smith is mentioned, or Joseph Smith is considered more important
   1 - only Brigham Young is mentioned, or Brigham Young is considered more important
   2 - the two leaders are considered equally important, or it is impossible to determine which man is considered more important since they are not compared in any way
   3 - neither Joseph Smith nor Brigham Young is discussed in the article

17. Content analysis section (USE ATTACHED TALLY SHEETS TO ANALYZE ARTICLES. RECORD TOTAL NUMBER OF TIMES REFERENCE IS MADE TO THE FOLLOWING CONCEPTS)

   A. Negative concepts

      1. Mormonism as a threat to the American political system_____
      2. Mormonism as a threat to the American economic system_____
      3. Mormonism as a threat to the American way of life_____
      4. Mormonism as heresy_____
      5. Unflattering description of Joseph Smith, of the origins of Mormonism, and of the religion itself_____
      6. Unflattering descriptions of the Mormon people_____
      7. Negative personal characteristics ascribed to the Mormons _____
      8. Unflattering descriptions of Mormon leaders and of the church leadership in general (DO NOT INCLUDE REFERENCES TO SEXUAL DEBAUCHERY IN CONNECTION WITH JOSEPH SMITH)_____
      9. Mormons as victims of unethical leaders _____
      10. Political control of LDS community by church (internal) _____
      11. Intolerant attitudes of Mormons toward non-Mormons _____
      12. Instances and accusations of murder _____
      13. Sexual debauchery, other overt sexual references _____
      14. Polygamy as a danger to the family as an institution, results of polygamy, general references to polygamy _____
      15. Unflattering descriptions of LDS proselytizing aims and techniques _____
      16. Other negative concepts, write in concepts and number

      _____

   B. Positive concepts

       1. Positive personal qualities of the Mormon people _____
       2. Positive qualities of the Mormon church leaders _____
       3. Positive religious qualities of the Mormons _____
       4. Mormons as achievers _____
       5. Desert transformed _____
       6. Mormon family _____
       7. Emphasis on youth _____
       8. Importance of education _____
       9. Patriotism, good citizenship _____
      10. Word of Wisdom _____
      11. Emphasis on culture and the arts _____
      12. Mormon tabernacle choir _____
      13. Sacred nature of marriage vows (temple marriage) _____
      14. In-group social and economic assistance _____
      15. Church Welfare Program and the "they take care of their own" concept _____
      16. Other positive concepts, write in concept and number _____
         _____

   C. Concepts peculiar to Mormon culture

       1. Negative concepts such as apostate, covenant-breaker, write in _____
       2. Positive concepts such as seagull, sego lily, write in _____

   D. References to RLDS Church (Saints' Church) or other splinter groups

       1. References to these groups that are positive _____
       2. References to these groups that are negative _____

18. General picture of Mormonism given in article

   A. Attitude expressed toward Mormon theological claims

       0 - Mormon theological claims treated as ridiculous and untrue either on the basis of historical evidence (attempting to prove that the Book of Mormon is untrue), on the basis that the story of the golden plates is preposterous, or on the basis of Joseph Smith's character
       1 - Mormon theological claims treated as untrue, but sensible enough to merit a serious attempt at refutation either through reference to logic or to the Bible
       2 - Mormon theological claims treated objectively; a socio-cultural description is given in which the attitude expressed is neutral
       3 - Mormon theological claims not mentioned in the article
       4 - Mormon theological claims are accorded the same stature as other religious claims (Mormon beliefs shown to be as likely logical, and acceptable as any other religious belief)
       5 - Mormon theological claims treated as unquestionably true

B. Attitude expressed toward Mormons as citizens

    0 - Mormons pictured as subversive of American political values, even as traitors to the American political system
    1 - Mormons seen as un-American, but not as dangerous to the political values of the rest of the country
    2 - Mormonism seen as no different from other religious belief as far as it affects American political values and patriotic ideals
    3 - Mormonism as it relates to American political life not mentioned in article
    4 - Mormons pictured as good citizens, positive exemplars of American political life
    5 - Mormons pictured as some of America's best citizens; 100% Americans

C. Attitude expressed toward Mormonism as it affects American family life

    0 - Mormons pictured as a threat to the purity of the American home, the honor of American womanhood, and American family structure in general
    1 - Mormon beliefs seen as destructive of acceptable family life within Mormonism, but not pictured as a threat to American social values and American family life in general
    2 - Mormonism seen as no different than other religious beliefs as far as family life and social values are concerned (i.e., neutral)
    3 - Mormonism as it relates to family life not mentioned in article
    4 - Mormon family life shown as a positive addition to the social make-up of the U.S., as a reflection of American ideals
    5 - Mormons pictured as having the most satisfactory, even ideal, family life in the United States

D. Attitude expressed toward Mormonism as it concerns morality/immorality

    0 - Mormons shown as extremely immoral and as such a danger to America and the American way of life
    1 - Mormons pictured as immoral, but not a danger to the rest of the country
    2 - Mormons pictured as any other American group as far as the issue of morality/immorality is concerned (i.e., neutral)
    3 - morals, morality of the Mormons not discussed in any way
    4 - Mormons pictured as a highly moral people (this category includes articles which explain how polygamy was carried out on a highly moral plane)
    5 - Mormons shown as highly moral, a group having greater moral strength than other American groups

19. Total effect of the article with regard to Mormonism, and the Mormon Church

    0 - Exposé, highly unfavorable to the church
    1 - Unfavorable to the church, but not in the character of an exposé
    2 - Neutral
    3 - Favorable to the church, but not in the character of an apology
    4 - Apology, highly favorable to the church

20. Questionnaire filled out by:

    0 - Jan Shipps
    1 - Tom Alexander

Notes

1. In a Fourth of July sermon, for example, the Mormon leader Sidney Rigdon threatened "a war of extermination" with "any mob that comes on us to disturb us." See Richard S. Van Wagoner, *Sidney Rigdon: A Portrait of Religious Excess* (Salt Lake City: Signature Books, 1994), 220.

2. For a classic example of persecution rhetoric, see James E. Talmage, *The Story of "Mormonism,"* a little volume for LDS missionaries that was published at the office of the *Millennial Star* in Liverpool, England, in 1907.

3. While most historians are aware that the "subterranean war" against the Saints continued "for at least another twenty years" after 1890, that is, until the reverberations from the U.S. Senate's investigation of Reed Smoot's right to a Senate seat had died away, the general consensus seems to be that the opposition to Mormonism ended around the same time that World War I ended. For discussions of the transition from antagonism to acceptance, see Klaus J. Hansen, *Quest for Empire* (East Lansing: Michigan State University Press, 1967; reprint, Lincoln: University of Nebraska Press, 1974), chapter 8; S. George Ellsworth, *Utah's Heritage* (Salt Lake City: Peregrine Smith, 1972), chapter 20; and my own "The Mormons in Politics: The First Hundred Years" (Ph.D. diss., University of Colorado, 1965), chapter 7.

4. Brigham H. Roberts and other Mormon apologists hold the position that the opposition to the church was mainly theological and therefore that Joseph Smith's murder made him a martyr to the faith. The Reverend R. G. McNiece, who spent twenty-one years in Utah, seemed to be less concerned about theology than about the fact that it was "grievously unjust . . . to put the Evangelical Churches of the country on a level with the Mormon Church and to claim that the latter is entitled to the same treatment as the former." See R. G. McNiece, "The Mormon Manifesto against Polygamy," *Our Day* 6 (December 1890): 420–21.

5. Caroline Hazard, review of *Early Days of Mormonism . . .* by J. H. Kennedy, *Andover Review* 10 (September 1888): 325 ("immorality cloaked" quote); Rollin Lynde Hart, "The Mormons," *Atlantic Monthly,* 85 (February 1900): 270 ("forty feet" quote); Petition, delivered to the Speaker of the House of Representatives during the debate on the seating of Brigham H. Roberts, a polygamist who was elected to Congress in 1898, reported in *New York Journal,* January 18, 1900 ("debased" and "purity" quotes). This petition had so many signatures that it made a stack seven feet high in front of the Speaker's platform (see *New York Journal* report).

6. Ruth Everett, "Woman's Life in Utah," *Arena* 21 (February 1889): 191.

7. L. A. M. Bosworth, "Mormonism the Same Yesterday, Today, and Forever," *Bibliotheca Sacra* 60 (January 1903): 172.

8. A particularly good example of a human interest story about the Saints that became news is the 1997 sesquicentennial reenactment of the Mormon trek. Accounts of the trek itself appeared in newspapers all across the nation, and the trek became the "lede" for in-depth television pieces and periodical articles, most notably a cover story, "Mormons, Inc.," *Time,* August 4, 1997, 50–59.

9. Sigmund Diamond, *The Reputation of the American Businessman* (Cambridge, Mass.: Harvard University Press, 1955), 3.

10. With the exception of the information about the number of missionaries assigned to the United States, the statistics in the table are taken from U.S. Census Bureau reports. Information about the Mormon missionaries was provided by Le-

onard J. Arrington, who, at that time, was church historian of the Church of Jesus Christ of Latter-day Saints.

11. In addition to making liberal use of interlibrary loan, this involved traveling to libraries at the University of Illinois and Yale, both of which have wonderful collections of nineteenth-century periodicals.

12. Donald L. Kinzer, *An Episode in Anti-Catholicism: The American Protective Association* (Seattle: University of Washington Press, 1964). In talking with him about what was written about the Latter-day Saints in the second half of the nineteenth century, I learned that many of the charges against the Latter-day Saints and stories about them were similar to (and quite often precisely the same as) charges against and stories about urban Catholics in the United States during the same time period.

13. An overall reliability coefficient of 0.892 was obtained when the way I scored positive and negative references to the Saints in the pretest instrument and the way Professor Alexander scored those references were correlated. The level of agreement was much higher for negative than for positive references; I found more positive references than he did.

14. Frank Luther Mott, *History of American Magazines*, 5 vols. (Cambridge, Mass.: Harvard University Press, 1957–58).

15. The circulation figures in the Rowell and Ayer directories were accepted at face value even though they were usually inflated to attract advertising. Trying to reconstruct more accurate figures proved to be an impossible task. The categories for information about the periodical and information about the article items were developed with the assistance of the late William E. Wilson, a member of the English department at Indiana University who wrote regularly for a great variety of periodicals for many years.

16. This dual approach proved to be of great value since almost half (48.2 percent) of the articles published between 1861 and 1896, well over a third (42.7 percent) of those published between 1896 and 1920, and a quarter (25.6 percent) of those published between 1921 and 1960 covered so many different aspects of Mormonism that it was necessary to code them in one of the "general" categories.

17. The only exceptions to the rule that the reference had to be explicitly positive or negative were references to polygamy, which were routinely coded as negative, and references to the murder of Joseph Smith and the early persecutions of the Saints, which were routinely coded as positive. In addition to the fifteen positive and fifteen negative concept categories, positive and negative "other" categories were included.

18. Richard L. Merritt, "The Emergence of American Nationalism: A Quantitative Approach," *American Quarterly* 17 (Summer 1965): 319–35; Richard L. Merritt, *Symbols of American Community* (New Haven, Conn.: Yale University Press, 1966); Louis Galambos, "The Agrarian Image of the Large Corporation, 1879–1920: A Study in Social Accommodation," *Journal of Economic History* 26 (March 1968): 341–62.

19. William A. Beatty, "A Practical Consideration of the Mormon Question," *Overland Monthly*, n.s., 4 (September 1884): 296; George F. Edmunds, "Political Aspects of Mormonism," *Harper's Magazine* 64 (January 1882): 285; Hazard, review of *Early Days of Mormonism* . . . by J. H. Kennedy, 327; Susa Young Gates, "Family Life among the Mormons," *North American Review* 150 (March 1890): 348; [Joseph Cook], "Utah at the Doors of Congress," *Our Day* 13 (May–June 1894): 233.

20. Hansen, *Quest for Empire*, 171.

21. Edward Leo Lyman, *Political Deliverance: The Mormon Quest for Utah Statehood* (Urbana: University of Illinois Press, 1986), 2.

22. As will readily be seen, the information contained in this and other summary graphs generally reflects the main outlines of Mormon/Utah and Mormon/American history from 1861 to 1960. This is crucially important because pictures markedly at odds with the ones many historians have drawn from a wide variety of sources throughout the years would automatically indicate that this methodological approach is suspect.

23. A chronological listing of the articles in the sample is in appendix B, which includes the overall ranking assigned to the article and the weighting factor used to take circulation numbers into account in the analysis.

24. Leonard J. Arrington, *Great Basin Kingdom: An Economic History of the Latter-day Saints, 1830–1900* (Cambridge, Mass.: Harvard University Press, 1958; reprint, Salt Lake City: University of Utah Press, 1993), 379.

25. Ellsworth, *Utah's Heritage,* 329. Thomas G. Alexander, *Mormonism in Transition* (Urbana: University of Illinois Press, 1986) extended the period of transition from 1890 to 1930.

26. Rollin Lynde Hart, "The Mormons," *Atlantic* 85 (February 1900): 261–72 (idea that it was not the Mormons but Mormonism that posed a problem); J. D Nutting, Reply to C. B. Spahr's "The Mormons," *Outlook* 64 (February 24, 1900): 469 (first quote); Frank J. Cannon and Harvey J. O'Higgins, *Under the Prophet in Utah* [serialized], *Everybody's Magazine* 24 (June 1911): 829 (second quote).

27. David Brion Davis, "Some Themes of Counter-Subversion: An Analysis of Anti-Masonic, Anti-Catholic, and Anti-Mormon Literature," *Mississippi Valley Historical Review* 47 (September 1960): 205–24.

28. See "No More Mormons on the Dole," *Literary Digest* 121 (June 6, 1936): 55.

29. No doubt the positive impact of these articles, plus items in "Life in these United States" and various fillers about the Saints, figured in the church's decision to pay for the placement of informational material in the *Reader's Digest* soon after it started to accept advertisements. See "Surveying the Mormon Image since 1960," herein, note 3.

30. In the first period, the percentage was 22.2; in the second period, it was 17.6; and in the third period, it was only 10.3.

31. Andrew J. Hanson, "Utah and the Mormon Problem," *Methodist Quarterly Review* 64 (April 1882): 214.

32. As will be seen in the next essay, the period in which the content of Mormon belief was less important than the sincerity with which it was held was short-lived. Renewed charges of Mormonism as heresy coincided with the growth from the 1960s onward of Protestant fundamentalism, evangelicalism, and pentecostalism at the expense of traditional mainstream Protestantism.

33. The witty Irishman's remark is adapted from J. B. Halsey, "Mormonism as It Is Today," *Era* 11 (June 1903): 511; the more modern description of Utah comes from Walter V. Woehlke, "The Garden of Utah," *Sunset: The Pacific Monthly* 29 (October 1912): 362.

3

Surveying the Mormon Image since 1960

An article written by Andrew Hamilton entitled "Those Amazing Mormons" was published in 1952 in *Coronet Magazine,* a *Reader's Digest* clone. Reviewing LDS history, it cast the early Saints as long-suffering heroes and heroines and described their descendants as hard-working people with all the Boy Scout virtues. The author asserted that they did not drink alcohol or anything containing caffeine, did not smoke, and consistently refused government assistance because they took care of their own.[1] This article is representative of a positive trend that, starting in the 1930s, would undercut the negative image that had been central to coverage of the Saints in the nation's periodical press during Mormonism's first hundred years. Marred mainly by a smattering of references to the continuing practice of plural marriage in Short Creek, Arizona, which many readers continued to connect with mainstream Mormonism, and by expressions that were a prelude to the growing concern of non-Mormon writers about the business activities of the LDS Church and its incredible wealth, press coverage of the Latter-day Saints remained positive, even laudatory, throughout the 1950s.[2] By that time, however, the Mormon image was no longer being shaped primarily by the print media.

To review, between 1847 and 1947, the great majority of Latter-day Saints had lived behind a "mountain curtain," in the Great Basin and along the Pacific, especially in southern California. During that period, the great majority of non-Mormon Americans gained most of the information they had about the Mormons by reading about them or by hearsay—hearing about them from someone who had read about them or, more rarely, from someone who had traveled through the West, seen Zion, and met a few Saints.

Just as the end of World War II brought change to many areas of American life, so it brought about a dramatic change in the opportunity U.S. citizens had to get to know members of the Church of Jesus Christ of Latter-day Saints. Although it would be decades before LDS wards and stakes would be organized throughout the nation, the end of the war accelerated the Mormon diaspora, as Saints started settling far beyond the boundaries of the state of Utah and the American West. By the 1950s, as a result of this "scattering of the gathering," people all across the country were beginning to learn about Mormonism first hand by meeting neighbors, people not unlike themselves, who happened to be Mormons. Moreover, as soon as the wartime dearth of automobiles for sale was replaced by the availability of reasonably priced new cars, a huge increase in recreational travel carried hordes of tourists to Mormonism's center place—Utah, particularly Salt Lake City.

Besides that, dramatic communications developments occurred at midcentury. Because of ever-cheaper versions of portable radios and the addition of radios as standard equipment in automobiles, radio became a natural adjunct to newspapers and magazines as a source of information. Moreover, phonographs with standard or "hi-fi" sound became the rage. Connected with this was growth in the sale of long-playing records, including performances of the Mormon Tabernacle Choir. Perhaps above all, this middle decade of the twentieth century saw commercial television rapidly take its place as a new communications medium.

In the wake of these developments, the positive image emanating from the periodical press of typical Mormons was matched by the presence on the national scene of a considerable number of appealing or impressive Mormon personalities, including the Pulitzer Prize–winning author and columnist Jack Anderson, the movie star Victor Jory, the golfer Johnny Miller, the swimsuit designer Rose Marie Reid, Michigan's Governor George Romney, Secretary of Agriculture Ezra Taft Benson, and, later, Donny, Marie, and the rest of the Osmond family.

Viewing the panorama of presentations of the Mormon image decade by decade from 1860 to 1960, as I did in my study of American perceptions of the Mormons, made me very sensitive to the fact that the decade of the 1950s was one of media transition. As the years passed, attractive aural and visual images started to complement and sometimes replace less illuminating and arguably more easily manipulated print portraits of the Saints. This was a change rooted in the way in which the culture was rapidly turning information into a commodity that would become quite as important to radio and television as entertainment is. Since advertising was an appendage to both, these developments called, in turn, for image management, and that made the work of public relations specialists important enough to add "PR" to the language. The consequence of the blurring of the line between news and entertainment and the dramatic expansion of advertising was that the content of paid promotions of everything from laundry soap to Latter-day Saints became a subgenre that would henceforth have to be taken into account in all image studies.[3]

Projecting a flattering Mormon image in the process, the church's Public Communications Division was able to take marvelous advantage of the many new venues for telling the Mormon story. These same communications advances, however, made it impossible for me to do a post-1960 study of perceptions of the Saints based—as my study of the century before 1960 had been—entirely on material appearing in the periodical press. Yet doing that earlier study had made me acutely conscious of media presentations of the Saints, both print and electronic. So much so that I am able to advance the following argument: if you take the electronic media into account, the decade or so between, say, 1963–64 and 1975–76 forms a unique period in the history of perceptions of the Saints.

During this time, the LDS Church had what Americans who embraced the civil rights movement regarded as a retrograde position on race, one noted and commented on in the print media, especially *Time, Newsweek,* the *Christian Century,* and elite newspapers on the East Coast and West Coast.[4] But that encumbrance was usually overlooked in radio and television broadcasts, which, almost as a reminder that the entire nation had not gone the way of the much-maligned, pot-smoking, flag-burning counterculture, featured all sorts of images of Mormons as neat, modest, virtuous, family-loving, conservative, and patriotic people.[5] The contrast with the radical Left made the image of the Saints even more appealing than it had been in the fifties, making this a time when at least middle America's perceptions of the Saints would be overwhelmingly positive. I am convinced that it was the dramatic discrepancy between clean-cut Mormons and scruffy hippies that completed the transformation of the Mormon image from the quasi-foreign, somewhat alien likeness that it had in the nineteenth century to the more than 100 percent super-American portrait of the late sixties and early seventies.[6] The situation was such that it became not at all uncommon to hear, in academic presentations at American studies meetings, that Mormons are "more American than the Americans."

It is true that members of the church had to maintain their distance from a growing body of so-called "new polygamists" by making sure that these schismatics were not confused with the genuine article, that is, "real" Latter-day Saints.[7] The LDS Church also needed to downplay the importance of a vocal and somewhat truculent group of former Saints by ignoring their efforts to scour the historical record and to find and publish information that helped them justify their turn away from the faith.[8] But the 1978 revelation permitting all worthy men to hold the priesthood appeared to put the troublesome race issue behind the LDS Church. On another front, despite the press brouhaha around the excommunication of the feminist Sonia Johnson and Utah's International Women's Year Convention debacle, the Mormon emphasis on family values seems to have trumped the church's anti-ERA stance in the eyes of a majority of those who thought much about the matter.[9] As a consequence, race and gender issues—they would now be described as political correctness issues—were apparently doing little to besmirch the positive Mormon image.[10]

People well acquainted with LDS history and culture are aware that many LDS Church members believe they need to be prepared to undergo persecution for their faith. By the time of the church's sesquicentennial, however, the internal excitement of exponential church growth started to create such a general atmosphere of hope and optimism that it looked as if the Latter-day Saints had little reason to anticipate much change in the salutary climate of opinion surrounding them. Many Saints were therefore both shocked and appalled at the appearance in the late 1970s and the 1980s of a negative subtext in a surprising number of media presentations of the Saints and their church.

Sometimes that subtext even became text, despite everything members of the LDS public communications staff did to provide information to head off the negativism. Several critical *60 Minutes* segments, for example, challenged the perpetually benign pictures of the church and positive depictions of Mormons as Saints almost too perfect to be believed.[11] A number of articles about the new polygamy were published, and documentaries that failed to make much distinction between the LDS Church and its schismatic offshoots were aired on network TV.[12] The *God Makers,* a film ridiculing Mormon doctrine, was promoted by conservative Protestants, who featured it in special services in many of their churches.[13] Reputable and well-known presses published several handsome books designed to reveal Mormonism's underside.[14]

One of the traditional ways of disseminating the Mormon image was (and still is) *Music and the Spoken Word,* the weekly Sunday morning television broadcast from the "historic Tabernacle standing in Temple Square at the foot of the eternal hills in Salt Lake City." Typically, along with a well-known Mormon hymn and a classical selection, the weekly Tabernacle Choir broadcasts include performances of some of the American people's best-loved inspirational music—some of it religious, some not. The spoken word is likewise inspirational, but generically so, with distinctive LDS doctrinal tenets either blunted or altogether missing. The effect is heartwarming, producing admiration for the performers and the people they epitomize. But however much this program elevates the spirit or motivates the observer, it reveals little or nothing about the idiosyncratic LDS doctrines that separate Mormonism from the historic forms of Christianity—Catholic, Protestant, and Orthodox.

Starting out as a radio broadcast in 1929, this program aimed to project an acceptable image of Mormonism. But like the images of practically everything else from the mid-twentieth century forward, by 1980 the Mormon image was not simply transmitted through Tabernacle Choir performances and the publication of engaging articles in the periodical press. It was being attentively shaped by skilled public relations people from whose offices issued a steady stream of press releases telling the world about the LDS Church and its members. By 1980, many of these releases diminished the distance between the Latter-day Saints and other religious groups with descriptions of instances demonstrating Mormon willingness to cooperate with members of other faith communities in delivering assistance in the face of natural disasters and helping in times of demonstrated human need.

Countless other press releases concentrated on LDS success by dealing in one way or another with church growth: the organization of new church units (branches, wards, and stakes) all across the nation and in many other parts of the world, the building of new temples, and the passage of million markers in numbers of members.[15] At the same time, Mormonism was becoming ever more visible. The Mormon church had been practically invisible outside the West as long as LDS missions in the various regions of the United States had been housed in large (usually Victorian) mansions purchased for that purpose. In the mid-twentieth century, however, the church emerged as a part of the nation's religious landscape as LDS stake houses and ward chapels (most of them looking very much alike) were built in cities and towns all across the nation.[16] To the surprise of many non-Mormons and the dismay of some, it suddenly seemed that Mormons were everywhere.

More disturbed about these developments than anyone else were members of new or recently revitalized conservative Protestant—evangelical, fundamentalist, and Pentecostal—bodies, a part of Christianity that was also growing exponentially. Leaders of these groups had long considered Mormonism to be one of four indigenous American "cults," and when it started to outstrip the others in both visibility and the number of converts, Mormons started to appear much more dangerous to them than the Christian Scientists, Jehovah's Witnesses, and Seventh-day Adventists.[17] In reality, what had been happening in the post–World War II era is that Mormons, evangelicals, and conservative Christians were all regarding the nation as a field ready to harvest. The problem was that workers from all these bodies were laboring in the same parts of the field, a competitive situation that seems to have caused conservative Protestants to regard the success of Latter-day Saints as illegitimate.

One result of this rivalry for religious commitments was that a good market existed for anti-Mormon materials, the most spectacular of which turned out to be the aforementioned *God Makers: The Mormon Quest for Godhood*. This fifty-six-minute attack film (also available as a video) and book with the same name (which reflects the content of the film) transformed Mormon theology into a science-fiction scenario and accused the Mormons of not being Christian. Produced by Ed Decker and Dave Hunt, with the assistance of Jerald Tanner, Sandra Tanner, and other ex-Mormons, the stated purpose of both the book and the film was unmasking the "myth of Mormonism" by revealing everything about the Latter-day Saints "from Family Home Evening through the actual secret temple rituals."[18] The book and the film were both distributed by Utah Missions, Inc. (UMI), publishers of the *Utah Evangel* (now simply the *Evangel*), a newsprint periodical devoted to "Exposing Mormonism."[19] Both the film and text versions of the *God Makers* helped advance UMI's clearly stated goals of turning Mormons away from Mormonism, "winning them for the Lord," and keeping potential LDS converts "from being deceived by the militant Mormon proselyting program."[20]

The *God Makers* was the most visible specimen of a whole genre of anti-Mormon literature that assailed Mormonism from the religious standpoint. Whether in broadsides, pamphlets, articles, books, or films, the central message was (and is) that Mormonism is not Christian but a heretical movement.[21]

In the days before the full-scale political and cultural mobilization of the religious right, this charge resonated soundly with members of certain conservative Protestant groups, a reality that became manifest when the Reverend Jerry Falwell organized the "Moral Majority," a political movement that sought to unite members of the Church of Jesus Christ of Latter-day Saints with members of fundamentalist and evangelical churches all across the country to exert pressure from within on the national Republican party. The famed pastor of the Thomas Road Baptist Church in Lynchburg, Virginia, was surprised to discover that many fundamentalist, evangelical, and Pentecostal Christians were unwilling to be united with Latter-day Saints under any circumstances.

During the 1980s, other indictments touching on the religious dimensions of Mormonism cast shadows on the Mormon image. Two books about the new polygamy, both quite obviously more subtext than text, appeared in 1981. Simon and Schuster's Linden Press issued Peter Bart's *Thy Kingdom Come,* a novel with a plot line that included the practice of polygamy at the highest levels of the LDS ecclesiastical hierarchy. Since the author acknowledged his debt "to the many kind people of the Mormon community who were . . . generous with their knowledge and hospitality" during the preparation of his work, this trade book was reputed to be a roman à clef, a novel in which real events and people were represented under the guise of fiction.[22]

That same year, G. P. Putnam's Sons, another New York trade press, published *Prophet of Blood: The Untold Story of Ervil LeBaron and the Lambs of God* by the Washington investigative journalists Ben Bradlee Jr. and Dale Van Atta. Although it dealt with a schismatic form of Mormonism, in the minds of readers unfamiliar with Mormonism this investigative report inevitably connected the Saints to the renewed practice of plural marriage as well as murder.[23]

These, however, were only the precursors of a series of books that are best characterized as neo-nineteenth-century exposé, a kind of exposé that deals almost entirely with the secular side of Mormonism. *The Mormon Corporate Empire* clearly fits into this category. Written by John Heinerman, a disillusioned Latter-day Saint, and Anson Shupe, a sociologist of good reputation who is best known for his earlier work on the Unification Church (the Moonies), this work was published by Beacon Press in 1985.[24] With information gained from the public record and investigative reporting that some people regard as "unethical snooping" since it sometimes involved misrepresentation on Heinerman's part, this work uses "chapter and verse" evidence to make the argument that the LDS Church is first and foremost a money-generating enterprise whose leaders are more concerned about adding to the fabulous wealth of the Mormon church than about anything else.[25]

Six years later, Shupe would publish *The Darker Side of Virtue: Corruption, Scandal, and the Mormon Empire,* a work designed to show that "behind the ideal image promoted by the LDS Church, a darker side of Mormonism exists." The dust jacket blurb continues, "The same Mormon ethos that has instilled many positive characteristics in its people has also led to dramatic instances of corruption, scandal, abuse of power, and even murder."[26] But long before Shupe's second work on Mormonism was published, a terrible Mormon tragedy precipitated what I have been calling subtext into the headlines in both the print and electronic media.

The Mark Hofmann saga catapulted the LDS Church specifically and Mormonism generally into public view in a way that combined accusations about religious illegitimacy and secular mendacity. While this is not the place to review the well-known Hofmann story, it is the place to point to how his forgeries and plagiarism—the production of spurious early Mormon documents, including the famed "Salamander letter,"[27] as well as holograph copies of such documents as Lucy Mack Smith's "Gospel Letter," which had only been available in printed form—and his subsequent murders of Steven Christensen and Kathy Sheets led to a convergence of the religious and the secular in multitudinous accounts of this gripping story. In the early news accounts, what had occurred was described as a secular story of murder and greed in which the protagonist simply happened to be a Mormon. When news organizations sent their crime reporters rather than their religion reporters to Salt Lake City to cover the story, however, those reporters soon realized that there was so much religion mixed up in the story that it could not be adequately covered without considerable familiarity with the LDS system of belief, Mormon history, and those who were writing that history.

Peggy Stack, née Fletcher, first put into words for me the dilemma the Hofmann story presented to newspaper editors and the supervisory staffs of other news organizations. Many of them soon realized that their crime reporters did not know enough about Mormonism to cover the story properly, but they were afraid that their religion reporters would not be able to describe what was happening satisfactorily because they did not know enough about crime and about the legal maneuvering that immediately started after Hofmann was charged with murder.

I quickly learned that Peggy Fletcher Stack was right. Probably because the University of Illinois Press had issued my *Mormonism: The Story of a New Religious Tradition* about six months before the story broke and because reviews published in the *New York Times Book Review,* the *New York Review of Books,* and elsewhere made much of my not being a Mormon, I started getting requests from reporters for phone interviews only one day after Hofmann's arrest. Subsequent telephone conversations revealed an abysmal lack of knowledge of Mormonism on the part of many of the journalists assigned to the story. For almost two weeks, I fielded so many phone calls from people writing for papers all over the United States as well as from the hosts of radio talk shows and researchers for television news programs that several staff members at IUPUI became convinced that I must be "somebody."[28]

Although most of the reporters who called had been in Salt Lake City long enough to have learned the identity of the first Mormon prophet, the great majority did not "speak Mormon" and needed a translator. Furthermore, most knew so little about the murderer's cultural and religious background and the religious significance of some of the forged items he had produced that I found myself endlessly repeating the introductory lecture on Mormonism that I had prepared for our religious studies department's "Introduction to Religion" course.[29]

The Hofmann story remained in the news long enough for most religion reporters to get a crack at it. It also became the basis for five full-length books, three published by trade presses, one published by a university press, and another written and published by Jerald Tanner and Sandra Tanner. The first to be published was *Salamander: The Story of the Mormon Forgery Murders*.[30] Written by Linda Sillitoe and Allen Roberts, both Latter-day Saints, this work presents the best balance of the secular and religious dimensions of this awful episode in the recent Mormon past. *A Gathering of Saints: A True Story of Money, Murder, and Deceit* was written by Robert Lindsey, a journalist who worked as a reporter and correspondent for the *New York Times* for twenty years. Well-written, this work reviews the Saints' trek from Iowa and their arrival in the Great Salt Lake Valley and alludes briefly to Mormon history where necessary for clarity. But Lindsey's narrative, which was published in 1988 by Simon and Schuster, a New York trade press, has a secular cast. In contrast, *Victims: The LDS Church and the Mark Hofmann Case*, written by the managing director of the LDS Church Historical Department, gives more weight to the story's religious aspects than to its legal aspects. The author, Richard E. Turley Jr., was trained as a lawyer, and his account of the legal aspects of the story is clear and precise, but the main purpose of the work was getting in the record the part the church played in the Hofmann story.[31]

From the standpoint of the Mormon image and most everything else, by far the worst of this quartet of books is the *Mormon Murders*, a work in which the authors Steven Naifeh and Gregory White Smith made an implicit comparison between the forger Mark Hofmann who produced counterfeit documents and the Mormon prophet who produced the Book of Mormon.[32] This widely advertised 1988 alternate Literary Guild selection was published in both hardcover and paperback.[33] Featured in bookstores all across the nation, including airport bookstores where it became a popular choice for travel reading, the *Mormon Murders* not only told the story of Mark Hofmann but also, according to the *Los Angeles Times* review quoted on the book cover, contained "a rich trove of details about the deceit, lying, and covering up by top [Mormon] church leaders."[34]

Prominently displayed on the back of the Naifeh and Smith book was its authors' claim that Hofmann's forged documents rocked "the very foundation and legitimacy of the Mormon church and its multi-million-dollar empire." Although this claim was mistaken, the tales of intrigue regarding the church's dealings with Hofmann as he produced one rare document after another, some of them threatening to discredit elements of the canonized story of the Mormon past, delivered a severe—though glancing—blow to the Mormon image.

Though glancing, the blow was fierce enough to spur damage control, first in the form of a rare press conference in which Gordon B. Hinckley, Dallin Oaks, and Hugh Pinnock, LDS general authorities who had met with Hofmann or had had dealings with him, made statements and answered the questions of dozens of reporters representing both local and national print and electronic media. Second, on August 6, 1987, after Hofmann had confessed and been imprisoned, a one-day church-sponsored public conference organized by the Joseph Fielding Smith Institute of Church History was held at Brigham Young University. Its purpose was to clear the air, to get the entire story on the record (including the part played by Dean Jessee, a scholar in the employ of the church, and other Mormon historians in clearing up the mystery of the forged documents), and to assess how Hofmann's forgeries might affect the way Mormon history would be written in the future.

Richard Bushman, author of *Joseph Smith and the Beginnings of Mormonism,* and I were asked to attend the conference, listen to the proceedings, and, at the end of the day, present our assessments of any enduring impact Hofmann's plagiarism might have on how the story of Mormon beginnings would be told in the future. To some extent, this was an ironic assignment because the two of us had participated in the opening plenary session of the August 1984 Sunstone Symposium, which had included what may have been the first *public* allusion to and discussion of the text of the so-called White Salamander letter.[35] Steven Christensen had issued a press release almost six months earlier (on March 7, 1984) acknowledging his ownership of a letter said to be from Martin Harris to William W. Phelps. In that announcement, the owner described his plans for authentication procedures and a research project he had organized to study the letter and place it in context. But that press release did not give the text of the letter or a description of its contents.

The final speaker at the BYU conference was Dallin Oaks, who took that "opportunity to speak for the record on a number of issues that have been of immense interest to scholars, church members, and the general public over the last several years."[36] His talk was important because it was the church's official answer to charges about alleged suppression of documents; its official explanation of how often and for what reasons Mark Hofmann gained interviews with Gordon B. Hinckley, the ranking member of the First Presidency, and with other church officials; and an official clarification of which Hofmann documents the church obtained through gift as opposed to purchases arranged by personnel in the church's Historical Department. The speech also provided factual clarification about the church's role in the aborted effort to facilitate purchase of the so-called McLellin collection so that it could be given to the church. Oaks lamented the fact that during the whole

Hofmann episode, members of the church saw "some of the most intense LDS Church-bashing since the turn of the century."

Oaks was absolutely correct about this negative media coverage, even though several writers in the audience who had been struggling for months to present the complicated story as accurately and evenhandedly as possible were outraged by his reference to church-bashing. I have recently reviewed the national print media's coverage of the Hofmann story, and it is obvious to me that while many reporters made a deliberate effort to convey the information necessary to make the story comprehensible without prejudice, national coverage (in contrast to most of the local Utah coverage) of the story contained an astonishing amount of innuendo associating Hofmann's plagiarism with Mormon beginnings.[37] Myriad reports alleged secrecy and cover-up on the part of LDS general authorities, and not a few writers referred to the way in which a culture that rests on a found scripture is particularly vulnerable to the offerings of con-artists.[38]

∽

Having so many full-length books devoted to the Hofmann story gave it a surprisingly long media life. After a while, however, normalcy reasserted itself. The church continued to grow by leaps and bounds. New temples were announced and built. Latter-day Saints rendered assistance to people suffering from the effects of natural disaster. Attractive Mormons made heartening news in the political arena, in sports, and in the entertainment world. Family values were in the ascendancy on the national agenda, and a positive shine once again appeared on the Mormon image.

Despite the allegations of dissimulation on the part of early Mormon leaders embedded in the *Mormon Murders* that were still making the rounds, the Mormon image was sufficiently positive not to be besmirched too much by the attacks on it in books written by Anson Shupe and by James Coates in 1991. Shupe's *Darker Side of Virtue* told of investment scams, accusations of child sexual abuse against pillars of the Mormon community, and a variety of other horrors. Moreover, using a strange and extraordinarily strained argument, Shupe implied that the LDS Church was at least complicit in causing the Shuttle disaster.[39]

Coates, a reporter for the *Chicago Tribune,* is the author of *In Mormon Circles: Gentiles, Jack Mormons, and Latter-day Saints,* a work filled with superficial caricature and a surprising number of statements that sound authoritative but are inaccurate, unreliable, distorted, or just plain wrong.[40] The book also contains a lot of material about what the author calls "the core LDS mysteries," provided mainly by Utah Lighthouse Ministry publications and

Jerald Tanner and Sandra Tanner, as well as information about the new polygamy furnished by members of those groups. Both of these exposés include chapters on the Hofmann episode, but neither adds new material to what was already known.

What these books by Shupe and Coates—and similar books and articles—purport to do is reveal hidden truths about Mormonism or take the lid off LDS conspiracies, which, they contend, need to see the light of day. What they actually do is focus attention on questions of wealth and power, questions that, at base, are secular questions. This may explain why these works, as loaded as they are with scandalous material, seem to have had little discernible impact on the Mormon image in the 1990s, a decade in which the main agenda for media treatment of Saints has been the way Mormonism functions in the religious realm.

Mark Silk, a former columnist for the *Atlanta Constitution* who is now director of the Center for the Study of Religion in Public Life at Trinity College in Hartford, Connecticut, is perhaps right about the media's not being as worldly as most people suppose. In any event, *Unsecular Media,* the title of Silk's most recent book, captures his argument that the media is not a secular wasteland where the attention paid to religion focuses on the way it impinges on the secular side of life.[41] The principal coverage of Mormonism in the 1990s would certainly suggest that Silk is onto something. My review of what journalists have considered newsworthy about the Saints in recent years indicates that the topics of greatest interest have nearly all had to do with the religious dimensions of Mormonism.[42]

Just think about noteworthy events, occurrences, and happenings, the news of which has made its way out of the "Valley" in the 1990s. Apart from the decision that the 2002 Olympic Games will be held in Utah (and related stories) and the recent hullabaloo about the continuing practice of plural marriage in Mormon country—about which more below—the principal subjects of national news stories that account for the contours of the modern Mormon image are stories about LDS missionary work; the changing of the wording in LDS temple rituals; the 1993 purge of dissident LDS intellectuals; the church's activity in locating sites for, building, and dedicating temples; tenure cases at BYU, all of which seem to have religious overtones; the change in the LDS Church logo; the baptizing of Holocaust victims; and the reenactment of the pioneer trek. Consideration of how these stories have been covered in both the print and electronic media provides some approximation of present-day perceptions of the Saints. But that approximation comes into sharper focus if it is set against that super-shaper of images in our nation nowadays: the portraits painted on *60 Minutes.*

In 1996, the Easter Sunday *60 Minutes* program included a segment on the Latter-day Saints that featured an extended interview with the church's president, Gordon B. Hinckley. In August of that year, my analysis of this interview was published in the *Christian Century* and reprinted in *Sunstone*.[43] I pointed to "what Mike Wallace missed," but of significance here is what the veteran *60 Minutes* newsman did not miss. While it is even more obvious to me now than it was at the time of the broadcast that the story of the recent transformation of Mormonism was almost entirely neglected, it is also clear that Wallace accepted what President Hinckley said as gospel. Wallace embraced a narrow concept of the LDS faith and its adherents and was satisfied to inform his audience that Latter-day Saints are attractive people, truly religious, and not weird.

In proper *60 Minutes* fashion, Wallace tested the "not weird" part of what Hinckley told him by asking questions about the wearing of ritual temple garments. But because the veteran interviewer and his program producer decided to use the words (and pictures) of Steve Young, Orrin Hatch, and Bill Marriott—three attractive, apparently truly religious, and certainly not weird Latter-day Saints who are clearly part of the American mainstream—to explain about the Saints living in a land of funny underwear, his discussion of this idiosyncratic religious practice had the effect of supporting rather than calling President Hinckley's depiction of the Saints into question.

Rereading the transcript with a different set of analytic glasses allowed me to see that the *60 Minutes* image of the Latter-day Saints was essentially a return to the Mormon image of the "golden age." As it happened, this program turned out to be a very public stand from which the LDS Church president was able to broadcast his message that Latter-day Saints are ordinary people to whom family and faith mean a lot. But two things are quite different now from what they were in that golden age. First, thirty years ago, the nation's attention was focused on Vietnam. In view of that, religious belief and practice seemed less important than one's patriotism (or lack of same), one's stand on war and civil rights, and so on. The second major thing that was different in the mid-1960s and early 1970s is that Latter-day Saints were still a religious minority then—Americans but quaint. They were a people not unlike the Mennonites, the Moravians, or (as they took care of their own) the Jews. While few Americans continued to think of the Saints as foreign or even as very strange, they were still *other;* however exemplary they might be, they were not quite "US." In the mid-twentieth century, the nature of the LDS belief system was not so much an issue for most Americans—fundamentalists, evangelicals, and Pentecostals excepted. What really mattered during that golden age was the obvious reality that Latter-day Saints were sincere about their beliefs.

In one of the sessions of the 1998 Sunstone Symposium, two journalism scholars from the University of Iowa presented a very interesting paper describing how the media started constructing the Latter-day Saints as a "model minority" in the middle years of the twentieth century.[44] What I am saying here is not meant to call into question what Chiung Hwang Chen and Ethan Yorgason said in their paper. Indeed, I am in perfect agreement with them that this is exactly what the media did, particularly in the 1960s and 1970s. Moreover, as these scholars demonstrated, in many of the presentations of Mormonism in recent years, including the 1997 *Time* magazine cover story, the Latter-day Saints continue to be set apart as a model minority.[45]

As such, the Saints are mostly admirable; they work hard, have wonderful families, and care for each other. But—and this is a qualifier that is nearly always present in substantial stories about the Saints—their alternative belief system not only leads to novel worship practices but also opens the way for the church hierarchy to exercise authoritarian oversight over everything from the intellectual lives of church members to the church's vast and, reflecting steadily escalating tithing revenue, expanding business and real estate holdings.

A close reading of the contemporary media picture suggests, however, that this practice of picturing the Saints as a model minority is gradually being superseded, for the clearly discernible reason that the Latter-day Saints no longer live in a self-contained culture, protected from the rest of the world by a mountain barrier. They reside on every continent and in countries all over the globe. Moreover, in the United States, the Church of Jesus Christ of Latter-day Saints is one of the nation's largest ecclesiastical institutions. While there are still more American Catholics, Baptists, Methodists, and Lutherans than American Mormons, there are more Latter-day Saints in the United States now than Presbyterians, or Episcopalians, or Disciples of Christ, or members of the United Church of Christ, that is, members of the churches that historically have stood at the very heart of the American Protestant mainstream.

The change becomes very obvious when one consults today's version of *Reader's Guide,* the Lexis-Nexis data base. I discovered this change while preparing the essay about the way the mainstream media handled the Southern Baptist Convention held in Salt Lake City in June 1998, which is included in this book. I assumed that I would be able to save time by calling up Lexis-Nexis references to Latter-day Saints/Mormons/Mormonism in the nation's twenty largest newspapers for the period between May 31 and June 31, 1998, to find out what journalists were saying about the situation. This assumption was wrong. Separating what I describe above as major stories—

stories, mostly syndicated, that appear in a large number of newspapers—from local news of Latter-day Saints in every large city in the nation is a tedious task. It is equally difficult to separate out the major news stories in regional newspapers. There is simply too much information being published about what local Latter-day Saints are doing (speaking at the Kiwanis Club, coaching Little League teams, winning beauty contests, sitting on school boards, being fined for speeding; and so on) for members of the Church of Jesus Christ of Latter-day Saints to retain their status as a "model minority." Unquestionably, Mormonism is rapidly losing the protection of minority *religious* status.

◦◦

This is no small matter. As long as the media set Mormonism apart, the church's distinctive doctrines could be (and have been) cloaked in what I have come to think of as LDS atonement discourse, a form of conversation and even sermonizing that asserts and emphasizes the critical importance of Christ's dying for humanity without going forward to specify how this atoning act is connected to the "fulness of the Gospel." Most especially, atonement discourse fails to link the atonement to that part of the "plan of salvation" that involves progression toward godhood, a topic President Hinckley and other Mormon leaders have been reluctant to discuss with the media.[46] Furthermore, as long as the media treated the Saints in holistic fashion, it was not simply the divergent doctrines separating Mormonism from traditional Christianity that could be protected with rhetorical barricades.

Something as countercultural as the new polygamy, which has been vigorously proscribed by the LDS Church but tolerated within the Mormon community, could be shielded, at least partially, from public view. In much the same manner that large extended families sometimes manage to keep pushing a skeleton back into the family closet, as long as the Saints remained a minority, their tacit acceptance of the practice of plural marriage in the LDS culture region did not become a scandal. Renewed practice of plural marriage flourished for decades within the larger LDS community without calling forth much police action or generating widespread media coverage. Even when exposés of this so-called new polygamy were published in books, magazines, and newspapers or shown on television, successful efforts to distance the church and its members from those engaging in plural marriage resulted in a diminution of media interest in the subject.

Things may be changing, however. The church itself has refused to sanction plural marriage for almost a century, of course. But now that these plural relationships once sanctified by the church have been tied to the victimization of women and children and possible abuse of governmental resources, continuing tolerance of the practice in the Mormon culture region will probably be less acceptable than it has been in the past half-century.[47] The state government of Utah, whose offices in the executive, legislative, and judicial branches are overwhelmingly filled with Latter-day Saints, can be said to reflect LDS culture, and pressure is likely to mount on the state government—and, by extension, the culture—to find some means of dealing with what is increasingly defined as a problem.

This is but one indication that the Latter-day Saints no longer have minority religious status and that what goes on within the LDS community is no longer protected from the inquiring minds of the general public. What happened in the summer of 1997 when the reenactment of the 1847 Mormon trek became a subject of widespread news coverage is a less obvious but more pregnant indication of the emerging situation in which what Latter-day Saints believe and what they and their leaders say and do are more likely to become grist for the media mill.

This trek reenactment was a not a Mormon PR ploy or even a church activity orchestrated by the LDS priesthood and Relief Society. Initiated by trail buffs, many of them non-Mormon, reenactment fever caught on at the LDS grass roots, giving the event a kind of energy that it might otherwise have lacked. For all that, through its Public Affairs Department, the church took advantage of the trek's sesquicentennial by creating a very professional and extremely attractive CD Rom file covering both the trek and modern Mormonism. This CD, called *Faith in Every Footstep: 150 Years of Mormon Pioneers,* was distributed to the media in much the same manner that news releases are scattered abroad. It generated a great deal of media interest and, perhaps because there was a date hook (July 24 was the hundred-and-fiftieth anniversary of the Saints' arrival in the Salt Lake Valley), articles about the reenactment and the church appeared in newspapers and magazines all over the country within a very brief period of time. In addition to the print media blitz, the trek and modern Mormonism were covered in substantial radio and television presentations, including segments on ABC's *World News Tonight,* with Peter Jennings, and on PBS's *NewsHour,* with Jim Lehrer.

Since I appeared in both these segments, I was close enough to their preparation to report that in both cases the producers were very much aware of the extent to which, by its very cooperation, the Public Affairs Department hoped to shape—not *control* but *shape*—the content of these segments. It seems to me, also, that by providing accurate information and access to President Hinckley and other LDS leaders, Public Affairs personnel did so to a considerable extent. Yet these presentations of the Saints were not shaped as they might have been if the ABC and NPR producers had followed Mike Wallace and been willing to construct the Mormons as a model minority. Aware of the exponential membership growth the church has been experiencing in recent years, neither producer treated the Saints as a religious minority, and the loss of minority religious status deprived the Saints of the protective tolerance that minorities ordinarily receive, especially regarding what they believe. In both segments, an idiosyncratic element of Mormon belief moved to the fore. In the ABC segment, Peggy Weymeyer described Mormonism's understanding of itself as Christian but gently called that into question for many viewers by focusing on the LDS belief about eternal progression toward godhood. The *NewsHour* devoted a considerable portion of its segment to Gail Houston, a BYU English professor, who answered questions about the Mormon belief in "heavenly mother" in her classes and the way her willingness to do so figured in her failure to gain tenure. In so doing, the producer (who, in this instance, was also the interviewer) directed attention not only to the LDS acceptance of a female deity but also to the church authorities' clear preference for keeping this part of the LDS belief system under wraps.

The loss of the protection that minority status afforded is extremely important.[48] On the one hand, the Saints will benefit because the LDS image will inevitably gain nuance if something other than their sincerity is featured. If the real version of their beliefs rather than a caricatured one becomes subject to media coverage, Latter-day Saints will no longer be stick figures capable of being captured in cartoons, as they were in the nineteenth century. Even the two-dimensional characters of the second half of the twentieth century will no longer serve.

On the other hand, the Saints will have to pay the cost. Just as the members of the Roman Catholic community have to live with their church's position on denying women's access to the priesthood, the anti-intellectualism of the Roman Curia, and the church's silencing of the theologian Hans Kung and the ethicist Charles Curran, so members of the Church of Jesus Christ of Latter-day Saints (whether they are called Mormons, Latter-day Saints, or Mormon Christians) will have to defend themselves against—or glory in— being a part of a church in which women have no access to the priesthood, a good portion of the church leadership adopts an anti-intellectual stance, and some BYU professors will fail to get tenure for religious reasons.

In 1989, President Hinckley told the media that with more than 99 percent of his sheep safe in the fold, where the others are does not really matter. In the *60 Minutes* interview, he responded to a question about the Mormon practice of plural marriage by saying "that was then; this is now." Such dismissive statements worked better when the media constructed Mormons as a model minority. As church membership continues to expand, things like the excommunication in a single month of a group of LDS intellectuals, collectively known as the September Six, will become far more significant— and not just to members of the faith. The same is true about Mormonism's distinctive beliefs, which are bound to receive increased scrutiny.

∾

Because this change will provide greater subtlety, it will probably be a blessing to the LDS Church and its members in the long run. As the change is taking place, however, the Mormon image is less than fixed. What that image will become in the new millennium is by no means clear. Moreover, as studies in perception go forward, things are changing so rapidly that I suspect soon it will not be legitimate (or even possible) to delineate *the* Mormon image. Despite the "cookie-cutter effect" of a carefully elaborated program the church has instituted in recent years to set standards for LDS belief and behavior, never again is there likely to be a single Mormon image. It is much more probable that along with nuance will come multiple images of the Latter-day Saints.

It is equally likely that these multiple images will be shaped as much by what goes on within Mormonism all across the world as by what occurs in the traditional Mormon culture region. This multiplicity of images is also likely to be viewed in multiple ways. Already, this appears to be happening as a result of the scandal that erupted over the strategies used by the Salt Lake Organizing Committee (SLOC) to secure the city's selection as the site of the 2002 Winter Olympic games. Despite revelations that the Utah capital is by no means the only city whose representatives employed questionable tactics in efforts to be chosen as Olympic sites, because the story of Olympic influence peddling first came crashing down on the city that is the Mormon center place, the actions of the SLOC were depicted as particularly shocking.[49]

Even so, this sad story is having a differential impact in Utah and elsewhere in the Intermountain West; the remainder of the United States; and the rest of the world. In the traditional Mormon culture region, the involvement of individual Latter-day Saints in unacceptable (and perhaps illegal) efforts to curry the favor of Olympic Committee members was a prominent feature of the coverage of the scandal, and there was considerable speculation about whether the church itself might somehow have been involved. But what happened in this instance in the very heart of Mormondom did not become a major Mormon story in the remainder of the nation; it was a Salt Lake City story, not a Mormon story. Outside the United States, however, the

Church of Jesus Christ of Latter-day Saints and Salt Lake City are so completely identified that any effort to separate these two quite separate entities is proving to be exceedingly difficult. The motivations of the Saints who were involved were probably more firmly rooted in their desire to improve the city's economic and civic life than in providing their church with an opportunity to be in the worldwide media spotlight for two full weeks. But reports from overseas indicate that if attempts to distance the institution (and Mormonism generally) from the actions of individual church members are being made, they are not working well enough to keep this story from reflecting negatively on the LDS Church. How the image of the Saints will come across during the games themselves is an open question.

What does not remain in doubt is that, whatever their character, during the 2002 Olympics the images of the Church of Jesus Christ of Latter-day Saints and its members will appear as often on the Internet as in the print and electronic media. Already such developments are taking place, and they will pose new problems for researchers trying to figure out what people think about the Saints and what their images are. Having made a good-faith effort to analyze what those images were in the print media in the nineteenth century and first half of the twentieth and having tried to describe what happened to the Mormon image with the shift from the print medium to the print and electronic media, I think I had better leave the tracking of new LDS images in a new media environment to scholars who are not as superannuated as I am.

Notes

1. Andrew Hamilton, "Those Amazing Mormons," *Coronet* 31 (April 1952): 26–30. The editors of *Coronet* decided to publish this article, written by a Latter-day Saint, even though they received a devastating prepublication critique from the LDS philosopher Sterling McMurrin, then dean of University College at the University of Utah, to whom the essay had been sent for review. McMurrin's reservations about the article ranged from what he regarded as inaccuracies in the historical portions of the manuscript to a romanticized picture of contemporary Mormonism. An extended exchange of letters between McMurrin and the *Coronet* editors is contained in the McMurrin Papers, Special Collections Division, Marriott Library, University of Utah, Salt Lake City.

2. A fine study of press coverage of Mormonism between 1950 and 1967 is Dennis L. Lythgoe, "The Changing Image of Mormonism," *Dialogue* 3 (Winter 1968) 3: 45–58.

3. A particular example of promotion paid for by the LDS Church that has to be taken into account in any study of the LDS image during this period is the series of eight-page inserts included in the *Reader's Digest* in the late 1970s and early 1980s. The figure most often cited as the estimated cost for these paid advertisements is $12

million. The extent to which these inserts were image constructions is one of the main points of an extended critique of LDS image-making written by the *Sunstone* editor Peggy Fletcher, "A Light unto the World: Image Building Is Anathema to Christian Living," *Sunstone* 7 (July 1982) 4: 17–23.

4. The race issue is covered in a study based entirely on the content of print media (newspapers as well as periodicals) between 1970 and 1976. See Stephen W. Stathis and Dennis L. Lythgoe, "Mormonism in the Nineteen-Seventies," *Dialogue* 10 (Spring 1977): 95–113. See "Mormons and the Mark of Cain," *Time*, January 19, 1970, 46–47, which, because of the magazine's huge circulation, was particularly important.

5. "Marketing the Mormon Image: An Interview with Wendell J. Ashton," *Dialogue* 10 (Spring 1977): 15–20. Initially organized in 1972 as the External Communications Department, the public communications arm of the church was given the official title Public Communications Department in 1973. Ten years later, the department was merged with the Special Affairs Department and renamed Public Communications/ Special Affairs. In 1991, the department's name was again changed, this time to Public Affairs. (I am grateful to Don LeFevre for this information.)

6. The "Homefront" series of public announcements for radio and television that were created in the early 1970s and started being broadcast soon thereafter added immeasurably to this perception of the Saints.

7. Although the policy regarding the way members of the Church of Jesus Christ of Latter-day Saints ought to be described by themselves and others was articulated in the press release that accompanied the adoption in 1995 of a new logo emphasizing the LDS Church's understanding of itself as a Christian church, the effort to replace *Mormon* with *Latter-day Saint* goes back at least to the 1960s. It seems likely that this earlier attempt at nomenclature adjustment was an effort to distance LDS Church members from modern polygamists.

8. Chief among this group were Jerald Tanner and Sandra Tanner, who, in the mid-1960s, established the Modern Microfilm Co. (now the Utah Lighthouse Ministry) as an outlet for mimeographed materials, pamphlets, a newsletter, and, eventually, books. Many of their publications include early Mormon documents that make it obvious that the Mormonism of the second half of the twentieth century differs, sometimes dramatically, from the LDS movement in its early years. They have also documented all the changes that have ever been made in the Book of Mormon and have published the purportedly secret LDS temple rituals. Generally, the Tanners have been a thorn in the side of the church as well as a boon to historians of early Mormonism. Their most famous publication is probably *Mormonism: Shadow or Reality?* 5th ed. (Salt Lake City: Utah Lighthouse Ministry, 1987). In the bookstore they maintain in Salt Lake City, they not only sell their own works but also the works of others. Like the bookstore's proprietors, many of the authors of the works sold by the Tanners were interested in making the case that Mormonism is by no means all that it claims to be.

9. A good account of Utah's International Women's Year Convention in 1977 and the Special Affairs Committee organized by the LDS Church to oppose ratification of the Equal Rights Amendment is found in Linda Sillitoe, *A History of Salt Lake County*, Utah Centennial County History Series (Salt Lake City: Utah State Historical Society, 1996), 251–58.

10. Although the interpretation in this essay might appear to be directly at odds

with Dennis L. Lythgoe's picture of a change from a positive to negative image of Mormonism when the 1950s are compared with the 1960s (and beyond), this disagreement is more apparent than real since his analysis was based entirely on the print media and this one is an effort to go beyond the print media to take the electronic media *and* the LDS Church's paid and unpaid advertising into account.

11. More than once, Mike Wallace or some other *60 Minutes* correspondent charged Mormonism with being more concerned about increasing its fabulous wealth than caring for the members of the LDS community, and Mormon women in Lovell, Wyoming, were once accused of mounting a conspiracy that destroyed the practice of the town's most prominent physician and brought about his imprisonment in the state penitentiary.

12. For a list of TV documentaries, see notes to D. Michael Quinn, "Plural Marriage and Mormon Fundamentalism," *Dialogue* 31 (Summer 1998): 1–68.

13. Jeremiah Films was the producer of this movie/video, which was apparently intended for rental or purchase by churches and church groups. Compared with the $7 cost of a book with the same name published in 1984 by Harvest House in Eugene, Oregon, the cost of the film was substantial: the rental fee was $87, and the original cost of a video cassette was $175.

14. Simon and Schuster issued Peter Bart's *Thy Kingdom Come* in 1981; G. P. Putnam issued *Prophet of Blood: The Untold Story of Ervil LeBaron and the Lambs of God* by Ben Bradlee Jr. and Dale Van Atta in 1981; Beacon Press issued *The Mormon Corporate Empire* by John Heinerman and Anson Shupe in 1985; and Addison Wesley issued *In Mormon Circles: Gentiles, Jack Mormons, and Latter-day Saints* by James Coates in 1991.

15. By 1980, church membership that had been less than 1.0 million at the end of World War II had soared to more than 4.5 million (4,633,000). Since 1945, stakes had been organized for the first time in Alabama, Alaska, Arkansas, Delaware, Florida, Georgia, Indiana, Kansas, Kentucky, Louisiana, Maine, Maryland, Massachusetts, Michigan, Minnesota, Mississippi, Montana, Nebraska, New Hampshire, New Jersey, North Carolina, North Dakota, Oregon, Rhode Island, South Carolina, South Dakota, Tennessee, Texas, Vermont, Virginia, West Virginia, and Wisconsin. In the nation's capital, a spectacular new Mormon temple had been built, and more than three-quarters of a million people had attended its open house. During the sesquicentennial year, the Seattle Temple was also dedicated.

16. Jan Shipps, "The Emergence of Mormonism on the American Landscape (1950–1965)," in *Historical Atlas of Mormonism*, ed. S. Kent Brown, Donald Q. Cannon, and Richard H. Jackson (New York: Simon and Schuster, 1994), 152–53.

17. See Anthony A. Hoekema, *The Four Major Cults* (Grand Rapids, Mich.: Erdmans, 1963). Still in print, this influential volume is generally in religious bookstores whose wares appeal to conservative Protestants.

18. The quotes are from an advertisement for the *God Makers*.

19. UMI was started in 1954 by John L. Smith, a Southern Baptist minister who served seventeen years in Utah.

20. *Utah Evangel* 33 (April 1986): 1.

21. The *God Makers* galvanized a rapid rebuttal in the form of a book, *The Truth about "The God Makers."* This page-by-page, line-by-line response was prepared by Gilbert W. Scharffs, who taught courses at the LDS Institute of Religion adjacent to

the University of Utah. Brought out in 1986 by the "Publishers Press," a Salt Lake City printer, it was not an official church publication.

22. Peter Bart, *Thy Kingdom Come* (New York: Linden, 1981), v.

23. The 1981 television drama *Child Bride of Short Creek* underscored the message of these two books: people connected with the Mormon church were still practicing polygamy. Throughout the decade, several news magazine television shows directed attention to the practice of modern plural marriage, with segments featuring the work of investigative journalists who interviewed some of the men and women involved.

24. Beacon Press is a reputable publisher of books on religion. A revised and updated version of this work was published in 1992 as *Wealth and Power in American Zion*. It was issued by the E. Mellen Press, a reputable but far less visible publisher.

25. In a very public exchange that occurred in one of the special seminars on American religion convened by the religious studies department at Indiana University in Bloomington during the 1989–90 academic year, I told Anson Shupe that it seemed to be common knowledge in Salt Lake City that Heinerman had misrepresented himself to gain information. Shupe acknowledged that this had "been necessary" in some cases. He went on to recount how he and a colleague had earlier misrepresented themselves to find out what they wanted to know about the "Moonies." Contending that the need for information to expose what is really going on inside a religious community legitimates a researcher's pretense to be someone he or she is not, he used a "higher law" argument to defend such misrepresentation.

26. Anson Shupe, *The Darker Side of Virtue: Corruption, Scandal, and the Mormon Empire* (Buffalo, N.Y.: Prometheus Books, 1991).

27. The Salamander letter was the most famous of the spurious documents produced by Mark Hofmann. Purported to be a letter from Martin Harris, one of Joseph Smith's earliest followers, to William W. Phelps, the text of the letter contained an allegation that a salamander had figured in Smith's discovery of the golden plates.

28. A local publication, *Indianapolis Woman*, published a profile of me in June 1986. Written by Barbara L. Waldsmith, who worked as the editorial assistant for the *Journal of the Early Republic*, then housed at IUPUI, it opened this way: "The telephone rings again as soon as she hangs up the receiver. She answers in half a ring, 'This is Jan Shipps.' On the other end of the line might be a reporter for the Indianapolis *Star*, or *Time*, *Newsweek*, the *Miami Herald*, the *Christian Science Monitor*, or one of a dozen other magazines and newspapers. If there is anything new in the world of Mormonism—and lately there has been a lot—Jan Shipps is the person people are calling" (17).

29. Over the next decade, I kept working on this lecture, which I thought of as "An Introduction to the Latter-day Saints." Eventually, it became the basis for the entry on Mormonism in the 1997 edition of the *Encyclopedia Americana*, 30 vols. (Danbury, Conn.: Grolier, 1997), 19:457–60. This is the entry on Mormonism in the "on-line" version of the *Encyclopedia Americana* as well.

30. This work was published in 1988 in Salt Lake City by Signature Books, a publishing house that has issued many important volumes about Mormon history and Mormonism generally, as well as a few volumes that do not touch on Mormonism in any way. Because Signature Books includes on its list many works that call parts of the canonized version of the LDS story into question, some Latter-day Saints regard it as an anti-Mormon press. I am convinced this is a mistake. I see it as an inde-

pendent press whose willingness to publish alternative interpretations of the Mormon experience has provided a richer picture of the LDS past than would otherwise be available.

31. His book, which was published by the University of Illinois Press in 1992, is set apart from the others by the fact that Turley had access to the journals and other records kept by the members of the church hierarchy who had dealings with Hofmann during his years as a dealer in (supposed) historical documents.

32. The connection was not lost on reviewers. For example, a blurb on the back of the book quotes a *Chicago Tribune* review that touted the work as "a fine study of detailed police and legal work; of the intricacies of the rare document industry, including the mechanics of forgery; and the development of the Mormon church."

33. The hardcover edition was published simultaneously in New York by Weidenfield and Nicholson and in Canada by General Publishing Co., Ltd. New American Library, a division of Penguin Books, published the paperback version. The year of publication for all three editions was 1988.

34. Michael Austin, "Troped by the Mormons: The Persistence of 19th-Century Mormon Stereotypes in Contemporary Detective Fiction," *Sunstone* 21 (August 1998): 51–71, classifies the works about the Hofmann episode by Sillitoe and Roberts, Lindsey, and Naifeh and Smith as "true-crime novels." His rationale for doing so is the extent to which the Latter-day Saints in them are "constructed" as nineteenth-century Mormon stereotypes. This classification is very appropriate for *The Mormon Murders,* less appropriate for *A Gathering of Saints,* and not appropriate at all for *Salamander.*

35. In view of what happened later, it makes sense to put the way that plenary session came about into the record. Since Steven Christensen was a member of the *Sunstone* board, Peggy Fletcher, the *Sunstone* editor, had hoped to open the symposium with a session on the Salamander letter somewhat analogous to the opening plenary session of the 1980 meeting of the Mormon History Association in Canandaigua, New York, in which Danel Bachman had projected the text of Hofmann's supposed Anthon transcript onto a screen. When Christensen and the scholars assigned to the research project to set the Salamander letter in context agreed that such a session would be premature, Fletcher turned to Richard Bushman; Valeen Tippetts Avery, coauthor of *Mormon Enigma,* a new biography of Emma Smith; and me. (My book, *Mormonism: The Story of a New Religious Tradition,* was still in press, but its publication was imminent.) Organizing the symposium's opening session as a panel, Fletcher asked the three of us to make twenty-minute presentations in which we would outline any new information about Joseph Smith and Mormon origins we had uncovered or new insights we had gained as we wrote our books.

Although Val Avery and her coauthor, Linda Newell, had used several documents Hofmann had produced in the writing of their biography of Emma Smith, Avery made no references to any of them in her presentation. Bushman made oblique allusions to the Salamander letter and an 1825 money-digging agreement, transcripts of both of which were circulating among the historians of Mormonism attending the symposium. His transparent purpose in doing so was warning the Saints, who made up most of the audience, not to be unduly disturbed by new evidence that was shortly to appear. Although I made no reference to the Salamander letter in the manuscript of my book, I had access to a transcript of it before my book went to press.

In my remarks, I said that I had seen only a typescript but that if the holograph proved genuine, it would likely lead to the same sort of investigation of magic at the beginnings of the Mormon movement that Morton Smith and others had been doing on the place of magic in the beginnings of Christianity. Since John Dart, a religion reporter for the *Los Angeles Times* who was attending the Sunstone Symposium that year, had written a book about Christian beginnings, he found my suggestion intriguing. He asked for a copy of my paper and subsequently wrote an article about the session that contained the first major news story alluding directly to the text of the Salamander letter. When Hofmann spoke to me after the session program was over, he asked where I had obtained a transcript of the letter, and he made it very clear to me that he was not pleased I had mentioned the letter's content in my remarks.

36. This talk was published in *Ensign* 17 (October 1987): 63–69.

37. The rise of the talk show phenomenon roughly coincided with the murders Hofmann committed. As a result, the Hofmann story became grist for radio talk shows, especially in the West. These were open to the wildest sort of speculation on the actions of the LDS Church in the entire Hofmann episode. While reviewing them for content is impossible, I was at the other end of the phone line on several of these shows. If the questions I was asked were at all typical, much talk-show conversation was animated by an astonishing level of suspicion on the part of those who posed call-in questions regarding conspiracy at the highest levels of the church designed to keep "the truth" about the Mormon past from coming out.

38. It is not without significance that *Refiner's Fire,* John Brooke's study of Mormon beginnings that emphasizes the significance of the occult to early Mormons, was—at least to some extent—generated by the Hofmann episode. Although he said that he came to understand fairly early on that the Salamander letter was a forgery, Brooke, the author of a prizewinning book on American colonial history, once told me that the text of that letter was one reason he decided to undertake a study of how Mormonism came into existence and why it succeeded. In any event, the final chapter of *Refiner's Fire* alleges that Mormons are unduly susceptible to scams of various sorts, something that, at least by implication, Brooke connects to a nonrational acceptance of the truth of LDS dogma. See John Brooke, *Refiner's Fire: The Making of Mormon Cosmology, 1644–1844* (New York: Cambridge University Press, 1994).

39. The malfunction of O-rings manufactured by Thiokol Chemical Corporation at its Wasatch Division in Brigham City, Utah, was pinpointed as the cause of the *Challenger* explosion. Shupe accepted the argument of several who testified during the 1986 booster-rocket controversy hearings that James Fletcher, the head of NASA, let the contract to Thiokol in response to pressure from LDS Church leaders. But Shupe took the argument further, charging, in effect, that the tragedy was the result of a Mormon conspiracy involving Fletcher; Senator Frank E. Moss, chair of the Senate's Aeronautical and Space Sciences Committee; and Nathan Eldon Tanner, a Mormon leader.

Pointing to an exchange of letters between Fletcher and Moss that his coauthor for *The Mormon Corporate Empire,* John Heinerman, found in the Moss papers in the Special Collections Division of the Marriott Library at the University of Utah, Shupe said that even though Fletcher knew (or should have known) that using Thiokol's O-rings would be dangerous, he let the contract for O-rings go to Thiokol because the LDS Church wanted business for the state of Utah. Shupe alleged that proof of this sinister conspiracy is found in an exchange of correspondence between Fletcher and Moss, especially a February 23, 1973, letter from Fletcher to Moss. In this letter (which Shupe quotes in full), the NASA head spoke of a conversation he had with Tanner, a member of the LDS First Presidency, in which he explained that his hands were tied as far as helping give the Utah economy a boost. Fletcher also complained to Moss that an unnamed member of the senator's staff had taken it upon himself to tell Fletcher that he had a "moral if not spiritual obligation" to give the contract to Thiokol since a member of the LDS First Presidency was anxious for the Utah company to have the business. Fletcher asked Moss to tell the staff member that he was out of line in suggesting that a Mormon government bureaucrat's church membership took precedence over his government responsibilities. Shupe used Fletcher's account of denying help to President Tanner and his asking Senator Moss to warn his staff member off as proof that his church was exerting undue influence on Fletcher.

Heinerman, whose photocopy of the February 23 letter was made with permission, supplied a copy to Shupe. Shupe's conviction that he was right about the conspiracy is supported by the fact that this particular letter disappeared from the Moss papers. To further support the conspiracy notion, Heinerman informed Shupe that the entry for the Moss-Fletcher correspondence had been expunged from the register of the Moss papers in the Special Collections section of the university's Marriott Library. This might well be, but since no specific reference was made to correspondence between Moss and Fletcher in the *Register of the Papers of Frank E. Moss,* which the library published in 1980, this must have involved the removal of some sort of interpolated entry describing the contents of either a box of materials about NASA in the Moss collection or a box of "Miscellaneous Correspondence." In any event, the disappearance of this letter led Shupe to the highly unlikely conclusion that a member of the Special Collections staff at the University of Utah either hid or destroyed the letter to protect the LDS Church. Failing to consider the possibility of misfiling after photocopying or some other innocent explanation, Shupe then read the presumed destruction of the letter as evidence of additional conspiracy and asserted that the disappearance of this letter from Fletcher to Moss was a deliberate effort to purge the public record of "smoking guns pointing to the [Mormon church's responsibility for the] booster rocket scandal" (*Darker Side of Virtue,* 160).

40. James Coates, *In Mormon Circles: Gentiles, Jack Mormons, and Latter-day Saints* (Reading, Mass.: Addison-Wesley, 1991).

41. Mark Silk, *Unsecular Media: Making News of Religion in America* (Urbana: University of Illinois Press, 1995).

42. This does not take into account the Salt Lake City Olympic scandal. Since this city was founded by the Latter-day Saints and is best known as the headquarters of the Church of Jesus Christ of Latter-day Saints, this has to be counted as a story connected to Mormonism. Yet it has not gained much traction as a religion story. From the national perspective, it seems to fit in with the stories about secular aspects of the city that have been much in the news in recent years, especially accounts of the success or failure of the Utah Jazz NBA basketball team and reports of skiing at Park City, Alta, Snowbird, and other nearby ski resorts, as well as stories about the area known as the Intermountain Silicon Valley.

43. *Sunstone* used the title I gave to this piece, "What Mike Wallace Missed," but

as originally published in the *Christian Century* 113 (August 14–21, 1996): 784–87, it was called "Mormon Metamorphosis: The Neglected Story."

44. Chiung Hwang Chen and Ethan Yorgason, "Those Amazing Mormons: The Media's Construction of Latter-day Saints as a Model Minority," *Dialogue* 32 (Summer 1999): 107–28.

45. Published on August 4, 1997, this story—now much expanded—has become the basis of Richard N. Ostling and Joan K. Ostling, *Mormon America* (San Francisco: Harper San Francisco, 1999). Richard Ostling was one of the authors of the *Time* story.

46. I have talked with many Latter-day Saints, not just "Sunstone types," who agree that President Hinckley "shocked many Mormons when [during an interview last year] he was asked if Mormons really believe God was once a man [and he] replied, 'I wouldn't say that. . . . That gets into some deep theology we don't know very much about.'" *San Francisco Chronicle*, June 6, 1998, A6.

47. One of the consequences of the presence of these schismatic groups in the Mormon culture region is a heated—and to non-Mormons extremely interesting— debate about whether members of these schismatic groups who accept the Book of Mormon and regard Joseph Smith as the founder of their faith communities deserve to be called what they call themselves, that is *Mormons.* See an exchange about this issue between Reed Neil Olsen and Thomas G. Alexander in the "Letters to the Editor" section of *Dialogue* 31 (Spring 1998): ix–x, and 31 (Fall 1998): ix–xi. There is a certain irony in all such discussions since Latter-day Saints who argue against allowing the Mormon tent to cover believers who, according to the LDS Church, are not orthodox also argue that the Christian tent should cover Latter-day Saints. According to many traditional Christian bodies, however, Latter-day Saints are not orthodox Christians. Alexander tries to remove himself from the horns of this dilemma by noting that (1) by practicing plural marriage, which is the defining characteristic of the new polygamists, they are breaking civil law; (2) members of the Church of Jesus Christ of Latter-day Saints are no longer motivated by revelation—indeed, they are no longer permitted—to break the civil laws; and (3) the new polygamists should therefore not be regarded as Mormon.

48. It is important to note that minority status afforded a certain amount of protection even in the nineteenth century when LDS belief was often either ridiculed or described as heresy and LDS behavior was described as criminal. As long as they remained behind the "mountain curtain," the Saints parried nearly every accusation with references to Constitutional guarantees of freedom of religion. When the press shifted over from constructing the LDS community as a dangerous minority to constructing it as a model minority, the right to privacy became their protective shield.

49. Utah's Governor Michael Leavitt has tried to make a silk purse out of this particular sow's ear by suggesting that what happened was a blessing in disguise: Latter-day Saints would be able to see to it that the Olympic Committee's selection process is cleaned up. This same "Saints will do the cleaning up" scenario was described to me by several Latter-day Saints I met when I was in Salt Lake City in the summer of 1999.

4

From Gentile to Non-Mormon:
Mormon Perceptions of the Other

The Book of Mormon, from its title page onward, speaks of Gentiles in the traditional sense, that is, their being the people who were not Jews. Quite as much as the New Testament, if not even more, the message of the Book of Mormon is that God's covenant with humanity is not a restrictive covenant. It is available to Jew and Gentile alike. Coming forth by way of Joseph Smith Jr., a Gentile seer, translator, and prophet, the Book of Mormon announced that after eons, during which the scattering and confounding of the house of Israel would occur, God would "raise up a mighty nation among the Gentiles." This nation would nourish the seed of Israel's house until it could again be gathered and the "covenants of the Father of heaven unto Abraham" could again be made known.[1]

Subsequent revelation delivered through the Prophet Joseph Smith made it clear that the United States was the mighty nation and that those who accepted the Book of Mormon's message as God's word and, with other believers, formed a "Mormonite" community would become the nucleus of the house of Israel gathered in the last days.[2] In keeping with this promise, as followers congregated in not one but two centers (Independence, Missouri, and Kirtland, Ohio), the young prophet, in pronouncing a blessing on his father's head, called Joseph Smith Sr. to be patriarch to the new Church of Jesus Christ, "prince over his posterity," the holder of "the keys of the patriarchal priesthood over the kingdom of God on earth." Accepting his divine mandate, Joseph Smith Sr. fulfilled the responsibilities of his office by administering patriarchal blessings to individual Saints.[3] Because they provided information to blessing recipients about their bloodlines and membership in the family of the patriarchs most often through Ephraim (but later, when Jews converted to Mormonism, Judah), these spiritual dicta were particularly significant in Mormonism's evolution as a religious tradition. As descendants of Abraham, Isaac, and Jacob (Israel), Latter-day Saints, who already understood themselves to be members of the only true Christian church then on the earth, also came to understand that, as a people, they were set apart from the Gentile multitudes.

Appropriately, therefore, the first LDS religious structure, built in Kirtland in the early 1830s, was not a church but a temple. Moreover, just as God had given Abraham's seed a promised land in the old world, these new world Saints were assured by revelation that, in this "new dispensation of the fulness of times," they had been given an inheritance in the form of land in Missouri.[4] Quite rapidly, Saints acquired a sense of themselves as categorically different from other folks. Where once they had been Gentile, they no longer had that status. The very blood flowing through the veins of the members of this new religious movement made them God's chosen people.

However much new religious movements differ in what they hold to be true and how they organize themselves, they have many things in common. One of the most obvious is that they erect substantial barriers between those who join the movement and those who do not. The sine qua non is a commitment to do much more than undergo an entry ritual, such as baptism. The new religions that survive and maintain their integrity compel from their members psychic separation from their friends and the members of their families who refuse invitations to come into the new movement with them. Often the leaders of the movement urge (or even demand) physical separation as well.

As Mormonism came into existence, Smith's followers responded to a "gathering" revelation that brought them together to await Christ's return at the opening of the new millennium. In the meantime, they set out to build up Zion, and if they did not construct literal walls around their settlements, they did put in place barriers that encircled Smith's followers, walling them off from non-Mormons.

Because truth is invariably at issue when new religious movements come into existence, a natural antagonism develops between the contenders for truth on both sides. This always strengthens the boundaries between inside and outside. Typically, issues of power as well as truth divide outsiders from insiders. When new movements flourish, establish geographical bases, and gain enough committed members to threaten the political and economic status quo, religious barriers turn into secular barricades. Suspicion, distrust, and paranoia abound both inside and outside the community. Apprehension turns into hostility that is manifested in physical struggle, a prelude to Armageddon not in future time but in real time.

As this pattern played itself out in early Mormonism, the people on both sides of the barricades developed mutually pernicious perceptions of those on the opposite side. These quickly became the basis of powerful and very negative mental abstractions that persisted, again on both sides, long after the murder of the Mormon prophet and the subsequent atomization of the Mormon movement. Because the Saints who followed Brigham Young to the Great Basin maintained and magnified the gathering pattern as they built an earthly kingdom in that mountain fastness and because they added the practice of plural marriage to the many other elements that made up the boundary between them and the rest of the world, their form of Mormonism lent itself to stereotype. From "Mountain Mormonism" was thus forged the steely LDS image that made the Saints seem so alien and dangerous from the middle of the nineteenth century onward.[5]

An unanticipated result of the analysis of the data set I gathered for my study of perceptions of the Mormons from 1860 to 1960 was the regularity with which the mountain Saints were described as foreign.[6] Although the elaborate scheme for content analysis of what was written about the Mormons that I used to create the "Satyr to Saint" data base allowed me to fashion rich descriptions of the shape and amplitude of the images of Latter-day Saints held by non-Mormons, my research results failed to yield any useful information about how important the Saints' belief that outsiders were Gentiles was in shaping the non-Mormons's images of the Mormons. A Mormon perception of themselves as divinely favored had been a critical factor in bringing on the Missouri Mormon War, but was it also one of the variables in the construction of the Mormon image? It is hard to say. The literary corpus about the Jewish experience in the United States suggests that the Jews' clear understanding that people not of their tribe were Gentile was one ingredient among several that accounted for how Americans thought about Jews. Likewise, that the Mormons came to understand that theirs was a special status was surely noteworthy, but I am convinced that this was merely one of many "otherizing" idiosyncrasies that made the Saints seem exotic, one far less consequential than the practice of plural marriage.

By contrast, for at least a century and perhaps longer, the central element in the Saints' conception of people who were not Mormon was that they were Gentile. A major reason this is true is that the LDS belief that people who refused invitations to accept the Mormon gospel were Gentile was a significant component of Mormon identity. Applying the epithet Gentile to non-Mormons was an effective (and expeditious) signal of the axiomatic outsider-hood of everyone who was not Mormon. At the same time, whenever Latter-day Saints used the word *Gentile* to describe someone—either someone they knew or someone they had only heard about—it dramatized for them their own membership in the family of God, enlarging their comprehension of their own special kinship with God as father and Christ as elder brother.[7] It is therefore not surprising that emphasis on the Gentile concept is key to understanding the history of Mormon perceptions of non-Mormons.

Across-time analysis of the data from which Americans constructed Mormon images revealed that changes in perceptions of the Saints were directly related to what the people in the nation read and heard about what was going on in the Great Basin. News from Utah about the theocratic form of government there and the Saints' effort to preserve plural marriage was critical to the construction of the menacing satyr image. While news about Utah's admission to the Union drained that frightening image of some of its power, the image's negativity was revitalized by the much publicized turn-of-the-century fights over whether to seat the polygamist B. H. Roberts in the U.S. House of Representatives and the LDS apostle Reed Smoot in the U.S. Senate. When subsequent news focused on the Saints' energy and commitment, their plain living and universal adherence to the Word of Wisdom, and, during the Great Depression, their Church Welfare Plan that allowed them to "take care of their own," the Mormon image was turned on its head.

This complete transformation was possible because the Mormon image in the American mind was almost pure stereotype. Practically no one had firsthand knowledge of the Latter-day Saints. The Mormon image was consequently an empty vessel that could be filled with whatever people heard or read about the Saints. The same was not true of the images of non-Mormons that Saints held.

Over the decades, a perceptual shift also occurred in the way in which Saints thought about people who were not Saints. This shift is connected with contemporary events, news about what the Saints were having to contend with outside the borders of the Great Basin kingdom, how they were being treated by non-Mormons, and the extent to which they were gaining respect in the outside world. The parallel between what happened to non-Mormon perceptions of Mormons and what happened to Mormon perceptions of non-Mormons does not go very deep, though. Whereas the American image of Mormons was virtually turned inside out, transformed not simply from evil to not-evil but also from evil to good, the Saints' image of outsiders never moved 180 degrees. Even though at different points in time the Saints' image of non-Mormons was inevitably affected by the extent to which the environment in which Mormonism existed was either malignant or benign, that image could only be altered, never turned inside out.

A total transformation could not occur because the image of non-Mormons in the minds of Latter-day Saints has never been pure stereotype. No matter how isolated they were, very few Saints had no acquaintance at all with people who were not Mormon. As a result, LDS perceptions of non-Mormons were not poured into an empty vessel. Rather than hollow stereotype, the Saints' image of non-Mormons was a null conception, a conception of what being "not them" was like. In other words, it was a mirror image. As a result, it inevitably changed as the Latter-day Saints themselves changed.

∽

The first thing I had to do before starting to track the alterations that changed people like me from "Gentile" to "non-Mormon" was to recognize and clarify the distinction between Gentiles and apostates. Once persons relinquish their Gentile status by becoming church members, there is no going back, even if they do not remain in the church. Throughout the years, many—a veritable multitude—joined the church only to leave, either because they were faint at heart or because they had never fully understood the implications of becoming Mormon. In the latter case, Saints have often looked upon such people with compassion. From the beginning, however, Latter-day Saints had little compassion for "apostates," that is, members who left the church because they concluded that Mormonism is not true or else because they decided that while the LDS Church is the true church, it is being led by the wrong men. Apostate status is not the same as Gentile status, and this has hardly changed over the years.

However, as articulated in LDS sermons and both official and unofficial writings, Latter-day Saints have regarded those who stand outside the LDS community with less consistency throughout the years. Gentiles, early on, were more often than not castigated as enemies and persecutors. For many decades, the term *Gentile* was rarely simply a descriptor indicating nonmembership; it meant a potential or actual adversary, unless a person somehow qualified as friendly.

But the likelihood that the term would be infused with negative meanings gradually lessened as more people who were technically Gentile were described as non-Mormon. To complicate matters, Saints have always considered those who stand outside the LDS Church as potential members. As a result, the effort to make those outside the faith less defensive conceivably had something to do with the fact that the designation *Gentile* has increasingly fallen into disuse among the Saints.

To see if I could figure out when the shift away from characterizing outsiders as Gentiles occurred and to see if I could suggest some reasons why, I used the same content analysis and general survey research method to study

Mormon materials that I used to study American perceptions of the Saints. For reasons set forth above, the results in this instance are far less precise, but they do call attention to changing conceptions of outsiders, which, in itself, is significant. If and when someone undertakes a more elaborate and detailed study, the results may substantiate what I outline here or may call this study into question. In any event, a more elegant research design developed with an eye to collecting more subtle variables that reflect the way the term *Gentile* was used—whether it was simply descriptive or had a negative connotation—is bound to clarify this study's somewhat superficial results.

Any study of posthumous perceptions depends on (and is limited by) a body of material whose content can be mined to create a data base for analysis. Although I did secondary research in preparing this piece for publication, I conducted the original research for this project in 1977 and 1978. Back then, locating an appropriate body of material to use was very difficult, mostly because no tidy body of systematically indexed Mormon materials analogous to those indexed in the *Reader's Guide* existed and no full-text data bases were available then.[8] Moreover, although numerous indexes—done by divers hands, apparently on the basis of divers principles of indexing—were available in Utah libraries, a surprisingly small number of entries were found under the headings of "Gentiles" and "Non-Mormons" and even fewer under such related headings as "Protestants," "Catholics," "Presbyterians," and so on. I found no references to material under either "Gentiles" or "Non-Mormons" in the index to the *Deseret Weekly News*, 1850–1900, for example, and none in the *Index to the Faith Promoting Series*, or the *Utah Genealogical and Historical Society Magazine Index*. Neither were they in the published indexes to *Books in the Noble Women's Lives Series*, the *Family Home Evening Manuals*, the *Relief Society Magazine*, 1914–1932, the *Relief Society Manuals, Handbooks, and Miscellaneous Materials*, the *Contributor* (vols. 1–17) or in the topical index to the *MIA and Priesthood Manuals*, 1898–1960. The only reference in the important children's periodical, the *Juvenile Instructor*, was to a story entitled "The Hammer of the Gentiles," and there was one reference in the *Young Woman's Journal* to an article warning that many young LDS women would be forced to marry Gentiles if plural marriage was truly at an end.

At the time I was working, the main resources I was able to use were materials to which I was led by references to Gentiles, non-Mormons, and related terms found in the published indexes of the *Documentary History of the Church*, the *Journal of Discourses*, the *Messages of the First Presidency*, *Tullidge's Quarterly Magazine*, *Conference Reports*, the *Improvement Era*, and the *Ensign*. All except *Tullidge's Magazine* are official publications of the LDS Church.

Because "Gentiles" and "Non-Mormons" are also headings in the card index to the Journal History, it would have been possible to use the great compilation of published and unpublished material documenting Latter-day Saint history available in the LDS Church Archives. But this is not something I managed to do. A separate analysis of these Journal History materials would be very helpful in verifying or calling the results of my work into question, mainly because the index to the Journal History is, among other things, a reasonably effective index to newspapers published in Zion. It would also be useful to compare the result of my analysis with an analysis of data drawn from published and unpublished materials containing references different Saints made to non-Mormons. Unfortunately, this would require checking many individual works because the index to Davis Bitton's *Guide to Mormon Diaries and Autobiographies* does not contain references to Gentiles or non-Mormons and because there is no other summary index of this nature to other Mormon materials, either published or unpublished.[9]

Despite the shortcomings of existing indexes, they perfectly exhibit one of the main difficulties with charting changes in LDS attitudes about non-Mormons through content analysis: indexes and the material to which the indexed items refer rarely indicate whether *Gentile* was being used merely as a descriptor or had a negative connotation. An important (but extremely eccentric) index illustrates this difficulty. The indefatigable researcher Stanley Ivins amassed a substantial and important collection of documents having to do with many different aspects of Mormon history, some of which were photocopies of original documents while others were copies he had personally transcribed.[10] When Ivins made an index to his huge collection, he placed only 15 items under the heading "Gentiles in Early Utah"; another 197 items were placed in a category he called "Mormon-Gentile Conflict." This indicates that, for Ivins, the term *Gentile* was obviously infused with a negative charge.

The linking of outsider and adversary into a single concept is also evidenced by the system of classifying items in the Journal History that was put in place in 1852. The "Gentile" category contained references to enemies of the Saints, while those who were not enemies but were also not LDS were classified as "friendly non-Mormons." This classification system was extended to the works in the LDS Church Library, where a "Gentile" classification was automatically assigned to the author of unflattering things written about the Saints, while a "Non-Mormon" classification was assigned to items written by those who were not Saints if what they had written was positive—or even reasonably neutral. That this system was still in place in the 1950s is illustrated by the fact that the librarian responsible for cataloging the work of Leonard Arrington was unaware that this eminent scholar, who would later become the LDS church historian, was a Latter-day Saint. His work was cataloged with other works by "friendly non-Mormons."

∽

During Mormonism's first century, the concepts of outsider and adversary were so often linked that when Mormons referred to Gentiles, the usage more often than not betokened opprobrium, disrespect, or worse. For purposes of my analysis, I therefore decided to place "Gentile" at the negative pole of a negative-positive continuum, hypothesizing that as the Saints moved away from the use of the term *Gentile*, LDS opinion of non-Mormons was moving in a positive direction. I considered using "anti-Mormon" as the negative extreme but decided not to do so because it refers more to what persons do than who they are. Using "anti-Mormon" would have given my analysis an essentially political character, with the result that much of what I wanted to investigate would have been hidden. The use of the Gentile concept is problematic, but my analysis generally bears out the fact that although this word and related concept had a negative meaning for many Saints for a very long time, it gradually lost its negative valence.

From the beginning, however, since the Saints themselves had, as George Q. Cannon once put it, "come through Gentile lineage," the negative weight borne by the concept as well as the specific descriptor was never as simple as Gentile equals evil adversary.[11] Moreover, in analyzing the meaning of references to Gentiles in LDS discourse, I had to make distinctions between scriptural allusions to Gentiles and general allusions to individuals and groups who were not Mormon, with those in the latter category subdivided as (1) persons and groups not part of the LDS community who were seen as potential, if not actual, enemies; and (2) persons and groups not Israelite/Mormon to whom the fullness of the LDS gospel had to be preached. Individuals and members of groups in the second subcategory had the option of accepting the LDS gospel, but revelation warned the Saints that most would reject its fullness. The term *Gentile* therefore had a double meaning.

This ambiguity was first established in the Book of Mormon, which states that "the Father" says that "Gentiles shall sin against my Gospel, and shall reject [its] fulness," and "shall be lifted up in the pride of their hearts above all nations . . . and shall be filled with all manner of lyings, and of deceits, and of mischiefs, and all manner of hypocrisy, and murders, and priestcrafts, and whoredoms, and of secret abominations." When they reject the gospel's fullness, "saith the Father, I will bring the fulness of my Gospel from among them; and then will I remember my covenant which I have made unto my people, O house of Israel, and I will bring my Gospel unto them; and I will shew unto thee, O house of Israel, that the Gentiles shall not have power over you." However, according to this new scriptural work, "if the Gentiles will repent, and return unto me, saith the Father, behold, they shall be numbered among my people."[12]

After the Saints settled in the Intermountain West and established a Mormon realm, the double meaning for *Gentile* became a complicated triple consciousness of the other. Turning on its head the situation in which the Saints had existed as outsiders, the settlement and organization of the Great Basin kingdom made the Saints insiders, and this made allusions to Gentiles take on an additional wrinkle. Not only were there scriptural references to Gentiles and references to those to whom the Saints were obligated to carry the LDS gospel in order for the times of the Gentiles to be consummated, but also there were references to the Gentiles who had been enemies of the Saints before they left the States and those in Washington, D.C., and elsewhere who continued to be their adversaries. Besides that, allusions to Gentiles increasingly pointed to the non-Mormon residents in Zion. These non-Mormon residents constituted a substantial contingent in the Utah Territory— by 1880, more than 10 percent—and LDS leaders often used them as convenient models of what being Mormon ought not to be.[13]

Data gathered for this study indicate that in the second half of the nineteenth century, during what they sometimes referred to as the final dispensation of the fullness of times, Mormon leaders very often used a complex formula of charges of iniquity, followed by the promise of acceptance, when they talked about people who remained outside the Latter-day Saint fold. The formula carried a dual message, suggesting that Gentiles were bad but that they had an opportunity to become good by converting to Mormonism, thereby relinquishing their Gentile status. But the Saints did more than simply present this dual message to potential converts. In a theological irony of sorts, the Saints preached the LDS gospel to the Gentiles for their own purposes. They needed to carry the gospel to the world, because when it had been preached to enough Gentile nations and Gentile individuals and when it had been rejected by a sufficient Gentile number, the "times of the Gentiles" would be used up and the fullness of the gospel could be carried to the house of Israel, a task that would have to be initiated before the millennium could be ushered in.

If the messages the Saints received from their leaders are organized chronologically, the double-edged character of LDS attitudes about the Gentiles can be seen. In times of stress and trouble, LDS leaders described the Gentiles in very negative terms, on the one hand, and called Saints to the task of preaching to them, on the other. For example, in 1855, when friction was building up in the face of LDS efforts to establish an outer cordon of settlements in areas already populated by non-Mormons, Apostle Orson Pratt said that "property is the Gentiles' god" and that "if there were no Gentiles among us, we could not see whether there was any integrity among the people."[14] But around that same time, he also said that "the gates of Zion shall not be shut day nor night, [so] that the forces of the Gentiles may flow into her."[15] This mixture of messages was reiterated the next day in a discourse in which Brigham Young described the necessity of gathering those of the blood of Israel from among the Gentile nations. Calling for the "brethren who have been selected to go and preach the Gospel [to] meet . . . in the Seventies' Hall, and the Twelve will meet with them, and the missionaries will there receive some instructions," he said that "the set time is come for God to gather Israel, and for His work to commence upon the face of the whole earth." Carrying the message to the world was necessary for the times of the Gentiles to be fulfilled, allowing the opening of the new millennium.[16] The clear implication of these and many other sermons preached in these stressful years was that proclaiming the gospel to the Gentiles was—whether or not they listened and responded positively—a prelude to ending the times of the Gentiles. Only when that came about would the way be cleared for the opening of the final dispensation of the fullness of times in which the earth would be renewed and the Saints would enjoy the presence of the Savior.

Throughout the nineteenth century and well into the twentieth, Saints repeatedly emphasized the same point. "And you have got to do a great deal of preaching before the times of the Gentiles are fulfilled," said Orson Pratt in 1859.[17] "When the times of the Gentiles shall be fulfilled, the power of God will be made manifest in the redemption of the House of Israel," Erastus Snow stated in 1880.[18] Quoting the New Testament, John W. Taylor declared in 1902 that "this gospel of the kingdom shall be preached in all the world for a witness unto all nations; and then shall the end come."[19] In 1920, Melvin J. Ballard proclaimed, "There shall come a day when the Gentiles shall reject this gospel, they will close their doors against it. . . . When that day comes then cometh the day of the redemption of Israel."[20]

Such messages promised reward to the Saints, but the Gentiles would likewise benefit. Again, it was Orson Pratt who sought to direct the Saints' attention to what their efforts could do in the way of protection for those not in the Great Basin kingdom: "There are great things in the future, and we are sometimes apt to forget them. We have been looking, for some time past, for

the Lord to accomplish and fulfill the times of the Gentiles." LDS missionaries have been "warning the Gentile nations [and] gathering out of their
midst, a few here and there of the believing Gentiles, away from the corrup-
tions of Great Babylon, preparatory to the destructions that are to be poured
out without measure upon the Gentile nations."[21]

⁓

If the Saints heard mixed messages, disparaging the character of the Gentiles
but exhorting them to carry the gospel to them so that their rejection of it
could be the agent of the much anticipated end of time, they also heard something else of great significance in making sense of the development of Mormon ethnicity in the nineteenth century and its disappearance at the end of
the twentieth century. On April 8, 1855, President Brigham Young included
in his conference discourse a description of the LDS belief that the Saints were
of the blood of Israel, which makes it very clear this was no mere symbolic
notion. "The Elders who have arisen in this Church and Kingdom are actually of Israel," he stated categorically. "Though the Gentiles are cut off, do
not suppose that we are not going to preach the Gospel among the Gentile
nations, for they are mingled with the house of Israel. . . . We want the blood
of Jacob, and that of his father Isaac and Abraham, which runs in the veins
of the [Gentiles]." He added, "You understand who we are; we are of the
House of Israel, of the royal seed, of the royal blood." Using the familiar
metaphor of the olive tree, he summarized the Prophet Joseph Smith's promise that "if the Gentiles are grafted into the good olive tree they will partake
of its root and fatness." This was not a metaphorical partaking: "Joseph said
that the Gentile blood was actually cleansed out of their veins, and the blood
of Jacob made to circulate in them; and the revolution and change in the
system were so great that it caused the beholder to think [that during bap-
tism] they were going into fits."[22] This explanation was as important in reassuring the members of the Church of Jesus Christ of Latter-day Saints that
they were chosen people despite their coming through Gentile lineage as it
was in explaining the difference between Mormons and Gentiles.

Moreover, in view of this potential for Gentiles to become Mormon, LDS
leaders made conscious efforts to eliminate the ambiguity about the Gentiles
that developed in Mormon minds as the LDS movement "rolled forward"
and as conflict with those who were not Mormon became a fact of everyday
life. In 1868, President Young explained that "'Gentile' or 'gentilism' applies
only to those who reject the gospel, and will not submit to and receive the
plan of salvation." He continued, "It does not apply to any, only those who
are opposed to God and His Kingdom. . . . [not] to a man because he is not

baptized. There are some of pure gentile blood will come into this Church." Then, echoing the Prophet Joseph Smith, he added, "When a person of real gentile blood, through honesty of heart, submits to the gospel and is baptized and receives the laying on of hands from a man duly authorized, you might naturally suppose, from the contortions of the muscles, that such a person had a fit, for the power of the Holy Ghost falls upon and renovates that rebellious blood and stirs it up . . . in consequence of the power of the Holy Ghost operating upon the power of the enemy within the individual."[23]

The general authorities of the church pointed out that by "grafting" Gentiles into the house of Israel, the church and the movement prospered. Still, as the transcontinental railroad neared completion and the Saints' Rocky Mountain Zion seemed about to be overrun with non-Mormons, the more negative aspects of being Gentile came to the fore, and the Saints' need to purify themselves "from every kind of corruption, from all the leaven of gentiles" became paramount.[24] The LDS theological understanding of the need to take the gospel to the Gentile nations and the belief that some Gentiles would continue to receive the gospel guaranteed that the double meaning for the term *Gentile* would never be entirely lost. Yet events in Utah, particularly after the railroad was completed in 1869, led to the virtual disappearance of neutral-to-positive references to the concept of non-Mormons as Gentiles who were not anathema to the Saints.

Chronologically ordered, the references that I gathered on those who stood outside of and apart from the church show that negative attitudes toward non-Mormons hardened throughout the 1880s. As Mormonism became locked in combat "with Babylon," LDS opinions and attitudes started to make a hard and fast association between the descriptive terms *anti-Mormons* and *Gentiles*. The two became synonyms, as sermons on the olive branch text disappeared from view. Saints were warned not to marry Gentiles, lest their children apostatize; trading with Gentiles was equated with apostasy; and the conflict between Mormons and Gentiles was reflected in newspapers, books, magazines, and official statements of nearly every kind.

Because the LDS story was first fully told, both from the inside and the outside, by the generation of Mormons and non-Mormons who lived through the events of the 1880s and 1890s and through the muckraking era when hostility toward the Saints was reignited by charges made during the Reed Smoot hearings, early histories of Mormonism organized the LDS past primarily around conflict, a format that emphasizes economics and politics.[25] Since what was occurring during the two decades on both sides of the turn of the century served as a lens through which the whole of the Mormon past was seen, it is not surprising that LDS history has so often been understood in the Stanley Ivins pattern, with a more than ten-to-one ratio of accounts of Mormon-Gentile antagonism set against descriptions of Mormons and non-Mormons managing to live in harmony. (While the analysis being presented here may be called into question if these findings are tested against an analysis of the materials in the Journal History, it is important to remember that this particular index was also a product of these years of conflict.)

My analysis seeks to move beyond the struggles—political, economic, and even social—that were faced by nineteenth-century and early twentieth-century Saints. In doing so, it calls into question an interpretation of the LDS past that presents the Mormon story mainly as a story of conflict. When the content (no matter how insignificant) of every reference indexed under "Gentile" and "non-Mormon" in the *Journal of Discourses*, the *Conference Reports*, the *Messages of the First Presidency*, et cetera is examined and the resulting data are organized chronologically, a pattern emerges that does not reflect years of unrelieved conflict between Latter-day Saints and Gentiles. *Enemies* is, far and away, the word most commonly used by Mormons to describe non-Mormons in the nineteenth century. Yet, if taken overall, these data show a fairly ambiguous attitude toward the Gentiles, which reflects an LDS understanding that Saints were once in the "Gentile" category and a hope that the Gentile multitudes will someday be moved over into the "Latter-day Saint" category. This attitude gave way to unrelieved animosity only at the height of the fight over plural marriage and the Mormon political kingdom. As that fight drew to its conclusion, less antagonistic attitudes reasserted themselves.

Moreover, the Saints used the term *Gentile* less and less after 1890, and when it was used, it generally referred to scriptural statements about Gentiles, especially the Gentiles in New Testament times. At least in its official statements, the LDS Church sought to sever the synonymous tie between *Gentile* and *anti-Mormon*. In a famous 1891 *Salt Lake Times* interview about the disbanding of the People's party, the management of this local newspaper posed a set of thorny questions about the Mormons in politics to the First Presidency of the church. The questions included numerous references to "the Gentiles." As framed by Wilford Woodruff and George Q. Cannon, the answers avoided the word *Gentile*. They referred to *non-Mormons* instead.[26] A dozen years later, President Joseph F. Smith talked about "insidious, wicked, unprincipled, hypocritical, lying, deceitful goats in sheep's clothing who are jealous and constantly raising a hue and cry against the covenant people of God," but he did not use the word *Gentile* as he said, "we will do them good if they will let us. We will do all we can to protect the rights of mankind."[27] By 1908, the shift was apparent at the annual conference, when Apostle Orson F. Whitney gave a talk in which he asserted that no adversarial relationship existed between Mormons and non-Mormons:

> Mormonism is not an enemy to the human race; it is not an enemy to the Gentiles. We do not recognize the word "Gentile" as an opprobrious term, though some of our outside friends take umbrage at it. . . . The word springs from "gentilis," which means of a clan, a family, a race, a nation. In the days of the Jewish commonwealth, Gentile simply meant one who was not a Jew; in the early ages of the Christian Church, it meant one who was not a Christian, and in these times it designates one who is not a Latter-day Saint. . . . We are not the enemies of the Gentiles, we are not the foes of the human race; our mission is friendship, peace, and good-will; our work is to preserve and bind together all that is good, both past and present, and to labor for the consummation of Christ's work in the great and wonderful future.[28]

The Saints did not stop—and may never stop—rehearsing the story of the persecution they suffered in the early days. The mobbings and drivings, Haun's Mill, and the martyrdom were probably as much a part of sacrament meeting talks after the turn of the century as they had been before.[29] But in conference talks, the enemies of the Saints were identified as "anti-Mormons," and the term *Gentile* was used less frequently.[30] By 1910, the old concern that Zion would be overrun by the Gentiles was tempered with Mormon practicality. Apostle Whitney reminded the Saints who remembered the "olden time" that the position often taken "suggesting that the Gentiles are coming in overwhelming numbers to outvote us" was a mistake. "If the Gentiles come to us," he said, "it will save us the trouble of going to them. Our mission is to the Gentiles, not from them. . . . If the Gentiles capture Mormonism, it will make Mormons of them—and that is just what we want. . . . Talk about the Gentiles overwhelming the Mormons and destroying the work of God! Yes, just as the Romans destroyed the Jews and the Christians."[31] Five years later, President Rey L. Pratt, of the Mexican mission, preached a conference sermon on the church's responsibility to take the gospel to the Gentile nations, only he did it without ever using the word *Gentile.* He instead referred to the members of the Seventies quorums who are expected to take the lead "in the work of preaching the Gospel to the nations of the world."[32]

☙

The shift in the attitudes of Mormons toward non-Mormons, the transformation in which outsiders were turned into "nonmembers," was far less

dramatic than the shift in American attitudes toward the Mormons. An antagonistic stance toward outsiders has not disappeared on the part of a certain element of the LDS community; perhaps it never will. But the turn away
from defining Gentiles as anti-Mormons that was so much a part of the late
nineteenth century came much more quickly within Mormonism than the
American change in attitude toward the Saints, which continued to be more
negative than positive until the 1930s.

An intriguing turn of events occurred with Mormons and non-Mormons
that deserves both comment and further investigation. As Latter-day Saints
discontinued the use of *Gentile* to describe those outside the faith, non-
Mormons living in the LDS community nearly universally adopted the noun
Gentile to describe themselves. I was aware that *Gentile* had become a verbal
Shibboleth, often used and widely understood by the residents of the Mormon culture region well into the twentieth century. But since I had spent most
of my Utah research time between 1965 and the 1990s in the company of
Latter-day Saints, I had started to believe that the use of the term *Gentile* was
increasingly anachronistic. Then, in 1997, while I was working on a new study
of religion in mid-size American cities that I began when I retired from teaching, I undertook the development of a religious profile of Salt Lake City that
called for interviewing Protestant, Catholic, Greek Orthodox, and Jewish
clergy as well as typical non-Mormon citizens. To my surprise, I discovered
that if *Gentile* is not being used by Latter-day Saints to describe them, non-
Mormons continue to use the term as a linguistic badge of identity separating them from members of the region's dominant community.

∾

A comparison of changing American perceptions of Mormons and changing Latter-day Saint perceptions of the other may be summarized as follows:
until the middle of the twentieth century, American attitudes toward the
Mormons mainly rested on hearsay, stories about the Mormons, gossip, and
exposé. Mormon attitudes toward non-Mormons rested on experience, on
close encounters, some of which led to tragedy and many of which resulted
in lesser forms of persecution. While the Saints sometimes "gave as good as
they got" in Missouri and Illinois, they truly suffered at the hands of the non-
Mormons both before and after they settled in the Great Basin. To them,
outsiders were actually dangerous. Yet Mormon attitudes toward non-Mormons were never as intensely negative as non-Mormon attitudes toward
Mormons.

This is not simply a matter of the Saints' turning the other cheek. Americans, and non-Mormons generally, were able to distance themselves from

the Saints, making it easy to define them as foreign and, primarily because of plural marriage, depict them as heathens who could and should be kept away from U.S. society. This psychosocial gulf allowed the nation to keep the humanity of the Saints at arm's length. Mormons were in a different situation. Try as they could, and they did try (the move to the Great Basin was clearly an effort the Saints made to separate themselves from the Gentiles), Mormons could not avoid contact with non-Mormons. The humanity of those they called Gentile was on display. While this allowed the Saints to experience the negative firsthand, it also allowed them to see the positive. As a result, Mormon attitudes toward non-Mormons were tempered with a hearty dose of reality.

Far more important in accounting for the fact that Mormon attitudes toward non-Mormons were extremely negative for only a few decades and that their attitudes became positive fairly rapidly after the terrible decade of the 1880s is the Saints' theological definition of Gentiles as people to whom the Saints must carry the fullness of the LDS gospel. Traditional Christianity might define Mormonism as heresy and its adherents as enemies of the Protestant and Catholic understandings of the gospel of Jesus Christ who had to be converted away from their faith or avoided. The situation was entirely different for the Saints. They were convinced that the "sectarians" were wrong, but they could not avoid contact with them. If they wanted to bring in the kingdom, they were required to preach the gospel to the Gentile nations. Besides that, while they themselves might have been born Mormon, their ancestors were Gentiles who had accepted the LDS gospel. In the end, American perceptions of the Mormons changed for the practical (and essentially secular) reason that the nation's citizens came to know and admire the Latter-day Saints. LDS perceptions of Gentiles changed because they learned what is fundamentally a religious lesson: when you meet the theological enemy and it is you, negative attitudes are hard to maintain for very long.

A development occurring within Mormonism in the latter part of the 1990s is an interesting and noteworthy coda to this study. When Bruce R. McConkie pulled together a description of Mormon doctrine in 1958, the belief that the Saints are actually of the blood of Israel was a hallmark of LDS understanding. Latter-day Saints understood this claim in literal terms and had done so for generations, as is evidenced by the testimony found in the letters and memoirs of thousands of Saints who, in serving their missions, say that they were convinced they were engaged in the gathering of Israel from among the Gentiles.[33] I find no direct evidence that the president of the church or LDS general authorities no longer hold to McConkie's declaration that "the Lord sends to earth in the lineage of Jacob those spirits who, in pre-existence developed an especial talent for spirituality and for recognizing truth; . . . [that] having the blood of Israel in their veins, [they find] it easy to accept the gospel."[34] But the belief that converts are individuals with "believing blood" is increasingly being watered down, as is the emphasis on birthright Latter-day Saints as the blood of Israel. This is happening so rapidly that it is now not surprising to hear Saints describe the notion that they are of the lineage of Jacob through Ephraim as symbolic rather than literal.[35]

Implications for the shift away from the Saints' regarding outsiders as Gentiles are direct and unmistakable. If what differentiates Latter-day Saints from those who are not Latter-day Saints is not corporeal bloodline but metaphorical tenet, then the separation is creedal rather than tribal. No longer are outsiders even "non-Mormon." They are what they are—Methodist, Baptist, Presbyterian, Catholic, nothing—and in relation to the Latter-day Saints, they are simply not members of the Church of Jesus Christ of Latter-day Saints.

Notes

1. Book of Mormon, 1 Nephi 22:3–10.

2. Doctrine and Covenants of the Church of Jesus Christ of Latter-day Saints, 45:25, 28–30.

3. Irene M. Bates and E. Gary Smith, *Lost Legacy: The Mormon Office of Presiding Patriarch* (Urbana: University of Illinois Press, 1996), 34, 37–38, 45–49.

4. Doctrine and Covenants, sections 58 and 84.

5. One of the great ironies of Mormon history is that even though this Hebraic dimension of Mormonism was far less significant to them than was the original claim to be the restored Church of Jesus Christ, the followers of the prophet who did not go west had to struggle to attain an identity apart from the "Brighamites." This was particularly the case for members of the Reorganized Church of Jesus Christ of Latter Day Saints. That the president-prophet of the Reorganized Church, Joseph Smith III, followed in the patriarchal priesthood line may account for this.

6. This description was correct in that converts from England and Scandinavia flowed in a great stream into the Great Basin kingdom. But the movement was not simply indigenous to the United States; it was led by U.S. citizens who proclaimed their allegiance to the nation.

7. Rooted in the positive embrace of LDS religious claims and the identification of outsiders as other, which gave a negative valence to outsiderhood, this understanding was critical to the development of Mormon ethnicity.

8. Even now, although the LDS Church has published and sponsored the publication of many periodicals over the years, no combined index directs readers to the contents of a combination of these publications in a style similar to that of the *Reader's Guide.*

9. Bitton's invaluable resource for the study of Mormon history was published by Brigham Young University Press in 1977.

10. After Ivins's death, this collection was deposited in the library of the Utah State Historical Society. (When I first used this collection in 1964, it was housed in cabinets and cupboards in Ivins's apartment in Salt Lake City, including—much to my surprise—his kitchen cupboards.)

11. This entire passage reads, "It is true we have been scattered among Gentile nations, and are called Gentiles, but nevertheless we are of the pure seed, having come through Gentile lineage that we may be the means of saving them, and through our faithfulness we shall stand at their head. This is the blessing which rests upon us as descendants of Abraham." *Journal of Discourses,* October 31, 1880, 26 vols. (Liverpool, England: F. D. and S. W. Richards, 1854–86; photo lithographic reprint, Los Angeles: Gartner Printing and Litho, 1956), 22:130.

12. This passage comes from the first edition of the Book of Mormon, 3 Nephi 7. Chapters in the 1830 edition of this work were not further subdivided into verses. Essentially the same message is found elsewhere in the Book of Mormon, as well as in the Doctrine and Covenants of the Church of Jesus Christ of Latter-day Saints.

13. *Journal of Discourses,* April 19, 1882, 23:58.

14. Ibid., April 7, 1855, 2:261; May 20, 1855, 3:16.

15. Ibid., April 7, 1855, 2:263. For a description of the emergence of friction in the outer cordon settlements, see Eugene E. Campbell, "Early Colonization Patterns," in *Utah's History,* ed. Richard D. Poll, Thomas G. Alexander, Eugene E. Campbell, and David E. Miller (Provo, Utah: Brigham Young University Press, 1978), 141–46.

16. *Journal of Discourses,* April 8, 1855, 2:267, 268.

17. Ibid., July 10, 1859, 7:186.

18. *Conference Report of the Church of Jesus Christ of Latter-day Saints,* April 6, 1880 (Salt Lake City: Church of Jesus Christ of Latter-day Saints, 1880), 89. The annual conference reports are now available on the *New Mormon Studies CD-Rom* (Salt Lake City: Smith Research Associates, 1998).

19. Ibid., April 6, 1880, 74.

20. Ibid., October 1920, 81.

21. Ibid., April 6, 1880, 86.

22. *Journal of Discourses,* April 8, 1855, 2:268, 269.

23. Ibid., August 16, 1868, 12:270–71.

24. Ibid., January 18, 1865, 11:56. The speaker was John Taylor, who would become president of the church.

25. This point is persuasively argued by Klaus Hansen in a brilliant summary article, which will appear in a forthcoming volume on Mormon historiography edited by Newell Bringhurst.

26. "Heads of the Church: Interview with President Woodruff and President Cannon on the Present Political Situation in Utah," *Salt Lake Times,* June 23, 1891.

27. *Conference Report,* April 6, 1903, 74.

28. Ibid., April 5, 1908, 93.

29. Gordon Shepherd and Gary Shepherd, *A Kingdom Transformed: Themes in the Development of Mormonism* (Salt Lake City: University of Utah Press, 1984). M. Guy Bishop published an informative review of the Shepherds' work in *Dialogue* 19 (Spring 1986): 180–81. Bishop summarized the Shepherds' findings as follows: "Mor-

mon leaders were primarily concerned about Church government, persecution, and the enmity of non-Mormons during the first three decades of Latter-day Saint history. From about the 1860s to 1890, their concerns shifted to plural marriage, Gentile antagonism, and obedience to gospel principles. Church (i.e., priesthood) authority and dedication to the gospel headed conference themes at the turn of the century, while missionary work and the divine nature of Joseph Smith's prophetic calling were stressed between 1920 and 1949. Post-war emphases have featured Jesus Christ, parenthood, and missionary work (76)." According to my cursory review of the contents of the *Ensign* and the *Church News* since the mid-1970s, there is much more emphasis in sermons and substantive articles on the history found in the scriptures, especially the New Testament and the Book of Mormon, than on early LDS history.

30. An electronic search of the volumes of the *Journal of Discourses*, which include major annual and semiannual conference addresses, indicated that the word *Gentile* went down from a high of 101 in volume 18, which includes sermons from 1875, 1876, and 1877, to less than 24 per volume for volumes 19 through 25. Volume 26 contained only 9 references to *Gentile*. This is a gross measure since what would be needed to clarify the situation more precisely would be an analysis of how many of the uses of the word or concept were scriptural references.

31. *Conference Report*, October 8, 1910, 52.

32. Ibid., April 4, 1915, 23.

33. In his discussion of the descriptions of proselyting in missionary diaries, Davis Bitton uses the phrase "searching out this wheat from among the flourishing tares." This reference is an appropriate one, often used in sermons by LDS leaders from the time of Joseph Smith and Brigham Young well into the 1960s, in describing the necessity of preaching the gospel to the nations because the blood of Israel (wheat) was thoroughly mixed with Gentile blood (tares). Davis Bitton, *Guide to Mormon Diaries and Autobiographies* (Provo, Utah: Brigham Young University Press, 1977), viii.

34. Bruce R. McConkie, "Believing Blood," in *Mormon Doctrine* (Salt Lake City: Bookcraft, 1958), 77–78. The entry in the second edition (1966) is the same as the entry in the first edition.

35. Nevertheless, I was surprised, nay astonished, when the *Los Angeles Times* reporter Teresa Watanabe told me that when she asked a member of the LDS Public Communications staff about the blood of Israel dimension of LDS belief, he assured her that while important, that part of LDS belief is "just symbolic." Telephone conversation with Teresa Watanabe following her interview with President Gordon B. Hinckley in June 1999.

5

Media Coverage of the Southern Baptist Convention in Salt Lake City

When the Southern Baptist Convention held its annual meeting in the heart of Mormon country in the summer of 1998, the *Deseret News* columnist Lee Benson welcomed the Baptists to the Utah capital with special enthusiasm. Alluding to his state's substantial restrictions on the sale and consumption of alcohol, he told them that theirs was "the first convention ever to come to Salt Lake City and not complain about the liquor laws."[1] While few other writers were so site specific, his was one of many observations that appeared in the national press about what is shared by the Church of Jesus Christ of Latter-day Saints (LDS) and the churches belonging to the Southern Baptist Convention (SBC).

Readers across the nation were informed that these two churches take almost interchangeable moral stances and that they have nearly identical social and political agendas. Both are conservative, virtually agreeing on family values (they are for them) as well as abortion, pornography, protected gay rights, drug use, and legislated gaming (they are against them). Voting Republican is the normal pattern for the great majority of Baptists and Latter-day Saints. Moreover, many members of both groups are clearly part of the Christian Right. But when Jerry Falwell, pastor of the Thomas Road Baptist Church in Lynchburg, Virginia, made an effort to create an umbrella organization that would include both—the Moral Majority—it foundered, at least in some measure, because Baptists were unwilling to be even loosely yoked to the Mormons.

The LDS Church and the churches in the SBC also share strategy in the religious arena. Both are mission-minded. SBC and LDS leaders have often told their flocks that every member must be a missionary. Latter-day Saints and Baptists routinely share their good news with anyone willing to listen.[2] Both organizations have large numbers of members. With more than 15 million members, the SBC is the largest Protestant denomination in the United States. The LDS Church, which now has more than 10 million members, with about half of them in the United States, is one of the nation's largest ecclesiastical bodies.

Nearly every time I have been interviewed about the Latter-day Saints in the last few years, I have been asked to explain Mormonism's immense and (to many non-Mormons) astonishing growth in recent decades. Six or seven reporters called me for information before they left for Salt Lake City to cover the SBC's annual meeting. All asked about the LDS Church's growth. But if the ones who called me were typical, neither Mormon growth nor what these two ecclesiastical bodies have in common was the topic in which the journalists who would be covering the convention were most interested. Those who called were much more anxious to hear anything I could tell them about what might happen when these formidable religious behemoths, somewhat like Jews and Palestinians, faced off against each other in the very shadow of the Mormon temple.

Those who had already seen the press packet prepared by the Baptist Press, the SBC news bureau, knew that Southern Baptists regard Mormonism as a form of counterfeit Christianity.[3] Every reporter headed to Utah to cover the story also seemed to have been aware that the Baptists would be spending up to $600,000 on local evangelism before and during the convention. They knew that in the weeks leading up to the conclave, radio and TV spots, huge billboard displays, and direct mailings to 400,000 Utah residents had been preparing the ground for the Baptists to launch a mission blitz the weekend before the convention opened.

With pun intended, Southern Baptists called this evangelical onslaught "Crossover, Salt Lake City." Sports clinics, block parties, and other gatherings would precede and follow up the main event: an all-out Sunday offensive in which Baptist missionaries planned to proclaim their message of salvation as they knocked on (presumably Mormon) doors all along the Wasatch Front. Local SBC evangelistic efforts were not new. In advance of the convention's opening every year, an evangelism campaign is conducted in the city where it is being held. But this time the SBC's executive committee had made a special effort to prepare the weekend missionary forces (the *New York Times* called them "Utah Shock troops") for their coming engagement with the Saints.

Interfaith Witness, a division of the SBC's North American Mission, had overseen the production of *The Mormon Puzzle*, a fifty-minute videotape describing LDS beliefs and charging that those beliefs differ so dramatically from evangelical dogma that Latter-day Saints are, in fact, cult members.[4]

Copies of this video, which includes instructions about how best to convince Saints that their church is not the way to salvation, had been mailed to all 40,000 Baptist churches that might be sending "messengers" (delegates) to Utah. Besides that, the SBC Sunday School Board printed 12,500 copies of a new book, *Mormonism Unmasked,* which put the "puzzle" together to picture a pseudoreligion that threatened evangelical Christianity. It is no wonder that the people who work in the mainstream media went to Utah expecting a battle. As it was put in a front-page article published in the *San Francisco Chronicle* on June 6, "the sacred heart of the Mormon Church" would be "the site of a weekend showdown between American evangelicals and one of the world's fastest-growing faiths."

While this annual SBC gathering had the smallest attendance since 1951, Herb Hollinger, spokesman for the SBC, told me that press attention increased. Convention press credentials were issued to more than a hundred journalists, a third of them from the mainstream/secular press. Although other conventions had attracted more correspondents for various religious and denominational presses, this was the largest contingent of reporters from the mainstream media ever to cover an SBC convention. One reason is that the South Baptist Convention's annual gathering has become increasingly newsworthy. In 1986 and 1987, it had made news by resolving that Baptists needed to evangelize Jews (lest they be lost as a consequence of not accepting Christ) and boycotting the Disney Company (because its actions appeared to legitimate a homosexual lifestyle and because so many of its films failed to reflect traditional moral values). This time, Hollinger said, the thing that drew the press to Salt Lake City was conflict. What the press clearly anticipated was a "wrestling match between two of America's evangelical juggernauts."[5]

Many of the articles published before the convention's opening indicated that a definition of the family would probably be added to the Baptist Faith and Message, the first addition since 1963 to the collection of statements that comes as close to a creed as Southern Baptists have.[6] Some preconvention articles mentioned the SBC's continuing battle with the Disney Company. More often than not, however, the interreligious mayhem that might occur as "thousands" of Baptists started going door to door in the Mormon heartland was the lead. On May 31, the *New York Times* warned readers to "expect a lively rumble among some champion proselytizers." In a June 6 article that, since it was syndicated, appeared elsewhere, the *Washington Post* said that if things went as the Baptists wanted, the Utah capital "will end up with fewer Mormons." Major news outlets, such as the *Los Angeles Times* (Larry Stammer's religion pieces are also syndicated), the *Dallas Morning News,* the *Min-*

neapolis Star Tribune, the *Louisville Courier-Journal*, the *Orlando Sentinel*, and even the overseas edition of the *Times*, all published articles in the next day or so to give readers an idea of the drama that could be expected. Nearly all used colorful phrases ("a missionary drive of biblical proportions" is my personal favorite) to depict what was about to happen.[7]

But there was no drama—not even much theater. Two thousand Baptists took part in the "Crossover" campaign, but there was no confrontation to report.[8] From the church president to the local ward bishops, LDS leaders asked their followers to respect members of all other faiths and encouraged them to be gracious hosts to Zion's Baptist visitors. Fully cognizant of a general Baptist feeling that "Crossover, Salt Lake City" would be "pay-back time" for all those occasions LDS missionaries had knocked on Baptist doors, Mormon leaders appealed to the Saints to be courteous to those who stood at their doors and knocked. The Saints complied. The conflict story evaporated.

Some 4,000 calls were received in Alpharetta, Georgia, on the toll-free number (1–800-JESUS-2000) appearing on the huge billboards in and around Salt Lake City, and 1,500 response cards were returned from preconvention direct mailings. The SBC reported 2,000 decisions for Christ. But these totals were reported after the convention adjourned. Precisely how many of them were made as a result of "Crossover" and how many were made by people who belonged to the LDS Church is not clear.[9] In Utah, the convention contented itself with passing a resolution reading the Latter-day Saints out of Christianity. But this was news only in the Mormon state.

With nary a skirmish to describe, not even doors slammed in Baptist faces, the mainstream press contingent shifted its attention to the convention itself and started focusing on the overwhelmingly conservative character of the SBC. Thirteen years ago, a conservative takeover of this ecclesiastical organization had been engineered by Judge Paul Pressler and the Reverend Paige Patterson, then a college student who, on the first day of the gathering in Utah, would be elected SBC president. In the years since then, Southern Baptist moderates have been pushed to the margins of the convention. Just how far is suggested by the low level of attendance at the convention.[10] The virtual absence of moderates was more clearly revealed in the vote to amend the Baptist Faith and Message by defining the family as society's "foundational institution" and spelling out the convention's conception of the proper structure of the intrafamilial relationship of husband, wife, and children.

After a debate that lasted only half an hour, less than 1.5 percent of the messengers cast dissenting votes to the 250-word amendment that implicitly rejects divorce, abortion, and homosexual unions: "A husband is to love his wife as Christ loved the church. He has the God-given responsibility to provide for, to protect, and to lead his family. A wife is to submit graciously to the servant leadership of her husband even as the church willingly submits to the headship of Christ. . . . [She has] the God-given responsibility to respect her husband and to serve as his helper in managing her household and nurturing the next generation. . . . Children are to honor and obey their parents." More than 98.5 percent of the roughly 7,000 messengers (three-fourths of them male) voted in the affirmative.[11]

Perhaps it was the absence of any semblance of a moderate-conservative balance as much as it was the need for an alternative captivating story to justify the concentration of so much attention to a religious body's annual meeting that caused journalists to focus so much attention on "gracious submission." Whatever it was, when the mainstream press reported on the amendment's passage, the lead was nearly always "Southern Baptists Declare Wife Should 'Submit' to Her Husband." This was the headline of Gustav Niebuhr's June 10 story in the *New York Times*. Its placement on the front page almost guaranteed that the story would be included on the network news. Moreover, the *New York Times* regularly provides grist for Jay Leno's mill. When Leno, the host of the *Tonight Show*, put a wife's "gracious submission" story into his patter, it quickly made its way onto the talk show circuit at the local and national levels. References to "gracious submission" also started appearing in political cartoons. *USA Today* was surely correct in saying that the convention's action had created "an unholy brouhaha."[12] The clamor was greater in the electronic media than in the print media.

As the story appeared in papers all across the nation, the intent of the Baptist Faith and Message amendment certainly seemed to be a guarding of the male prerogative. But there was more to it than that. For all practical purposes, the floor debate on the amendment had been one-sided, essentially dismissing out of hand the moderate position regarding the way spouses ought be in relationship with each other and where authority rests within the family. After its passage, however, print coverage of the story turned out to be a venue for full expression of the moderate as well as the conservative position on intrafamily dynamics.

On June 9, even before the amendment was considered, the *Louisville Courier-Journal* story warning that the statement on families would divide Baptists included the observations of both conservatives and moderates. Mary Mohler, a member of the committee that framed the statement, was quoted as saying that "it's a Biblical issue. . . . a strong statement and one that may be viewed with disdain by the world. But we stand by it." The conservative Debra Bell, a messenger who had been married thirty-five years, was quoted as saying, "I feel very strongly that if a man has been led by Christ, he should be head of the household," while the moderate Robert Parham anxiously commented, "They hope to make June Cleaver the Biblical model for motherhood."[13]

On June 11, *USA Today* quoted Martin Marty, an expert on the history of American religion, as saying that the statement is "a recruiting device for a church competing with nondenominational megachurches and the media-savvy men from Promise Keepers." But the same story also quoted Paige Patterson's observation that he had "been a bit surprised that anyone would be surprised by this," and Eunice Smith, a member of the SBC resolutions committee, who asserted, "You have to understand it in the full context of scripture."[14]

The account in the *Atlanta Journal and Constitution* quoted the chair of the amendment drafting committee on the committee's work: "We are saying to the culture this is God's plan for family life." Several conservative messengers from Georgia were also quoted. The *Chicago Sun-Times* story featured only those who were angered by the statement. Most of the major newspapers' substantial articles on the convention's action did not simply report the position of one side or the other, however. Exemplary balanced articles include the one by Richard Vara and Cecile Holmes published in the *Houston Chronicle,* Stammer's article in the *Los Angeles Times,* and Don Lattin's piece in the *San Francisco Chronicle.*[15]

Indeed, nearly all of the articles in the mainstream press balanced conservative positions and moderate ones. The *Chicago Tribune's* Steve Kloehn, for example, pointed to the way in which the SBC is using this new definition of the family as a means of engaging the culture by placing Reverend Patterson's position that "it's only hot language to someone not familiar with the Bible" alongside the text of a substitute statement proposed by moderate pastor Tim Owings. The defeated statement read, "Both husbands and wives are to submit graciously to each other as servant leaders in the home," a moderate position close to the one articulated by Catholic bishops.[16]

From Salt Lake City, David Briggs wrote in the *Cleveland Plain Dealer* that James Uline from Parma, Ohio, said that the amendment spoke to men as well as women. "Men are wimps," Uline said, "they don't want to take that leadership role." Briggs also quoted Paige Patterson and Patterson's wife, Dorothy, who both pointed to a scriptural basis for the statement. In the same article, however, he noted that others condemned the Baptists "for treating women as 'auxiliaries' to their husbands" and gave voice to Andrea M. Johnson, director of the Virginia-based Women's Ordination Conference, who said, "I don't think they have a prayer of succeeding in pushing us back . . . but they are going to try."[17]

As the story took off, many articles were focused on what local Southern Baptists had to say about their denomination's new definition of the family. As such stories often do, those in the *Baltimore Sun,* the *Louisville Courier Journal,* and the *Detroit News* all balanced conservative observations with more moderate ones. Another type of article moved beyond the Southern Baptists to report the opinions of leaders from other denominations or experts in the study of American religion. These, too, tended to offer a balanced perspective.

From time to time, in a newspaper article or item about the convention on radio or TV, some brief comparison of the SBC amendment and the LDS statement on the family would surface. Dean Bill Leonard of Wake Forest University suggested that geography could have played a role in the decision to bring this amendment to the floor because Mormons have held the "high ground" on families. But as the media's attention increasingly centered on "gracious submission," the convention's location became irrelevant.[18]

Still, a comparison of the Baptists and the Mormons could be helpful here. If the coverage of an addition to what amounts to the Baptist creedal declaration had been about an addendum to Mormon doctrine, the efforts of journalists to represent a wide range of LDS positions in reporting such a development might have been interesting, but they would have had no effect whatsoever on whether Latter-day Saints in local wards (congregations) complied. Whether they submitted graciously or grudgingly, Saints would have had to accept such a change because authority in their church moves from the center out to the periphery.[19] This is not the case with the Baptists. However dictatorial the actions of the convention might seem to people who are not Baptist, there is a long-standing Baptist congregational polity (to which the SBC subscribes) that allows every congregation to decide whether it will adopt this or any other amendment to the Baptist Faith and Message. This means that, in a quite substantial way, mainstream press coverage of a convention action became a surrogate for open debate on the convention floor.

∽

This review of the press coverage of the convention has a moral arising from what could have almost been an artificially structured experiment. Expecting a Mormon-Baptist clash, religion writers and mainstream journalists prepared themselves by researching the Latter-day Saints as well as the Southern Baptists. The conservative accord and corresponding pattern of gospel spreading in these two clearly defined religious groups operated as a set of controlled variables. The outcome is that the print reportage of the gathering of Southern Baptists in Utah yielded surprisingly sophisticated treatment of the complex doctrinal and theological issues that separate the Latter-day Saints and the largest Protestant denomination in the United States.

As Marty King, director of public relations for the North American Mission of the SBC, said, "On the whole, the media got the story of the difference in the belief systems of the Mormons and Southern Baptists accurately." The staff of the LDS Public Affairs Department was also satisfied, expressing no complaint about the media's characterization of Mormon theology and doctrine and the way they differ from Baptist belief.[20] These are meaningful encomiums because they come from professionals whose task is, at least in part, to monitor the way their belief systems are described in the press.

King added, however, that reporters were disappointed when the expected clash between the two failed to take place. Once the media turned its attention to the amendment to the Baptist Faith and Message, King noted, "the story was so focused on the passage about the gracious submission of a wife to her husband that it failed to point to the way the amendment defined the family so that it excluded same-sex marriage."

For this review of the coverage of this story, I examined some 125 stories from the mainstream press, a surprising portion of which were at least eight hundred words long. In general, I agree with the LDS and SBC public communications professionals. If the descriptions of the expected conflict were sometimes overwrought, the comparisons and contrasts of these two religious organizations imparted a great deal of information to the public clearly and, for the most part, were right on the mark.[21] When coverage in the mainstream press moved to the convention's amending the Baptist Faith and Message, considerable complexity was sacrificed for description and discussion that generated a powerful picture of the Southern Baptist Convention as a politically incorrect institution. But the conservative-moderate balance in that coverage reminded the world that while moderates no longer attend SBC conventions, the term *moderate Southern Baptist* is not an oxymoron.

AN AFTERTHOUGHT

Comparison of the LDS "Proclamation on the Family" and the Baptist 250-word family amendment to the Baptist Faith and Message, which was added in the 1998 meeting of the SBC, suggests that, at least in these very public statements, the LDS Church's picture of proper male-female relationships within the family is more moderate than the picture of those same relationships limned by the action of the Southern Baptist Convention. Set side by side, both these statements clearly reject a family headed by two members of the same sex. But however much the effect of the two statements might be the same, the description of how authority is to be structured within the family differs on a key point.

In both statements, a wife is pictured as being equal to her husband in theological terms, that is, in the sight of God. In the business of managing the household and caring for the children, however, there is a significant difference. The relevant section in the Baptist statement reads:

> The marriage relationship models the way God relates to His people. A husband is to love his wife as Christ loved the church. He has the God-given responsibility to provide for, to protect, and to lead his family. A wife is to submit graciously to the servant leadership of her husband even as the church willingly submits to the headship of Christ. She, "being in the image of God" as is her husband and thus equal to him, has the God-given responsibility to respect her husband and to serve as his "helper" in managing their household and nurturing the next generation.[22]

On the same points, the LDS "Proclamation on the Family" reads, "By divine design, fathers are to preside over their families in love and righteousness and are responsible to provide the necessities of life and protection for their families. Mothers are primarily responsible for the nurture of their children. In these sacred responsibilities, fathers and mothers are obligated to help one another as equal partners."[23]

Both of these official statements make it clear that the husband is to lead (the Baptist language) or preside (the LDS language). The husband is likewise given the responsibility of protecting and providing for the family in both statements. As for managing the household and nurturing the next generation, however, the Baptist statement says that a wife is to be her husband's "helper," while the LDS statement says that husbands and wives must "help one another as equal partners."

Many of the observations made to journalists by Baptist husbands and wives suggest that, from a practical perspective, there is probably very little difference. But for the record, on this particular and very important point, the LDS Church, which is sometimes pictured as the most conservative of all conservative religious bodies, is the more moderate of the two.

Notes

1. Lee Benson, "Will Baptists Stir Up Big News Again?" *Deseret News,* June 8, 1998.
2. The LDS Church has a much more massive missionary army than that sent out

by the SBC. At their own expense, young LDS adults go on missions in which the "sisters" spend eighteen months and the "elders" spend two years in full-time service to the church. In the summer of 1998, more than 58,000 LDS missionaries were in the mission field. Southern Baptists support 5,000 missionaries, whose entire careers are typically spent in the mission field, plus smaller numbers of mission pastors, missionary associates, apprentices, and missionaries in other categories, who serve for limited terms.

3. Not many members of the press were aware that these two groups have been stumbling over each other for years as they attempted to work the same mission fields. Moreover, practically nobody outside these two religious communities knew that Utah Mission, Incorporated (UMI), an organization spearheaded by a Southern Baptist minister, has been publishing for over seventeen years an impassioned newsletter, the *Utah Evangel*, whose stated goal is turning Mormons away from Mormonism and "winning them for the Lord" while keeping potential LDS converts "from being deceived by the militant Mormon proselyting program."

4. This is a kinder and gentler video than *The God Makers*, but the message of the two films is the same: Mormonism is a cult, and it is not Christian.

5. Jeffrey Weiss, "Southern Baptist Meeting Enters Heavily Mormon Salt Lake City; Leaders of Highly Evangelical Faiths Pledge Friendly Week," *Dallas Morning News*, June 7, 1998, A1.

6. At least three weeks before the convention opened, the Religious News Service released an article about the impending consideration of the marriage issue. See "Baptists Tout Marriage Statement," *New Orleans Times-Picayune*, May 16, 1998, B4. The first paragraph read, "A committee of the Southern Baptist Convention plans to recommend an addition to the denomination's statement of faith that affirms heterosexual marriage and declares the husband is responsible for the family and the wife should 'submit graciously to the servant leadership of her husband.'"

7. Robert Parham, "Disney Baptists Remain at Odds," *Orlando Sentinel*, June 7, 1998, G1; "Fundamental Differences," *New York Times*, May 31, 1998, sec. 6:19; Caryle Murphy, "A Gathering Full of Purpose: Baptists Put Mormons, Marriage on the Agenda," *Washington Post*, June 6, 1998, B9; Larry B. Stammer, "Evangelicals Crusading in Mormon Utah," *Los Angeles Times*, June 8, 1998, A1; Giles Whittell, "Baptist Legions Storm Mormons' Utah Stronghold," *Times* [overseas news], June 10, 1998; "Baptists Gear Up for Blitz on Mormons' Home Turf," *Louisville Courier-Journal*, June 6, 1998, A1.

8. It is difficult to determine exactly how many of the two thousand were knocking on doors in Utah since a simultaneous "Crossover" effort was being made in Idaho Falls, Idaho.

9. Peggy Fletcher Stack, "Baptists Boast Success with Utah Evangelism," *Salt Lake Tribune*, June 9, 1998, reported that Crossover organizers "acknowledged that 'the primary evangelistic harvest was not among the Mormon faithful.'"

10. The largest number of messengers voting on any measure was 8,540. Compared with the more than 40,000 messengers who attended the convention in 1985 when the moderate-conservative struggle was occurring, this is a small number.

11. David Briggs, "Southern Baptists Amend Tenet," *Cleveland Plain Dealer*, June 10, 1998, A1.

12. Cathy Lynn Grossman, "Baptists Explain Moral Tone," *USA Today,* June 11, 1998, D6.

13. Leslie Scanlon, "S. Baptists Urge Wives to 'Submit' to Spouses," *Louisville Courier-Journal,* June 10, 1998, A1; Leslie Scanlon, "Statement on Families Divides Baptists, *Louisville Courier-Journal,* June 9, 1998, A1; Gustav Niebuhr, "Southern Baptists Declare Wife Should 'Submit' to Her Husband," *New York Times,* June 10, 1998, A1.

14. Gossman, "Baptists Explain Moral Tone," D6.

15. Gayle White, "Georgia Delegates Support Biblical Marriage Structure," *Atlanta Journal and Constitution,* June 10, 1998, A3; Ernest Tucker, "Baptist Battle; Decree That Wives Should 'Submit' Angers Some," *Chicago Sun-Times,* June 11, 1998, A5; Richard Vara and Cecile S. Holmes, "Baptists Stand by the Man," *Houston Chronicle,* June 10, 1998, A1; Larry B. Stammer, "A Wife's Role Is 'to Submit,' Baptists Declare," *Los Angeles Times,* June 10, 1998, A1; Don Lattin, "Baptists Say Wives Must Submit," *San Francisco Chronicle,* June 10, 1998, A1.

16. Steve Kloehn, "Southern Baptists Approve Submissive Wives Doctrine," *Chicago Tribune,* June 10, 1998, 1. The text of the proposed substitute statement was widely reported in the press. See, for example, Lois M. Collins, "Southern Baptists Adopt 'Bible Definition' of a Family," *Deseret News,* June 10, 1998. As noted, this substitute statement was closer to the one articulated in 1993 by the National Conference of Catholic Bishops. The pastoral letter the bishops issued that year acknowledges that male and female marital roles are different, but it did not call for wifely submission. The wording of this part of their pastoral letter said that "mutual submission, not dominance by either partner, is the key to genuine joy."

17. Briggs, "Southern Baptists Amend Tenet," A1.

18. This was brought home to me when the segment on the Southern Baptist Convention aired on *Religion and the Media,* hosted by Bob Abernathy. Before "Crossover, Salt Lake City" began and it still looked as if conflict between the Baptists and the Saints would be the main story of the convention, the show's director had engaged a crew in Indianapolis to videotape an interview with me. I spent an hour or so with the crew, which put a good twenty minutes on tape. By the time the program aired, however, the conflict story had fizzled, and attention had turned to the submission story. The segment started with less than a minute of the interview in which I answered questions about the Saints' relationship with conservative Protestants, and then it turned immediately to a debate about the amendment to the Baptist Faith and Message.

19. Authority in the LDS Church continues, for the most part, to be perceived as coming from the top down. In view of the geographical expansion of the membership of the church, "from the center to the periphery" is a more apt description. But this in no way changes a "flow-chart" description of authority flow from within the church.

20. Telephone interviews with Marty King and Bruce L. Olsen.

21. By far the most complete and, in many ways, most knowledgeable press coverage of the story is in the *Deseret News* and the *Salt Lake Tribune.* To a certain extent, this is to be expected, since it was a local story. But there is more to it. The writers for both papers have extensive experience in covering the Mormon-evangelical story, and since the LDS Church's "Proclamation on the Family" has often been in the

news in the Intermountain West, these writers had already dealt with a story not unlike the "wifely submission" story.

In a public forum at the 1998 Sunstone Symposium, the Reverend Mike Gray, pastor of the largest Southern Baptist Congregation in the Salt Lake Valley, said that he was very pleased with the local coverage of the convention. This seems to me high praise indeed.

22. "Report of Committee on Baptist Faith and Message, June 9, 1998," <http://www.sbc.net>.

23. "The Family: A Proclamation to the World," <http://www.lds.org>.

PART 2

HISTORY, HISTORIOGRAPHY, AND WRITING
ABOUT RELIGIOUS HISTORY

During my years in residence on the faculties of the history and religious studies departments at Indiana University–Purdue University, Indianapolis, I had many colleagues who could not understand why I often settled on the introductory course when I had a choice between teaching one of the lower division (freshman/sophomore) or upper division (junior/senior) courses in one or the other department's curricular array. I did so because it was both a privilege and a pleasure to teach our "Introduction to Religious Studies" and "Introduction to Historical Studies" courses. Since neither one assumed previous knowledge on the part of the students, each time I taught one of these courses, it allowed me to explore with students the nature of history or the nature of religion.

Starting with the fundamentals—beginning at the beginning, as it were—required a good deal of ingenuity. I had to generate lessons and discussion that would open the minds of the students to new understandings of what history is and how it is written as well as how religious traditions come into being. Naturally, how I did so varied both with the composition of the classes—whether they were made up of students fresh from high school, or so-called returning students with lots of life experience, or, most likely, a mixture of both—and with what I happened to be working on in the research and writing side of my life. When a course was going well, lively class discussion generated so many probing (and often unanticipated) questions about these basic arenas of human existence that I stopped being the instructor and became a partner in the learning process.

Among the many valuable lessons I gleaned from these discussions, two of the most important are the usefulness of developing clear and meaningful categories and the need for clarity—straight talk rather than academic jargon. Both make addressing elemental questions about history and religion more fruitful. Both, it is to be hoped, are reflected in the selections in this section that have to do with determining what history is and with writing about the past, most especially the writing of religious history.

∾

With the exception of the last of the five selections in this section, all have been previously published. Most, however, appeared in places where even Mel Bashore's exhaustive bibliographies of recently published works on Mormonism failed to pick them up.[1] And for good reason in the first instance. Neither Mormonism nor the LDS experience is mentioned in "History, Her-Story, and Our Story," a set of reflections that opens this part of the book. I decided to include it in this account of my life among the Latter-day Saints because it represents part of the development of my own understanding of history as a class of literature and a particular variety of intellectual endeavor that always reflects and often plays a fateful role in the generation in which it is written.

When I wrote this little piece, I was serving as a member of the advisory board of the National Historical Society, an "outfit," as I sometimes called it, that published *American History Illustrated,* the magazine in which it appeared. Unlike the American Historical Association and the Organization of American Historians, professional associations whose members were primarily working historians, the National History Society was a commercial enterprise.[2] The company's staff had two main tasks: arranging package tours to places where significant historical events had occurred and publishing magazines that went against the grain of what appeared to be happening in the historical profession in the 1960s and 1970s, a time when historians, fascinated with theory, quantification (percentages, measures of statistical significance, and so on), and other aspects of social history, seemed to be writing for one another rather than for the world at large.[3]

Although I was doing a good deal of quantification myself in my studies of public opinion, I was pleased to be associated with a publication designed for those sometimes described as history buffs, people who are as fascinated by what happened in the past as by what is going on in the present. But I also sympathized with the editors of *American History Illustrated* who sometimes grew frustrated when their readers exhibited more interest in the minutia of history, the specifics of what happened on battlefields—what the soldiers wore, what sorts of weapons they carried, the tactics and strategy—than in the outcome of the battle or its place in the larger scheme of things. This essay was my response to a request for a short editorial that would encourage their readers to think about history as a genre and to think about how we are affected not only by what happened in the past but also by the way in which the past is described in what we read.

Had I been writing this editorial at the end of the twentieth century, I would have added "and by what we see." Probably more of what the public knows about the past nowadays comes from film than from words printed on the pages of books and magazines. In fact, I would be willing to wager that any random sample survey of what the general public knows about LDS history would reveal that more of its information about the Mormon trek came from Lee Groberg's *Trail of Hope* video presentation than from all the books written about that signal part of the Mormon past put together.

The *Wilson Quarterly* (in which my "Capsule Bibliography of Mormonism," the second essay in this section, first appeared) is aimed at a very different sort of reader.[4] The tag line printed underneath its logo, "published by the Woodrow Wilson International Center for Scholars," suggests that this is a journal designed to appeal to an audience of sophisticated consumers of information. In addition to articles written by philosophers, scientists, political theorists, and psychologists, the editors of the *Wilson Quarterly* make every effort to publish articles that bring international perspectives to bear on the American experience. In keeping with this effort, they asked Malise Ruthven, an English journalist who specializes in religion, to prepare an article about modern Mormonism. Ruthven accepted this commission and wrote "The Mormons' Progress," which was published in 1991.[5]

To accompany his article, the editors commissioned two sidebars; they asked me to prepare a bibliography, and they asked Peggy Fletcher Stack, who was working in New York as the associate editor of *Books and Religion,* to write something about Mormon women.[6] I used this opportunity to survey the history of writing about Mormonism for a general audience, partly because it seemed to me that readers of the *Wilson Quarterly* were unlikely to be familiar with the work of the scholars who know the most about Mormonism and partly because it seemed important to locate the observations of an English writer who was essentially a stranger to Mormonism in the complex body of literature about its history.

My abbreviated survey is reprinted here as it was published except that I have placed the citations in notes rather than in parentheses. As readers peruse what I wrote, they should keep in mind this was written at the very beginning of the 1990s, a decade that saw the publication of many important works of LDS history as well as several informative and extremely valuable articles that are true historiographical essays.[7] While I stand by what I said, this piece is included here because it reveals the contours of my thinking about Mormon historiography at that point in time, placing on display some ideas I thought might be helpful to people who did not know much about the history of Mormon history as well as discussing a few exemplary works that illustrated the points I was making.

"Remembering, Recovering, and Inventing What Being a People of God Means: Reflections on Method in the Scholarly Writing of Religious History" is located in the center of this section on history, historiography, and writing about religious history. It is truly the centerpiece of the section because it pulls together the critical elements of my approach to writing religious history. The title was adapted from the name of a fascinating book by the noted scholar of Islam Bernard Lewis, a work that presents examples of remembering, recovering, and inventing various parts of the history of the Near East.[8] Originally presented as one of many papers given by historians and sociologists of religion at the National Humanities Center during a 1992 conference that considered the question of whether the scholarly writing of denominational history is "an oxymoron," it was subsequently published in *Reimagining Denominationalism: Interpretive Essays*, edited by Robert Bruce Mullin and Russell E. Richey.[9]

This essay is the one place in the material I am including in this book where I made a conscious effort to bring together some of the things I have learned from reading widely in the history of my own denomination (Methodism) with what I have learned from reading and writing the history of the Latter-day Saints. While it employs a variety of examples from and observations about Mormonism to make my points, LDS history is not its main focus. It is here, more than in anything else I have written about historical method, that I have made an effort to set writing Mormon history in a larger context.[10]

"Dangerous History: Laurel Thatcher Ulrich and Her Mormon Sisters" is the fourth essay in this section. Laurel Thatcher Ulrich is the author of *A Midwife's Tale: The Life of Martha Ballard Based on Her Diary, 1785–1812*, a prizewinning work that was probably primarily responsible for Ulrich's selection as a recipient of a MacArthur "genius grant" as well as her appointment to the Harvard University faculty. In 1992, many intellectuals in the Mormon community were stunned to hear that this eminent LDS woman would not be allowed to present the keynote address at the 1993 Annual Women's Conference at BYU, and reverberations of the decision made by the university's board of trustees that she should not do so made their way into the nation's scholarly community. "Dangerous History" started out not as an article about religious history but as an effort to make sense of this decision, which appeared on the surface to be one more of the LDS Church's efforts to halt the spread of feminism among Mormon women.[11]

The original intent of this piece, which was written for the *Christian Century* and first published there, was to explain what had happened in the Ulrich imbroglio.[12] As I worked on it, however, I concluded that this situation was not entirely unlike the situation eight years earlier in which Linda King Newell and Valeen Tippetts Avery, the coauthors of a controversial biography of Emma Smith, were "silenced." That being the case, the issue was not merely whether these particular women should be allowed to speak in gatherings organized or sponsored by the LDS Church. What had happened had to do with the church's exercising control over the platforms from which Saints are addressed in official gatherings and with the larger issue of the history of Mormon women. It is that larger issue that makes this particular piece appropriate for this part of this book.

"Thoughts about the Academic Community's Response to John Brooke's *Refiner's Fire: The Making of Mormon Cosmology, 1644–1844*" is the final selection included in this section. Except for a reference to Brooke's work in my introduction to *The Journals of William McLellin, 1831–1836*, and a statement about *The Refiner's Fire* that was printed on the dust jacket of his book, this is the first time I have written anything about his controversial tome.[13] Here I propose an answer to the question of why, despite the almost universally negative response the book received from LDS scholars, it was selected by both the Bancroft Committee and the Prize Committee of the Society for Historians of the Early American Republic (SHEAR) as the best work on early American history published in 1994. I suggest that although it is conceivable that the main reason Brooke's work appealed to so many non-Mormon scholars is his secular explanation for Mormon beginnings and the appeal of the movement, there are additional factors that need to be taken into account.

Notes

1. Bashore's valuable bibliographies are published periodically in the *Mormon History Association Newsletter*.

2. My membership on the National Historical Society advisory board came mainly through the offices of a great historian of the American South, Bell I. Wiley, who had taken an interest in my writing about the Latter-day Saints. While board members were never paid for their services, each year they were permitted to recommend recipients of a thousand-dollar grant to an institution or organization that would use money to support the cause of history. In 1980, the year I served as president of the Mormon History Association, my recommendation (which was accepted) was that "my" thousand dollars should go to the Mormon History Association to help underwrite the expenses of the 1980 annual meeting held that sesquicentennial year in Canandaigua, New York. Although the National Historical Society no longer exists as such, I am pleased to take this opportunity to express my gratitude to Robert Fow-

ler, the magazine's founder, and this corporation for its generosity to the Mormon History Association.

3. Probably the most famous and successful of the National Historical Society publications was *Civil War Times*. All its periodicals were for sale on newsstands and were in competition with *American Heritage*, a more lavishly illustrated magazine of popular history.

4. *Wilson Quarterly* 15 (Spring 1991): 48–50. This title is new. When it was initially published, this little survey was simply called "Background Books."

5. Malise Ruthven, "The Mormons' Progress," *Wilson Quarterly* 15 (Spring 1991): 22–50. Ruthven, best known for his work on Islam, wrote *The Divine Supermarket: Shopping for God in America* (New York: William Morrow, 1989). This work is an account of the author's travels through the United States looking for the interesting, unusual, and exotic in American religion. As one might expect, it contains a section on Mormonism. While interesting, Ruthven's work often emphasizes the elements of religious systems that seem to him strange, even bizarre.

6. This article was also accompanied by sidebars prepared by Ruthven, "Portraits of Zion" and "LDS, Inc." In another sidebar, headed "The World beyond Salt Lake City," the editors reprinted a piece on Mormon missionaries written by James Fallows, which first appeared in *U.S. News & World Reports*, May 2, 1988.

7. For a review of significant works on Mormonism published in the 1990s, see Richard D. Ouelette, "Mormon Studies," *Religious Studies Review* 25 (April 1999): 161–69. I have also seen in draft two really substantive essays about the "New Mormon History," one written by David Paulsen and the other by Klaus Hansen. Hansen presented a condensed version of his essay, which will appear in a volume about Mormon history currently being edited by Newell Bringhurst, at the 1999 Sunstone Symposium. The title of the paper, to which I gave a response, was "Mormon History and the Conundrum of Culture."

8. Bernard Lewis, *History—Remembered, Recovered, Invented* (Princeton, N.J.: Princeton University Press, 1976).

9. Jan Shipps, "Remembering, Recovering, and Inventing What Being a People of God Means: Reflections on Method in the Scholarly Writing of Religious History," in *Reimagining Denominationalism: Interpretive Essays*, ed. Robert Bruce Mullin and Russell E. Richey (New York: Oxford University Press, 1994), 177–97.

10. In *Mormonism: The Story of a New Religious Tradition* (Urbana: University of Illinois Press, 1985), I made an explicit comparison of the beginnings of this new tradition with the beginnings of Christianity and Judaism, but I made little effort to address the question of denominationalism.

11. The church's opposition to the Equal Rights Amendment and its efforts to stop its passage, already well publicized, had given the church an antifeminist reputation.

12. Jan Shipps, "Dangerous History: Laurel Ulrich and Her Mormon Sisters," *Christian Century* 110 (October 20, 1993): 1012–15.

13. Jan Shipps, "Another Side of Early Mormonism," in *The Journals of William McLellin, 1831–1836*, ed. Jan Shipps and John W. Welch (Provo, Utah, and Urbana: *BYU Studies* and University of Illinois Press, 1994), 11n8; John Brooke, *The Refiner's Fire: The Making of Mormon Cosmology, 1644–1844* (Cambridge: Cambridge University Press, 1994).

6

History, Her-story, and Their Story

As a youngster going to school in Alabama back in the days before social studies entered the curriculum, I was in a class that had history lessons the first four days of the week. On Fridays, we had current events. Our history books stayed in our desks, and we read the *Weekly Reader,* a newspaper covering contemporary topics designed for our grade level. This way of separating things taught us that history was about the past. The present was covered in current events. This neat and logical division stayed with me until 1960, when I returned to college. As I read a standard textbook for a history course, I discovered that the author was treating as history what I regarded as current events.

This made me feel old. It also puzzled me. Did current events turn into history after five or ten years? Or had I been wrong to think that history only concerned the distant past? Did the present also have something to do with history? In time, I learned that students are not the only ones who question the relationship between past and present in history. Many books have been written describing what history is, how it is written, and the impact of accounts of the past on what happened as people reacted to the history that appeared on the printed page.

One of the best ways to understand the direction American history is currently taking is to envision history as a bridge connecting the present to the past. Information drawn from surviving records provides the building material for this "bridge." As the "builders," historians select materials from the available supply and decide how to use them, always looking back from the present to the past. Historians thus span the chasm between then and now, showing how the unalterable events of the past are having an effect on the present, that is, on current events.

Since every historian's interpretation of the past is influenced by the prevailing social attitudes of his or her own time, it is virtually impossible to write a historical account that will never need to be rewritten. The shifting interest of each "new" present tends to stimulate so many revisions of the past (in which things previously overlooked or ignored are seen) that history itself has a history.

Future historians who study the United States as it developed between the end of World War II and the end of the twentieth century will discover they need to describe a profound cultural change that grew out of—or at least accompanied—the development of self-consciousness, first among racial and ethnic minorities and then among women. They will also find it necessary to describe a revolution in the approach to writing about American history, one that gained momentum in the 1960s. Until then, nearly all historians organized their narratives into chronological and geographical segments or into specialized aspects of American experience, such as its political, social, and economic dimensions. Whatever the breakdown, the study of the American past emphasized a white, mainly Anglo-Saxon, Protestant elite. Since most of the history was written by men, the past was revealed as a man's world: men explored the wilderness, settled the nation, created and peopled its institutions, fought its wars. Women rarely ever played anything other than supporting roles, while Native Americans, African Americans, and other ethnic minorities existed only as foils for the dominant white male population.

Progress toward equality has by no means been uniform in the past half-century. Yet the system symbolized by seats in the back of the bus for blacks, marriage and motherhood as the only options for women, poverty-ridden reservation life for Indians, and mudsill status for Latinos and Chicanos no longer operates unimpeded. American culture has opened up enough to make a place for a cadre of African American leaders, to make way for women to move into and make upward progress in nearly all areas of national life, and to allow American Indians, Latinos, Chicanos, and members of other ethnic minorities to achieve an uncompromised American citizenship.

These changes have inevitably made their way into American history. Nearly every major college and university history department in the nation started offering courses in black history and women's history and sometimes courses on the history of American Indians, Latinas/Latinos, and Chicanos/Chicanas as well. Book publishers, whose output once celebrated "the [white] men who made America great," started adding to their lists books about blacks and women and Indians—most often called Native Americans—and nearly every other minority (including gays and lesbians from the mid-1980s onward). Editors of history periodicals began to publish articles dealing substantially or even exclusively with the history of once-excluded subcultures.

More significant than all the developments directed toward recovering the heritages of women, African Americans, and other ethnic minorities are the new histories that weave all their stories into the fabric of the American past. Such integrated histories are not simply efforts to seduce a market that rarely accepts a U.S. history textbook unless significant pages in it are devoted to minority groups. Nor do they reflect intellectual "fads" destined to die out when affirmative action programs disappear from the scene. Despite the current conservative thrust, people living in a world ushered in by the civil rights and women's movements are not about to be pushed out of the mainstream of American life. American history will have to be "her story" and "their story," too, or it will fail to serve as a bridge connecting today to the glory and the tragedy of the nation's past.

7

A Capsule Bibliography of Mormonism

For Latter-day Saints, "once upon a time" was yesterday. Things are changing rapidly, but the great majority of today's adult Saints grew up in a different universe, one insulated from the larger culture, a world that was divided between "them" and "us." In that place, young Saints learned how to recognize "the other" before they learned their ABCs. So much has been altered that, by 1980, according to Martin Marty, a religious historian and frequent commentator on American religion, the Mormons were not much different from everyone else in the United States.

The earlier Mormon-Gentile dichotomy dominated the literature of Mormonism until the middle of the twentieth century, though. Works about the Saints could be conveniently divided into pro- and anti-Mormon categories. Joseph Smith, the founder of the faith, was either a prophet or a profiteer—a religious genius, divinely called to lead a new dispensation, or a humbug, an outright fraud. Those who responded to his call were either progenitors of a new chosen people, called out from among the nations, or simply followers of a compelling charismatic figure whose message was nothing but Christian heresy.

After World War II, a new type of Mormon literature came into existence: well-trained Mormon scholars started examining critically their own history and culture, and non-Mormon scholars began investigating Mormonism without preconceptions. This new age in Mormon studies was ushered in by the publication between 1945 and 1958 of four remarkable books: *No Man Knows My History: The Life of Joseph Smith, the Mormon Prophet* by Fawn McKay Brodie; *The Mountain Meadows Massacre* by Juanita Brooks; *The Great Basin Kingdom: An Economic History of the Latter-day Saints, 1830–1900* by Leonard J. Arrington; and *The Mormons* by Thomas F. O'Dea. Taken together, they illustrate the change that occurred in Mormon studies as the "olden days" slowly started to pass away.[1]

Fawn Brodie was reared in Utah. As a niece of David O. McKay, who became president of the LDS Church in 1951, she grew up among the LDS elite. But she departed from Zion when she went to study literature at the University of Chicago. Her beautifully written biography of the prophet was published in 1945 when she was only thirty, but it was the work of a mature scholar and represented the first genuine effort to come to grips with the contradictory evidence about Smith's early life. The canonized history of LDS beginnings is contained in the first six volumes of the *History of the Church of Jesus Christ of Latter-day Saints.*[2] Brodie used non-Mormon sources as well as the evidence in this history to reach a noncanonical conclusion: Smith was a gifted young farmer who dabbled in folk magic and made up a story about golden plates that he himself later came to believe. The Saints were exceedingly offended by this interpretation, and Brodie was excommunicated. The influence of her book could not be expunged, though.

Mormonism, unlike other modern religions, is a faith cast in the form of history. For a very long time, any "profane" (i.e., secular) investigation of that history was like trespassing on forbidden ground. Causing nearly as much stir as Brodie was Juanita Brooks in her book *The Mountain Meadows Massacre.* In 1857, during the Utah Mormon War, a group of Mormons and American Indians had murdered every adult in a California-bound wagon train as it tried to pass through southern Utah. Brooks, who lived in that part of Zion, came to distrust official LDS accounts that denied church complicity in the terrible tragedy. She retrieved the story piecemeal from pioneer letters and diaries and interviews with Saints whose ancestors had participated in the horrible misadventure. Her account of the massacre explained the actions of both victims and perpetrators in terms of wartime hysteria, which vividly evoked the intensity of the "them and us" mind-set on both sides.

Unlike Brodie, Brooks continued to affirm her faith in public and, perhaps for that reason, managed to retain her membership in the church. She became living proof that a Mormon historian need not ignore evidence placing individual Mormons and their church in a bad light.

Leonard J. Arrington's *Great Basin Kingdom* explained much of Mormon history up to 1900 in terms of the marketplace. The Saints were able to make "the desert blossom as the rose" not so much because "the Lord caused his face to shine on them" or even because they were worthy and hardworking but because Salt Lake City became an entrepôt for would-be miners traveling to California during the gold rush. Arrington's interpretation sounds hardly shocking to non-Mormons now. But this is not exactly the way Boyd K. Packer, an LDS Church apostle, and other churchmen prefer to have the story told. Even today Mormon students are instructed to "see the hand of the Lord in every hour and every moment of the church from its beginning till now."[3] Despite being an active churchman, Arrington told the Mormon story using the kind of explanations that would have described ordinary human beings just as well as they did chosen people living in the promised land.

Brooks and Arrington thus set the pattern for "the new Mormon history," which has now become the standard academic approach to the Mormon past. Independent university presses—particularly the University of Illinois Press—became the usual publishers for this approach that did not question the legitimacy of Mormonism but required scholars to place the movement in context and to use the full range of available resources and analytical techniques. Two outstanding general histories written in this new objective vein were James B. Allen and Glen M. Leonard's *Story of the Latter-day Saints* and Leonard J. Arrington and Davis Bitton's *Mormon Experience: A History of the Latter-day Saints.*[4] The remaining work in the original quartet of studies, Thomas F. O'Dea's *Mormons,* was not history so much as it was a cultural inquiry. O'Dea, a Roman Catholic sociologist, analyzed the Mormon belief system, arguing that, as Tolstoy had asserted years before, Mormonism is "the American religion," impossible to understand apart from the culture of its time. "Mormonism represents a theological version of the American attitude of practical activism," O'Dea wrote. It "elaborated an American theology of self-deification through effort, an active transcendentalism of achievement."[5]

The new era in Mormon studies was thriving by the mid-1960s when *Dialogue: A Journal of Mormon Thought* was launched. This independent periodical treated controversial topics and welcomed Mormon and non-Mormon points of view. Church officials were obviously uncomfortable when *Dialogue* intellectuals confronted such issues as the prohibition against black priests, but they did not interfere. Their policy of toleration was further tested when the more radical *Sunstone,* which began as a student publication but fairly quickly became what Peggy Fletcher Stack would call "a Mormon magazine," was willing to publish articles about the subservient role of Mormon women and the murky origins of the Book of Mormon.[6]

Today, one of the controversial areas in Mormon studies follows in the tradition started by Thomas O'Dea, trying to fit Mormon history into the context of American culture. Lawrence Foster's *Religion and Sexuality,* for example, shows that in nineteenth-century America the Mormons were far from alone in sexual experimentation.[7] From the Shakers, who tried to give up sex altogether, to the Oneida community, which practiced a complex free-love system, there was a general search in the new democracy for alternatives to traditional family structures.

Foster's (and O'Dea's) question about where Mormons fit in the spectrum of American culture and history is one of the great controversies among the historians of Mormonism today. At one end of the debate is Mark Leone's *Roots of Modern Mormonism,* which makes the Marxist argument that Mormonism is "a religion for subordinates which serves to maintain their condition intact."[8] At the other end is Kenneth H. Winn's *Exiles in a Land of Liberty: Mormons in America, 1830–1846,* which sees the Saints and their opponents as siblings in a new republic, both claiming to embody republican ideology, both decrying "the growing economic in-egalitarianism of Jacksonian society."[9]

Klaus J. Hansen's *Mormonism and the American Experience* makes the interesting and important point that Mormonism was merely temporally "out of step with [American] social reality."[10] Although the early Mormons were "building their anti-modern kingdom of God," Hansen says, even in the nineteenth century they were already developing "those modern habits of initiative and self-discipline that helped dig the grave of the kingdom and ushered in a new breed of Mormon thoroughly at home in the corporate economy of America."[11] Hansen concludes that it is "nothing less than a modern miracle" that "within a generation a people that had been the very epitome of an anti-bourgeois mentality became one of the mainstays of the American middle-class culture."[12]

A final important category of Mormon studies is that which considers Mormonism first and foremost as a religion. Sterling M. McMurrin's *Theological Foundations of the Mormon Religion* compares Mormonism with other religious movements in the Western world. McMurrin describes Mormonism as a form of Christianity that could well have emerged in ancient times if St. Paul had not challenged the Jewish apostle Peter for leadership of the Christian community.[13] My own *Mormonism The Story of A New Religious Tradition* argues that Mormonism is related to existing forms of Christianity (and Judaism) in much the way that early Christianity was related to the Hebrew tradition of its day.[14]

When we compare Mormonism with other religions, we can see why the historical transformations in the church were not the "fault" of the U.S. government or any other agency. Those transformations are changes that take place in every religion as it learns to live "in the world but not of it." The Saints are no longer all gathered into their own kingdom in the West. They are everywhere, and, like the early Christians, they have had to learn to live in the world. As late as midcentury, being born a Mormon was analogous, in relation to the larger American society, to being born Jewish; today it is perhaps not much more different from being born into a conservative Protestant family. Within the sacred space of the Mormon temple rituals, the Saints remain a chosen people. Outside, in everyday life, they are simply members of a church, the Church of Jesus Christ of Latter-day Saints. The rest of us are no longer even Gentiles. We are merely nonmembers.

Notes

1. Fawn McKay Brodie, *No Man Knows My History: The Life of Joseph Smith, the Mormon Prophet* (1945; 2d ed., rev. and enl., New York: Alfred A. Knopf, 1976); Juanita Brooks, *The Mountain Meadows Massacre* (Stanford, Calif.: Stanford University Press, 1950; new ed., Norman: University of Oklahoma Press, 1962; reprint, with foreword and afterword by Jan Shipps, Norman: University of Oklahoma Press, 1991); Leonard J. Arrington, *Great Basin Kingdom: An Economic History of the Latter-day Saints, 1830–1900* (Cambridge, Mass.: Harvard University Press, 1958; reprint, Salt Lake City: University of Utah Press, 1993); Thomas F. O'Dea, *The Mormons* (Chicago: University of Chicago Press, 1957).

2. B. H. Roberts, ed., *History of the Church of Jesus Christ of Latter-day Saints: Period I, History of Joseph Smith, the Prophet, by Himself,* 6 vols. (Salt Lake City: Deseret News, 1902–12). This work is sometimes referred to as the "Documentary History."

3. Packer's injunction "to see the hand of the Lord," which comes from an address presented at the Fifth Annual Church Educational System Religious Educator's Symposium held on August 22, 1981, at Brigham Young University, was drawn from an address that church president Joseph F. Smith gave in the Seventy-fourth Annual Conference in 1904 (see *Seventy-fourth Annual Conference of the Church of Jesus Christ of Latter-day Saints* [Salt Lake City: Deseret News, 1904], 2). Packer's address was printed as "The Mantle Is Far, Far Greater than the Intellect," *BYU Studies* 21 (Summer 1981): 259–78. The quotation appears on 261. The wording of the quotation used here is taken from an article about D. Michael Quinn's challenge to Packer in a speech to BYU graduate students in Kenneth L. Woodward, "Apostles vs. Historians," *Newsweek,* February 15, 1982, 77.

4. James B. Allen and Glen M. Leonard, *The Story of the Latter-day Saints* (Salt Lake City: Deseret Book, 1976); Leonard J. Arrington and Davis Bitton, *The Mormon Experience: A History of the Latter-day Saints* (New York: Alfred A. Knopf, 1979).

5. O'Dea, *The Mormons,* 154.

6. For several issues, *Sunstone: A Mormon Magazine* appeared on the title page, but the subtitle has not been used for years. I originally thought *Sunstone* was begun by Brigham Young University students, but it was actually founded by Scott Kenney, a graduate student at the Graduate Theological Union in Berkeley, California. See [Robert] Lee Warthen, "History of Sunstone, Chapter 1: The Scott Kenney Years, Summer 1974–June 1978," *Sunstone* 22 (June 1999): 48–61.

7. Lawrence Foster, *Religion and Sexuality: The Shakers, the Mormons, and the Oneida Community* (1981; reprint, Urbana: University of Illinois Press, 1984).

8. Mark P. Leone, *The Roots of Modern Mormonism* (Cambridge, Mass.: Harvard University Press, 1979), vi.

9. Kenneth H. Winn, *Exiles in a Land of Liberty: Mormons in America, 1830–1846* (Chapel Hill: University of North Carolina Press, 1989), 5.

10. Klaus J. Hansen, *Mormonism and the American Experience* (Chicago: University of Chicago Press, 1981), 206.

11. Ibid.

12. Ibid., 205.

13. Sterling M. McMurrin, *The Theological Foundations of the Mormon Religion* (Salt Lake City: University of Utah Press, 1965).

14. Jan Shipps, *Mormonism: The Story of A New Religious Tradition* (Urbana: University of Illinois Press, 1985), 41–65.

Remembering, Recovering, and Inventing What Being a People of God Means: Reflections on Method in the Scholarly Writing of Religious History

The fire fed by the bodies of Bishops Latimer and Ridley in 1555 still burns, but scholarly studies of the Reformation seem almost to have reduced the story of how the blood of Anglican martyrs became the seed of English Protestantism to that lovely quotation from Foxe's account in which Latimer told Master Ridley to "be of good cheer." For, said he, "we shall this day light such a candle, by God's grace, in England, as I trust shall never be put out."[1] This is not to say that modern critical histories of the English Reformation entirely ignore religious matters or even that they completely neglect the story of the persecutions the Protestants endured during Queen Mary's reign. What happened, where, when, and to whom, is typically described, sometimes very well indeed. But modern scholars tend to look beyond religion for explanation, predicating the establishment of the Anglican church on the crisis in the aristocracy, the politicization of the culture, the rise of the middle class, and other social factors.[2] Similarly, the flame that warmed John Wesley's heart flickers only faintly in the accounts of scholars who see the modernization of England in Methodism and use the Wesleyan movement to explain the "making of the English working class."[3]

Many critically acclaimed scholarly studies focus on these and other religious events, dealing with them directly and thoroughly. Yet because the authors of so many of these histories explain what happened to the faith of people, as well as the organization of the ecclesia, primarily in terms of politics, economics, social class, or—since it is English history—the amorous desires of kings, it is hard to find among them many particularly fine models for the scholarly writing of England's *religious* history. Many historians also describe religion in the United States as a means to some end, a way to make Americans, for example, or a means of masking the seeking of power and social status.[4] Such studies explain a great deal about American society and culture, but they do not recount and explicate what happened in a manner that makes their histories meaningful for members of faith communities.

This historiographical circumstance points to the fact that two audiences exist for histories of religion. One is made up of the members of communities of believers—in common parlance, the church. The other audience is the general public that has increasingly been represented by academia since the oft-lamented disappearance of the so-called public intellectual by and large left the reviewer's task to members of the faculties of the nation's colleges and universities.[5]

Yet, no matter which audience they intend to address, those who write the history of the religious dimension of human experience, especially as it is manifested in corporate forms, must deal with essentially the same historical sources, the same data sets. At the same time, the concerns of the historians who write for communities of believers and of those who write academic treatises diverge. As a consequence, these two groups of historians pose different questions and thereby produce distinctively different accounts of what happened.

In the United States before World War II, it was not really obvious just how different these two forms of history are, at least insofar as the history of American religion is concerned. Before this conflict that was such a watershed in the American experience, this nation's multicultural character was hidden beneath a widely shared impression of North America as a white, Anglo-Saxon, Protestant culture, and the bases for such a perception were not hard to find. Despite constitutionally mandated church-state separation, school prayer became virtually a universal ritual from early in the twentieth century; religious rhetoric has always been a staple of our political discourse; and all sorts of civic occasions open with invocations asking for the blessing of Almighty God and close with benedictions that end by calling on "the name of Jesus Christ." And they always have.[6]

Since these symbols and rituals represented the religion of white, Anglo-Saxon Protestants, they and other symbols and rituals present at key points in the public arena supported the conception of a WASP-ish "Christian America." Furthermore, whether they were Protestant, non-Protestant, non-Christian, or even unchurched, most citizens of the United States saw the nation's Constitution as a civic covenant and consequently understood themselves as somehow exceptional, a covenanted people. This understanding was supported by the narratives that informed Americans of their past, especially the texts used in the public schools that emphasized Puritans and pioneers and scripted the settlement of the country as a journey to a land of promise.[7]

Back then, the lines of demarcation between audiences in faith communities and those in the larger culture were not so sharply drawn. As a result, the histories that interested one type of audience very often appealed to the other. This is not particularly surprising since institutions and leaders were emphasized in both. Whether describing the building of America for a scholarly or for a popular audience, the authors of histories of the nation concentrated on key figures—founders and pacesetters—and on the structures of government, business, and society. Whether penned by ministers or by members of college or seminary faculties, histories of American religion focused on the clergy and institutions, bricks and mortar.[8]

In such a situation, religious history was almost as acceptable as a scholarly pursuit as the political and economic and what then passed for social history that provided the foundation for scholarly accounts of the nation's past. Surveys of national history rarely recounted the story state by state, proceeding chronologically and thematically instead, while American religious history was generally organized within a denominational framework. But each had a major theme. Civic history rang the changes on the growth of freedom (including religious freedom) and democracy. Religious history privileged Protestantism and pictured non-Protestant faith communities as more or less marginal. Like U.S. history texts, religious history was also written in a triumphal vein, and, because both kinds of historical accounts were dominated by the actions of white Anglo-Saxon men, religious history was as chauvinistic as the political and economic history of the day.

There were important differences, however. In spite of the fact that the importance of women to the religious life of the nation was seriously underestimated, they were at least integrated into the main text of religious histories. By sheer dint of numbers, Roman Catholics also generally became a part of the narrative, even though an earmark of American religious history was its clear qualitative differentiation between Catholic and Protestant Christianity. But Protestant or not, the faith communities that historians of American religion regarded as sects and cults were relegated to the margin that brief capsule accounts signify. By cultural definition, Jewish and African American communions likewise inhabited the margins, and they, too, were fortunate if capsule accounts of their past were included.

In the decades following World War II, the assumptions underlying civic history started to unravel, as did the unquestioning acceptance of mainstream Protestant hegemony, and historians and their readers alike began to be dissatisfied with a historiographical situation that posited substantive agreement about the way things were and are. In the area of religious history, the civil rights and the women's movements of the 1960s and 1970s started to make denominational histories that focused almost exclusively on white men seem outdated. Furthermore, the reality of religious pluralism made accounts that privileged Protestantism appear hopelessly old-fashioned, particularly to intellectuals aware of the magnitude of the changes going on in American culture.

In addition, perceptions about the pertinence of standard denominational history were revised as many people switched their denominations as well as their residences when they moved from place to place. Left with what might be described as religious orientations rather than enduring affiliations with particular faith communities, many readers became less interested in the details describing a specific denomination's unfolding doctrine, institutional development, reform movements, and schisms.

Moreover, it was not just the audience for religious history that changed. Many of the historians who had engaged in the writing of religious or (as it was then called) church history—and many more of their students—also became dissatisfied with its conventional forms. This is evidenced by the shift that took place after midcentury away from the study of ecclesiastical and institutional matters and toward a focus on the experience of the people in the pews, especially the women and the minorities who theretofore had been left out. Although Sydney Ahlstrom's classic *Religious History of the American People*, which was published in 1972 was, finally, more distinctive in the way it was organized than in the approach to the topic revealed through the text, the shift in focus pushed religious history toward social history, a disciplinary subfield that, as a result of the increasing ease of electronic data manipulation, was itself in the throes of methodological transformation. Consequently, a number of church historians, chiefly those holding faculty positions in public institutions and private colleges and universities without close denominational affiliations, became enamored of technology and statistics.

It would be an overstatement to say that church historians suddenly discovered power, money, and social class where before they had placed the people in the communities of faith they studied in lay and clerical categories and along continua that ranged from pious to apathetic, active to inactive, and generous to parsimonious. Yet it is certainly true that when some of them started to take advantage of the data preserved in census reports and church statistics, they began to write a very different kind of history. Moreover, if there were not really large numbers of church historians who themselves started to draw detailed information about occupation, economic status, location and size of residence, and birthplaces of citizens and their parents (that is, ethnic data) from the manuscript census and then to link census and church records for sequential decades both to determine demographic and social mobility and to define the ethnic character of local congregations and denominational bodies, the profession was influenced, perhaps inordinately, by those who did. Histories that failed to address questions of social class, ethnicity, and the place of women in the organization took on a musty, antique tone.

At about the same time (the 1960s and early 1970s), the altered cultural situation also led scholars who wrote synthetic treatments of American religion to become more inclusive, incorporating and frequently giving at least equal, and sometimes more than equal, time to the stories of many of the communities of faith that once had appeared to be marginal. This mandated a more empirical approach that sometimes led scholars (sociologists more often than historians) to organize the nation's multiplicity of religious groups according to criteria that made more sense in the academy than in chapels, churches, synagogues, or mosques.

The expanding fissure in the audience for studies of religion in the United States may be detected by examining the reaction to the altered approaches to the history of faith communities both in academia and in the communities themselves. In the Church of Jesus Christ of Latter-day Saints, I watched as the "new Mormon history" became a matter of concern to church authorities at the very highest level.[9] If this LDS example is at all indicative of a general trend, the change in the way professional historians were beginning to write religious/denominational history proved much less satisfactory to the faith communities whose histories were being written than to the scholarly community as that community is reflected in the book review sections of historical journals, as well as in the annual, semiannual, and regional meeting programs of the American Society of Church History and the North American Religion Section of the American Academy of Religion.

The principal ground for the dissatisfaction of both the leaders and the rank-and-file members of religious communities was (and is) not that the works themselves are filled with mistakes so much as that scholarly works somehow seem to tell their stories from the wrong angle, addressing questions of greater importance to the culture than to the faith community. In academia, the new history describing the interpenetration of religion and culture and measuring the impact of culture on religion was (and is) highly praised.[10] Traditional narrative histories of faith communities have often been criticized as old-fashioned and their lack of intellectual rigor has been derided.

Few academicians seemed to appreciate how religious history serves faith communities as a sort of holy grail. They failed to realize that history is a vessel that contains the stories of beginnings and of God's dealing with humanity in past times and that it sparks faith and passes belief from one person to another and from one generation to the next. But religious history does this only if it is the sort of account in which the hand of God is not removed from the action, if it is a narrative that preserves the religious story and provides in it a recognizable place for believers in both past and present times. For faith communities, the new social history and those revisionist histories that explain religion almost entirely in human terms simply do not fill the bill. Yet they are precisely the kinds of studies that receive scholarly acclaim.[11]

Despite the dramatic changes in the culture and in the scholarly approach to the study of history sketched above, denominational histories written by members of the academy have not disappeared from the scene. Seminary faculty members and members of the history faculties of various institutions of higher learning continue to compose such accounts, often of their own denominations' histories. But a process that had been under way for decades—a process that transformed storytelling into an academic discipline—steadily accelerated after World War II; what once had been a steady stream was reduced to a trickle. Neither historians nor religious authorities seem to have fully anticipated what turning the chronicler's vocation into a profession would mean for the writing of histories of faith communities.

∿

The emerging prominence of social history generated a substantial literature on method in the late 1960s and the 1970s, much of it having to do with the application of statistical techniques and sociological analysis to historical data.[12] For the most part, these methodological discussions recommended that religion be treated as one among a variety of variables to be investigated as a part of multivariate analysis. The goal was a demonstration of the direct connection between religious leadership and economic power, for example, or between gender and piety, or between any number of other pairs of variables. But the sanguine expectation that religion—and practically everything else—could be explained if enough data that could be digitized could be collected and analyzed did not go unchallenged. The late 1970s and the 1980s saw the emergence of neopragmatism in philosophical theology, a movement that generated a substantial body of discussion about how historical reality emerges from historical interpretation. William D. Dean, one of the leading thinkers in this area, described this as "an unexpected development in recent American intellectual history" and pointed out that, among other things, neopragmatism calls into question the "cliometric historicism that seeks verification of historical claims through the strict use of quantitative methods."[13]

Notwithstanding this postmodernist critique (to which historians of religion would do well to pay close attention), the work of Paul Kleppner, Richard Jensen, Robert Swierenga, Philip R. VanderMeer, and a host of others demonstrates that explorations treating religion as a function of economic status, ethnicity, or social class can be perfectly legitimate and sometimes extremely useful academic enterprises.[14] But as long as they treat religion as secondary and deal with membership in faith communities as just one of several key variables to be analyzed to explain what happened in the past, historians end up writing about the belief and the behavior arising from faith commitments without addressing the fundamental question of religion. They reduce it instead to something that occurs with and seems to result from something else, turning it into an epiphenomenon.

While the discussion of how to handle the study of religion as it functions in and is influenced by culture has proceeded apace, the bifurcation of the audience for works on religion has thus far failed to prompt much explicit methodological inquiry regarding writing about the faiths around which communities of believers coalesce and about the history of the experiences of believers in such communities. There is an increasing awareness, however, that historians cannot treat religion as a dependent variable if they wish to study communities of faith and preserve religion as an irreducible element in the histories they write. That awareness was one of the basic reasons for the consultation that gave rise to the book in which this essay originally appeared.[15]

What follows are some observations, reflections, and recommendations about the writing of the histories of communities of faith by someone who has been directing her energies to that enterprise for decades. I begin with some general observations about an approach that holds out the possibility of building a bridge between religion as a part of social and cultural history (what many academics describe as the "scholarly" approach to religious history) and the scholarly enterprise of writing the history of faith communities. I then move on to some suggestions about how the work of historians of tightly bonded faith communities might be of help to those who write about communities of faith—particularly mainstream Protestant denominations—whose boundaries are so highly permeable in both directions that it is sometimes difficult to make distinctions between faith communities and the surrounding culture. Then I end with some observations about the advantages and the disadvantages of writing religious history from outside and from inside particular faith communities.

To diminish the distance between history written for the church and that written for the world, historians of communities of belief, who for the sake of convenience will hereafter be called denominational historians, should pay close attention to religion itself. One way a historian can do this is by naming and defining religion's constituent elements and pointing to their embodiment in the denomination under consideration. Referring with specificity to myth (which, in addition to scripture, includes the stories of those who first believed), institutional structure (formal and informal), doctrine, ritual, and the social, ethical, and experiential dimensions of the religion being studied provides a set of categories, a shared language of analysis that makes intellectual rigor easier to demonstrate to the scholarly world. When historians explore the interactions of these elements and dimensions, they can more readily illustrate how religion generates belief and behavior that are amenable to analyses in which belief is treated as the independent variable, with behavioral variables dependent on belief—and vice versa. If it is used skillfully, this approach does not make the denomination's story inaccessible to the members of the faith community.

Of perhaps even greater importance from the standpoint of reimagining the scholarly writing of denominational history, this set of categories allows denominational historians to explore the interaction between scripture, history, and faith. Such an examination inevitably leads to the recognition that early histories written by or about the founders of religious communities are not ordinary histories. This approach is helpful to denominational historians as they go about their work, and it also allows them to explain convincingly that, as the world understands history, such accounts are, in fact, not histories at all. In the eyes of the members of the faith communities in question, they take on the characteristics of scripture (which is true by definition), instead of being seen merely as accounts and interpretations of what happened, accounts that are always open to continuing revision on the basis of new evidence. Since the narratives of faithful history tell of a time of direct divine-human interaction, within the bounds of faith communities such accounts are sacred history and must be so recognized.

In addition to exploring sacred history, denominational historians are in a good position to treat the issue of canonization in connection with the religious history of the faith communities they study. While the canonizing of historical accounts occurs in the political as well as the religious arena—as studies of the histories of the former Soviet Union are making clear—the canonizing process is rarely well documented and consequently is often ignored. But canonization is sometimes so overt and so easily traced in religious communions that denominational historians can make significant contributions to historical knowledge by recognizing and describing the processes of canonizing history in the faith communions they study.

As is the case with so much else in denominational history, both the recognition of the historical accounts that have gained the status of sacred history and the explication of the process of canonization are easier to accomplish when fixed and stable boundaries surround a community of faith.[16] This is, however, only one of the exceptional advantages that come with studying communities of faith that are so tightly bonded they function as ethnic groups.[17] Even when these communities are what sociologist Bryan Wilson calls "world-indifferent" rather than "world-denying," they maintain sharp and well-defined boundaries between themselves and others, insiders and outsiders, "them and us."[18] Consequently, positive as well as negative identities are provided to participants in sectarian and cultic groups and also to members of non-Protestant and non-Christian communities. From the standpoint of their relationship with the divine, they know who they are (chosen, saved), as well as who they are not (Gentile, damned). Furthermore, because all communities of faith have a mechanism for conscious appropriation of membership (for example, confirmation, adult baptism, affirmations of faith), being a part of the community is, at least theoretically, voluntary. There is, however, a great deal that is involuntary about being a member of such communities, and this involuntary side of things is likewise a part of the identity of community members.[19]

This two-sided aspect of personal identity is illuminated, as is so much else, by the work of sociologists of religion. In a printed forum discussion on religion and personal identity, Robert Wuthnow separated personal identity into its *ascribed* and *achieved* dimensions, with the former referring to given attributes (such as gender and ethnicity) and the latter to statuses or features that are embraced or earned (church member, college graduate).[20] Using these sociological categories as an analytical device reveals more than one might expect about the population of tightly bonded communities of faith.

If members are "birthright" members of a religious community or members of very long standing, they not only are connected to the group through the continuing affirmation of its religious claims that regular and wholehearted participation in public and private worship signifies but also are tied to it ethnically and culturally, thus unifying the ascribed and the achieved dimensions of their personal identities within the framework of the faith community. Even if, at some point in their lives, members reject the theological and doctrinal underpinnings of the community's institutional structure and make a conscious decision to disclose this, they do not so easily shed the eth-

nic and cultural dimensions of their identity. As a result, much of its mean-
ing-making and value-imparting structure stays with them.

By way of illustration, I recall the remark of a Latter-day Saint who had
been "born in the covenant" but had lost faith—no longer believing that the
Book of Mormon is what it claims to be and no longer certain that Joseph
Smith was a prophet or that the church he founded is the restored Church
of Jesus Christ. Refusing an offer of coffee—as all Mormons must if they
comply with the Mormon prophet's Word of Wisdom, which forbids the
consumption of hot drinks—he said ruefully, "There's just no 'checkoutabil-
ity' in this system." In LDS circles, he was one of those who had moved over
into the Jack-Mormon category in matters of belief, but what had happened
to him with regard to behavioral practice is not unique to Mormonism. Many
(perhaps all) faith communities have such categories—examples include
cultural Jews, ethnic Catholics, and backslid Baptists. The people in these
categories have given up active participation in the strictly religious facets of
the corporate life of the community, but the cultural aspects of being what
they were remain so embedded in them that they retain their understanding of themselves as community members and often continue normal interaction with others in the community.[21]

This is not to say that people do not leave Mormonism, Roman Catholicism, the more sectarian forms of Protestantism, or any of the many other
communities of faith that maintain high boundaries between themselves and
others. Many do. But they seem to have more difficulty simply drifting into
inactivity than do the many Protestants in the American mainstream who
move away from birthright denominational domiciles. Some do not drift
away, of course; they are converted to the acceptance of alternative theological and ecclesiastical systems, but their difficulty in fully "checking out,"
escaping the ethnic and cultural dimension of the personal identities that
were ascribed and internalized as they grew up, is captured in the names of
the groups some of them join: Jews for Jesus, for instance, or Saints Alive in
Christ. Recognizing the dual character of personal identity also helps in
making sense of how some denominations seem to make converts readily yet
have real difficulty in turning them into members who stay the course.

From the perspective of denominational history, it is interesting to note
the incredible interest in the history of their community shown by many of
the people who have forsworn the theological tenets that are the reason for
the community's existence and have rejected the authority of the institution
around which it is organized. In some (perhaps many) instances, study of the
community's history appears to be a surrogate for lost faith. In other in-

stances, however, it becomes an effort to find hard evidence that can serve as justification for abandoning the community's creedal base. If it is the latter and if the interest in history becomes a preoccupation that leads to writing about the community, very often the outcome is history that is tendentious in the extreme—history the community dismisses as "apostate." Although such slanted accounts do not provide good models for the scholarly writing of denominational history, they are useful to scholars as evidence of what can happen when the religious basis of personal identity is shattered.

Scholars who have learned to appreciate the utility of membership profiles from social history can take advantage of personal identity's double strand by drawing from within the community's belief and behavior patterns measures of the intensity of members' identification with the community along both dimensions. For the religious dimension, some possible measures are level of attendance and participation in worship, offices filled, and contributions of time and money; for the ethnocultural dimension, some possibilities are level of interaction with other members in community activities that are not specifically religious (parent-teacher organizations, service clubs) and commitment to the preservation of the community's cultural heritage. Although gathering such data would be very difficult and time-consuming, it would be feasible to use such measures to construct membership profiles of the community at different points in time.[22] These profiles would very probably differ from socioeconomic profiles of the same community at the same points in time, but perhaps not. Correlating the place of individuals in religiocultural profiles with their place in socioeconomic profiles of faith communities would surely be extremely revealing. Perhaps correlations of this sort could even provide enough convincing empirical evidence about the connection between money, power, and religion to test theories about their interconnections. But even without the socioeconomic comparison and rigorously constructed statistical profiles constructed from measures on the ascribed and the achieved dimensions of personal identity, an analysis that takes account of the double strand of members' identities may come closer than strict socioeconomic analysis to describing the faith community as experienced at different points in time.[23]

In this same vein, historians may make efforts to describe the community as experienced by directing attention to the part of personal identity that stipulates the nature of divine-human relationships. Although such knowledge is ultimately purely perceptual, the student of communities in which the notion of being the chosen people or the perception of presiding over the sole avenue to salvation is present has the benefit of being able to determine whether tensions in the community are a part of intragroup dynamics or come from

the outside. Moreover, explorations of the mechanisms of boundary maintenance and the impact of perceptions of chosenness on individual and group
behavior are also fruitful lines of inquiry that can open to view the specifically religious dimensions of the life of communities of faith.

Yet another advantage in studying communities that have both well-
defined boundaries and authoritarian systems (historic Roman Catholicism,
Mormonism, the Unification Church) is that historians have no trouble recognizing who speaks for God within the community. With such a fundamental "fact" established, delineating human responses to what are understood
as divine mandates is a much simpler task than is the case when both mandate and response must be teased out of the sources—diaries, letters, personal
essays, sermons, testimonies—that open individual perceptions to history.
In this and many other ways, definite boundaries lend a clarity and a power
to a faith community's story that is often missing when boundaries are in-
definite and porous, allowing members to move in and out as the winds of
faith blow hot and cold.[24] Historians of denominations without clear and
unmistakable boundaries cannot manufacture them to make consideration
of a particular denomination's history more accessible to analysis. But if
tightly bonded communities are treated as something like ideal types, comparison on points of structure, the various elements of personal identity,
intragroup dynamics, and other factors might shed light on the workings of
communities whose boundaries are so porous they are almost nonexistent.

Despite all the advantages of doing the history of tightly bonded communities of faith that traditionally have been at the margins of American
religion, questions about the scholarly writing of their histories are probably more pervasive and pressing in these communities than they are in mainstream American Protestantism.[25] The reasons are not hard to find. The stories of the genesis of such indigenous religions as Mormonism, Christian
Science, and the Unification Church make these communities particularly
vulnerable to apostate accounts and exposé, but they are not alone. Almost
any faith community founded or led by a charismatic leader is vulnerable to
historical accounts that, at the very least, are unflattering. The history of such
communities reveals that most of their leaders have understood that unanswered negative versions of their history pose a danger, not so much to their
image in the world as to the health of the communities themselves. Accordingly, community leaders have a record of countering negative renditions of
their history by issuing histories that are subsequently recognized by the
communities as their official (that is, canonized) histories, reissuing previously canonized histories in a more accessible format—often in larger print
with pictures added—or commissioning or otherwise putting their stamp

of approval on new renderings of the conventional canon.[26] Confronted with the cool medium of scholarly history, however, many leaders and most rank-and-file members have not been entirely sure how they ought to respond.[27]

If the scholarly writing of denominational history seems a cool medium to the community of faith, however, it often seems just the opposite to historians in the academy. This may simply be the nature of things, but if the scholarly writing of denominational history is separated from the traditional kind, the situation can be clarified, and an answer can be advanced to the question of whether scholarly writing of denominational history is an oxymoron. Consideration of the several kinds of accounts of the history of communities of faith also points to connections, not only between religion and personal identity but also between religion and ethnicity.

⟨⟨⟩⟩

When the Islamic specialist Bernard Lewis delivered the Gottesman lectures at Yeshiva University in 1974, lectures that were subsequently published as *History—Remembered, Recovered, Invented,* he was more concerned about the connections between history and contemporary events than about the association of religion, history, identity, and ethnicity.[28] But because he dealt with the history that religious people write and how such history serves to locate modern believers inside their respective traditions, Lewis's division of history into remembered and recovered varieties, as well as his reflections on how history is invented, can be used to make distinctions not only between the types of religious history written for the church and the world—that is, traditional (or confessional) history and scholarly (or critical) history—but also between subdivisions within the genre of confessional history.

With regard to this last, since the Protestant Reformation and the division of Protestantism into denominations, denominational history (at least in English) has nearly always been written by Protestants. The same cannot be said for faith communities outside the Protestant mainstream. Roman Catholic history was written by both Catholics and rabidly anti-Catholic Protestants, and the outcome was not just history seen from two angles but two very different histories. Two different histories of the Shakers, the Mormons, the followers of John Humphrey Noyes, the Christian Scientists, and many other communities of faith outside the Protestant mainstream also exist. But as different as the two basic renderings of each community's history are, both must be classified as confessional, for each version reflects and is determined by the different authors' particular understandings of reality, truth, and the historical process.

In an admirable discussion of denominational history, Russell F. Richey, an eminent Methodist historian, avers that whatever the situation for the scholarly writing of denominational history, the confessional genre is alive and flourishing inside nearly all faith communities.[29] Written by insiders for insiders, these accounts are, finally, not efforts to recover history so much as they are a form of corporate remembering whose purpose is preserving particular understandings of the past. Whether the subject is the recent period of a particular faith community's experience or the beginnings of a religious movement (the story of its founders and early adherents, apostles, and church leaders), the goal of remembered history is effective communication, history written so that it will be meaningful to new generations of readers.[30]

That most examples of this type of remembered history are Whiggish in interpretation and supportive of the status quo is to be expected. But it is not always so. Even when denominational historians write from the inside, they also manage to find, in the existing storage bin of available incidents to recount and stories to tell, precedent for reform, change, and a turn to new directions. For all that, however, if the truly significant difference in confessional and scholarly history is to be isolated and named, it is crucially important to recognize that regardless of whether they are trained as professional practitioners of Clio's discipline, historians who do confessional history must work within a genre whose resources are limited to a particular body of data.

Although it often appears to historians in the academy that historians who write confessional history are forever "pulling their punches," a close analysis of any large bibliography of confessional history reveals that this is not what always happens in such writing. While there are people who write denominational history by doing little more than recycling existing accounts, there are also many denominational historians who employ the canons of the profession in gathering evidence; determining whether each source from which data are to be drawn is authentic and, if so, whether it is trustworthy; and deciding where each piece of evidence fits in the overall context of the community's history. Within the confessional form of the genre, however, the historian's main purpose is not discovering new information about the past—that is, recovering history—but strengthening the chain of corporate memory by writing an account that stretches from the very day in which the history is being written back through time to the point of beginnings and then returning by moving forward through the ages to the present.

While the program of the writer of confessional history is thus essentially circular, it is not merely "painting by the numbers." In accomplishing their task, confessional historians are, in fact, at liberty to paint the story as they believe it should be painted, as long as they do not mix new colors. What this less than subtle analogy intends to suggest is that the authors of confessional history cannot reach outside what amounts to a canonized body of evidence composed of the testimony believers have left behind in their writings and in the stories of their lives, as well as in the records kept by the members of the faith community. When denominational historians extend their search into other portions of the historical record, they are constrained to include only that which serves to support and confirm the memories of believers.

Circumscription of the available body of evidence has an inevitable impact on the history that can be written, for it removes the chronicling of events from the ongoingness of experience, producing a narrative that—for all its detail, its precise location in particular times and places—stands outside history. Confessional accounts are, finally, ahistorical because all explanation is internal to the community. Latter-day Joshuas fight battles in which they are outnumbered a hundredfold, but the walls come tumbling down nonetheless, and there is one and only one acceptable explanation—as an actor in the drama, God determined the outcome. Evidence drawn from outside the community might be available to establish the existing weakness of the walls and the likelihood that they would have crumbled in any case, but historians who write confessional history learn to use such evidence sparingly, if at all.[31] No matter how sophisticated the handling of the evidence drawn from the recorded memories of believers, and it is often very sophisticated indeed, the result is a history shot through with accounts of divine-human interaction that do not lend themselves to disinterested historical analysis.[32]

As explanation and support for a community's most-favored-people status, confessional history does more than strengthen and fortify the faith of individuals. It also serves to connect individual religious experience and corporate perceptions of the faith community as a distinct and esteemed people with whom the divine is directly concerned. A shared history in which divinity and humanity have participated jointly provides a basis for kinship that may begin as fictive and symbolic but across the generations becomes the real kinship that underlies ethnicity.

Even though confessional history written from the inside is vital to the life of the community, such accounts rarely go unchallenged for long. Whether written before or after a faith community's story assumes its elemental configuration, history written by nonbelievers very often becomes a mirror image of the community's faith story. Instead of depending primarily or exclusively on evidence drawn from the memory of believers, the historians who write this sort of history base their accounts on the memories of those who were present at the creation but failed to participate, those who never

believed, or—more important—those who believed for a while before becoming disillusioned and leaving the movement, carrying with them a plentiful supply of insider information. Fashioned into narrative, the histories
based on this class of evidence picture the faith community's leaders and
members alike in terms that are all too human—the former are filled with
cupidity, sexual desire, and a yearning for power, while the latter seek protection, psychic security, and an opiate that will alleviate the pain of the human condition. In all events, any manifestation of the divine is noticeably
absent from such narratives.

While the historians composing such accounts may be skilled gatherers
of information who carefully evaluate the authenticity of the evidence they
use and assess its trustworthiness, they are constrained by a limited corpus
of available evidence. They also draw on a fixed body of data: the memories
of those who did not believe, plus the generally ample evidence drawn from
any religious community's historical record that can be used to bolster a picture of human folly. As in all history, the result is an account that reflects the
historian's mind-set and perceptions of reality—and, of course, the historical process. The difference is that, to those who are not directly involved,
confessional history written by believers is filled with leaders and people who
are just too good to be convincing, whereas confessional accounts written by
historians preoccupied with their unbelief are filled with leaders who are so
bad that they are unconvincing and followers who seem more like caricatures
than living souls.

Although scholars may write confessional history of either variety, confessional history is not the sort of scholarly history that is the hallmark of
the best historical writing, either in or out of the academy. This is to say that,
as good as some confessional history is, because its practitioners allow themselves to be bound by informal but nevertheless very real limits on the evi-
dentiary sources from which they draw their data, the accounts they write
cannot be classified as critical history. This matter of not muzzling the ox as
the grain is being treaded out is, it seems to me, the crucial distinction between traditional and scholarly history. Those who do scholarly history must
be able to proceed through the evidence untrammeled by blinders that place
whole categories of evidence off limits.

When beginning history students are introduced to the concept of perspective, some of them immediately jump to the conclusion that history is
all interpretation. Without appreciating what they are doing, these initiates
move toward the position of some postmodern philosophers of history who,
in response to deconstruction and the limits of historicism, have concluded
that, at bedrock, history—even critical history—is ultimately nothing more

than an interpretation of reality fabricated from interpretation "all the way down." While I recognize that the emphasis I place here on the crucial importance of full and unlimited access to the historical record to doing critical history could be read as an effort to reclaim the integrity of the idea of a past as it actually was, I do not mean to go so far as to suggest that full recovery of that past was—or ever will be—possible. What I intend, rather, is to defer the issue of interpretation until the matter of putting together the building blocks from which histories are constructed can be addressed.

While fiction may theoretically issue ex nihilo from an author's pen, history never does; the story of the past is fashioned from existing elements into which historians must breathe life and "vent in" meaning. If any history— whether of nations or denominations—is to represent something more than an individual historian's idea of what happened, as scholarly history must, then gathering sufficient data to answer questions about who, what, where, and how must antedate the creation of that literary invention called narrative history. Historians who are willing to follow the evidence wherever it leads in the search for answers to fundamental questions can and do write scholarly history. When they take a particular faith community as the subject of their historical inquiry, whether what they write can be classified as scholarly history primarily depends on the locus of their inquiry.

If the story of the faith community is treated as a case study and analyzed as a means to further exploration of such larger questions as modernization, the politicization of the culture, or the nature and management of power, then the result is quite obviously scholarly history. Yet such studies are not examples of the scholarly writing of denominational history. When historians turn their attention to the communities themselves, when they describe them in a manner that fully credits their character as communities, and when they make a conscientious effort to represent what happened in a way that the participants themselves would recognize, then they are engaging in the scholarly writing of denominational history.

But how are historians to meet the requirements that turn scholarly history into denominational history without returning to the genre of confessional history? These observations will be brought to a close with some final reflections on method that speak to this question.[33] Again, the key concept is identity, this time not the identity of the objects of inquiry but the identity of the historian making the inquiry.

Scholars (especially those in the academy) who want to write a scholarly history of their own denominations cannot go back inside, using their status as believers to privilege their own denominations. They must always keep in mind their status as historians and proceed in accordance with their historical training, refusing to neglect the canons of history. In gathering evidence, they must as far as possible consider all the available data, assessing the reliability (or lack thereof) of evidence and authenticating any that is questionable. In doing so, they must apply the rules of evidence evenhandedly, and—although a denomination's fundamental religious claims are generally ahistorical—they must determine where and how evidence just coming to light fits into the larger contemporaneous body of historical data. Nevertheless, this does not mean that those who are worthy of being called professional historians must write a secular history of faith communities or a necessarily unsympathetic one.

Listening to what the data really appear to be saying is just as important as using the rules of evidence to determine what occurred. Here believers have an advantage, for they speak the language and can recognize nuances easily missed by scholars unfamiliar with a denominational idiom. Insiders are also familiar with the faith community's formal institutional system as well as the informal manner in which it operates at both the administrative and the congregational levels. Moreover, in assessing meaning and significance and determining how evidence is connected to later events, historians can look to religious studies, anthropology, and the sociology of religion for interpretive models that describe how religion works and how it fits into culture. Such a program for the scholarly writing of denominational history requires insiders to become "outside-insiders," who know their denominations intimately but are willing to develop the ability to see them from the disinterested perspective of the outside.

At the same time, it is equally possible but, in different ways, just as (or even more) demanding for outsiders to engage in the scholarly writing of denominational history. If insiders have to become "outside-insiders," then outsiders must become "inside-outsiders." Before they can apply the rules of evidence, which may be easier for them than for insiders, they must learn enough about the denomination to collect data efficiently. Since the bulk of the historical sources are often held by the denomination, this very often involves gaining the trust of denominational officials. To determine the meaning of the evidence they gather, outsiders have to learn both the theological and the popular religious language of the denominations they study. They also have to guard against analyses that make too much of petty intradenominational squabbles, on the one hand, and fail to credit fully the importance of believers' commitments to theological positions and worship practices, on the other.

Finally and, it seems to me, of the greatest importance when writing about denominations from either inside or outside, historians whose goal is writing scholarly history need somehow to bracket and suspend judgment about a faith community's truth claims. Unless this approach to basic beliefs is taken, insiders will almost inevitably write tendentious accounts that amount to a defense of the denomination, and outsiders will write tendentious accounts that call the denomination's legitimacy into question. A willing suspension of belief (or disbelief) makes it less likely that what a historian writes will be confused with efforts at faith promotion or exposé. But if the basic elements and dimensions of religion are kept to the fore, the suspension of belief (or the lack of it) will not prevent the composition of sensitive accounts of the denomination's past. Such a strategy can provide both inside-outsiders and outside-insiders with a place to stand, one where they can be interested and fair at one and the same time.

More than anything else, this place of observation may be the key to the scholarly writing of denominational history, for if the disinterestedness that is at the heart of fine history starts to disappear, then what started out as an effort at composing a scholarly account of a faith community's experience will revert to a variant form of confessional history, and the historian will have failed to write a scholarly history. But as the foregoing suggests, this in no way means that the scholarly writing of denominational history is a contradiction in terms.

Notes

1. John Foxe, *The Acts and Monuments of John Foxe,* 8 vols. (New York: AMS Press, 1965), 7:550. This passage is found in many books of quotations, including several editions of Bartlett's *Familiar Quotations* and the *Oxford Dictionary of Quotations.*

2. An early example of works in this genre is Conyers Read, *Social and Political Forces in the English Reformation* (Houston, Tex.: Elsevier, 1953). See also Steven Gunn, *Recent Perspectives on the Henrician Reformation* (Leicester, England: UCCF Associates, 1985).

3. Among such works, the best known and most influential is E. P. Thompson, *The Making of the English Working Class* (New York: Vintage Books, 1963). A second, expanded edition was published in 1968.

4. R. Laurence Moore, *Religious Outsiders and the Making of Americans* (New York: Oxford University Press, 1986); Paul E. Johnson, *A Shopkeeper's Millennium: Society and Revivals in Rochester, New York, 1815–1837* (New York: Hill and Wang, 1978). In an important paper presented to a joint session of the American Society of Church History and the American Historical Association in December 1990, Stephen Marini directed the attention of the profession to the way in which religion historians are increasingly interpreting religion as an epiphenomenon.

5. The disappearance of the public intellectual from the American scene is one of the major concerns that William D. Dean deals with in *The Religious Critic in American Culture* (Albany: State University of New York Press, 1994).

6. Robert N. Bellah, "Civil Religion in America," *Daedalus* 96 (Winter 1967): 1–21.

7. Timothy L. Smith, "Religion and Ethnicity in America," *American Historical Review* 83 (December 1978): 1155–85, reminded us that journeys to lands of promise are "theologizing experiences."

8. Denominations were species of the genus Protestantism, and their individual histories were species of the genus American church history. Individual denominational histories written during the first half of the twentieth century consequently reflected the same attitudes and narrative patterns as did sweeping surveys of the nation's religious history.

9. This concern was expressed in negative reactions to James B. Allen and Glen M. Leonard, *The Story of the Latter-day Saints* (Salt Lake City: Deseret Book, 1976). See Jan Shipps, *Mormonism: The Story of a New Religious Tradition* (Urbana: University of Illinois Press, 1985), 106–7. See also Boyd K. Packer, "The Mantle Is Far, Far Greater than the Intellect," *BYU Studies* 21 (Summer 1981): 259–78. It was clear that the LDS apostle Packer spoke for the church in this warning against professional history. Further evidence of the concern of LDS general authorities about new historical writing was supplied when Linda K. Newell and Valeen T. Avery, the authors of *Mormon Enigma: Emma Hale Smith, Prophet's Wife, "Elect Lady," Polygamy's Foe, 1804–1879* (Garden City, N.Y.: Doubleday, 1984; 2d ed., Urbana: University of Illinois Press, 1994), a critical biography of the Mormon prophet's first wife, were forbidden to talk about their work at LDS women's groups or any official church meetings. (See "Dangerous History: Laurel Thatcher Ulrich and Her Mormon Sisters," herein.)

10. A prime example in the first category is Ernest Lee Tuveson, *Redeemer Nation: The Idea of America's Millennial Role* (Chicago: University of Chicago Press, 1968). As for the impact of culture on religion, no major work surpasses Nathan Hatch, *The Democratization of American Christianity* (New Haven, Conn.: Yale University Press, 1989).

11. See "Thoughts about the Academic Community's Response to John Brooke's *Refiner's Fire,*" herein.

12. Many monographs on method in social history have been published since the late 1960s and early 1970s. Early examples are Charles Dollar and Richard Jensen, *Historian's Guide to Statistics: Quantitative Analysis and Historical Research* (New York: Holt, Rinehart and Winston, 1971); and Robert P. Swierenga, ed., *Quantification in American History: Theory and Research* (New York: Atheneum, 1970). *Historical Methods Newsletter* (now *Historical Methods*) began publication in 1967. The *Journal of Social History,* which places major emphasis on method, began publication that same year.

13. William D. Dean, *History Making History* (Albany: State University of New York Press, 1988), contains a broad-ranging and intelligible discussion of this intellectual movement. The quotations are from the preface, x.

14. Paul Kleppner, *The Cross of Culture: A Sociological Analysis of Midwestern Politics, 1850–1900* (New York: Free Press, 1970); Richard J. Jensen, *The Winning of the Midwest: Social and Political Conflict, 1888–1896* (Chicago: University of Chicago Press, 1971); Robert P. Swierenga and Philip R. VanderMeer, eds., *Belief and Behavior: Essays in the New Religious History* (New Brunswick, N.J.: Rutgers University Press, 1991).

15. Robert Bruce Mullin and Russell E. Richey, eds., *Reimagining Denominationalism: Interpretive Essays* (New York: Oxford University Press, 1994), is the work that

emerged from the conference entitled "The Scholarly Writing of Denominational History: An Oxymoron?" The subtitle, according to the editors, reflected "the disdain that those involved in denominational studies had experienced from university colleagues who conveyed in one way or another the impression that the denomination was not worth intellectual attention" (6).

16. To some extent, this is explained by the distinctiveness of the stories of the genesis of such communities. When such stories are not widely shared outside the community, they ordinarily do not become subject to multiple interpretations.

17. Whether denominations are ethnic groups or whether religious communities simply function as ethnic groups is one of the basic questions animating ongoing discussion among scholars on the relationship between religion and ethnicity. See the section on ethnic studies in Russell E. Richey, "Institutional Forms of Religion," in *Encyclopedia of the American Religious Experience: Studies of Traditions and Movements,* ed. Charles H. Lippy and Peter W. Williams, 3 vols. (New York: Charles Scribner's Sons, 1988), 1:44–47. Although I believe this is a fruitful arena of scholarly inquiry, I do not mean to claim anything more here than that tightly bonded religious communities function in much the same way that ethnic groups do.

18. Bryan Wilson, *Religion in Sociological Perspective* (New York: Oxford University Press, 1982), 111–13.

19. I have made an effort to generalize from my own work both because Mormonism is the case I know best and because the Mormon examples are so clear and unambiguous.

20. Robert Wuthnow, "Religion, Identity and Ethnicity: A Forum," *Religion and American Culture* 2 (January 1992): 2–8.

21. Prominent examples of this pattern in Mormon circles are the feminist activist Sonia Johnson and the philosopher Sterling M. McMurrin, the late LDS philosopher who once served as U.S. commissioner of education. See Sonia Johnson, *From Housewife to Heretic: One Woman's Spiritual Awakening and Her Excommunication from the Mormon Church* (New York: Wildfire Books, 1989); and the interview with Sterling M. McMurrin published in *Seventh-East Press* 17 (January 1983), 5–7, 9–11.

22. I once made an effort at classification not unlike the one suggested here, but it is extremely rudimentary and does not make use of the conception of identity as a combination of ascribed and achieved dimensions. See Jan Shipps, "Beyond the Stereotypes: Mormon and Non-Mormon Communities in Twentieth-Century Mormondom," in *New Views of Mormon History: A Collection of Essays in Honor of Leonard Arrington,* ed. Davis Bitton and Maureen Ursenbach Beecher (Salt Lake City: University of Utah Press, 1987), 342–62.

23. See Jan Shipps, "Making Saints in the Early Days and the Latter Days," in *Contemporary Mormonism: Social Science Perspectives,* ed. Marie Cornwall, Tim B. Heaton, and Lawrence A. Young (Urbana: University of Illinois Press, 1994), 64–83.

24. Examples of studies supporting the claim that distinct boundaries make for historical clarity include Jay P. Dolan, *The American Catholic Experience: A History from Colonial Times to the Present* (Garden City, N.Y.: Doubleday, 1985); Robert A. Orsi, *The Madonna of 115th Street: Faith and Community in Italian Harlem, 1880–1950* (New Haven, Conn.: Yale University Press, 1985); Ann Taves, *The Household of Faith: Roman Catholic Devotions in Mid-Nineteenth Century America* (Notre Dame, Ind.: University of Notre Dame Press, 1986); Jack Wertheim, ed., *The American Synagogue:*

A Sanctuary Transformed (Cambridge: Cambridge University Press, 1987); Leonard J. Arrington and Davis Bitton, *The Mormon Experience: A History of the Latter-Day Saints* (New York: Alfred A. Knopf, 1979); and Klaus J. Hansen, *Mormonism and the American Experience* (Chicago: University of Chicago Press, 1981).

25. In recent years, probably no issue has generated more attention, both in articles published and in letters to the editor, in *Dialogue* and *Sunstone*, major journals of opinion in the LDS intellectual community. Within conservative evangelicalism, fundamentalism, and pentecostalism, the matter of the scholarly writing of denominational history has also generated a whole corpus of scholarly books and articles, as well as a professional organization of conservative historians that devotes its sole attention to faith and history. See the ample bibliography of secondary works in Grant Wacker, *Augustus H. Strong and the Dilemma of Historical Consciousness* (Macon, Ga.: Mercer University Press, 1985).

26. The canonized *History of Joseph Smith, the Prophet,* a portion of which is included in the Pearl of Great Price, one of the three new books of scripture of the Church of Jesus Christ of Latter-day Saints, originated, as the first verse says, as a response to the "many reports which have been put in circulation by evil-disposed and designing persons in relation to the rise and progress of The Church of Jesus Christ of Latter-day Saints, all of which have been designed by the authors thereof to militate against its character as a Church and its progress in the world." Another example of official reaction to negative history is found in the biographical studies and the several official histories of the Church of Christ, Scientist, written by Robert Peel. These are works clearly designed to answer unflattering pictures of Mary Baker Eddy and the beginnings of Christian Science, such as the one found in Edwin Franden Dakin, *Mrs. Eddy* (New York: Grosset and Dunlap, 1929), and in several subsequent accounts that the church has perceived as nothing more than scurrilous attacks.

27. A case in point is the cool, clearly hands-off response of Oral Roberts and his followers to David Edwin Harrell Jr., *Oral Roberts: An American Life* (Bloomington: Indiana University Press, 1985), a sympathetic biography of the faith healer.

28. Bernard Lewis, *History—Remembered, Recovered, Invented* (Princeton, N.J.: Princeton University Press, 1976).

29. Richey, "Institutional Forms of Religion," 1:32–34.

30. Confessional history must communicate effectively not only to new generations based on age groupings but also to generations of new believers, that is, to new converts to the faith.

31. A pertinent example of this pattern can be drawn from an incident in the recent history of Mormon historiography. The "miracle of the seagulls" is the well-known part of the LDS story that recounts the appearance of gulls to ingest the hordes of crickets that threatened grain fields whose harvest was crucial to the Saints' survival during their first year in the Great Basin. Memorialized in a stone monument that presides over Salt Lake City, as well as in countless numbers of "faith-promoting" narratives, it has assumed such a sacred character that a friend of mine who was a historian in the employ of the CES, the LDS Church's seminary and institute system, was roundly criticized for praising an article in which William G. Hartley looked outside the circle of acceptable sources and reported that at the time there were many keepers of conscientious chronicles in the area who failed even to mention the

seagulls, much less to note that a miracle had occurred. The article in question was William G. Hartley, "Mormons, Crickets, and Gulls: A New Look at an Old Story," *Utah Historical Quarterly* 38 (Summer 1970): 224–39.

32. Note that throughout I have conscientiously avoided using both the word and the concept of *objectivity*, a more extreme version of disinterestedness. While this is an issue of great importance, a discussion of objectivity and the extent to which it is possible to attain it is less important to the matters with which I am concerned than the effort to find a reasonably disinterested perspective from which to write denominational history.

33. These reflections are drawn directly from my own experience as a birthright Methodist who has continued to maintain that denominational connection while devoting nearly four decades of my life as a professional historian to a study of the Latter-day Saints.

Dangerous History:
Laurel Thatcher Ulrich and Her Mormon Sisters

A Latter-day Saint born and bred, with a genealogy that stretches to the beginnings of Mormonism, Laurel Thatcher Ulrich moved into the world of
historical scholarship while rearing five children. As she earned her degrees,
worked toward tenure at the University of New Hampshire, and wrote two
remarkable books about women in colonial America, she still managed to
be a model Mormon wife and mother. This "feminist historian" stays active
in the Church of Jesus Christ of Latter-day Saints and its women's auxiliary,
the Relief Society. Despite the renown she received after her second book won
awards (including a Pulitzer Prize and a Bancroft Prize), after she was tapped
for one of the so-called MacArthur genius grants, and after she was hired as
a professor in the history department at Harvard University, she continued
as a senior editor of *Exponent II,* an independent quarterly for Mormon
women that she helped establish in 1974.[1]

Because many Mormon women must also juggle family, church, and work
responsibilities, it is small wonder that this celebrated sister is regarded as a
paragon or that LDS feminists consider her to be particularly worthy of
emulation. Neither is it surprising that the planning committee for the 1993
Brigham Young University–LDS Relief Society Annual Women's Conference
proposed Ulrich as a keynote speaker. What does seem remarkable, at least
initially, is that the committee's proposal was vetoed.

While the veto was decided on during a meeting of the university's board
of trustees in November 1992, no public announcement of the ruling was
forthcoming. Since no formal invitation had been issued, the matter of the
keynote speaker for the women's gathering was probably treated as an internal matter. But the women who had submitted Ulrich's name were under-
standably disappointed, even outraged. Rumors about the board's decision
started to circulate before Christmas of that year, although a full three months

passed before Peggy Fletcher Stack, the religion writer for the *Salt Lake Tribune,* broke the story. The decision not to invite a Mormon Pulitzer Prize–winning historian to speak at BYU became news, making its way into newspapers outside Utah and into the *Chronicle of Higher Education.*

Since the Ulrich affair came soon after the promulgation of a new statement specifying limits to academic freedom at the university, some observers viewed this episode as an early indication of the deleterious consequences of such limits. Certainly the statement does seem to require all campus speakers, not just faculty, to be, as the religion department chairman Robert L. Millet approvingly stated, "less concerned with what the academy thinks of their labors than what the Lord and the board of trustees think." Yet the university's honors division had made Ulrich welcome earlier in 1992 when it sponsored a lecture at which she spoke about her work in colonial history to a thousand students and faculty and received a standing ovation. It is obvious that something more than academic freedom was at stake when the LDS decision-making cadre decided that she should not speak from the dais during the annual women's conference.

Responding to press inquiries about the decision, Margaret Smoot, the BYU spokesperson, affirmed the university administration's "great respect" for Ulrich's scholarship, explained that no one meant to "embarrass her publicly," and refused further comment. Like many such statements, this was a nonexplanation. It did not clarify the extent to which the ruling was a university ruling as opposed to a ruling that reflected the wishes of the church's governing hierarchy. It also failed to make clear whether the reference to not intending to embarrass Ulrich "publicly" was meant as a warning that something about her private life had led "the Brethren" to consider it unwise to allow the church's most eminent female historian to speak to its women.

Even though Laurel Ulrich's bishop received a call "from Salt Lake" asking about her, Ulrich's private life is almost certainly not the reason why the committee's preliminary invitation was not followed up with a formal invitation to speak. A much more plausible explanation is that the members of the church's First Presidency and Council of the Twelve who were serving as BYU trustees were, in this instance, not concerned about whether Ulrich's presenting a keynote address at the university would be an appropriate university activity. They were concerned about a much larger issue. They did not want to take a chance that this dynamic and very knowledgeable LDS scholar would talk about Mormon women and history from a platform that implied the blessing of the LDS priesthood.

Ulrich's articles and editorial observations in *Exponent II* (as well as a short piece reprinted in *Women and Authority,* a volume of collected articles on "reemerging Mormon feminism") were all available for the Brethren's review.[2] Since her writings expressed Ulrich's concerns about the church's apparently equating priesthood and maleness ("almost like mistaking a utility pole for electricity or a sacrament cup for water") and since some of her articles pointed to an earlier era in which church leaders had encouraged prominent LDS women to become active in feminist causes, they no doubt proved troubling to the members of the LDS First Presidency and Council of the Twelve. Because the BYU board of trustees is made up of apostles who sit on the Council of the Twelve plus the heads of two women's auxiliaries, the decision against Ulrich's speaking was probably a church decision rather than a university decision.

If this reading is accurate, the decision ought not to be interpreted—as it sometimes has been—as a warning from the church hierarchy that LDS women should not pursue academic careers or call themselves feminists. Instead, it can be read as a reflection of concern among the church leaders about how Mormon women's history was being (and continues to be) used to call into question the church's conservative stance on the role of women and also how history seemed to be driving the development of an LDS feminist theology centered on the Mormon concept of a Mother in Heaven, a deity (consort to God the Father) whose existence was described in an 1845 poem written by Eliza R. Snow (arguably the most notable female Mormon in the history of the movement).[3]

The Church of Jesus Christ of Latter-day Saints is hardly alone in trying to grapple with changes in female roles without alienating women or undermining the foundations of tradition. But the problem of preserving LDS custom, style, and social practice without estranging female members is particularly formidable on two counts. First, however much the church aims to preserve and protect families, its theology and doctrine are utterly patriarchal both in approaching life in the here and now and in enshrining traditional female roles for time and eternity.[4] Second, the church's task of making "being Mormon" as satisfying to women as it is to men has to be taken up in the context of an institution whose history is complex and paradoxical. In this essay, I focus on the second issue.

As is well known, the Church of Jesus Christ of Latter-day Saints sanctioned the practice of plural marriage for almost half a century before 1890. This means that Mormonism was once as emphatically radical in its challenge to the nuclear family as it is now insistent on sacralizing it. The dynamics of this shift are too complicated to be easily summarized. But it is important to keep in mind that while much in the religious as well as the cultural realm has changed for LDS women, much that is fundamental has stayed the same for LDS men, including the practically universal ordination of males to offices in one of the priesthood orders. The only significant difference between how things used to be for male Latter-day Saints and how they are now is that in the past ordination generally occurred in early adulthood, whereas now it typically occurs at age twelve. This allows time for boys to grow into the responsibilities of priesthood as they become men; it also gives them time to learn how to preside.

Now, as in former times, priesthood holders preside in both the home and the ecclesiastical offices to which they are called. In the pioneer period, however, many men had multiple families over which to preside. Additionally, men were often called away on church missions, regardless of whether they had a family or families to support. As a result, nineteenth-century Mormon women had substantial practical autonomy in running their households and supervising their children. Oftentimes, too, circumstances forced wives to find ways to support themselves and their children. This implicit although limited sovereignty in their homes and families was bolstered by the calling of women to exercise spiritual powers by performing certain priestly rituals, especially blessing their children and washing, blessing, and anointing their sisters with holy oil for healing.[5]

Modern fathers still preside over their homes and families, but the task of pastoring congregations and fulfilling local church responsibilities is now much more widely dispersed within the church's lay priesthood than it was in the nineteenth century. Besides struggling to support their wives and, more often than not, a stairstep progression of children, active LDS men are now frequently called on to shoulder time-consuming ecclesiastical duties at the local level.

Mormon women are thus still left with a great deal of responsibility for maintaining their homes and overseeing the lives of their children. Moreover, even though church leaders instruct wives and mothers to avoid working outside the home if at all possible, economic realities force many into the workplace. Now, however, women no longer have the limited spiritual sovereignty that the right to seal blessings and conduct anointings gave to their foremothers.

As the definition and clarification of the rights and responsibilities of those who hold various priesthood offices proceeded in the late nineteenth century and early twentieth, the callings that women had once held were restricted to ordained men.[6] This has forced women to be passive in the spiritual realm. They are no longer able to participate in the performance of any priesthood ritual whatsoever. Even participating in the ordinance analogous to christening in which babies are named and blessed is specifically forbidden to LDS mothers. Thus, while the male priesthood role remains essentially unchanged in the home and has expanded in the ecclesiastical realm, women's role in initiating and performing rituals and thereby filling a meaningful role in communal religious life has been severely curtailed. A woman is now enjoined to study and pray and teach the gospel to her children. If she needs a blessing or if other LDS women turn to her in distress, she must call for members of the priesthood to seal the blessings and perform the anointings that endow her prayerful requests with ritual emphasis.

As an arena for education and compassionate service, the Relief Society has paralleled the priesthood since 1842. It has served as Mormon women's public sphere. But whereas women once presided over their own auxiliary, maintained their own buildings, collected and dispersed their own monies, and had their own magazine (reporting to the ecclesiastical authorities only at the very highest level), this changed in the 1960s and 1970s. The *Relief Society Magazine* is no longer published since all LDS adult periodicals were merged in 1971 to create the *Ensign,* a general church magazine. No longer is the women's auxiliary permitted to collect its own money or maintain a separate budget, and the line of its reporting authority is considerably modified. The Relief Society's president in a local ward (parish) is now a member of the bishop's (that is, pastor's) cabinet, which makes coordinating ward members' care much easier and more effective but also means that the society reports to the priesthood at the local level, a change that at least symbolically takes from women autonomy that was once theirs.

A discrepancy also exists between the public role that LDS women were asked to play historically and their current role. In the late nineteenth century and early twentieth, church leaders encouraged LDS women to work for universal suffrage and women's rights.[7] Today, a Mormon woman is expected to take a stand for "family values." The Equal Rights Amendment was officially opposed by the church, and women were instructed to work for its defeat. Women who believe that abortion is a woman's choice are discouraged from publicly identifying themselves as Latter-day Saints.

All this makes the history of Mormon women potentially dangerous. Church leaders have therefore started to oversee the preparation and presentation of LDS women's history whenever its exposition suggests any touch of official sanction and whenever the presentation is to an LDS audience, especially an audience of Mormon women. One of the most obvious efforts to influence Mormon women's understanding of women's history centers on whether the Relief Society was originally conceived as an auxiliary priesthood. In the excellent official history of the organization published in 1992 by Deseret Book Company, the official LDS press, the three female authors place a conservative interpretation on what the Prophet Joseph Smith meant when he said that he had organized the women "in the order of the priesthood after the pattern of the Church" and, as Eliza R. Snow said in recording the event, "turned the key to them."[8] This interpretation was subsequently canonized by the LDS apostle Dallin Oaks in a semiannual conference talk presented on the occasion of the Relief Society's sesquicentennial. This member of the church's highest ecclesiastical quorum appeared to be speaking for the church's general authorities in honoring the women of the church and celebrating the Relief Society's contribution to the cause of Christ's kingdom. But Oaks, who was a sitting justice on the Utah Supreme Court when he was called to be a member of the Council of the Twelve, also rendered what the church has taken to be the final verdict in this case: "No priesthood keys were delivered to the Relief Society."[9]

Oversight of LDS women's history was also exercised by another highly placed LDS leader: Loren C. Dunn, a member of the church's First Council of the Seventy. As a part of the Relief Society's sesquicentennial celebration, an exhibit on its history was mounted at the LDS Museum of Church History and Art in Salt Lake City. When Dunn reviewed the exhibit only three hours before its formal opening, he ordered quotations from Joseph Smith, Bathsheba Smith, and Eliza R. Snow removed because they referred to women as "queens and priestesses." His explanation was that the quotations were "too sacred" to place on public view.[10] But the fact that they dealt with the question of women and the priesthood can hardly be overlooked.

Maintaining control of history is never easy, however. It is particularly difficult at a time when women's journals, diaries, and writings from the nineteenth century and early twentieth are being published or reprinted. An outpouring of Mormon women's history can be seen in books and Mormon periodicals that have no official connection to the church—most especially *Dialogue: A Journal of Mormon Thought, Sunstone, Exponent II,* and the *Journal of Mormon History,* all of which have, or recently have had, women as editors. Access to this plethora of historical information is creating an LDS women's intellectual community, most of whose members are stalwart but increasingly independent Saints. It is important to note, however, that this amorphous group is mainly composed of birthright Saints or longtime converts—women who, for all practical purposes, are ethnically Mormon. Knowledge about the LDS past may provide enlightenment and understanding, but it rarely destroys their faith or causes them to leave Mormonism.

But the church is growing rapidly, and many of its new members do not have a similar ethnic grounding. With more than ten million members world-wide, the church is overwhelmed with converts who need milk, not meat. From history, they require faith-promoting accounts of the lives of Saints that can be internalized and assimilated to contextualize their new faith. Cognizant of this need, LDS leaders, instead of drawing female role models and precedents them from church history, are increasingly pointing in their sermons and their writings to stories from the Book of Mormon and other scriptures that provide timeless and immutable models but in which women are virtually absent.

Yet history is always there to provide a subtext, an alternate voice, reminding the Saints that role models change and that precedents point in more than one direction. For that reason, in addition to their straightforward attempts to control history itself, LDS leaders are making an effort to control the church's pulpits and podiums to be sure that the history dispensed from them is faith-promoting and that it provides acceptable models for modern members of the church.

In this instance, the concern was Mormon women's history. The church leadership wanted to be confident that anything said about the LDS women's experience would hold up female models that priesthood leaders would regard as appropriate for the end of the twentieth century. It is easy to see, looking back from the end of the twentieth century, that what happened to Laurel Ulrich fits squarely into the defensive program with which the church guards its fortress against heterodoxy by exercising close oversight of public discourse about sensitive dimensions of LDS history, public conversation about the meaning of scripture, and unauthorized explications of dogma.

The standard pattern for controlling church rostrums had been established in 1985 with the silencing of Linda King Newell and Valeen Tippetts Avery, coauthors of *Mormon Enigma*, an unauthorized biography of the wife of the Prophet Joseph Smith. Their work, published in New York by Doubleday in 1984, was a sympathetic portrayal of the prophet's wife, one of the preeminent female models for Mormon women. At the same time, the biography included a picture of the prophet as seen through the eyes of his suffering wife on whom the introduction of plural marriage took a terrible toll. No doubt this less than sympathetic "nontraditional" depiction of the prophet was, in itself, disturbing to LDS Church leaders. What was more alarming however, was that the work, which became a prizewinner, generated enough interest to make it practically a best-seller.[11] Almost inevitably, its authors became the recipients of numerous invitations to speak, often to LDS women's groups and adult "firesides."

Newell and Avery were never informed exactly who made the decision that such presentations should not be allowed or when that decision was made. But soon after their book received the prestigious Evans Award for Biography, instructions not to allow them to speak about their recently published book or any other "aspect of religious or church history in any Mormon church-related meeting or institution" went out to priesthood leaders and local LDS authorities throughout the West.[12] Although this ban was widely reported in the press, the ruling that they were not to have access to any LDS dais was not communicated personally to them.

When the church's control of access to platforms from which to speak to LDS audiences was reconfirmed in the Ulrich case eight years later, no church leader communicated the church's decision directly to Laurel Ulrich either. Just as Newell and Avery had been baffled by the edict that silenced them, so Ulrich was perplexed by the decision. She was more puzzled than angered or hurt. In a telephone conversation, she asked me, "If I'm not safe to speak at BYU, then who is?" In view of her lifelong efforts to fulfill all the responsibilities of Mormon womanhood even as she worked to achieve distinction as a scholar, it is easy to understand her bewilderment.

It is also easy to understand the anger and confusion of many LDS women reacting to the news of what had happened to her. But the decision of the church leaders is also understandable, even sensible from their perspective. They were confronted with either acceding to or disapproving the planning committee's proposal to invite as an official women's conference keynote speaker not Sister Ulrich, the faithful (if feminist) Mormon, but Laurel Thatcher Ulrich, historian. Those in authority decided against allowing her to speak probably because they knew that her standing in the professional community gave this gifted historian a commanding presence among LDS women and because they were aware that, in preparing a keynote address, Ulrich would be able to call on the record of the experience of LDS women, which is filled with many examples embodying their independent spirit.

If the Newell and Avery silencing was a prelude to what might be called "the Ulrich affair," neither of these incidents involved formal church discipline. What happened caused suffering, especially in the Newell and Avery case,[13] but these three women were not disfellowshipped or excommunicated. During 1992–93, the same year the Women's Conference Committee attempted to get an invitation issued to Laurel Ulrich to be their keynote speaker, six prominent Latter-day Saint intellectuals were disciplined, however. Moreover, an official statement from the First Presidency—reflecting some LDS general authorities' concern about what they regarded as the ersatz versions of church history and mistaken interpretations of scripture, theology, and doctrine that were being presented on the programs of Sunstone symposia (held annually

in Salt Lake City and in other large urban areas across the nation) and dis-
seminated through the sale of tape recordings of the symposia sessions—
warned members of the LDS community against attending symposia and
other gatherings in which presentations are made by "alternate voices."

Although the episodes in which the church excommunicated five members of the Mormon intellectual community and disfellowshipped another
(all within one month in 1993) were officially unrelated, if these disciplinary
actions are considered in conjunction with the disapproval of the Ulrich
invitation and the issuing of the warning against listening to alternate voices,
it is obvious that all were part of the church's struggle in the late 1980s and
the early 1990s to gain control of the LDS intellectual ambience by limiting
what the Saints were exposed to when they attended not only church-sponsored gatherings but also independent symposia.[14]

The issues involved in all six disciplinary cases were complex, but LDS
women's issues were critical in at least four of them. Among those excommunicated were two women: Lavina Fielding Anderson and Maxine Hanks.
Anderson, a seventh-generation Mormon, once worked as associate editor
of the *Ensign* (the official magazine of the church). She is now both propri-
etor of Editing, Inc., and editor of the *Journal of Mormon History*, the highly
regarded voice of the Mormon History Association. Hanks is the editor of
Women and Authority: Re-emerging Mormon Feminism, the collection that
reprinted Laurel Ulrich's essay connecting new LDS feminist theology with
the history of female Saints.[15] One of Hanks's own essays was included in this
collection. Another woman, Lynn Kanavel Whitesides, president of the feminist Mormon Women's Forum, who had publicly questioned the explicit
instructions of the church leadership not to pray to Mother in Heaven, was
disfellowshipped. *Women and Authority* also included an article written by
another excommunicant, D. Michael Quinn, the well-known (and since his
excommunication, much published) historian of Mormonism. In his *Wom-
en and Authority* essay, Quinn argued that the history and the language of
temple ordinances make it clear that LDS women have held the priesthood
since 1843.[16] While not as directly involved with women's history, another
excommunicant, the lawyer Paul Toscano, coauthored with his wife, Margaret, *Strangers in Paradox*, a work of "speculative theology."[17] Margaret
Toscano is an outspoken LDS feminist theologian.

∽

The 1993 semiannual conference of the LDS Church was held October 2–3,
following hard on what Lavina Fielding Anderson in an interview on National
Public Radio called the church's "fall housecleaning."[18] Characterized by an

unusual dialectic, the conference talks given by the members of the First Presidency and Council of the Twelve combined appreciation for and concern about women with warnings about apostasy and definitions of it. But if some connection between the two emphases was implied, it was not spelled out. *Apostasy* was defined as behavior in which members "repeatedly act in clear, open, and deliberate public opposition to the Church or its leaders" and in which church members persist in "teaching as Church doctrine information that is not Church doctrine after being corrected by their bishops or higher authorities."[19] Whether public presentation and publication of those parts of LDS women's history that are not included in the church's "approved curriculum" is flirting with apostasy the Brethren did not say.

Since the *Church Handbook of Instructions* issued in 1998 includes both the warning against symposia and the explicit definition of apostasy set forth in the 1989 *General Handbook of Instructions* and reiterated in the 1993 semi-annual conference, it is not at all clear that intellectual free agency will remain in place for Laurel and her sisters.[20] Yet one thing is certain: at least in the foreseeable future neither Ulrich nor other Mormon women historians will be permitted to exercise authority—even apparent authority—in interpreting Mormon history.

Notes

1. With the change of editors in 1996, *Exponent II* reorganized its editorial staff so that it no longer has senior editors. As a result, Laurel Ulrich's name has disappeared from the masthead.

2. Laurel Ulrich, "On Appendages," in *Women and Authority: Re-emerging Mormon Feminism,* ed. Maxine Hanks (Salt Lake City: Signature Books, 1992), 94–96, was originally published in *Exponent II* 11 (Winter 1985): 9. That this volume, which reprinted several essays challenging the church's position on women, was published only a few months before the matter of asking Ulrich to speak at the Women's Conference came up could have figured in the decision against issuing an invitation to her to do so. When I told her that her 1985 essay was included in this volume, Ulrich was surprised. She had not been asked for permission and was unaware that her essay had been reprinted.

3. This poem, "O My Father," became a cherished LDS hymn. The relevant lines read, "In heav'ns are parents single? / No, the thought makes reason stare! / Truth is reason; truth eternal / Tells me I've a mother there." See Elaine Anderson Cannon, "Mother in Heaven," in *Encyclopedia of Mormonism,* 5 vols., ed. Daniel H. Ludlow (New York: Macmillan, 1992), 2:961.

4. The church's "Proclamation on the Family" was introduced "to the church and to the world" on September 24, 1995, when church president Gordon B. Hinckley read it to those in attendance during a General Relief Society meeting. The text was printed in the *Deseret News* of the same date, and it has often been reprinted since.

5. See Linda King Newell, "The Historical Relationship of Mormon Women and Priesthood," *Dialogue* 18 (Fall 1985): 21–32. A revised and expanded version of this article was printed as "Gifts of the Spirit: Women's Share," in *Sisters in Spirit: Mormon Women in Historical and Cultural Perspective*, ed. Maureen Ursenbach Beecher and Lavina Fielding Anderson (Urbana: University of Illinois Press, 1987), 111–50. This article was reprinted under its original title but with material from the "Gifts of the Spirit" revision in *Women and Authority*, ed. Hanks, 23–44.

6. The version of Newell's essay that appeared in *Sisters in Spirit* is especially good on the relationship between the ever clearer definition of priesthood and the restriction of spiritual sovereignty (as called forth through ritual) to members of the priesthood. See 132–43.

7. For more on the change described here, see Jan Shipps, "*Exponent II*: Mormonism's Stealth Alternative," *Exponent II* 22 (Summer 1999): 28–33.

8. Quoted in Jill Mulvay Derr, Janath Russell Cannon, and Maureen Ursenbach Beecher, *Women of Covenant: The Story of Relief Society* (Salt Lake City: Deseret Book, 1992), 41, 49.

9. Annual conference addresses are published in the *Ensign* in May of each year. See the *Ensign* 22 (May 1992): 34.

10. Quoted in "Relief Society Exhibit Censure," *Sunstone* 16 (February 1992): 66.

11. When the second edition of this book appeared in paperback in 1994 under the University of Illinois Press imprimatur, the book had sold 37,000 copies and has since sold over 6,000 more.

12. The general authorities made no attempt to prevent Newell and Avery from talking about their research at the annual meetings of professional organizations.

13. Linda King Newell and Valeen Tippetts Avery, *Mormon Enigma: Emma Hale Smith*, 2d ed. (Urbana: University of Illinois Press, 1994), xii.

14. In a related development, members of the faculty at BYU and other LDS intellectuals who worked in the Church Educational System or the expanding church bureaucracy were counseled against participating in Sunstone symposia.

15. See note 2 above.

16. D. Michael Quinn, "Mormon Women Have Had the Priesthood since 1843," in *Women and Authority*, ed. Hanks, 365–410. This essay was first published in *Sunstone* 6 (September–October 1981): 26–27.

17. Margaret Toscano and Paul Toscano, *Strangers in Paradox: Explorations in Mormon Theology* (Salt Lake City: Signature Books, 1990).

18. Transcript of interview, *Sunstone* 16 (November 1993): 69.

19. Quoted in James E. Faust, "Keeping Covenants and Honoring the Priesthood," *Ensign* 23 (November 1993): 38 from *The General Handbook of Instructions: Book 2*, Priesthood and Auxiliaries (Salt Lake City: Church of Jesus Christ of Latter-day Saints, 1989), 10–13. The definition also specifies that following the teachings of apostate cults (such as those advocating plural marriage) is apostasy.

20. *Church Handbook of Instructions: Book 1, Stake Presidencies and Bisphoprics* (Salt Lake City: Church of Jesus Christ of Latter-day Saints, 1998), 153 (warning against "alternative voices" under the heading "Symposia and Similar Gatherings"), 95–96 (definition of apostasy in the section entitled "Church Discipline").

Thoughts about the Academic Community's Response to John Brooke's Refiner's Fire

In 1986, John Brooke, a member of the history department at Tufts University, presented a paper at the annual meeting of the Mormon History Association (MHA) in Salt Lake City. In it, he reported some of his early findings about the Prophet Joseph Smith's ancestors in England as well as those on this side of the Atlantic. As a non-Mormon scholar of early American history, he had only recently embarked on a study of the first Mormon prophet and early Mormonism, and he was a newcomer to the MHA.[1] Nine years of exhaustive research and writing later, he once again appeared on the MHA program, this time as the author of *The Refiner's Fire: The Making of Mormon Cosmology, 1644–1844,* a new and prizewinning book about Mormonism that was heralded by a scholar of no less stature than Martin Marty as "a model of the historian's enterprise."[2] The committee charged with selecting the 1994 Bancroft Prize agreed with Marty, identifying this book, which was issued by the Cambridge University Press, as one of the year's two best books in early American history. The Society for the Historians of the Early American Republic (SHEAR) also honored Brooke's work, giving the work its Best Book Award for 1994.

These judgments and Marty's description of Brooke's book as a model history notwithstanding, Brooke's presence in an MHA "Scholar Meets the Critics" session was not an occasion for the sort of unalloyed accolade that he and his work seemed to be earning from "the world." One of the critics in the session, Princeton's Alfred Bush, described *Refiner's Fire* as a "stunning book," a work "revolutionary in its perspective" and in its "amazing deconstruction of the Mormon past." But critiques presented by the other two commentators, Grant Underwood from Brigham Young University at Hawaii and David J. Whittaker from the University Archives at Brigham Young University in Provo, challenged the work on the twin bases of the author's failure to use a variety of significant documents (which had been available for study while he was doing his research) and his flawed interpretation. While these two critics were more respectful of Brooke and slightly less disparaging of his efforts, their critiques were not unlike already published (or about-to-be published) reviews of the Tufts professor's work by other LDS scholars who have studied early Mormonism. Many of these reviews written by Latter-day Saints were lengthy, erudite, detailed, and sometimes vituperative denunciations, excoriating the author for "methodological leaps," "factual errors," the "forcing of evidence," and an egregious misreading of texts.[3]

A general negative critique by Latter-day Saints is not surprising in view of Brooke's explanation in strictly human terms of virtually everything the Saints hold sacred—the Book of Mormon, which Joseph Smith said he translated with spiritual assistance; the restoration of their church and priesthoods; and the prophet's revelations, particularly the revelations outlining the LDS "Plan of Salvation," which includes preexistence, multiple heavens, and eternal progression toward godhood. Nor was it shocking to see that the most extended, scathing, and downright ugly reviews of *Refiner's Fire* were written by scholars connected with the Foundation for Ancient Research and Mormon Studies (FARMS), now located at Brigham Young University.[4] This is what one would expect: Brooke's work calls the ancient origins of the Book of Mormon and the LDS belief system into question, and the primary purpose of FARMS is to demonstrate and clarify the ancient origins of both.[5]

Although most reviews of Brooke's work by non-Mormons praised it highly while most reviews by Latter-day Saints condemned it roundly, two Latter-day Saints wrote assessments of the work that stand out because of the balance they brought to their reviewing task. Richard Bushman wrote an essay, published in the *Journal of the Early Republic,* that he called "The Mysteries of Mormonism," and Philip Barlow wrote an extended review for the *Christian Century* that he entitled "Decoding Mormonism."[6] Both authors recognized that Brooke carried out research that could be useful, but both were convinced that he made too much of what he found and were critical of how he interpreted his evidence. Although they apparently did not compare notes about what they would write, both also pointed to Brooke's failure to recognize how much of what he described as hermetic or occult came directly from the New Testament. Moreover, both authors denounced Brooke's last chapter, in which he made an effort to assess the long-range effects on Mormonism of accepting religious claims rooted in the hermetic tradition. Barlow suggested that this chapter came close to "cultural slander." These two LDS authors also agreed that, in the final analysis, *Refiner's Fire* is not a work that generates confidence in the author's reading of the mass of evidence he uses to make his case that Mormonism's roots are to be found in the occult and the hermetic tradition.

Notwithstanding these evaluations that fail to fit squarely into one category or the other—one of the best or one of the worst books ever written on Mormonism—there is still much to be said about where this work fits into the study of Mormonism and the study of American religion during the 1820s, 1830s, and 1840s. At its most basic level, *Refiner's Fire* is an effort by a respected historian of early (colonial and antebellum) America not merely to place the development of Mormonism in the context of the history of England's North American colonies and the United States in the early nineteenth-century but also to set it down firmly in the history of Christianity in Europe and the United States.[7] Yet this work is not the history of the founding of a new religion so much as it is a social and intellectual history that seeks to delineate the transmission and working out of a particular set of ideas and beliefs in the new United States. Perhaps it is this more than anything else that motivated certain defenders of the faith not only to criticize the work but also to chastise the press for publishing it.[8] Some of the same critics have also reproached me (who "ought to know better") for allowing my opinion of the book as being important to the study of American religion generally—and not simply to Mormon studies—to be printed on the dust jacket.[9]

What, then, is this *Refiner's Fire,* a book that has received both the highest praise and a level of negative response that has moved beyond criticism of the work itself to admonishment of both the press that issued it and those who find the book meritorious enough to recommend it to other readers? What is it about this book that might have led non-Mormons to give it such enthusiastic reviews and members of the Bancroft and SHEAR prize committees to give it such high honors?

Many LDS scholars seem to think the positive responses to Brooke's work are latter-day expressions of prejudice against Mormonism, the academic equivalent of the accusation that Mormonism is a cult that is so often made by members of fundamentalist and evangelical denominations. Perhaps there is something to this, but it seems to me that locating Brooke's study in the historiography of American religion—and not just the historiography of Mormonism—suggests quite a different explanation.

Since the 1850s, historians have been writing the story of American religion in terms of a particular metaphor: the American Protestant *mainstream.* Although actually peopled in the nineteenth century more by Methodists and Baptists than by members of other denominations, the mainstream also included that part of the "Magisterial Reformation" that established itself institutionally in Congregational and Presbyterian forms of Anglicanism. The putative mainstream also included what became of the Anglicans who held on to the episcopalian organizational pattern after the American Revolution (i.e., Episcopalians) and the Lutherans, as well as the upstart Campbellites (the Disciples of Christ). But it was the Methodist, Baptist, Presbyterian, and Congregationalist mainstream—primarily in its WASP formulation—that came to stand at the heart of a prevailing consensus about the faith of the nation. After Perry Miller's rediscovery of the Puritans in the first half of the twentieth century, the Puritan tradition was assimilated into this mainstream metaphor, and together they appeared to answer all the important questions about religion in the United States. Despite Richard Bushman's warning that Puritans rapidly turned into Yankees, Sydney Ahlstrom and a host of others came dangerously close to explaining the mainstream entirely in terms of the Puritan tradition.[10]

Two things happened to this explanation after the 1950s. The first was that the mainstream itself experienced a decline in numbers of adherents, particularly young ones. The other was that this decline underscored one of the critical elements of what may properly be called the Puritan interpretation of the nation's religious life—*declension*. The United States, the Protestant nation whose mountain top had been the days in which "visible saints" were the intellectual and cultural leaders of society, appeared to be spiraling steadily downward toward secularity.

This summary of the state of the study of American religion in the 1960s and 1970s is drawn more from survey texts than from the flood of monographs that lent both substance and nuance to the "Righteous Empire" story.[11] But as superficial as this description may be, it does not overstate either the significance of Puritanism or the pervasiveness of the mainstream metaphor in the way the story of American religion was—and sometimes still is—told. In those same years, however, the shape of American Protestantism was being dramatically and permanently altered by a resurgence of Protestant fundamentalism and an almost exponential growth of conservative evangelicalism and various forms of pentecostalism.[12]

To find an explanatory analogue clarifying what happened in the wake of this change, it is helpful to remember how race emerged in our national consciousness in the wake of the civil rights movement. Before the 1960s, black children who attended "white" movies saw themselves stereotyped as servants and buffoons, always ancillary to the main story line. Moreover, as was made clear in Malcolm X's *Autobiography*, they could not even find themselves in the history books, except as an incidental part, almost a footnote to the larger story of the nation. Since the 1960s, an important part of the cultural resolution of such oversight has been that real black people, not just stereotypes,

started appearing in the movies and on television. Moreover, the story of African Americans' own past, separate and apart from the white mainstream,
has been added to the history books and the history curriculum.

During these same years, something not unlike this was happening in
American religion. Throughout the twentieth century, especially after H. L.
Mencken, *Elmer Gantry,* and the Scopes trial provided a base for stereotypes,
a great multitude of Christian believers who stood outside the Puritan tradition and the liberal mainstream churches also suffered an image problem.
If they were included in the American story at all, they were usually pictured
as poverty-stricken anti-intellectual boobs with one eye on the collection
plate and the other on the Second Coming. More often than not they were
pictured as residing in Appalachia or in blue-collar ghettos of large metropolitan areas.[13] The notions feeding this abstraction included the widespread
perception that such Protestants were at the bottom of the social ladder and
the idea that their worship forms whipped up extreme emotionalism. Still,
as early as the late 1960s and certainly in the 1970s and 1980s, the emergence
of a vital conservative religious movement on the American (and world)
scene stimulated what can now be clearly recognized as consciousness-raising in the religious arena that was not unlike the consciousness-raising that
was occurring in the racial and gender arenas.

In this case, too, history became a potent weapon for combating popular stereotypes of fundamentalists, evangelicals, and Pentecostals. As early as
1957, Timothy L. Smith used a massive body of evidence in *Revivalism and
Social Reform* to assert that conservative Protestants who expected the millennium to commence shortly were really as much a part of America's religiocultural center as were the members of more liberal denominations. In
subsequent work during his notable clerical—Smith was an ordained minister in the Church of the Nazarene—and professorial career, Smith put forth
the idea of a *mosaic* as a metaphorical alternate to the mainstream for describing American religion and culture, a metaphor that did not so easily lend
itself to characterizing winners and losers. In continuing to search for the
historical and cultural roots of that part of American Christianity that has
always inhabited the banks of the religious mainstream, Smith's students and
friends, especially George Marsden, Nathan Hatch, and Jonathan Butler,
produced some of the most outstanding and influential volumes in the field
of American religious history that have been published in recent years. Marsden's *Fundamentalism in American Culture: The Shaping of Twentieth-Century Evangelicalism, 1870–1925,* Hatch's *Democratization of American Christianity,* and Butler's *Awash in a Sea of Faith: Christianizing the American People*
were all prizewinning volumes, and all have contributed mightily to a grow-

ing understanding of the metaphorical poverty of the idea of a (or the) Protestant mainstream as a key to understanding American religion.[14]

In a very broad sense, it is possible to say that Marsden, Hatch, Mark Noll, Grant Wacker, and a host of other scholars whose work deals with fundamentalism, evangelicalism, and pentecostalism have been trying to recover the roots of their own faith traditions. This is not true of John Brooke. Since he described himself as a secular humanist (in the MHA session mentioned above), his historical pilgrimage to the roots of America's radical religion can be interpreted as a search for his own religious heritage only if freethinking is understood to be a type of radical religion. Even so, the fruits of Brooke's search, so richly detailed in the *Refiner's Fire*, carry the labors of Timothy Smith and all those who followed in his footsteps a long way forward—or backward into the past.

What Brooke has done, by concentrating on the Mormons rather than on some variety of Protestantism that needed to be kept separate from all the others, is to trace virtually all of the radical religious forms in America—including the Quakers and the Methodists—not simply back to England but through England back to the European continent and the very heart of the radical Reformation.[15] This is no mean achievement, especially since in so doing Brooke has carried forward the work of demolishing the concept of Puritanism as the only touchstone really needed to understand the United States and its religious faith. I am convinced that this contextual aspect of Brooke's work (which consumes nearly a third of his book) goes a long way toward explaining why it received so many reviews in which it was called an outstanding book. That the *Refiner's Fire's* received both the Bancroft Prize and the SHEAR Prize is probably due to its placing radical religion at the very heart of the American religious commonwealth.

༄

Yet the subject of Brooke's work is the origins of Mormonism itself, not just the origins of its distinctive (and radical) theology. On that score, what is its bequest to Mormon studies? Does *Refiner's Fire* add to the store of knowledge about Mormon beginnings and, if so, in what way? Here the praise of those thoroughly conversant with the tradition Brooke describes has been far less enthusiastic, considerably qualified. This is partly due to the failure of the press and the author to ask for a prepublication reading from a Latter-day Saint scholar. A critical reading by a Latter-day Saint specializing in the history of early Mormonism might have pointed to particular discourse constructions that were sure to signal the author's less than complete comprehension of things Mormon.[16] Of much greater importance, a reading from someone with an experiential acquaintance with the LDS scriptures and belief system, as well as familiarity with LDS history and the historical sources available to the scholars who wish to understand the tradition fully, could have pointed the author to additional sources and simultaneously alerted him (and his press) to points where his conclusions needed shoring up.

For all that, in the long run, the value of Brooke's work is not likely to hinge on the extent of his intimate knowledge of every Mormon jot and tittle or the particular points where he has posited connections that are too tenuous. To a much greater extent than many reviewers noted, assessment of *Refiner's Fire* as a work of history is likely, finally, to rest on how well this author has made his argument that the Mormon prophet himself and those who became Mormon converts were a "prepared people."

In and of itself, this idea of Mormons as a prepared people is astonishingly helpful. Brooke's working it through in his extended study demonstrates that much. But even though this dimension of his work is its greatest strength, it is also its greatest weakness. Brooke's notion of how prophet and people were prepared turns out to be assailable because he focuses on the arcane and cryptic rather than the discernible and explicit. In *Refiner's Fire,* Brooke asserts that before they became Latter-day Saints, Joseph Smith himself and many of his followers were prepared for Mormonism by their involvement with hermeticism, magic, alchemy, and other radical forms of religion. In the case of the Mormon prophet's paternal and maternal families, as well as the families of many early converts, Brooke traces connections to radical Christianity that extended back for several generations (although the connecting lines were sometimes less than direct—second cousins, great aunts, and so on). Although he was mainly concerned about demonstrating that those who became followers of the prophet were already involved with or had an interest in the magical, hermetic, and alchemical components of early Mormonism, Brooke also cites numerous instances of what might be described as theological preparation, in which converted Saints recalled that they seem to have believed the gospel even before they heard it. Perhaps because he was attuned to the abstruse and esoteric while being scripturally tone-deaf, he did not pursue the significance of this type of readiness to hear the Mormon message.

Although this conception, this idea of a prepared people, is not entirely novel, Brooke's work provides a fine-screened grid of supporting evidence that is helpful in accounting for Mormonism's appeal to particular people and certain groups in England as well as in the United States. But as serviceable as this idea of a prepared people is in explaining the appeal of Mormonism, Brooke concentrates too much on the recondite and radical aspects of this new faith. At no point does he acknowledge that the religious and cultural situation into which Mormonism made its way was one in which, despite Tom Paine and other skeptical Deists, authority continued to rest in the Bible—the Bible alone, *sola scriptura.*

Surely an intense fascination with alternative routes to the supernatural was present in the nation during the childhood, adolescence, and adulthood of Joseph Smith Jr. But as Nathan Hatch pointed out more than a decade earlier, for most people the scriptures were the source of information and truth.[17] For all Brooke's diligent digging into the proto-Mormon past, he fails to acknowledge (and perhaps even to understand) that for many—and quite possibly most of those who became Saints—all it took for them to join the ranks of the people prepared to hear the "restored gospel" was a literal reading of the Bible and a certain acceptance that prophecy would be fulfilled.[18] Moreover, such converts to the new faith were not all consigned to the ranks of virtually nameless followers who played little role in shaping Mormonism.

Mormons themselves have long known how critical a literal Bible reading was to the development of Mormon theology and doctrine, and it has also often been pointed out to the scholarly world. In particular, it was the subject of Marvin Hill's 1968 University of Chicago dissertation. It was also documented by Gordon Irving in a major *BYU Studies* article in 1973, and in the first three chapters of Philip Barlow's Harvard dissertation, which was published in 1991 as *Mormons and the Bible: The Place of the Latter-day Saints in American Religion.*[19] This characteristic of the faith was powerfully reinforced by none other than Timothy L. Smith himself in one of the two inaugural Mormon History Association Tanner Lectures in 1980, a lecture subsequently published in the *Journal of Mormon History.*[20] Although Grant Underwood's *Millenarian World of Early Mormonism* was not published until 1993, when Brooke's manuscript was already in press, Underwood had been pointing out the extent to which belief in the Bible was a main feature of early Mormonism in papers given in the annual meetings of several different professional organizations.[21]

The existing work on early Saints who were mainly, if not solely, prepared for Mormonism by their knowledge of the Bible was underscored and carried forward by the discovery and ensuing publication of the missionary journals of William E. McLellin.[22] These rare documents, which the forger Mark Hofmann once claimed to have found, were located in the vault of the First Presidency of the LDS Church in 1986, but their discovery was not announced until 1991.[23] At the request of the general authorities of the LDS Church, I had read these journals before that announcement was made, and I realized they are some of the most extensive and informative documents covering the period between 1831 and 1836 in Mormon history that have ever come to light.[24] They reveal that it was his biblical knowledge alone, not any background of inquisitiveness about or interest in alchemy or the occult, that prepared this Illinois schoolteacher to receive the Mormon message. After he joined the church in 1831, he became a leading elder, an apostle, who was called to be a member of the first "traveling high council," or, as it is better known, the Council of the Twelve.

Published the same year that Brooke's book was, these contemporaneous journals do not add much to the existing store of historical evidence that must be drawn on to develop pictures of the Mormon prophet himself or what was going on at the very center of the movement. But they do provide a full and clear picture of how this new gospel was presented to potential converts. Perhaps of greater significance here, these intimate accounts say a great deal about how leading Mormons talked about their new belief system among themselves and about how the gospel was preached to nascent congregations of church members between 1831 and 1836, years that coincide with the building of the first Mormon temple in Kirtland, Ohio.

McLellin was one of those who sometimes sat in the councils of the mighty—and who talked at length with those who were in the prophet's inner circle—and although his writings do not cover the entire movement as it came into existence, they provide an incredibly rich picture of Mormonism as it took shape in the midwestern and northeastern United States and the southern Ontario countryside in the early 1830s. In McLellin's meticulous entries about 434 preaching appointments, accounts that usually note the exact biblical text as well as the topics on which more than thirty Mormon preachers expounded, and the more than 603 separate topics they considered (71 percent are described in some detail), this astonishing resource opens wide a hitherto clouded window.[25] Through this opening, it is possible to see how Mormonism was presented and to some extent how it was perceived by those who joined the movement during the very same period in which many of the alchemical elements deriving from Masonry would have to have been fused with radical Christian beliefs to, in Brooke's felicitous phrase, "make the Mormon cosmology."[26]

None of us knew about these journals when most of the research for *Refiner's Fire* was being done. Although I sought permission from LDS authorities to undertake a scholarly edition of these documents almost as soon as I completed my first reading of them, I had not seen them when I read Brooke's manuscript. Had I known what they contained, I surely should have advised him (and his editor at Cambridge University Press) of their existence and their content. But since they were not available as his manuscript took shape, Brooke could not have known that these magnificent accounts of the early years of the church contain absolutely no direct evidence and almost no indirect evidence to support his picture of a movement and an institution whose grounding and superstructure were permeated with esoterica. The absence of such evidence in the earliest extended contemporaneous LDS source cannot, of course, be taken as evidence that hermetical/alchemical elements were not present; indeed, evidence to the contrary is abundant in the Mormon historical canon.[27] But the lack of references to this aspect of Mormonism indicates that it could not have been as pervasive at the movement's outset as Brooke argues in *Refiner's Fire.*

In the preface to his work, Brooke acknowledges that he has made no effort to tell the whole of the story of Mormon beginnings. That concession notwithstanding, the subtitle of his work is *The Making of Mormon Cosmology, 1644–1844*. This seriously overstates the case. In failing to point to all that the Saints took from the Bible—and to those who were prepared to hear the Mormon message simply because they were familiar with the Old Testament and the New Testament—*Refiner's Fire* neglects definitive components of that cosmology and an ingredient in the LDS mix that is absolutely critical to explaining Mormonism's appeal, not simply to the thousands who responded to the message during the prophet's lifetime but also to the millions who have been responding ever since.

For that reason, despite the significant contribution this study makes to our overall understanding of the history of religion in the colonial period and in the era of the early republic and despite what Brooke has added to our knowledge of important features of the early LDS story, I think it is unlikely *Refiner's Fire* will become a standard work, one of those about which a scholarly consensus develops regarding whether it is essential to the study of American religion or the study of Mormonism. For the foreseeable future, no adequate bibliography for a graduate paper on the history of religion in American culture or on early Mormonism will be complete without it. Nevertheless, because, after the first third of the book, this work is so focused on Mormonism, it will not take its place alongside more general works (such as those written by Jon Butler and Nathan Hatch) for the study of religion and American culture. Moreover, because its LDS focus is so foreshortened, capturing a significant part but by no means the whole, readers wanting to understand the beginnings of Mormonism are still likely to turn to older works: Fawn McKay Brodie's *No Man Knows My History* (first published in 1945); Donna Hill's *Joseph Smith, the First Mormon* (1977); and Richard Bushman's *Joseph Smith and the Beginnings of Mormonism* (1984).[28]

Notes

1. The programs of the annual meetings of the Mormon History Association bring together people who either write Mormon history or have an intense interest in the subject to hear papers in which LDS historians, RLDS historians, non-Mormon historians, and, much more rarely, anti-Mormon historians describe their work-in-progress or report on studies that have been completed.

2. John Brooke, *The Refiner's Fire: The Making of Mormon Cosmology, 1644–1844* (New York: Cambridge University Press, 1994); Martin Marty, "Saints for These Latter-days," *Commonweal* 122 (March 10, 1995): 26.

3. William J. Hamblin, Daniel C. Peterson, and George L. Mitton published an exhaustive critique in *Reviews of Books on the Book of Mormon* 6, no. 2 (1994): 1–58. An abridged version of this unflattering appraisal was published in *BYU Studies* 34, no. 4 (1994–95): 167–81. For another negative assessment of the book, see Davis Bitton, review of *The Refiner's Fire*, by John L. Brooke, *BYU Studies* 34, no. 4 (1994–95): 182–92.

4. The goal of this elaborate and expanding undertaking involving many LDS scholars is to encourage and support research on the Book of Mormon and other ancient scriptures.

5. According to the statement of purpose published in its newsletter, the main research interests of FARMS are ancient history, language, literature, culture, geography, politics, and law relevant to the scriptures. Its publication list reflects these interests, but it also includes a variety of items that deal with the coming forth of the Book of Mormon, as well as with its context and content.

6. Richard Bushman, "The Mysteries of Mormonism," *Journal of the Early Republic* 15, no. 3 (1995): 501–55; Philip Barlow, "Decoding Mormonism," *Christian Century* 113 (January 17, 1996): 52–53.

7. Brooke's critics dispute whether he is respected by quoting the most negative statements that can be found in the reviews of his first book, *The Heart of the Commonwealth: Society and Political Culture in Worcester County, Massachusetts, 1713–1861* (New York: Cambridge University Press, 1989). Despite reviews that were not filled with unqualified praise, this work was also a prizewinning book, having shared one of the major prizes awarded annually by the Organization of American Historians.

8. In a telephone conversation, Frank Smith, Brooke's editor at Cambridge University Press, acknowledged receiving a letter from scholars at BYU chiding the press for publishing the book.

9. Louis Midgley, "The Shipps Odyssey in Retrospect," *Review of Books on the Book of Mormon* 7, no. 2 (1995): 231.

10. Robert Baird, *Religion in America; or, An Account of the Origin, Progress, Relation to the State, and Present Condition of Evangelical Churches in the United States, with Notices of the Unevangelical Denominations* (New York: Harper and Brothers, 1844); Perry Miller, *New England Mind: From Colony to Province* (Cambridge, Mass.: Harvard University Press, 1953); Perry Miller, *Errand into the Wilderness* (Cambridge, Mass.: Harvard University Press, 1956); Perry Miller and Thomas H. Johnson, *The Puritans* (New York: Harper and Row, 1963); Richard L. Bushman, *From Puritan to Yankee: Character and Social Order in Connecticut, 1690–1765* (Cambridge, Mass.: Harvard University Press, 1967); Robert T. Handy, *A Christian America: Protestant*

Hopes and Historical Realities (New York: Oxford University Press, 1971); Sydney Ahlstrom, *A Religious History of the American People* (New Haven, Conn.: Yale University Press, 1972).

11. Just as the "Great Basin Kingdom" took on reality in space and time after the Mormon kingdom was so described by Leonard J. Arrington in the title of his magisterial economic history of the Latter-day Saints in the second half of the nineteenth century, so "Righteous Empire" took on reality in space and time after Martin E. Marty used the expression as a way of summing up the Protestant experience in the United States. His influential work won the National Book Award. See Leonard J. Arrington, *Great Basin Kingdom: An Economic History of the Latter-day Saints, 1830–1900* (Cambridge, Mass.: Harvard University Press, 1958; reprint, Salt Lake City: University of Utah Press, 1993); and Martin Marty, *Righteous Empire: The Protestant Experience in America* (New York: Dial, 1970).

12. In the 1980s, the changing shape of the conservative Christian community became evident in the growth of megachurches and the expansion of several highly visible television ministries. See Dean M. Kelley, *Why Conservative Churches Are Growing: A Study in the Sociology of Religion*, new and updated ed. (San Francisco: Harper and Row, 1977); Wade Clark Roof and William McKinney, *American Mainline Religion: Its Changing Shape and Future* (New Brunswick, N.J.: Rutgers University Press, 1987); and Robert Wuthnow, *The Restructuring of American Religion: Society and Faith since World War II* (Princeton, N.J.: Princeton University Press, 1988), especially chapters 7 and 8.

13. There is a remarkable affinity between this image and the image of the Mormons in the late nineteenth century and early twentieth. Both were outsiders, but while the Latter-day Saints were perceived as foreign, the fundamentalist/evangelical/Pentecostal image was an image of domestic aliens. Polygamy was missing from the latter image, but in both cases the image was of anti-intellectual—nay unintelligent—zealots focused on the end time. In both cases, the leaders were also depicted as a greedy and probably dishonest lot. In sum, members of both groups were clearly "other."

14. Timothy L. Smith, *Revivalism and Social Reform* (New York: Harper and Row, 1957); George Marsden, *Fundamentalism in American Culture: The Shaping of Twentieth-Century Evangelicalism, 1870–1925* (New York: Oxford University Press, 1980); Nathan O. Hatch, *The Democratization of American Christianity* (New Haven, Conn.: Yale University Press, 1989); Jonathan Butler, *Awash in a Sea of Faith: Christianizing the American People* (Cambridge, Mass.: Harvard University Press, 1990). Marsden's, Hatch's, and Butler's works all received major prizes awarded by the American Society of Church History (ASCH). Stephen J. Stein's monumental study, *The Shaker Experience in America* (New Haven, Conn.: Yale University Press, 1992), also won top ASCH honors. All four of these books were concerned with American religion outside the traditional mainstream.

15. For some suggestions about the radicalism of early Methodism, see Nathan O. Hatch's 1994 Tanner lecture, "Mormonism and Methodism: Popular Religion in the Crucible of the Free Market," *Journal of Mormon History* 20 (Spring 1994): 24–44.

16. As a non-Mormon historian of Mormonism, I became aware of the importance of getting details correct early on. It happened this way. Once, when I was doing research for my doctoral dissertation in the collections of the Utah State Historical

Society in 1964, I overheard two LDS historians (whose identity I still do not know) discussing a recently published article written by Howard Lamar, a distinguished member of the history department at Yale University. In the article, "Statehood for Utah: A Different Path," *Utah Historical Quarterly* 39 (Fall 1971): 307–27, "Latter-day Saint" had been written as "Latter Day Saint."

One of the historians asked, "What did you think of Howard's article?" The other replied, "Well, he might be on to something. But you can be pretty sure that anyone who doesn't know that Latter-day Saint is spelled with a hyphen and a little *d* can't possibly know too much about Mormon history." While this may seem extreme, the very process of getting details right is not simply of intrinsic importance. It also leads to an increased understanding of someone else's religious tradition and can thus help avoid misrepresentation.

17. Nathan O. Hatch, "*Sola Scriptura* and *Novus Ordo Seclorum*," in *The Bible in America: Essays in Cultural History*, ed. Nathan O. Hatch and Mark A. Noll (New York: Oxford University Press, 1982), 59–78.

18. See "The Reality of the Restoration in LDS Theology and Mormon Experience," herein.

19. Marvin S. Hill, "The Role of Christian Primitivism in the Origin and Development of the Mormon Kingdom, 1830–1844" (Ph.D. dissertation, University of Chicago, 1968); Gordon Irving, "Mormons and the Bible in the 1830s," *BYU Studies* 13 (Summer 1973): 473–78; Philip L. Barlow, *Mormons and the Bible: The Place of the Latter-day Saints in American Religion* (New York: Oxford University Press, 1991). On several occasions, Grant Underwood and Barlow presented papers at professional meetings, including meetings of the American Society of Church History and the Mormon History Association, touching on the Saints' regard for the biblical text.

20. Timothy L. Smith, "The Book of Mormon in a Biblical Culture," *Journal of Mormon History* 7 (1980): 3–21.

21. Grant Underwood, *Millenarian World of Early Mormonism* (Urbana: University of Illinois Press, 1993).

22. Jan Shipps and John W. Welch, eds., *The Journals of William E. McLellin, 1831–1836* (Provo, Utah, and Urbana: *BYU Studies* and University of Illinois Press, 1994).

23. As far as can be determined, these journals had lain there unnoticed and undisturbed since they were purchased by the church for $50 in 1909 and placed in the First Presidency's vault rather than the archives, probably because Joseph F. Smith, who was church president at the time, wanted to "prevent the writings of this unfortunate and erratic man, whose attitude after his apostasy was inimical to the Prophet Joseph Smith from falling into unfriendly hands." Richard E. Turley Jr., *Victims: The LDS Church and the Mark Hofmann Case* (Urbana: University of Illinois Press, 1992), 249.

24. This request was transmitted to me by the managing director of the LDS Church's Historical Department, Richard E. Turley Jr., who indicated that Richard Bushman and I were being asked to read the journals before their discovery was announced because "the Brethren" were concerned that the Hofmann connection and the fact that McLellin had left the church and had been branded as apostate could lead to renewed speculation in the press about what these journals contained and to charges that the church had been hiding them. If questions arose about the content of the journals, they could be referred to Bushman or me.

25. M. Teresa Baer, "Charting the Missionary Work of William E. McLellin: A Content Analysis," in *The Journals of William E. McLellin, 1831–1836,* ed. Shipps and Welch, 379–405.

26. The subtitle of Brooke's *Refiner's Fire* is *The Making of Mormon Cosmology, 1644–1844.*

27. Richard L. Bushman, *Joseph Smith and the Beginnings of Mormonism* (Urbana: University of Illinois Press, 1984), argues that such elements were a part of the premodern universe the Smith family and other early Mormons inhabited. See also D. Michael Quinn, *Early Mormonism and the Magic World View,* 2d ed. (Salt Lake City: Signature Books, 1998), especially chapters 5 and 6.

28. Fawn McKay Brodie, *No Man Knows My History: The Life of Joseph Smith, the Prophet* (1945; 2d ed. rev. and enl., New York: Alfred A. Knopf, 1976); Donna Hill, *Joseph Smith, the First Mormon* (Garden City, N.Y.: Doubleday, 1977); Bushman, *Joseph Smith and the Beginnings of Mormonism.*

PART 3

PUTTING RELIGION AT THE HEART OF
MORMON HISTORY AND HISTORY AT THE
HEART OF MORMONISM

Throughout my years of teaching at IUPUI, my joint appointment in religious studies and history complicated my academic life. Always I had a double dose of department meetings to attend and committee assignments to fulfill. I also had to contend with dual sets of departmental requirements for everything from promotion and tenure to negotiating release time and research support. But my teaching assignments were not doubled; they were split between history and religious studies. Typically, in each semester's history department offerings, I would teach a sophomore U.S. survey course on the history of the nation before 1865 or after 1865. In the religious studies department, I was nearly always assigned to teach a section of the introductory course. In alternate semesters, I taught upper-division (i.e., junior or senior level) courses in history and religious studies.

In the semester in which I taught an upper-division history course, it was usually a course on the Civil War and Reconstruction.[1] In the semester in which I taught an upper-division religious studies course, it was usually "Varieties of American Religion," Indiana University's name for a course about the "alternative" religious groups outside the mainstream (which by this time reflected the sociologist Will Herberg's *Protestant, Catholic, Jew* configuration). Preparing lectures for two upper-division courses in two disciplines kept me very busy.

Even though I had done well in the graduate course on the Civil War and Reconstruction that I took to make up for what I failed to learn at Utah State about this part of the nation's past, I very quickly discovered that while the subject is fascinating, it is very complicated. Getting ready to present lectures and lead discussion in classes that invariably included history buffs who knew more about the Civil War battles than I did turned out to be a chore. In the alternate semester, when I switched gears into religious studies, I also had to spend enormous time and effort to "get up to speed" so that I could present lectures on all sorts of different religious groups in the United States, from Shakers and Quakers to Santeria, B'hai, and beyond.[2]

As I look back, my first few years of teaching seem more than anything else to be a monographic blur. Knowing I must add substance to the quite rudimentary lectures I had prepared in my first pass through teaching these demanding upper-division history and religious studies courses, I read and read and read about battles and leaders (to use a Civil War term) and about religion outside the American mainstream. Then, to "publish rather than perish," between semesters I conducted further research, wrote articles, started preparing a manuscript on Mormon history, and struggled to keep up with the expanding body of LDS scholarly literature.

Like most instructors in their initial years of college teaching, I found myself under tremendous pressure. I was always working to get specific lectures prepared and to get certain research and writing tasks done, so much so that I never seemed to have time to step back to look for connections among all the things I was reading. What happened instead is that I created for myself two separate spheres, one for history and the other for religious studies.

After I had been teaching for several years, the curriculum committee of the School of Liberal Arts decreed that freshman seminars should be developed in every department except foreign languages. Since one of the purposes was to counter the anonymity that seemed to accompany attending classes in what was rapidly becoming a large urban university, registration in each one would be limited to fifteen students. This requirement was not a problem for the religious studies department because our "Introduction to Religious Studies" class could easily be adapted to a seminar format. In the history department, however, a seminar that would be called "Introduction to Historical Studies" had to be developed. Our resourceful departmental chair made an agreement with the dean that would allow faculty members willing to develop and offer an experimental section of this seminar to be relieved of teaching their usual upper-division courses for one semester. The opportunity to do so was open to one faculty member who specialized in American history and one who specialized in European history.

Jumping at the chance to skip a semester facing all those military history buffs with their urgent questions about such things as the difference in the buttons on the uniforms worn by the members of various regiments in the Union army, I volunteered to develop the history department's introductory course. The upshot was that during the 1978 fall semester I taught two freshman seminars, one designed to enlighten students about history, what it is and how it gets written, and the other intended to acquaint students with the religious studies discipline, a main goal of which was clarifying the relationship between religion and culture. Because I had been concentrating so heavily on the Civil War, on one hand, and on various nonmainstream religious groups, on the other, I was still working within two more or less self-contained disciplines at that point.

Although my work on Mormonism could well have served as a bridge between history and religion, it had not done so.[3] During the semester in which I led introductory seminars in both history and religious studies, however, connections that had theretofore been obscured came flooding to the surface. So much so that, at certain points, I discovered that what we were considering in one of these seminars was appropriate for the other, and what I was teaching in both spilled over into my work on Mormonism.

◌◦

Trying one day to help students in the history seminar understand the difference between history as it happens (raw experience), the historical record (surviving accounts of events), and a historian's reconstruction of what happened in the past (e.g., written history), I hit on what I dubbed an X-Y-Z method of explanation. To make the necessary distinctions clear, I drew a set of boxes on the chalkboard (see figure 9). This was my way of setting forth clear distinctions between the past; firsthand and secondhand accounts of events (technically primary and secondary evidence); and later reconstructions of the same events, X, Y, and Z. My original reason for designing this explanatory device was quite simple: I wanted students to understand and be able to articulate their understanding of the correspondence between a historical event and firsthand accounts—say in a letter or diary—and secondhand accounts—say in a newspaper—of that same event. At the same time, I was anxious to make sure they realized that when historians reconstruct events (create "Z's"), they do not have direct access to those events (X) but must work from the historical record (Y). This explanatory device did far more than I expected, for it became the basis for symbolic discourse that everyone in the class understood.

Most of the fifteen students in the seminar were very bright, and all were extremely interested in the topic. As a result, when I used commonsense examples, drawn mainly from my reading of Civil War history, and asked the students to use my X-Y-Z distinctions in considering how an account of a military engagement might differ depending on the place the observer hap-

X = *The Past* everything that ever happened	Y = *The Historical Record* written visual aural & artifactual	Z = *Reconstruction* *of the Past* what results when historians do history

Figure 9

pened to be standing and how a history written by a Southerner might differ from one written by someone from the North, an exciting class discussion ensued. It ranged across such complicated historiographical issues as the
difference in the value of historical accounts that rest on firsthand as opposed
to secondhand reports of events; the difference in the value of carefully preserved statistical data as opposed to estimates recorded by well-informed
observers; and whether, to someone doing history, a picture is worth a thousand words. Another dimension of historiography that made its way into the
discussion was the importance of the perspective from which historians do
history, as well as the influence of their training, or lack of same, on the way
they use the historical record to reconstruct the past. Moreover, without being
prompted, members of the class brought up the important matter of the
difference in historical accounts and narrative reconstructions made by men
and women and people of different races, classes, and so forth. From that
point, no matter what the assigned readings or topics considered were, the
level of discourse never returned to the level usually present in class discussion among freshmen in public institutions of higher learning, especially one
with virtually open admission policies.

The elevated discourse level was particularly evident in a discussion of
George Orwell's famous novel *1984*, which is essentially a treatise on the
power of history and how, in a radically authoritarian state, history can be
controlled and manipulated. Because this class was being offered when Wa-
tergate was still fresh in American minds, the question of the connection
between history and the government's desire to control information during
the Vietnam War made the reading of Orwell's work considerably more than
an ordinary academic exercise.

With the questions the history students conjured up after I drew those
X-Y-Z boxes on the chalkboard and their observations about *1984* still reverberating in my mind, I entered into a discussion in the "Introduction to

Religious Studies" seminar in which the topic was the difference between scripture and history. One of the texts I had selected to illuminate the religion-culture interface was John G. Gager's *Kingdom and Community: The Social World of Early Christianity,* a work in which the beginnings of Christianity are presented from a perspective that does not privilege canonized accounts of what happened.[4] Working through this text with a seminar in which several of the students came from fundamentalist and evangelical Christian backgrounds proved to be so difficult that I began to wonder if I had chosen the wrong text. But after I imported the X-Y-Z device from the history seminar into the religious studies seminar, students started to see that a canonized account is one of many reconstructions of events that happened in the past, but because it is the one defined as correct by a religious institution, it is the one that members of that institution regard as true. After that, students in the religious studies class found the concept of canonization easy to understand, and from that point on, not only the students but also the instructor made clearer distinctions between the historical record, profane (i.e., secular) history—history "as it actually happened," to use Leopold von Ranke's telling phrase—and the past as it is captured in scripture.

Perhaps it was coincidence, but during this same semester I starting working on an interrelated set of thorny Mormon history problems having to do with the nature of history, how history figured in the Book of Mormon, and so on, problems that would eventually be addressed in my first book. I was initially surprised and then delighted to discover that making use of the X-Y-Z device allowed me to formulate new questions, questions that could be answered only if I stopped putting religion and history in separate spheres.

Although I cannot point to a "Eureka" moment in which all became clear, before the end of the semester in which I led these two freshman seminars I recognized in the LDS experience an intimate relationship between religion and history. Unlike William Miller, the founder of the Adventist movement who returned from the War of 1812 to search the scriptures and find in them a calendar on which he could read the day and the hour of Christ's Second Coming, Joseph Smith Jr. was not simply one more earnest but unlearned interpreter of scripture. Unlike the Campbells, father and son, who found a warrant in the existing scriptures for the organization of the (Campbellite) Church of Christ, a new denomination whose goal was ending all Protestant denominational division, young Joseph did not conclude as a consequence of careful reading of the Old and New Testaments that the "true Church of Jesus Christ" was not on the earth in the 1820s and that it had not been on the earth since the time of a "Great Apostasy" at the end of the apostolic age.

Casting the story within a developmental metaphor, during Mormonism's gestation and parturition, not only the Mormon prophet but also all the neophyte Saints engaged in a process that is comparable to and understandable as "history making." In a very real sense, these Mormonites, as they were called, became historical revisionists. They added what they were confident was reliable new evidence (i.e., the Book of Mormon) to what was then known about the history of Christianity, and they reinterpreted situations and events described in both Old and New Testaments in light of this new evidence.

Their revised understanding of Christian history set Joseph Smith's followers apart. Along with most American Protestants, they believed that Roman Catholicism was allied with Satan, but they also rejected and were rejected by what they described as "sectarian Christianity." Moreover, in spite of a body of seekers who moved in and out of various "new moves," the Saints shared no real common ground with any of the multitude of religious innovators in the New World Eden that had somehow managed to get itself organized as the United States. Mormonism was not just a new denomination, not just a new church. Its firm grounding within a radically altered historical framework allowed Mormonism to become for its adherents the "restoration of all things," including priesthood and ancient ordinances of comfort and salvation, as well as a divinely legitimated ecclesiastical institution. Significantly, also, Mormonism became the vehicle for the reconstitution of the family of Abraham and the gathering of the Saints in Zion, God's "new Israel" on the American frontier. As all this happened before their very eyes, the Mormons carried the ancient Hebrew story and its early Christian recapitulation with them as they moved into a "new dispensation of the fulness of times."

Introducing the very notion of what history is to beginning history students and considering, at length and essentially from the outside, what happened in the earliest time of Christian beginnings allowed me to see that the history making that goes on at the genesis of a new religion differs from ordinary history making. The history of religious beginnings involves the irruption of the sacred into the profane realm in an event or series of events that are sufficiently anomalous to sustain supernatural explanation. This is the sine qua non. Yet in every known case of the beginnings of significant religious movements, reconstructions of what happened come from both the inside and outside.

History making of even the most rudimentary sort—say the kind that goes on as professionals argue about what sorts of structures deserve places on the National Register of Historic Places—leads to a struggle over control of the past. In the religious arena, the arguments are deeper and more complex because they have to do with supernatural as well as natural things, with types and antitypes, prophecy and its fulfillment. But struggles over the proper way to preserve and recount the story of a nation's history and struggles over the composition of a canon of scripture both involve the preservation of corporate memories.

The poet Wallace Stevens is said to have held that humanity does not live in a place so much as in the memory of a place. This suggests that perceptions of reality are social constructions. If this is so, then history making is not an inconsequential enterprise that a society can turn over to amateurs and dilettantes—or entirely to professional historians. Furthermore, students of what might be called secular history sometimes fail to recognize what all students of religious studies seem to know almost instinctively: historical narrative is not the only manner in which corporate memory is preserved. Symbols, rituals, liturgical formulations, pageants, and pilgrimages also capture, preserve, and transmit memory.

✧

Yet history is crucially important to the continuing life of faiths as well as nations. This is obvious in the way in which the stories of their beginnings are told. Much of the new Mormon history has been devoted to the beginnings of Mormonism.[5] Carrying that discussion forward is not the purpose of this section of this book, however. Instead, my purpose is to demonstrate that it is not merely at a religion's beginnings that the sacred may be discerned in history.

The three historical essays in this section are about three different chronological periods in LDS history. The first is a description of how an understanding of the truth of the Old Testament was conjoined to the appearance of the Book of Mormon to demonstrate to the early Saints the sacredness of what they were experiencing, making their understanding of the restoration literal rather than symbolic. This essay was published in a collection edited by Richard T. Hughes called *The American Quest for the Primitive Church.*[6] It was originally prepared for a conference entitled "The Restoration Ideal in American History," held at Abilene Christian University in 1985.

In 1983, Ron Watt, who was responsible for putting together a Utah State Historical Society/Sons of the Utah Pioneers Lecture Series, invited me to present a lecture on Brigham Young. I later turned this lecture into an article for publication in a special issue of *Journal of the West* devoted to religion in the American West.[7] It describes the extent to which Young's effective leadership during the Mormon trek and, more especially, in the Great Basin kingdom has been interpreted in secular terms and argues that Young's long-term importance to Mormonism lies in the manner in which he realized the vision the Prophet Joseph Smith set forth.

The final essay in this section moves forward in the chronology of Mormonism and describes the Mormon diaspora and the creation of outposts of Zion all across the United States in the fifteen years or so after the end of World War II. The story of the way in which building meetinghouses in the mid-twentieth century recapitulated building Zion in the nineteenth century is remarkable, and it places religion at the heart of making LDS history in the modern context. This essay began as a Juanita Brooks Lecture presented at Dixie College, a version of which was published as a pamphlet by the college.[8] It was the inaugural lecture given on the occasion of my dear friend Doug Alder's inauguration as president of Dixie College.

All three of these essays were written after I first taught those two introductory courses and after I completed the manuscript of *Mormonism: The Story of a New Religious Tradition,* a work that also is concerned with the interaction of history and religion. In all three, although not brought to the surface, my X-Y-Z approach to the past is a critical part of my argument.

Notes

1. I was not a specialist on the history of the Civil War. As a result of negotiating a half-time appointment in the history department (which would locate me in the discipline in which I had been trained), I had to take "potluck" with regard to what upper-division history course I would teach. It was up to me to learn enough to teach it. Because of the unexpected death of the professor who usually offered the popular and often oversubscribed Civil War and Reconstruction course, this was the course the department asked me to teach.

2. As can be imagined, I was always pleased to reach the point in this course where I could turn the spotlight onto LDS history.

3. My perception of myself as a historian obscured connections between the disciplines of history and religious studies. This perception flowed from my graduate training. My dissertation and the articles derived from it were history, as was my investigation of perceptions of the Saints. I had borrowed from sociology, but what I wrote was not sociology but history. My work on Mormonism to this point in my career had all been done within the history sphere.

4. John G. Gager, *Kingdom and Community: The Social World of Early Christianity* (Englewood Cliffs, N.J.: Prentice-Hall, 1975). This was one of the volumes in the Prentice-Hall Studies in Religion Series edited by John P. Reeder Jr. and John F. Wilson.

5. Some of the more important essays in this literature are in George D. Smith, ed., *Faithful History: Essays on Writing Mormon History* (Salt Lake City: Signature Books, 1992).

6. Jan Shipps, "The Reality of the Restoration and the Restoration Ideal in the Mormon Tradition," in *The American Quest for the Primitive Church*, ed. Richard T. Hughes (Urbana: University of Illinois Press, 1988), 181–95.

7. Jan Shipps, "Brigham Young and His Times: A Continuing Force in Mormonism," *Journal of the West* 23 (January 1984): 48–54.

8. Jan Shipps, *The Scattering of the Gathering and the Gathering of the Scattered: The Mid-Twentieth-Century Mormon Diaspora* (St. George, Utah: Dixie College, 1991).

11

The Reality of the Restoration in LDS Theology and Mormon Experience

The concept of restoration can be found in the Judeo-Christian scriptural materials from the biblical story's first major turning point, when Eve and Adam were thrust from the garden, to its last, when John the Apostle was banished to the Isle of Patmos and there beheld a series of apocalyptic visions. What may properly be described as a restoration motif can be identified in the different parts of the Old Testament, as well as in the New Testament, although its presentation takes different forms. It is especially evident in the Psalms and in the postexilic materials. Again and again Hebrew psalmists and prophets speak of returning to a paradisaical situation wherein the earth will be renewed, the blind will see, the lame will leap for joy, hunger will be satisfied, righteousness and truth will prevail, and the covenant between God and his people will be reinvested with meaning. In addition to restoration references of a general character, the Old Testament includes restoration passages that are very specific. Following the division of Israel into northern and southern kingdoms, and after the desolation of Jerusalem, the destruction of the temple, and the Babylonian captivity, Isaiah, Jeremiah, Ezekiel, and other prophetic figures predict the reunion of Jacob's family through an in-gathering of the members of the scattered tribes. With the "whole body of Israel" restored, they look forward to the restoration of the kingdom of God that would include rebuilding both the city of Jerusalem and the temple, restoring them to the glory they had possessed in King Solomon's day.

In the New Testament, itself the canonized story of a restoration movement, the Old Testament's generalized restoration motif is reflected in the various Gospel accounts that picture Jesus feeding the hungry, healing the sick, making the lame man "take up his bed and walk," and causing the blind to see. Although his followers believed that Jesus was the son of a virgin, that he was Immanuel, whose coming the prophet Isaiah had foretold, the crucifixion frustrated further fulfillment of specific restoration prophecy having to do with the Messiah's bringing about the restoration of a civic kingdom of God. The cross, signifying the crucifixion, became the symbol of a new covenant that brought Gentiles as well as Jews into a covenantal relationship with the divine. As is detailed in the Acts of the Apostles, the apostolic church became the guardian of the social reality of the new covenant. The concept of the kingdom of God as a precise place in space and time gave way to the "gospel of the Kingdom of God" and the idea that "the kingdom of God is within you," that is, within the Christian community and, by extension, within individual Christians. Yet the enormous appeal and continuing power of restoration promises that admit interpretations of great specificity are clearly indicated by the inclusion of the Book of Revelation at the end of the New Testament canon.

Considering the emphasis on restoration found in the Bible—obvious even from the foregoing bare-bones review—it is not surprising that so many movements in the modern history of the Judeo-Christian tradition have a restorationist base. (In the same vein, in view of its firm rooting in the Judeo-Christian tradition, it is not surprising that the United States has become the primary political agent for the "redemption of Zion" since the close of World War II.)

It is somewhat surprising, however, that so many Christians have understood restoration to be virtually synonymous with New Testament primitivism. Whether it represents little more than a vague longing, a nostalgia for living in Christianity's golden age, or whether it represents a rigorous, full-scale, good-faith effort to restore "the essentials of primitive Christianity" in an institutional context, the search for the restoration *essence* (as it would be stated in Platonic terms) has been concentrated on the apostolic era.

Mormonism is a conspicuous departure from this pattern.[1] Without question, the biblical account of the church during the apostolic age was important to seekers who followed the Mormon prophet. But unlike the restorationist understandings of the Campbellite, Seventh-day Baptist, and other American primitivist movements, Mormonism's understanding of itself as a restoration movement began with the belief that the Church of Jesus Christ was removed from the earth when direct communication between divinity and humanity ceased at the end of the apostolic age. Furthermore, Mormonism's understanding of itself as *the* (not "a") restoration proceeded from the assumption that restoration could and would come about when *and only when* direct communication between humanity and divinity was reopened. This is to say, before restoration could occur, one who could speak for God, a prophet, would have to come forth.

The belief that Joseph Smith Jr. was such a person and that through him restoration was effected arises from an extraordinary set of theological claims that together establish for Mormons *an unbroken line of fulfilled prophecy* from Isaiah, Ezekiel, and Daniel, through Revelation to Joseph Smith and beyond. Whereas from outside the faith these claims may appear as "a silly mess of stuff" (the phrase is from the early Mormon leader Parley Pratt), the Mormon conviction that they were directly connected to both Old and New Testament restoration promises, plus the fact that these claims are internally consistent, proved to be a motive force powerful enough to bring a new religious tradition into being.[2]

The main elements of the early Mormon story are very familiar. In addition to the prophet's autobiographical statement, which has been canonized, many historical narratives outline Joseph Smith's career.[3] They describe the First Vision, in which the future prophet saw God and Jesus as distinct personages and learned from them that all the churches then existing were false and that he would be the agent of the restoration of the true church. These accounts tell of Smith's finding a set of golden plates on which an ancient record was engraved in "reformed Egyptian"; they tell about his "translating" this record to bring forth the Book of Mormon and describe the establishing of the Church of Jesus Christ. Fundamentally historical rather than theological in nature, these accounts of the beginnings of Mormonism go on to picture Smith leading the Latter-day Saints forward into a "new dispensation of the fulness of times." But there is no systematic theological statement on the order of an LDS *Summa Theologica* that organizes and clarifies the theological claims supporting the Mormon restoration.[4]

The Book of Mormon and Smith's early revelations (many of which appeared in the Book of Commandments in 1833) provided the basis for the Mormon theological system, but Mormon beliefs were elaborated and interpreted in other writings of Joseph Smith, in early Mormon pamphlets, and in LDS sermons and addresses. The most significant sermons and addresses were delivered by an important group of LDS leaders between 1847 and 1890. Recorded by scribes, the discourses of Brigham Young, John Taylor, Wilford Woodruff, Lorenzo Snow, Orson Pratt, Parley Pratt, Daniel H. Wells, George Q. Cannon, Joseph F. Smith, and at least a dozen others were published serially in England and distributed in the United States.[5] The members of this group were such influential interpreters of the Mormon belief system that they may well be described as the church fathers of Mormonism.

The intent of this essay is gathering Mormon theological claims from these diverse places, organizing them, relating them to restoration promises found in biblical materials and in the LDS canon of Scripture, and suggesting their impact on Latter-day Saint history. Before proceeding to that task, however, it is vitally important to take up the matter of the first Mormon prophet's own conception of his role in the Mormon restoration. This is an especially significant issue in view of the results of recent research that is providing direct evidence to establish beyond dispute conclusions that an impressive body of less direct evidence has long suggested.[6] Joseph Smith, his father, and possibly one or two of his brothers were practitioners of folk magic.[7] The future prophet had been actively involved in the practice of using seer stones, or "peepstones," as a means of "divining" the location of lost treasures before 1827, when he reported finding a cache of gold plates whose surfaces were covered with engravings and some "ancient seers" known as the "Urim and Thummim." Connecting this report with Smith's earlier divining ventures, many of the inhabitants of the area of western New York where he lived dismissed his prophetic claims and continued to regard him as a folk magician.

The future prophet could very well have been employing the magic arts when he sought treasure in the Hill Cumorah, where he said the plates were found. But since religion and magic were not mutually exclusive in either European or American folk culture, his having been involved in folk magic does not indicate that the psycho-biographer Fawn M. Brodie was necessarily correct in describing Joseph Smith as a village scryer who engaged in conscious deception.[8] In fact, the evidence that emerges from the holograph copies of the history left by the Mormon prophet's mother, Lucy Mack Smith, and the testimony of his wife, Emma, and of the followers who assisted him as scribes points away from Brodie's conclusion that he created a work of fiction that he afterward came to accept as true.[9] It seems much more likely that as the text of the Book of Mormon started to take shape, Smith became convinced that the words he dictated to his scribe came from the "sealed book" to which the prophet Isaiah referred in 29:11–14.

Whether this young New York farmer actually found metal plates or whether he worked from plates that he could see only with "spiritual eyes," the future prophet prepared a document containing characters copied off the plates, some of which he said he translated "by means of the Urim and Thummim."[10] He gave it to his scribe Martin Harris so that it could be taken to the East for examination by eminent linguists of the day. In his account of the beginnings of Mormonism written in 1838, Smith reported that Harris returned from visiting Columbia College saying that he had given the paper to a great authority, Professor Charles Anthon, but that Anthon could not read the hieroglyphics on the page. Determining exactly when Smith started to identify himself as the unlearned one to whom a sealed book was delivered is difficult.[11] Yet it stands to reason that Smith recognized the significance of Isaiah 29 when he was dictating the section of the Book of Mormon known as 2 Nephi.

Although the biblical account says only that the unlearned man protested that he was not learned and that the Lord promised to do "a marvelous work and a wonder," a corresponding passage in Smith's "gold bible" is more informative. Chapter 27 of 2 Nephi includes much of the content and even much of the actual wording of Isaiah 29. But it is more explicit about the connection between the unlearned man and the marvelous work, making clear that the unlearned would "read the words which I [the Lord] shall give unto thee."

A 1980 work by the Lutheran minister Robert Hullinger, *Mormon Answer to Skepticism: Why Joseph Smith Wrote the Book of Mormon,* made an elaborate and sustained argument that Martin Harris's journey was undertaken by design, that Smith sent him to the East to show the characters presumably copied from the plates to highly respected scholars of the day because their failure to read the document would mean that the Isaiah 29 prophecy was being fulfilled.[12] Hullinger, agreeing with Fawn Brodie, believes that the episode was deliberately set up, as it were, to make Smith's book more appealing by establishing a clear connection between the Book of Mormon and the Bible. Although Hullinger and Brodie differ on the matter of Smith's motive—he believes that the Book of Mormon was written to combat skepticism, whereas she apparently thought that the project was initially a mercenary enterprise—they use similar circumstantial evidence to make their cases. But even if Hullinger and Brodie are right, even if Harris was sent to the East so that Smith could claim he was the unlearned man who could read what the learned could not, the only available primary source material, the manuscript of a history of these early years written by the prophet's mother, gives absolutely no indication that Smith ever doubted that he was the person to whom the ancient prophet made reference. Smith believed that this was an incident in which prophecy had been fulfilled, and those who followed him concurred.

The first chapter of one of the earliest and most often reprinted LDS proselyting tracts, *A Voice of Warning and Instruction to All People,* is a good example of the significance of this linkage with the Bible. The author, Parley P. Pratt, ranged all across the Old and New Testaments citing example after example of fulfilled prophecy. His intent was to show that "the predictions of the Prophets can be clearly understood, as much so as the almanac when it foretells an eclipse." Moreover, he said, quoting 2 Peter 1:20 as his authority, "no prophecy of the Scripture is of any private interpretation"; prophecies have been and will be *literally* fulfilled. To emphasize the importance of this message, Pratt placed the motto "What is Prophecy but History reversed?" at the head of the *Voice of Warning*'s second chapter, "On the Fulfillment of Prophecy Yet Future." It is a motto that could have stood as well at the head of many of the early accounts that the Latter-day Saints wrote telling their own stories.[13] Such works show that the concept of a literal fulfillment of prophecy was, to borrow a phrase from *A Voice of Warning*, the "definite rule of interpretation" used by the Saints, both in reading Scripture and in trying to comprehend the meaning of their own individual and corporate lives.

A description of the combination of theological elements that serve as a foundation for the Mormon restoration will illustrate the significance to LDS theology of this same "definite rule of interpretation." A caveat is in order, however. In reading this description of the claims supporting the Mormon restoration, one should remember that the various LDS interpretations of events as prophecy fulfilled were not introduced sequentially. Nor were all such interpretations regarded as equally important by the early Saints. Moreover, the elaborate interrelated set of fulfilled prophecy claims are not emphasized in modern Mormonism in the same way they were emphasized in the nineteenth century. The fundamental import of assertions that prophecy had recently been fulfilled and that it continues to be fulfilled was the reassuring message that "the heavens are no longer brass," that direct communication between divinity and humanity had been reopened.

Since the early twentieth century, that message has increasingly been communicated to Latter-day Saints through the First Vision story, an account of a theophany in which God and Jesus appeared to fourteen-year-old Joseph Smith in the spring of 1820 in the spot now known as the Sacred Grove.[14] But this episode was apparently not often described during the period of Mormon beginnings; the message that God was starting to speak again first appeared in Mormonism in very specific claims about fulfilled prophecy.

Identification of Joseph Smith as Isaiah's unlearned man set the stage for the Mormon restoration. The Book of Mormon was identified as the "marvelous work and a wonder" foretold in verse 14 of Isaiah 29. "And in that day," verse 18 of the same chapter reads, the deaf shall "hear the words of the book and the eyes of the blind" shall be opened. "The meek also shall increase their joy in the Lord and the poor among men shall rejoice in the holy one of Israel," verse 19 says, conjuring up one of the many generalized restoration pictures found in the Old Testament materials. But exactly what connection could be established between the coming forth of the book that the learned could not read and the opening of the LDS restoration? The fulfillment of a second prophecy was more specific.

Almost nowhere in the Old Testament is there a more dramatic rendering of the coming restoration of Israel than that found in Ezekiel 37. The hand of the Lord set the prophet down in the valley of dry bones and caused him to prophesy, whereupon the bones were resurrected into the whole house of Israel. Then the word of the Lord came again, instructing the prophet to write a history for the "stick of Judah" and another history "for Joseph, the stick of Ephraim." When that was done, the Lord would take the two sticks and "make them one stick" and one nation in his hand. Two passages in the Book of Mormon relate Smith's "gold bible," as his contemporaries called it, to Ezekiel's prophecy. The first, a part of a great vision given to Nephi of the grand sweep of history up to the early nineteenth century, tells of a time when the history of the Hebrew peoples who had come to the New World before the Babylonian captivity would be joined to the "record of the Jews." The other, from 2 Nephi 3:12, says that "the fruit of [the loins of Joseph] shall write"—a clear reference to Joseph Smith—"and the fruit of the loins of Judah shall write," and these writings "shall grow together."

By themselves, these two passages might not have been strong enough to support an interpretation of the Book of Mormon as fulfillment of Ezekiel 37. But other evidence attests to the prominence Mormons gave to this connection during the years when Mormonism was coming into being and when the theological tenets that would undergird the Mormon community were being put in place. In August of 1830, a revelation given through Joseph Smith spoke of Moroni, the angel, as the one "to whom I [the Lord] committed the keys of the record of the stick of Ephraim."[15] In addition, early broadsides advertising the Book of Mormon described the work as "the stick of Joseph taken from the hand of Ephraim."[16] The message being transmitted ran as follows: because the Book of Mormon was "the stick of Ephraim," its coming forth signaled the beginning of the restoration of Zion.

An examination of references to the new dispensation and the restoration, cited in the index to the sermons delivered by the aforementioned LDS Church fathers and published in the *Journal of Discourses,* further indicates how the Book of Mormon was linked to the Bible and how its coming forth was presented as the first step in the restoration. Besides citing Isaiah 29 and Ezekiel 37, these LDS leaders sometimes referred to a third Old Testament passage, "Truth shall spring out of the earth, and righteousness shall look down from heaven," to prove that the Book of Mormon, translated as it was said to have been from gold plates found in the ground, was a fulfillment of prophecy.[17] But of all the biblical passages that they used to make this point, these leaders most often cited a passage from the Revelation of St. John to associate the coming forth of the Book of Mormon and the opening of the final dispensation and the beginning of the restoration. The same August 1830 revelation (Doctrine and Covenants 27) that made reference to Moroni's possession of the keys to the record of the stick of Ephraim also indicated that the Book of Mormon contained "the fulness of the everlasting gospel." This phrase directed the attention of early Mormons to Revelation 14:6, and a positive identification was quickly made. The heavenly being that led Smith to the Hill Cumorah was none other, the Mormons came to believe, than the angel that flew "in the midst of heaven having the everlasting gospel to preach unto them that dwell on the earth," and this specific claim was made repeatedly in nineteenth-century LDS sermons and gospel tracts.[18]

The attention that LDS speakers directed to this reference from the Book of Revelation brought the Saints close to the many other American Christians of their day who were mightily concerned about the Second Coming of Christ and the inauguration of the millennium. Yet it was a proximity more apparent than real. Accepting the Book of Mormon as scriptural fulfillment of Old Testament as well as New Testament prophecy set the Saints on a path that would separate them from other forms of Christianity on the basis of doctrine, as well as from the more obvious perspectives of marriage practice (polygamy), politics, economics, and, in time, geography.

The early Saints also applied literal fulfillment as the definite rule of interpretation to other Mormon scriptures. Recognizing the Book of Mormon as the "translation" of "an account written by the hand of Mormon upon plates" meant recognizing, in turn, that in the day when the writings of the fruit of the loins of Joseph and Judah "grew together," God would raise up a "choice seer," whose name like that of his father would be Joseph. He would be one who would be mighty among the people, who would "do much good both in word and in deed," who would "work mighty wonders" and bring to pass the restoration of Israel.[19] As a result, his followers not only allowed Joseph Smith Jr. to lead them but also expected him to prophesy, to speak for God. In their eyes, this was a sure sign that the gospel was restored.

Given this Book of Mormon prophecy, it was reassuring that "thus saith the Lord" was the form of address that Smith used in calling his father, his brother Hyrum, Oliver Cowdery, and others into God's service.[20] It meant that the heavens were opened, that prophecy was fulfilled then and there, not in some far distant future. The restorations of the ancient priesthoods of Aaron and Melchizedek that Joseph announced were likewise reassuring; they fit clearly into the category of "mighty wonders" that were inaugurating the restoration. Moreover, that this was a restoration of something more than the so-called primitive church was made crystal clear when revelation formally authorized the authority of the Mormon leader. On April 6, 1830, the day when the Church of Jesus Christ was formally reorganized, revelation designated Smith as seer, prophet, and translator, as well as apostle of Jesus Christ and elder of the church.[21] The lack of a carefully drawn distinction between forms of authority drawn from the Old and New Testaments (and from the Book of Mormon) is an early signal that when the Mormon restoration was fully in place, it would be nothing less than the "restoration of all things."[22]

As momentous to Smith's followers as were the restoration of the ancient priesthood and the reorganization of the church, it is likely that the fulfillment of two of Smith's prophetic utterances in September 1830 was of greater consequence in turning the Mormon restoration into a literal, actual living reality. One of these, now numbered section 27 in the LDS Book of Doctrine and Covenants, is a revelation saying that the hour approached when the Lord would come "to drink the fruit of the vine" with his Saints on earth. With him would come Elias and Elijah, and Jacob, Isaac, and Abraham, plus John the Baptist and Peter, James, and John. To Elias, the revelation said, had been committed "the keys of bringing to pass the restoration of all things, spoken by the mouth of all the holy prophets since the world began." To Elijah, continued the revelation, had been committed "the keys of the power of turning the hearts of the fathers to the children and the hearts of the children to the fathers." The second significant prophecy given through Joseph Smith that same month was a revelation that dealt with the gathering of the Saints and, using the imagery of John's revelation, prophesied the end of time.

Fulfillment of these prophecies came in reverse order. The gathering of the Latter-day Saints started on the morrow of Smith's announcement of the prophecy, if not before. Prior to the issuing of the revelation about the gathering of the Saints, missionaries had been making preparations to carry the message of the Book of Mormon to the Indians on the Missouri frontier. Smith admonished them to keep their eyes open. Even as they told the Indians how the Book of Mormon revealed that the American natives had a Hebraic heritage, the missionaries should keep watch for a likely place where the Saints could gather. Chapter 29 of 3 Nephi had promised that when the words from the plates came forth, the Saints would know "that the covenant which the Father hath made with the children of Israel concerning their restoration to the lands of their inheritance" was beginning to be fulfilled. If a suitable place could be found and set apart, then the Latter-day Saints, God's chosen in the new dispensation, could claim their own inheritances and the building up of God's kingdom in the new world could begin even before the rebuilding of his kingdom in Palestine.[23]

The first gathering place was not to be so far west, however. In early 1831, the prophet and most of his followers left western New York en masse to gather in Kirtland, Ohio, where a Campbellite minister, Sidney Rigdon, had been converted to the "restored gospel" and, in turn, had converted his entire congregation to Mormonism. In the astonishingly short period of two to three years, Smith and his band built up such a thriving settlement that it transformed this tiny hamlet into a good-sized Ohio town. As in ancient days, the Saints constructed a temple to serve as Kirtland's focal point, its center. Thus it was that the early Mormons, believing that the heavens had opened and that prophecy was being fulfilled in their own day, began to bring about the fulfillment of prophecy themselves. As Leonard J. Arrington, Feramorz Fox, and Dean L. May demonstrated in their study of early Mormon communitarianism, *Building the City of God: Community and Cooperation among the Mormons,* this became the LDS pattern.[24] Prophecy was fulfilled; things came to pass because the Saints—believing that the restoration had commenced—made them come to pass.

While this is a process that is certainly related in some manner to the concept popularly known as "self-fulfilling prophecy," it was (and is) by no means an uncomplicated process in which (1) prophecy can be equated simply and directly with stimulus and (2) fulfillment can be equated simply and directly with response. That the issue is far more complex and complicated is indicated by the fact that before this pattern was truly established, one more dramatic fulfillment of prophecy occurred to set the LDS restoration firmly on course.

On April 3, 1836, climaxing the week in which the Kirtland Temple was dedicated, Joseph Smith and Oliver Cowdery went behind the temple veil, and there, in what can be interpreted as fulfillment of the prophet's September 1830 revelation (although the Saints do not universally interpret it as such), the prophet and the "first elder" of the church were visited, they reported, by the Lord of Hosts. He accepted the temple, said his name should be there, and promised to manifest himself to his people therein. Then, the report continues, Moses, whose coming had not been prophesied, appeared and committed "the keys of the gathering of Israel" to the Mormon leaders. After this, Elias, whose appearance had been foretold, committed to them "the dispensation of the gospel of Abraham," telling Smith and Cowdery that in them and their seed all future generations would be blessed. Finally, Elijah stood before them, they said, and committed to them the keys of this, the new and last dispensation of the fullness of times. With that, the restoration of all things could truly begin.[25]

The outlines of the story of what happened to the Saints as they engaged in the most radical restoration project ever undertaken in the American West are familiar. But only those who find sermons as well as settlement patterns interesting would know that even though the Saints were driven from the nation, they saw their going out as a literal fulfilling of Revelation 18:4: "Come out of her [the world], my people, that ye be not partakers of her sins and that ye receive not her plagues."

Acts 3:21, that favorite text from the New Testament, was used again and again to describe the character of the Great Basin kingdom, most especially by Brigham Young and future church presidents John Taylor and Wilford Woodruff. The Saints did not believe that their new dispensation superseded all previous dispensations; *it fulfilled them*. Flowing into this new dispensation were all that had before been revealed. As is well known, for the nineteenth-century Saints in the West, this dispensation included a political kingdom organized in the manner of the kingdom of God in Solomon's day, under what they regarded as ancient ordinances administered in temples— most particularly, plural marriages and baptisms for the dead—as well as a church organized, they believed, as it had been organized in the days of the apostles.

It would be an exaggeration to say that, as a reality, the radical restoration was an unqualified success. But it was successful enough to lead the Saints to believe that another of Isaiah's prophecies was about to be fulfilled: the kingdom established in the tops of the mountains shall "be exalted above the hills and all nations shall flow into it." The Saints had learned, as Woodruff said, "to take God at his word."[26] Moreover, they knew, as Taylor said of the Almighty, that "he does not run on a narrow track as we do," and they depended on the coming reality of Daniel's vision of the stone cut out of the mountain without hands as a means by which the Mormon kingdom would break in pieces and consume all other kingdoms and stand forever.[27]

But history proved that literal fulfillment of this prophecy would not come in North America at the end of the nineteenth century. The Saints' success in building, inside the boundaries of the United States, a kingdom of God that operated according to ancient principles generated powerful non-Mormon opposition. By the 1890s, this opposition became so intense that, for self-protection, Mormonism had to shift away from its radical restorationist mode to what may best be described as a mode of conservative preservation. Exchanging the political kingdom and the practice of plural marriage for Utah statehood, the Saints preserved the restored gospel, the restored priesthood, the reorganized church, and the kingdom *idea*. But the LDS civic kingdom was no more.

The fact of the kingdom's demise caused an enormous wrenching within Mormon culture and even within the LDS religious realm. The most visible evidence of the tumult was the bewilderment and chaos infecting Mormon culture after the Saints were directed by the president of the LDS Church—their prophet, seer, and revelator—to discontinue their practice of plural marriage. The demise of the Mormon political party and the division of the Saints into the Democratic and Republican parties also generated confusion in the culture. These conspicuous evidences of turmoil in the LDS community were but signals of the critical situation in which Mormonism found itself as it moved away from its period of beginnings, which the Saints had confidently regarded as the "winding-up scene," toward a new world in which the LDS Church would be the reality and the literal restoration as it manifested itself in the Mormon kingdom would be idealized and preserved in memory.

In the half-century after 1890, Mormonism changed dramatically. Its ecclesiastical structure was streamlined and its theology systematized, and the everyday experiences of ordinary Saints slowly but very surely started to resemble the everyday experiences of Christians who are Protestants and Roman Catholics.[28] As the LDS Church has expanded beyond the confines of the Great Basin, first to California and then to the remainder of the United States and outward to the world, its doctrine has been organized and elaborated in such a way that it can be communicated across linguistic and cultural barriers. As this has happened, the reality of the Mormon restoration seems to have receded in importance, whereas its significance as ideal increases. As temples are built throughout the world and the Book of Mormon is emphasized, the difference between Mormonism and other forms of Christianity becomes sharper. The apostolic era is an era of great consequence to the Saints, but in many Mormon hearts and minds "restoration" corresponds to an LDS golden age when Zion stood in the tops of the mountains for all to see.

Notes

1. The *New Mormon Studies CD-Rom* (Salt Lake City: Smith Research Associates, 1998) has the full text of virtually every reference to which I refer in this essay and many others as well, including numerous nineteenth- and early twentieth-century LDS periodicals, *Sunstone,* and *Dialogue;* the *Journal of Discourses;* the full run of *LDS Conference Reports;* and many historical and contemporary studies of Mormonism.

2. Parley Pratt, *A Voice of Warning and Instruction to All People; or, An Introduction to the Faith and Doctrine of the Church of Jesus Christ of Latter-day Saints,* 13th ed. (Salt Lake City: Deseret News, 1893), 133. This is perhaps the greatest of all early Latter-day Saint proselyting tracts. As indicated in the introduction to this section, the argument that Mormonism is not a denominational, heretical, or fraudulent form

of Christianity but a new religious tradition is made in Jan Shipps, *Mormonism: The Story of a New Religious Tradition* (Urbana: University of Illinois Press, 1985).

3. From the standpoint of the LDS Church, the most authoritative of these quasi-canonized narratives are two composed by general authorities of the LDS Church: B. H. Roberts, *A Comprehensive History of the Church of Jesus Christ of Latter-day Saints,* 6 vols. (Salt Lake City: Deseret News, 1930); and Joseph Fielding Smith, *Essentials in Church History: A History of the Church from the Birth of Joseph Smith to the Present Time, with Introductory Chapters on the Antiquity of the Gospel and the "Falling Away"* (Salt Lake City: Deseret News, 1922), both of which were published by a press controlled by the LDS Church. The best narrative accounts currently available are James B. Allen and Glen M. Leonard, *The Story of the Latter-day Saints* (Salt Lake City: Deseret Book, 1976); and Leonard J. Arrington and Davis Bitton, *The Mormon Experience: A History of the Latter-day Saints* (New York: Alfred A. Knopf, 1979). However, because these accounts of the LDS past are written from the perspective of a particular form of Mormonism, the fracturing of the Mormon movement after Smith's death is not emphasized. Because quite different understandings of the meaning of the concept of restoration developed between the Saints who followed Brigham Young to the Great Basin and those who stayed in the Midwest and were "reorganized" under Joseph Smith III, the breakup of the movement that occurred between 1844 and 1860 is important here. Paul M. Edwards, *Our Legacy of Faith: A Brief History of the Reorganized Church of Jesus Christ of Latter Day Saints* (Independence, Mo.: Herald Publishing House, 1991), is the best narrative history of the reorganization. Inez Smith Davis, *The Story of the Church: The History of the Church of Jesus Christ of Latter Day Saints and Its Legal Successor, the Reorganized Church of Jesus Christ of Latter Day Saints,* 4th ed. rev. (Independence, Mo.: Herald Publishing House, 1948), remains the canonized history of the RLDS Church.

4. The most important compendia include James E. Talmage, *The Articles of Faith [of the] Church of Jesus Christ of Latter-day Saints* (Salt Lake City: Deseret News, 1901), of which many reprints are available; and Bruce R. McConkie, *Mormon Doctrine,* rev. ed. (Salt Lake City: Bookcraft, 1966). A compilation of radio talks presented in 1944 by Joseph Fielding Smith has been brought together in a volume entitled *The Restoration of All Things* (Salt Lake City: Deseret Book, 1973). Although this work enumerates and explains many of the theological points that will be dealt with here, it is in no way a work of systematic theology.

5. *A Book of Commandments for the Government of the Church of Christ, Organized according to Law on the 6th of April, 1830* (Zion: W. W. Phelps, 1833). A facsimile of this work was reprinted by Herald House in 1972. The Book of Commandments was incorporated into the *Doctrine and Covenants of the Church of the Latter Day Saints: Carefully Selected from the Revelations of God,* comp. Joseph Smith Jr., Oliver Cowdery, Sidney Rigdon, and Frederick G. Williams (Kirtland, Ohio: F. G. Williams, 1835). Changes in numbering and alterations in wording of the revelations as they appeared in the Book of Commandments and the first version of the Doctrine and Covenants are documented by Lyndon W. Cook in his extremely valuable volume, *Revelations of the Prophet Joseph Smith: A Historical and Biographical Commentary of the Doctrine and Covenants* (Provo, Utah: Seventy's Mission Bookstore, 1981). The sermons of LDS leaders were recorded in shorthand as they were delivered and were published in the 26-volume *Journal of Discourses,* published serially in Liverpool and London

in the nineteenth century. A photo lithographic reprint of these sermons was published in 1956 (Los Angeles: Gartner Printing and Litho).

6. A summary of the evidence about Joseph Smith's connection with the group sometimes called the "Palmyra magicians" is found in Fawn McKay Brodie, *No Man Knows My History: The Life of Joseph Smith, the Mormon Prophet*, 2d ed. (New York: Alfred A. Knopf, 1976), chapter 2 and appendix A; see also Marvin S. Hill, "Brodie Revisited: A Reappraisal," *Dialogue* 8 (Winter 1972): 72–85; Marvin S. Hill, "Joseph Smith and the 1826 Trial: New Evidence and New Difficulties," *BYU Studies* 12 (Winter 1972): 223–33; and Jan Shipps, "The Prophet Puzzle: Suggestions Leading toward a More Comprehensive Interpretation of Joseph Smith," *Journal of Mormon History* 1 (1974): 3–20.

7. A narrative description of this connection is found in the early chapters of Richard L. Bushman, *Joseph Smith and the Beginnings of Mormonism* (Urbana: University of Illinois Press, 1984). In addition, two book-length studies dealing with magic and the occult are now available: D. Michael Quinn, *Early Mormonism and the Magic World-View*, 2d ed. (Salt Lake City: Signature Books, 1998); and John L. Brooke, *The Refiner's Fire: The Making of Mormon Cosmology, 1644–1844* (New York: Cambridge University Press, 1994). A number of articles about Joseph Smith and folk magic published between 1984 and 1986 are not included here because some of the evidence on which they were based was drawn from documents forged by the document dealer Mark Hofmann. None of the books listed above depends on material that passed through Hofmann's hands.

8. Brodie, *No Man Knows My History*, 49.

9. The collection of holograph pages from which came Lucy Smith's *Biographical Sketches of Joseph Smith the Prophet and His Progenitors for Many Generations* (Liverpool, England: S. W. Richards, 1853) is in the LDS Church Archives in Salt Lake City. Although similar to the published work, these holograph pages give a more immediate picture of the prophet's mother's understanding of the coming forth of the Book of Mormon. Pages 107–38 of the printed version (published in an Arno reprint edition in 1969) recount the coming forth of the work and her own reflections on what her son had told her about it. Emma Smith's understanding of the translation process is described in Linda King Newell and Valeen Tippetts Avery, *Mormon Enigma: Emma Hale Smith*, 2d ed. (Urbana: University of Illinois Press, 1994), 21–23. Even though Oliver Cowdery, the prophet's primary scribal assistant, left the church, he never denied that the Book of Mormon was exactly what it purported to be.

10. B. H. Roberts, ed., *History of the Church of Jesus Christ of Latter-day Saints: Period I, History of Joseph Smith, the Prophet, by Himself*, 6 vols., paperback ed. rev. (Salt Lake City: Deseret Book, 1978), 1:19.

11. A clear photostat and a transcription of a note that Smith wrote on the back of a copy of the document Harris is said to have carried to show Professor Anthon is included in Dean C. Jessee, ed., *The Personal Writings of Joseph Smith* (Salt Lake City: Deseret Book, 1984), 284. This document turns out to have been a forgery, however.

12. Robert N. Hullinger, *Mormon Answer to Skepticism: Why Joseph Smith Wrote the Book of Mormon* (St. Louis: Clayton Publishing House, 1980). This work was republished in 1992 by Signature Books under the title *Joseph Smith's Answer to Skepticism*.

13. A particularly important example of such an account is the diary of Wilford Woodruff, one of Smith's first followers, who became the fourth president of the LDS Church. Beginning in 1983, this diary was published in typescript in nine volumes by Smith Research Associates in collaboration with Signature Books. Other examples are found in the writings of Jedediah Grant published in Gene A. Sessions, *Mormon Thunder: A Documentary History of Jedediah Morgan Grant* (Urbana: University of Illinois Press, 1982); and the various writings of LDS women published in Kenneth W. Godfrey, Audrey M. Godfrey, and Jill Mulvay Derr, eds., *Women's Voices: An Untold History of the Latter-day Saints, 1830–1900* (Salt Lake City: Deseret Book, 1982).

14. James B. Allen, "Emergence of a Fundamental: The Expanding Role of Joseph Smith's First Vision in Mormon Religious Thought," *Journal of Mormon History* 7 (1980): 43–61.

15. Doctrine and Covenants, 27:5.

16. A photograph of one of these broadsides is included in Allen and Leonard, *The Story of the Latter-day Saints,* 49.

17. See, for example, *Journal of Discourses,* 8:367.

18. References to Revelation 14:6 are found in at least twenty of the talks given between 1855 and 1880 that are printed in the *Journal of Discourses.*

19. Book of Mormon, 2 Nephi 3:24.

20. Doctrine and Covenants, 2, 3, 6, 8, 10.

21. Ibid., 21.

22. This expression, often used to describe the form of Mormonism that included temple ordinances, plural marriage, and a literal kingdom structured on the model of Solomon's kingdom, is adapted from Acts 3:21, which speaks of "the times of restitution of all things which God hath spoken by the mouth of all his holy prophets since the world began."

23. On June 7, 1831, revelation specifically designated Missouri as the "land of your inheritance." Doctrine and Covenants, 52:42.

24. Leonard J. Arrington, Feramorz Y. Fox, and Dean L. May, *Building the City of God: Community and Cooperation among the Mormons* (Salt Lake City: Deseret Book, 1976; 2d ed., Urbana: University of Illinois Press, 1992).

25. Doctrine and Covenants, 110.

26. *Journal of Discourses,* 2:195.

27. Ibid., 26:107. The best discussion of the Mormon expectation that their kingdom would rule the kingdoms of the world is Klaus J. Hansen, *Quest for Empire: The Political Kingdom of God and the Council of Fifty in Mormon History* (East Lansing: Michigan State University Press, 1967; reprint, Lincoln: University of Nebraska Press, 1974).

28. The best treatment of this era is Thomas G. Alexander, *Mormonism in Transition: A History of the Latter-day Saints, 1890–1930* (1986; reprint, Urbana: University of Illinois Press, 1996).

12

Brigham Young and His Times:
A Continuing Force in Mormonism

In accounts of Mormonism written before 1860, Joseph Smith was nearly always cast as the star of the Latter-day Saint (LDS) drama. While Mormon writers, who believed him to be a prophet, always pictured Smith as a hero, Gentiles (non-Mormons) usually described him as a villain. Either way, Smith was the Mormon that mattered in the early years. My careful review of the literature on Mormonism published in American periodicals demonstrates dramatically, however, that the emphasis shifted in the late 1860s and 1870s away from the first Mormon prophet to a new hero/villain, Brigham Young.[1] A casual survey of any substantial library collection on Mormonism indicates that journalists were not the only writers in the post–Civil War years to focus on "Brother Brigham," as his followers called him. The authors of book-length works also started to find President Young more fascinating than his predecessor.

Since Catherine Waite's *Mormon Prophet and His Harem* (1866), Ann Eliza Webb Young's famous *Wife No.19; or, The Story of a Life in Bondage* (1876), and a host of other exposés of Mormonism featuring the LDS marriage system found ready markets, it is obvious that the practice of plural marriage—polygamy—was partially responsible for this shift.[2] Yet interest in Brigham Young was not limited to curiosity about his domestic situation. Long after the practice of polygamy ceased, Young's story continued to fascinate people. Furthermore, when they read about him, people outside as well as inside the LDS community wanted to read something more substantial than repetitious accounts of Young as a "dirty old man." To name only a few of the many popular book-length works about this LDS leader, Frank Cannon's *Under the Prophet in Utah* (written with Harvey J. O'Higgins) and his *Brigham Young and His Mormon Empire* (written with George L. Knapp), M. R. Werner's *Brigham Young,* Preston Nibley's *Brigham Young, the Man and*

His Work, Milton Hunter's *Brigham Young, the Colonizer,* and Ray B. West's *Kingdom of the Saints: The Story of Brigham Young and the Mormons* all deal with Young as premier pioneer, prominent politician, beloved (or feared) ecclesiastic, and gifted kingdom builder, as well as awesome patriarch.[3] Whether negative or positive in tone, these books, and many others, including the influential works by Edward Tullidge and the Stenhouses, show Young, for good or ill, as such an important and powerful LDS leader that they skew Mormon history away from the Prophet Joseph Smith.[4]

The so-called frontier school in American history was a strong factor in this tendency in early modern times to elevate Brigham Young to first place in the development of Mormonism. His role was given special weight in virtually everything written about this movement in which the frontier as the location of the action was emphasized. Young's reputation also benefited from unsympathetic studies portraying Joseph Smith as a mentally unbalanced megalomaniac. These laudatory, filiopietistic biographies of "Brother Brigham" that stressed his strength, practicality, and virtue caused most non-Mormons and even some Latter-day Saints to regard Young as the "genius of Mormonism." This idea did not originate with Bernard De Voto, but the Ogden sage, who made good in the New York literary world, gave it classic expression when he described Mormonism's phenomenal success, cited Young's multiplicity of leadership qualities, compared his abilities to those of the first Mormon prophet, and concluded that the significance of Joseph Smith for Mormonism lay almost entirely in his choice of the right time and place to get himself martyred. Young's career, he said in an article entitled "The Centennial of Mormonism," published in the *American Mercury,* explained the survival and success of the LDS movement.[5]

De Voto and the other journalists and scholars who give Young credit for saving Mormonism from Joseph Smith's "follies" all base their conclusions on two important assumptions. The first comes directly from the history of Mormonism canonized by the LDS Church headquartered in Salt Lake City. It is the supposition that while a few of the Saints went with James J. Strang to Michigan after Smith's murder and a few others stayed in the Midwest waiting for the prophet's eldest son to become old enough to lead the church, most of the Saints left Nauvoo, Illinois, and—as a part of a corporate move— followed Young to the Intermountain West.[6] The second assumption is that the martyrdom was a unifying force in Mormondom.

Both of these assumptions were incorrect. Sophisticated modern demographic analysis makes it clear that large numbers of Saints stayed behind when Young led his followers westward. Perhaps as many as 40 percent of the LDS population did not go, among whom, significantly, were a great many of the Mormons who had been born in the United States.[7] The popular perception that the murder of Joseph Smith unified the Saints is not directly attributable to the canonized *History of the Church,* but the official depiction of the situation in Nauvoo between 1844 and 1846 is designed to reveal a consensus that suggests unity. In fact, however, the Mormons were not united by the death of their prophet. Instead, the martyrdom laid bare a deep division within the community that reflected a serious theological rift among the Mormons.

The fundamental issue about which the Saints disagreed was whether Mormonism was primarily an idiosyncratic version of primitive Christianity—a reformation, or forming again, of the ancient apostolic church accompanying the restoration of the Christian gospel—or whether it was a far more complex restoration of all things, the "gospel of the God of Abraham" as well as the "gospel of Jesus Christ," a restoration that called for a renewal of temple rituals and other Old Testament practices, such as plural marriage. This division, which figured prominently in the struggle for authority and power that constituted the "succession crisis," expressed itself in a variety of ways. Most particularly, it worked itself out in disagreement about whether the Saints should persevere in their compliance with the principle of the "gathering." Those in the "Christian camp," as it might be called, believed that continuing the gathering that had made Nauvoo the largest city in Illinois in the early 1840s would be dangerous. Suspecting that Smith's murder and the threat of fresh persecution were responses to the presence in the western part of the state of a powerful, virtually independent corporate body, these Saints favored the scattering of the LDS community and the ensuing development of separate congregations. Those in the other camp—it might well be called the Camp of Israel—regarded continuation of the gathering as mandatory because they believed it was the literal reversal of the dispersion of the chosen people in biblical times that was a necessary prelude to the millennium.[8]

The official accounts of Brigham Young's accession to LDS leadership feature stories of a transfiguration in which Young appeared to the Saints in the "form, size, countenance, and voice of the martyred prophet" and convinced them that the Council of the Twelve Apostles should lead the church.[9] Young, who stood at its head, and the members of the council claimed they were the ones closest to the murdered prophet. They also said they knew he was fully committed to an LDS theology that emphasized the restoration of all things from the beginning of the Old Testament forward and, thus, to the importance of temple rituals, plural marriage, and the continuance of the gathering. These accounts give the impression that, with unimportant exceptions, the Saints all agreed this was the Mormonism of Joseph Smith.

While De Voto and other journalists and scholars of a secular bent, who failed to appreciate these crucial theological complications, were persuaded that Brigham Young saved the LDS movement by rescuing it from the follies of its founder, the Latter Day Saints who did not go west interpreted Young's words and actions in a different fashion. In particular, the "Josephites," who "reorganized" the Church of Jesus Christ of Latter Day Saints under the leadership of Joseph Smith III, said that Young and his "Brigham-ite" followers had perverted Mormonism, turning it away from its original pure form. Adamant above all about their belief that plural marriage was a practice introduced into Mormonism by Young rather than Smith, these Saints were certain that the LDS movement in the Great Basin was not the same Mormonism as the one through which primitive Christianity had been restored to the world by Joseph Smith, the prophet.[10]

Scholars who have kept up with what has gone on in LDS studies know that in the past several decades a main item on the Mormon history agenda has been a broad-based attempt to assess the extent to which Young ought to get the credit for the survival and endurance of Mormonism. Even more important, from the standpoint of faithful Saints, is investigation of the issue of whether the Mormonism of Brigham Young and the Utah Saints was the Mormonism of Joseph Smith. The three scholars whose work deals most directly with these questions were Eugene England, Ronald K. Esplin, and Leonard J. Arrington.[11] Their research revealed that the Mormon "restoration," which took shape in the Great Basin under Brigham Young's guidance, reflected a pattern that Joseph Smith set forth in Nauvoo during the final years of his life. While Linda Newell, referring specifically to the history of the women's Relief Society, pointed out correctly that correspondence between the actions of Young and those of the first Mormon prophet were not always as exact as is sometimes claimed, England, Esplin, Arrington, and others argued that since his conception of Mormonism came directly and exclusively from the Prophet Joseph Smith, it is a mistake to say that Young saved Mormonism from the excesses of its founder.[12] Instead, they argued the reverse, suggesting that one can comprehend Young's career properly only by beginning with the realization that "Brother Brigham" was first and foremost a "follower of the prophet." He understood his task was transforming Smith's mature vision of Mormonism into reality. That this was a task for which he was superbly equipped and one that he realized magnificently may prove, LDS scholars said, that Young was an able and gifted leader, but it does not prove De Voto's assertion that without Young "the church must have perished."

Although ample evidence supports the interpretation of Young as entirely committed to the form of Mormonism that Smith had revealed in its fullness in Nauvoo, the argument must not be carried so far that it turns Brigham Young into little more than a carbon copy of his predecessor. Without any doubt, both Young and his followers believed that the "mantle of Joseph" rested securely on his shoulders. Yet even in the eyes of the Saints in Utah, Young was more than the Prophet Joseph transfigured. Perhaps, as Eugene England said, Young "gives us the real Joseph Smith," but "Brother Brigham" did not simply do what the first Mormon prophet would have done had he been permitted to live long enough to build up the kingdom.[13] Many personal accounts written by those who had dealings with Young reveal that he was his own man and that he made his own contribution to Mormonism. That contribution profoundly influenced the Church of Jesus Christ of Latter-day Saints and the entire LDS movement. For that reason, isolating, identifying, and recognizing it as separate from—if not inconsistent with—Joseph Smith's contribution to Mormonism will make it possible to clarify the role Brigham Young played in the development of the movement and to make a more accurate assessment of its significance.

But describing Young's contribution as unique raises the question of what Brigham Young did that was crucially important—what he did that differed significantly from what Smith had done and, for that matter, what subsequent LDS prophet-presidents would do. Such a question is not easy to answer because there are literally thousands of deeds, even important ones, that Young did that neither Smith nor the LDS leaders who came after Young did, and there were literally hundreds of activities he engaged in that all the other LDS leaders did not engage in. He was, for example, the practical commander who worked out the fine points that made institutional leadership by the Council of the Twelve Apostles effective; he selected the Great Basin as a place for Mormon settlement; he was the colonizer extraordinary, the prime mover in building the Utah Central Railroad, in directing cooperative merchandising among the Saints, in establishing Brigham Young Academy (now Brigham Young University), and in constructing temples in Saint George, Manti, Logan, and Salt Lake City; and he did so much more that the sheer magnitude of any enumeration of his activities and accomplishments would be hard to comprehend fully. Yet other leaders might have done many, if not most, of the things that Young did, and they might have done them almost as well.

It is nevertheless clear that Young did two things that other LDS prophet-presidents not only did not do but quite possibly could not have done: he led the Saints through the wilderness to the Great Salt Lake Valley, which he then insisted that they identify as Zion, the promised land; and he was in charge during the years in which the Saints built up a kingdom appropriate to that place and learned to live as chosen people there. In the process,

Brigham Young presided over the "making of Saints," an accomplishment of a wholly different order. It required more than the superior organizational skill and outstanding leadership talents that have so often been mentioned by Young's secular admirers. It required more, too, than faith, fortitude, and the ability to inspire the same in others, his qualities most often celebrated by the Saints.

From a miscellaneous collection of European and American Protestants, with a few Roman Catholics and a few Polynesians thrown in—by no means all of whom had joined the Mormons during Joseph Smith's lifetime—Young created a cohesive, self-conscious body of Latter-day Saints whose primary identity was Mormon and whose understanding of Mormonism paralleled his own. Since the creation of this body was Young's signal achievement and since it was created during the Saints' journey across the plains and mountains and their building up and living in the kingdom, the nature of Brigham Young's contribution to Mormonism can be identified and its importance can be best understood through a brief consideration of his leadership during the trek and his thirty-year career as the preeminent authority in Zion.

Rather than examine these decisive episodes in the Mormon past with an eye for their congruence with Joseph Smith's vision of Zion, however, this consideration needs to go forward from another direction, and it must proceed at several levels. So that the permanent tangible outcome of his leadership will not be neglected, the Mormon trail and Great Basin kingdom need to be considered at the practical level. The logistical maneuvers that made possible the movement of an army of people from Illinois to Utah and all the problems involved in turning a desert into a suitable place of habitation for Saints must be examined. The events of the journey from Nauvoo to the Great Basin and the events of the period of building and settlement must likewise be considered at the experiential level. The meaning that traveling on the Mormon trail and living in the LDS kingdom had for those who were actually involved is as important to these considerations as the material results of the Saints' activities. Furthermore, Young's leadership in these "Saint-making" situations must be considered at a deeper, symbolic level. This allows one to discover what meaning the journey and the kingdom took on when the early Saints paused to reflect on what had happened to them and to learn what significance these events have had for the Mormon community as successive generations of Latter-day Saints have learned about their past. By examining the data in this fashion, it is possible not only to establish Brigham Young's role in the development of Mormonism but also to suggest why he remains a continuing force in the LDS movement. It also helps identify some of the elements that make the Mormons a "peculiar people," setting their religious tradition apart from the traditional Christianity that other pioneers took to the non-Mormon portions of the American West.

The story of the journey that carried the Saints away from Nauvoo and across the plains to the Salt Lake Valley is too well-known to require much elaboration. Brigham Young served as organizer and leader, making practical decisions about wagons and oxen, resting places and recruiting stations, which travelers should be assigned to the main body of Saints, which ones should lead out, and which ones should take up the rear. To counteract melancholy and aid the Saints, as Andrew Jensen noted in the sketch of Young in the *LDS Biographical Encyclopedia,* in "the exercise of cheerful hope, President Young would have them meet around the campfire and engage in songs and instrumental music."[14] He established Winter Quarters, consulted with Jim Bridger, and settled on a place to take his homeless followers that held out the possibility of supporting their physical needs, once the irrigation ditches could be dug to bring water to the arid valley, and the possibility of providing protection from those who, with mobbings and drivings, had cast the Saints out of the parts of the United States people regarded as civilized.

At a deeper level, the trek, as experienced by the pioneers themselves, was clearly separated from other treks in which pioneers traveled west along the Oregon Trail or the Sante Fe Trail. The Saints were a part of "The Camp of Israel," not attached to a secular band. They were organized into tens, and fifties, and hundreds, with captains over them. Prayer was as much the order of every day as harnessing oxen or cooking over campfires. Death was a constant companion, but there were also healings and comfortings that made bearable the dust and desperation of the trail. At this experiential level, President Young was far more than a trail captain. Drawn together by the proclamation of a new dispensation, the Saints knew that, despite everything, they could trust President Young when he said that he was satisfied with the course they were taking and that "there had never been a body of people since the days of Enoch placed under the same circumstances where there was so little grumbling." If "Brother Brigham" was "satisfied that the Lord was pleased with the majority of the 'Camp of Israel,'" they knew, too, that the Lord was with them, leading them to a new gathering place.[15]

At the deepest level, the journey of the Saints from Nauvoo to the Great Basin was a part of a complicated *recapitulation process* wherein the Latter-day Saints *lived through* the history of the Hebrews. Historical accounts of the corporate movement of the Saints from Illinois to the Great Salt Lake Valley are rarely written without mentioning that the Saints who followed Young westward resolved themselves into a Camp of Israel and organized into companies in the same manner that the ancient Israelites had been organized during their journey from Egypt to the Promised Land in Palestine. But the real extent of the Exodus-like character of the journey is fully disclosed only when it is remembered that after weeks of "running ice," which made crossing the Mississippi River difficult and dangerous, the departure of the Saints from Nauvoo was facilitated by an "ice bridge" that allowed some of the Saints to walk across the river without getting their feet wet, in somewhat the same manner that the followers of Moses had walked across the Red Sea dryshod. That fact alone serves as a means of separating the Mormon trek from the treks of other westering pioneers, but there is more. Starving and desperate Saints reported miracles in which quail and a mannalike substance called honeydew kept them from perishing.[16]

The astonishing thing about Brigham Young is not that he presided over the Saints as the community negotiated this corporate movement across the American continent but that as he presided over the Saints, he participated with them at all three of these levels. He was the gifted practical administrator who led the pioneers to the valley. He organized way stations, chastised LDS counterfeiters (who apparently were using some sort of "despoiling the Egyptians" rationale to justify their activities), found the best roads and camping locations, and somehow managed the thousand and one other things necessary to allow the move to take place. At the same time, Young fulfilled his calling as the Lion of the Lord by serving as religious leader and spiritual counselor. Sustained as prophet, seer, and revelator, as well as the church's chief administrator, Young kept before the Saints the realization that theirs was the new dispensation; they were God's chosen people in these latter days, and the presence of this perception in their minds gave the suffering and hardship they experienced a meaning that transcended relief based on sheer survival. More than anything else, however, Young's leadership turned an extremely difficult trip across the plains and mountains into an Exodus event. Furthermore, at that deepest level, Young did not allow this exodus to fade into the ordinary past. Remembering that the journey's result was the "making of Saints," he was not satisfied merely to get the Mormons to the Great Basin. He kept the journey alive in LDS minds, both by retelling and, in a very real sense, celebrating the story in his sermons and in the annual ritual re-creations of the final "entry into the Promised Land" episode of the Exodus and by seeing that the journey, itself, was replicated again and again during the remainder of his lifetime. By establishing the Perpetual Emigrating Fund, encouraging the Handcart Brigade, and generally supporting the immigration of ever larger numbers of Saints, Young kept reminding those who were already in the valley that the pathway to Zion proceeded through the "wilderness."

In Mormon history, the three decades between 1847, the year the Saints reached Utah, and 1877, the year of President Young's death, are best understood in terms of kingdom building. The Great Basin kingdom came into existence during this time. When this segment of the LDS past is subjected to a schematic analysis, similar to the one used to consider the trek, Young's same pattern of multilevel participation with the Saints appears. It shows Young to have been an extremely effective director and counselor at the level of concrete accomplishment, all the while filling majestic roles at the experiential and symbolic levels.

All the biographical studies, including those that cast him in an unfavorable light, make it clear that overseeing the settlement of Utah was an immense responsibility, one that Young discharged with distinction. The demands he had to meet to ensure the very survival of the pioneer band are hard to comprehend. But accounts of frequent wolf hunts, hordes of locusts devouring everything in sight, and descriptions of such ingenious traps as buckets full of water with greased boards balanced on the edges sloping inward, allowing as many as sixty mice to be caught in a single evening, are reminders that simply keeping starvation at bay was a dreadful task.[17] In this space that was practically without form and void, Young had to establish and maintain order, create a community structure, deal with the area's native population, and direct the exploration and settlement of contiguous areas. As if these internal requirements were not sufficient, he had also to superintend the Saints' relationship with the Gentile world, which, as it turned out, meant the U.S. government.

Although he was extraordinarily successful as the community's pioneer leader, earning the title of "Brigham Young, the colonizer," his unique contribution to Mormonism is more transparent if attention is turned to the Saints' own perceptions of living in Utah when the "Lion of the Lord" was there to lead them. Thousands of pioneer diaries have been left behind to testify that the Latter-day Saints did not inhabit an ordinary pioneer outpost on the edge of civilization. They lived in the kingdom of God, established, as it was often put, at the beginning of the "winding-up" scene. As governor, Young stood at the head of a political entity existing at one and the same time in nineteenth-century America and in a very different age.

As patriarchs had presided over multiple families in the kingdom of David and Solomon, so men married many wives and presided over them and their progeny in this latter-day Zion. "Brother Brigham" was not the first Mormon prophet to marry into plurality, but in Joseph Smith's time the practice had been hidden. Such was the nature of the LDS kingdom in the Great Basin, however, that Young maintained an official residence, the Lion House, wherein he installed his multiple families and from which he presided over the realm as patriarch. While living in a culture in which polygamy was thus celebrated might have been sufficient to set the Saints apart, another activity drawn from the biblical kingdom was carried on in this land: temple building. Unlike the pattern of temple construction in the Old Testament, LDS temple building was not concentrated in a single locale; even as Mormons created their kingdom in the West, they expected to return to Jackson County, Missouri, which revelation to Joseph Smith had identified as the "new Jerusalem." For all that, the construction of those extraordinary temples in Saint George, Logan, Manti, and Salt Lake City was as significant as the practice of plural marriage in the process of realizing—in the sense of making real—the validity of Young's claim that this LDS Zion in the American West was, in fact, the kingdom of God.[18]

So rich are the sources that it is not difficult to find indications of the symbolic importance of Young's role during the kingdom-building years. At first, of course, he was both governor of the State of Deseret (afterward Utah Territory) and "Prophet, Seer, Revelator, and President" to the Saints, with no necessity for some symbolic significance of his place. When the United States confronted the reality of the existence of the Mormon kingdom, however, rumor went out that the LDS leader would be removed from civil office. Responding to that rumor, Young told the Saints that he was and would be governor until the Lord Almighty said, "Brigham, you need not be Governor any longer," because "no man can thwart the plans of the Almighty for he will carry them out and none can stay His hand."[19] This prediction would appear to have come to naught, since Young's office was taken away; yet the historical record indicates otherwise. The nation settled its agents in the territorial governor's chair, but Young remained governor de facto throughout his lifetime. More significant for this consideration is the symbolic import of the history of the State of Deseret. An often acrimonious debate has been going on for years over the purpose of the organization and legislative deliberations of this so-called Mormon ghost government, which, following adjournment of the territorial legislature, met annually in the 1860s to hear messages from "Governor Young" and enact legislation for Deseret. Without entering into this debate, if Deseret's history is taken into account, it is easy to see that Young's position at the head of the government was, in the eyes of the Saints, not simply de facto. To the citizens of Deseret, "Brother Brigham" was sovereign in the land.[20]

The multilevel character of Young's "progressions" through the territory serves as a further indicator of the multiple roles this amazing LDS leader assumed as the kingdom was being established. These periodic visits to the

Saints who lived at some distance from Great Salt Lake City were, first of all, practical personal surveys that allowed Young to measure the progress of settlement and assess the Latter-day Saints' state of being. They were also ecclesiastical events, occasions on which the Saints experienced the presence of a prophet, seer, and revelator in their midst. Of greater consequence here, those visits took on the character of royal progressions through a kingdom over which a monarch ruled. The mode was regal and the reaction appropriately adulatory. Notwithstanding their points of origin—Liverpool, Nauvoo, Copenhagen, or wherever else—in their responses to Young's presence, the people of this movement revealed that their connection to Mormonism was deeper and more complex than religious affiliation alone; they had been turned into citizens of the LDS kingdom, in a word, Saints.

The foregoing sketch fits readily into the timeworn pattern of telling stories of the Mormon "trek" and Utah pioneer period that make Brigham Young the central figure and give him the lion's share of the credit for moving the Mormon community from Illinois to Utah and getting it established in the Great Basin, but it can do more than illuminate the Mormon leader's personal biography. This examination points beyond the story of "Brother Brigham" to disclose, through its multilevel approach, that traveling to Zion and living in that land in the pioneer days were transformative experiences. They served as passageways ushering individuals into Sainthood and as experiential corridors in which the Saints were corporately transmuted from their miscellaneousness and variableness into an ethnic body whose shared heritage was a wilderness journey and lives lived out in Zion. Their Mormon ethnicity set the Saints apart, permitting—perhaps mandating—the creation of an LDS culture that would survive not only the death of Brigham Young but also the demise of the practice of plural marriage and the disappearance of Mormon political and economic hegemony and the natural barriers that surrounded the LDS culture region in the nineteenth century.

Young's crucial role in the creation of this LDS culture proves that the notion that he saved Mormonism from the follies of its founder is entirely wrongheaded. Instead of rescuing Mormonism from Joseph Smith, Young took the lead in creating a form of Mormonism that so fully explored the implications of the fullness of the first LDS prophet's visions that it was more esoteric, more communal, and, from the standpoint of traditional Christianity, more heretical under Brigham Young than it had been during the lifetime of Joseph Smith.

If Young did not save Mormonism from his predecessor's follies, what role did he play in the development of Mormonism after Joseph Smith's death? Many observers suggest, as indicated, that Young was responsible for Mormonism's survival in the wake of the prophet's murder, but any survey of Mormon history that takes in a spectrum wide enough to include the Saints who did not go west, as well as those who did, proves this popular notion to be in error. Mormonism was "reorganized" in the Midwest under the leadership of Joseph Smith III and institutionalized as the Reorganized Church of Jesus Christ of Latter Day Saints, with headquarters in Independence in Jackson County, Missouri, where it still survives.[21] This means that although Brigham Young played a critical role in the development of Mormonism, it was a role played out as the leader of the Mormons *who went west.* Yet his role still ought not to be described in De Voto's terms. Perhaps, indeed, "the church must have perished" without his leadership, but in view of the survival of an astonishing number of variant forms of Mormonism, that is improbable.[22] More likely, had Young not been there to turn the Mormon trail into an exodus route and had he not seen to it that the Great Basin was turned into God's kingdom, Mountain Mormonism would never have become the creative combination of ethnicity and ecclesiology, church and culture, that set it apart for a full hundred years after the Saints reached the Great Basin and that, even now, gives it enormous internal vitality, making it a force to reckon with on the world's religious scene.

Notes

1. According to my "From Satyr to Saint" data base, over 53 percent of the articles published between 1861 and 1895 in which Joseph Smith and Brigham Young were mentioned emphasized Brigham Young more than Joseph Smith; 24 percent emphasized Joseph Smith more than Brigham Young; and 23 percent accorded reasonably equal treatment to the two Mormon leaders.

2. Catherine Van Valkenburg Waite, *The Mormon Prophet and His Harem; or, An Authentic History of Brigham Young, His Numerous Wives and Children* (Cambridge, Mass.: Riverside, 1866); Ann Eliza Webb Young, *Wife No. 19; or, The Story of a Life in Bondage, Being a Complete Exposé of Mormonism, and Revealing the Sorrows, Sacrifices and Sufferings of Women in Polygamy* (Hartford, Conn.: Dustin, Gilman, 1875; reprint, New York: Arno, 1972).

3. Frank J. Cannon and Harvey J. O'Higgins, *Under the Prophet in Utah: The National Menace of a Political Priestcraft* (Boston: C. M. Clark, 1911); Frank J. Cannon and George L. Knapp, *Brigham Young and His Mormon Empire* (New York: Fleming H. Revell, 1913); M. R. Werner, *Brigham Young* (London: J. Cape, 1925); Preston Nibley, *Brigham Young: The Man and His Work* (Salt Lake City: Deseret News, 1936); Milton Hunter, *Brigham Young, the Colonizer* (Salt Lake City: Deseret News, 1940); Ray B. West, *Kingdom of the Saints: The Story of Brigham Young and the Mormons* (New York: Viking, 1957).

4. Edward Tullidge, *Life of Brigham Young; or, Utah and Her Founders* (New York: Tullidge and Crandall, 1876); Fanny Stenhouse, *"Tell It All": The Story of a Life Expe-*

rience in Mormonism (Hartford, Conn.: A. D. Worthington, 1874); T. B. H. Stenhouse, *Rocky Mountain Saints: A Full and Complete History of the Mormons* (New York: D. Appleton, 1873).

5. Bernard De Voto, "Centennial of Mormonism," *American Mercury* 19 (January 1930): 1–13.

6. The major canonized histories of the LDS Church are B. H. Roberts, *A Comprehensive History of the Church of Jesus Christ of Latter-day Saints*, 6 vols. (Salt Lake City: Deseret News, 1930); B. H. Roberts, ed., *History of the Church of Jesus Christ of Latter-day Saints: Period I, History of Joseph Smith, the Prophet, by Himself* and *Period II, From the Manuscript History of Brigham Young and Other Original Documents*, 7 vols. (Salt Lake City: Church of Jesus Christ of Latter-day Saints, 1902–32); and Joseph Fielding Smith, *Essentials in Church History: A History of the Church from the Birth of Joseph Smith to the Present Time with Introductory Chapters on the Antiquity of the Gospel and the "Falling Away,"* 26th ed. (Salt Lake City: Deseret Book, 1973).

7. Dean L. May, "A Demographic Portrait of the Mormons, 1830–1980," in *After 150 Years: Mormonism in Sesqui-centennial Perspective*, ed. Thomas G. Alexander and Jessie Embry (Provo, Utah: Charles Redd Center for Western Studies; distributed by Signature Books, 1983), 37–69.

8. Douglas D. Alder and Paul M. Edwards, "Common Beginnings, Divergent Beliefs," *Dialogue* 11 (Spring 1978): 18–28.

9. The description quoted here comes from the entry on Brigham Young in Andrew Jenson, *Latter-day Saint Biographical Encyclopedia*, 4 vols. (Salt Lake City: Andrew Jenson Publishing, 1901), 1:11. This apparent manifestation of the spirit, which occurred on August 8, 1844, is often referred to as Young's receiving "the mantle of the prophet." Descriptions of the event were recorded by several different Latter-day Saints. Especially well known, perhaps because they are included in a note in the *History of the Church of Jesus Christ of Latter-day Saints* (7:236), are those recorded by George Q. Cannon, William C. Staines, and Wilford Woodruff. Leonard Arrington described this momentous event in *Brigham Young: American Moses* (New York: Alfred A. Knopf, 1985; reprint, Urbana: University of Illinois Press, 1986), 114–15.

10. Richard P. Howard, "The Reorganized Church in Illinois, 1852–82: Search for Identity," *Dialogue* 5 (Spring 1970): 62–75.

11. Eugene England, *Brother Brigham* (Salt Lake City: Bookcraft, 1980); Ronald K. Esplin, "The Emergence of Brigham Young and the Twelve to Mormon Leadership, 1830–1841" (Ph.D. diss., Brigham Young University, 1981); Arrington, *Brigham Young: American Moses*. All three scholars also made many presentations dealing with Young and published articles on the subject.

12. Linda Newell's observation was made in response to a paper presented by Eugene England (see note 13) at the annual meeting of the Mormon History Association in Omaha, Nebraska, in May 1983.

13. Eugene England, "Brigham Young's Rhetoric: The Language of Tradition and Persuasion" (paper presented at the annual meeting of the Mormon History Association, Omaha, Nebr., May 1983).

14. Jenson, *Latter-day Saint Biographical Encyclopedia*, 1:12.

15. Roberts, ed., *History of the Church of Jesus Christ of Latter-day Saints*, 7:608.

16. Jan Shipps, *Mormonism: The Story of a New Religious Tradition* (Urbana: University of Illinois, 1985), 41–65, is a full exploration of this recapitulation process. For

an account of the "honey-dew" miracle, see Carol Lynn Pearson, "'Nine Children Were Born': A Historical Problem from the Sugar Creek Episode," *BYU Studies* 21 (Fall 1981): 443. A similar "miracle" was reported to have taken place during the period of "kingdom-building." See *Deseret News,* August 22, 1855.

17. For a firsthand description of the difficulties the Saints experienced in the early days in the Salt Lake Valley, see Isabella Hale, "Migration and Settlement of the Latter-day Saints," manuscript, n.d., Bancroft Library, University of California at Berkeley. It includes a description of the mousetrap.

18. Young's references to the kingdom of God were sometimes ambiguous, but his sermons in the *Journal of Discourses* make it obvious that his listeners could have understood his references to it as a proclamation that Zion and the "kingdom" were one and the same. See especially *Journal of Discourses,* 26 vols. (Liverpool, England: F. D. and S. W. Richards, 1854–86; photo lithographic reprint, Los Angeles: Gartner Printing and Litho, 1956), 5:327, which includes the direct statement, "This is the Kingdom of God on the earth."

19. Ibid., 1:187; David Pettigrew, Journal (photocopy), Manuscript Collections, Utah State Historical Society, Salt Lake City.

20. The debate over the purposes of the formation and activities of the "State of Deseret" centers on the question of whether this organization was the political arm of the kingdom of God. See especially Klaus J. Hansen, *Quest for Empire: The Political Kingdom of God and the Council of Fifty in Mormon History* (Lansing: Michigan State University Press, 1967; reprint, Lincoln: University of Nebraska Press, 1974); D. Michael Quinn, "The Council of Fifty and Its Members, 1844 to 1956," *BYU Studies* 20 (Winter 1980): 163–97; and Peter Crawley, "The Constitution of the State of Deseret: A Keepsake [essay] Issued by the Friends of the Harold B. Lee Library in Commemoration of the Library's Two-Millionth Volume," *Friends of the Brigham Young University Library Newsletter* 19 (November 1982): 1–27.

21. It seems, however, to be an open question as to how long the Mormon connection will have much meaning to the Reorganized Church, which appears to be making a real effort to become a "peace church." Furthermore, for the first time in its history, the RLDS Church no longer has at its head a member of the family of the prophet, a direct descendant of Joseph Smith.

22. De Voto, "Centennial of Mormonism," 9; Charles C. Rich, *Those Who Would Be Leaders (Offshoots of Mormonism),* 2d ed. (Provo, Utah: Brigham Young University Extension Publications, 1967).

13

The Scattering of the Gathering
and the Gathering of the Scattered:
The Mid-Twentieth-Century Mormon Diaspora

By revelation given in 1830 through the Prophet Joseph Smith, God called the members of the Church of Jesus Christ, newly organized in April of that year, to gather themselves together as baby chicks are gathered under a mother hen's wing. At that time, the prophet and most of the Latter-day Saints expected the imminent ushering in of the millennial kingdom. The Saints' corporate response to the gathering revelation heightened the millennial expectations of the whole group, and this, in turn, released an incredible amount of what some would call psychic energy but others would describe as religious or spiritual commitment. The gathering of the Saints, which came about first in Kirtland, Ohio, also led to an astonishing willingness on the part of the Saints to make huge portions of their meager resources available for building up the kingdom.

The result was that a great variety of people from diverse backgrounds who believed they were God's chosen people in these latter-days of the last dispensation of the fullness of times rapidly coalesced into a communion of Saints, a new community. The members of this community generally gave assent to the complex set of theological claims on which Joseph Smith's standing as a prophet rested, so they shared not only millennial expectations but also understandings of the sources of legitimate authority in both the civic and religious realms.

The Kirtland Temple, which the Saints constructed according to specifications given through their prophet, symbolized their shared convictions. It gave them a holy place literally in the geographic center of the community, and it was the setting for the extraordinary corporate baptism by the spirit that the Saints experienced during the building's dedication. Indeed, insofar as the Mormon kingdom is regarded as synonymous with the kingdom of God, it can be said to have commenced during the transfigurationlike happening that stood at the heart of the dedication of the Kirtland Temple.

As important as that corporate spiritual experience was, however, a sense of oneness, of true community, did not occur in an instant. Communities are not like popcorn; they do not spring full-blown into existence. Everyday ordinary social intercourse surrounded the kernels of shared religious beliefs and shared spiritual experience. In direct contrast to most Protestant parishes made up of congregations whose members worshiped together on Sundays but returned during the week to a pluralistic (albeit Protestant) culture, the Saints who attended sacrament meetings or heard sermons from less than imposing stands on Sundays lived out their ordinary weekday lives in close proximity to one to another. As a result, Mormons started thinking of themselves as Saints in the secular as well as religious dimensions of their lives. The Mormon gathering thus shaped the way Saints thought about themselves, not just from the standpoint of exclusivist religious claims to being the chosen, God's new Israel led by a living prophet, but also from the practical, pragmatic perspective of sharing the more mundane joys and sorrows of everyday life. Mixed in with spiritual highs were low points precipitated by the deaths of loved ones, the loss of economic security, and, just as important, such ordinary exasperations as bread that would not rise or seeds that would not sprout. Together with their shared religious beliefs, the physical gathering of the Saints led to the development of such a strong Mormon identity that the Saints gave up existing birthrights and past identities.[1]

The significance of the gathering for Mormon self-understanding was not lost on non-Mormons. In Ohio, Missouri, and Illinois, the corporate character of Mormon life frightened those who stood on the outside. Assessing the extent to which it was politics, or religion, or economics that turned non-Mormon fright to active hostility is interesting but extremely difficult. It is, however, easy to see that opposition gave the Saints something to stand over and against: Christians versus the lions; Saints versus a Gentile world. Saints had no choice except to take sides, and as they did so, their identification with Mormonism intensified. The vicissitudes the movement suffered in Ohio, Missouri, and Illinois therefore strengthened LDS self-understanding.[2]

Elsewhere I have argued that the trek west and the experience of living in the kingdom, set apart by both geography and the institution of plural marriage, functioned as cultural "glue," calling into existence not just a chosen people in the religious sense but also a new ethnicity as fully rooted in self-understanding as in common religious belief.[3] Heretofore, my argument has emphasized the intangible but very real impact of a shared sacred history and shared symbols of kinship (i.e., plural marriage, the adoption ordinance, genealogy, and temple work). Examining the impact of the gathering is a reminder that there is yet another body of evidence showing the strength of LDS identity and the existence of a Mormon ethnicity. This is the ability the community of Saints repeatedly demonstrated of incorporating large numbers of people from many different cultures who had accepted the Mormon gospel. Historians and folklorists can separate out culture areas in Utah—the Danes in San Pete County (especially Manti) and Box Elder County (especially Brigham City), for example—and British, German, and Swiss cultural areas elsewhere in the Great Basin. In discussing immigration to the Mormon kingdom in the nineteenth century and early twentieth, observers often point to the widespread retention of native languages through at least the first generation, as well as the existence of German- and Danish-language newspapers. But unlike the situations in American Lutheran and Roman Catholic folds, where German Lutherans and Swedish Lutherans, Irish Catholics and Italian Catholics, and so on were assimilated into American culture but not into a pan-Lutheran or pan-Catholic culture, the nineteenth- and early twentieth-century gathered community of Saints turned Danes into Mormons, Britons into Mormons, Germans into Mormons, and so on.[4] Although the Manifesto of 1890, which announced the demise of plural marriage and Mormonism's accompanying loss of the politico-economic independence it had enjoyed during its kingdom period, was traumatic, these stunning developments affected the gathering only indirectly. They did not weaken the gathering—quite the reverse. For the LDS Church, the decades between 1890 and the end of World War I were not marked by vigorous external growth. But because the Saints continued to "gather to Zion" from their homes in the "mission field," the LDS population in the area often described as the Mormon culture region increased more rapidly than total church membership.[5]

During the ecclesiastical administration of church president Joseph F. Smith (1901–18), Senator Reed Smoot and other influential Mormons worked hard in Washington, D.C., and in overseas embassies to reverse the U.S. immigration officials' practice (if not policy) of disallowing the applications of Mormon converts who wished to gather to Zion.[6] Unfortunately for the gathering Saints, however, the Great Basin did not lend itself to intensive population settlement as long as agriculture was the primary means of earning a living there. LDS Church authorities soon came to realize this, and, therefore, even as they were successful in their effort to change the situation regarding LDS immigration, the church itself changed its attitude toward the gathering revelation.

This change did not come in a single dramatic announcement that made the 1830 revelation null and void. It came instead in a series of shifts that effected an official reinterpretation of the meaning of the gathering revelation. Whereas the church had long held that converts should flee out of "Babylon" to join the Saints in Zion, President Smith started saying to European Saints in 1910 that "at present" they did not need to "trouble themselves too much about emigration."[7] He told his Swedish listeners that they did not need to be troubled even about the temple ordinances, "for if death should intervene before the ordinances were performed, their children could see to it that the work was done."[8]

Douglas D. Alder, in his 1950 Master's thesis on the German-speaking immigration to Utah, summarized the steps that brought about this complete policy change and the subsequent reinterpretation of the gathering revelation. He suggested that President Smith's use of the phrase "at present" indicated a lack of agreement among the LDS general authorities about a definite policy change on this matter. If Alder's suggestion is correct, and it stands to reason that it is, the evidence indicates that the policy question was settled by 1921. On October 18 of that year, the First Presidency issued an official statement urging missionaries to stop preaching immigration. This statement gave economic rather than religious reasons for this counsel, however. Not until 1940 did religious justification for the Saints' staying put resume priority. That year, the Saints were directed to "gather out of spiritual Babylon, out of the midst of wickedness," but they did not need to go so far as to gather in Utah. This same general counsel has been given to Saints throughout the world since then. In the words of Spencer W. Kimball in 1955, "[R]emain [in your own land] and build up a people to the Lord."[9]

While this policy turnabout was by no means limited to Saints outside the United States, in the years before World War II, Saints in this country continued, for the most part, to live in the traditional Mormon areas of Utah, southern Idaho, western Wyoming, eastern Nevada, northern Arizona, and eastern New Mexico.[10] There were exceptions, of course; throughout the years, individual Saints or single families left "the valley" for various reasons. A good number departed the intermountain area because they were disenchanted with Mormonism, but the great majority of those who left probably did so for economic reasons. Some in this latter group maintained their allegiance to the LDS Church even though they established homes so far from organized LDS bodies that their ties to the Saints could be maintained only by receiving mail, entertaining traveling Mormons, or going "home to Zion" for visits. Some settled close enough to participate actively in the programs of the church as members of LDS branches primarily peopled by Saints who had joined the church but had never participated in the gathering. In the pre–World War II years, however, the organizational situation was different outside the Mormon culture region because branches were generally attached to missions and because mission presidents who oversaw the activities of the church's comparatively small bands of missionaries also presided over local branches of Latter-day Saints.[11]

The main exceptions to this pattern before the end of the Great Depression came with the organization of the Union stake in Oregon in 1901 and the opening up of a Mormon region in southern California during the early years of the administration of Heber J. Grant, who served as president of the church from 1918 to 1945.[12] The first LDS stake established in California was established in Los Angeles in 1923. A second California stake was organized in Hollywood in 1927, and a third was organized that same year in San Francisco.[13] Before World War II, nine other stakes were organized in California. Such units were also organized in several major urban areas in other parts of the United States: New York (1934), Chicago (1936), Portland, Oregon (1938), Seattle (1938), Denver (1940), and Washington, D.C. (1940). A stake was also organized in Laie, Hawaii (1935) before the beginning of World War II.

Even so, developments that led once and for all to the permanent, apparently irreversible policy that "Zion is where the people of God are" did not come until the end of World War II. Moreover, when it came, the scattering of the gathering that carried so many Saints away from the "kingdom in the tops of the mountain" came about without direction from the church. Many service people, returning from wartime tours of duty, sought employment outside the Great Basin because they (or their parents) remembered how hard the Great Depression had been in the Mormon culture region. As a result, they took advantage of occupational opportunities elsewhere. With G.I. benefits available to them, Saints were attracted to "Gentile" colleges and universities and, thereafter, very often to work outside and away from Zion.

The natural increase that came to most American families during the postwar "baby boom" came "in spades" to these Mormon families that had settled in the "mission field." As a result, in a surprisingly short time significant numbers of Latter-day Saints scattered all across the United States, with many settling either in the environs of major universities or in the suburbs of the nation's great cities. By 1960, only Kentucky, Tennessee, and the Dakotas could not claim at least a thousand members of the LDS Church. Of particular importance to the post–World War II scattering was the spread of Mormons across the southern United States, the Midwest—particularly Indiana and Illinois—and the Pacific Northwest.

The out-migration of Saints from the Great Basin and surrounding areas and the difficulty of calculating the size of natural increase in Mormon families in the traditional Mormon culture region relative to those in other parts of the nation make it almost impossible to compare with any real precision the levels of church growth in and outside the Mormon culture region during the first decade and a half after the war. But as table 2 demonstrates, if the organization of new stakes is used as a measure, Mormonism's changing geographical profile is easy to discern.

Table 2. New Stakes Organized in the United States, 1946–65

	1945–50	1951–55	1956–60	1961–65	Totals
Mormon culture region	31	17	22	41	111
Other parts of U.S.	50	10	22	48	130
Totals	81	27	44	89	241

Source: The history of the formation of stakes is in every *Church Almanac,* issued biennially by Deseret News in cooperation with the Historical Department of the Church of Jesus Christ of Latter-day Saints.

From 1960 onward, despite a higher birthrate among Latter-day Saints than among non-Mormons, the number of convert baptisms has been greater than the number of members added to the church membership rolls from natural increase.[14] The extraordinary level of church growth throughout the nation and the church's manner of reporting on membership make it almost impossible to make comparisons that will reveal anything much more precise about the scattering of once gathered Saints in the late 1940s and the 1950s. But impressionistic perceptions of an LDS Church led in the areas outside the Mormon culture region by members of the LDS priesthood who were reared in the Great Basin before the war are so commonplace that it is obvious a dramatic scattering of the gathering occurred in the decade or so following the war.

Other post–World War II phenomena, the increasing use of tape recorders and the growing importance of oral history, make it possible to reconstruct what happened as Latter-day Saints settled all across the country. At least two oral history sources are available to researchers: materials gathered through the James Moyle Oral History Program, established by the LDS Church during the "historical administration" of Leonard J. Arrington, and an oral history project that was conducted in local stakes and wards in which a more or less haphazard selection of LDS bishops and former bishops who served outside the LDS culture region were interviewed.

These oral histories reveal that there was a good deal of trying first this and then that on the part of the church administration as the implications of the scattering became clear.[15] Moreover, while considerable variation characterized the good-faith attempts the general authorities made to give individual attention to each situation, a programmatic pattern of church response to the scattering gradually developed. That response is described below.

∾

To understand fully the pattern that developed, it is important to remember that the LDS Church has no professional clergy. The Saints have a lay priesthood organized into quorums of the Aaronic (or lower) priesthood and the Melchizedek (or higher) priesthood. These quorums are ranked from lowest to highest, with the deacons, teachers, and priests quorums in the priesthood of Aaron, while quorums of elders, seventies, and high priests are in the priesthood of Melchizedek. Latter-day Saint males are generally ordained as deacons in the Aaronic priesthood at the age of twelve. Ordinarily, LDS males move through the teachers and priests quorums in their teens and are elevated to quorums of elders in the Melchizedek priesthood when they go on missions or move into adult life. If they become inactive for some reason, they are not automatically moved into the higher priesthood but retain their status as members of the Aaronic priesthood.

During the war, huge numbers of young Saints had gone into the service while they were still members of Aaronic priesthood quorums. When the war was over, the returning servicemen who failed to resume active participation in the church became, by default, members of a large and unwieldy Mormon group known as "Adult Aaronics." Having joined or been drafted into the service at just the age when adult perceptions of identity are in the process of becoming fixed, having been propelled into the fellowship of wartime service units, and having settled outside the Mormon culture region after the war, many of these young men were nominal Mormons, at best. When what I am calling "mission field" bishops referred to the large numbers of young adult males in their wards, many of whom did not think of themselves first and foremost as Mormons, these exasperated local church leaders often used the phrase "adult inactives" rather than "Adult Aaronics." Sometimes they used both descriptors, as did Bishop La Farr P. Astle in describing his ward in Pittsburg, California. He recalled that his ward "had a little over 100, at times, inactive Adult Aaronics."[16]

Inactive young men were not Bishop Astle's only problem, however, for in his ward, "out of 150 families, more than half were what we call split families with just one member, usually the woman, belonging to the church."[17] This was not an isolated situation limited to one area of the country in the late 1940s and the 1950s. Many young LDS women had married non-Mormon servicemen during the war and had left the Mormon culture region to settle elsewhere with their husbands before their identities were fully formed. As a result, their perception of themselves as Mormons was also threatened. As they became mothers in the early years after the war, however, many of these young wives sought both support and spiritual succor among the Saints. Naturally, they took their young children with them as they began to attend meetings in local wards. For this reason, the demographic profiles of many (perhaps most) of the new wards formed in the mission field in the decade after the war were skewed by the presence of many active young women, huge numbers of very young children, and very few active men. With only a scattering of males above ten years of age and with practically no active members who held rank in the Melchizedek priesthood, creating a full-scale ward program was sometimes, as they say, an act of faith. One bishop of a ward in the New York Stake reported that he had only one active Melchizedek priesthood holder, for example. Yet this bishop and hundreds of others somehow managed to establish full-scale programs.

By and large, this is what occurred. The first step in re-gathering the scattered Saints in the early years after the war was the identification of a worthy layperson who could be called to serve as the ward leader in an area where an LDS ward had not before been organized. Typically, this was done by LDS authorities, usually a mission president, ward bishop, or stake president in an adjacent area. When enough Saints had settled in the new area to justify the formation of a ward, this person would be called as the ward bishop, the LDS nomenclature for congregational leader. Sometimes these about-to-be-called bishops had a history—however short—of being reasonably active in LDS endeavors while the area was still unorganized, often indicating their suitability for the assignment by the simple act of driving with their families for a considerable distance to attend Sunday School and sacrament meetings. But as often as not, a bishop was called to serve as much on the basis of his record of youthful prewar church activity in a Great Basin ward or stake as on his activity in the area where the new ward was being formed.

I discerned this pattern of identifying bishops from the information in the oral histories of "mission field" bishops in the LDS Church Archives, documents that do not contain individual narrative accounts of each bishop's experience so much as answers given by the mission field bishops to a standard set of open-ended questions. These queries began with a request to each bishop to recount his personal history as a Latter-day Saint. Of the scores of documents I examined, very few—probably less that 10 percent—contained references to a bishop's having grown up outside the Mormon culture region. Nearly all grew up in Utah, eastern Nevada, or southern Idaho.

At the same time, however, very few of these postwar "mission field" bishops were closely connected to renowned LDS families in Utah. As a group, they were men from families whose members had "followed their file leaders" (priesthood authorities) in the early part of the twentieth century. Because so many moved up through the ranks to become stake presidents and, in some cases, moved on into the LDS hierarchy, this pattern of calling men from families whose record of church service was solid but not particularly noteworthy turned out to be a pattern of infusing new blood into the church's administrative structure. If most of the priesthood leaders who would become general authorities were still closely connected to the leadership cadre that D. Michael Quinn identified in *The Mormon Hierarchy: Origins of Power* and *The Mormon Hierarchy: Extensions of Power,* these "mission field" bishops became the foundation of a formidable middle-management corps that made it possible for the church to manage the growth and geographical expansion that would take place after 1960.[18]

The first tasks a new bishop had to perform were calling the scattered Saints together, finding a place for them to meet, and establishing a regular schedule of meetings. On Sundays, these included a priesthood meeting, Sunday School, and a sacrament meeting. During the week, LDS auxiliary activities included "Primary" for the youngsters; Boy Scouts, which—for all practical purposes—became an official LDS auxiliary; youth activities (still called "Mutual" in those days) for any teenagers in the ward; and Women's Relief Society. Moreover, there was ward teaching (in which two members of the priesthood were responsible for visiting the Saints in their own homes at least once a month). Bishops and their counselors were also responsible for organizing welfare projects by which the ward could earn enough to underwrite the welfare assistance that, from time to time, bishops needed to dispense to Saints in trouble. All this, it must be kept in mind, had to be done as these (sometimes quite young) LDS ex-servicemen were moving into new jobs or trying to get professional careers established.

Managing all this was exceedingly difficult, especially in mission field wards, which tended to be "bottom-heavy," that is, wards in which there were rarely enough members of the priesthood to direct and carry out these many functions. Often, even if they were "on the books," not enough priesthood members could be rounded up to do the ward's work because the level of Adult Aaronic inactivity was so high. The good Bishop Astle's hundred inactive Adult Aaronics would seem to have been about average. Many bishops remembered that at least 50 to 60 percent of the men in their wards were inactive. Moreover, given the demographic makeup of the mission field wards in the late 1940s, it was not at all unusual for a ward to have so few deacons of the usual age for passing the sacrament (i.e., from twelve to fifteen years old) that this duty had to be performed by Adult Aaronics, who were also scarce. Bishop Doyle N. Hawkins, who conducted several of these interviews, remembered it was very difficult to find enough home teachers to serve all the members of his ward. He said they sometimes had to assign seven or eight members to a single pair of home teachers, and, even then, a senior companion often had no junior companion.[19]

The gravity of the situation in those early postwar years was summed up in the response given by Wilford Thomas Webb, who, after years of service as a counselor in a bishopric and service on a high council, was called to be chairman of the stake's genealogy committee. In accepting his new assignment, he told President Harold B. Lee that it might not really be much of a change. He had, he said, been "chasing live dead ones" for fourteen years.[20] Clearly, something needed to be done to remind these scattered Saints of their Mormon heritage and LDS identity.

This "something," in nearly every case, turned out to be the building of a ward chapel. As the bishops' oral histories indicate, this often pulled the Saints together spiritually as well as physically, reminding them that they had been and still were Latter-day Saints. Bishop George Mortimer remembered that when his ward built the Short Hills Chapel, "it brought a lot of people into activity that otherwise wouldn't have been."[21] On this subject, Bishop Astle said:

> The church building turned out to be a little short of what I had envisioned, but it served our purpose for over twenty years. . . . [Working together] pulled the Saints together spiritually, and the Lord's will was done. . . . As far as getting inactive people into activity, we were able to use our building program quite a good deal in this area. We had quite a number of inactive Adult Aaronics come and work on the chapel; then after a few months they would occasionally show up at church. Some of them even became holders of high positions in the ward.[22]

Karl George Jellinghausen's description sums up the importance of building chapels with such a clear understanding of the importance of this activity in these years of recongregating the scattered gathering that it bears quoting at length:

> It seems that I've been in a building program ever since I came back into activity in the church. I appreciate it because I realize if the Church isn't growing we may become stagnant. But here in this area [northern California] alone we've had so many experiences where building programs have brought

people into activity and given them opportunity to participate in these programs. . . . We had one of those building plans where the members had an
opportunity to go out and work on it . . . they don't work that way anymore.
It used to be that they sent a Building Supervisor or Superintendent out from
the church. . . . and he went around from one building to another . . . most
of [the work] was donated labor. . . . Now we contracted out some of the
plumbing. We contracted out all the brick work—the block work and everything. But for the most part most of the men and many women would go
down evenings and work and we spent Saturdays over there working. It was
really quite a thing to go down on Saturday because we had a feed at noon.
It was fit for a king. . . . The [sisters would] bring food down. And the brotherhood and companionship that developed out of this was good. . . .

I miss that part of the building program. There is a brotherhood that you
don't get when you just associate with them in going to meetings: There is
this brotherhood that comes from working with people that you don't get
when you are just making cash contributions.[23]

The story of the significance of building chapels to what became a reified
gathering that turned mission field wards into miniature Mormon culture
regions is probably best captured not in some bishop's narrative but in the
final chapter of *Rocky Mountain Empire,* a book about Latter-day Saints in
the twentieth century, written by Sam Taylor. In a chapter called "The Wasatch Front," he describes the building of a chapel by the members of the
Redwood City Ward in northern California.[24]

Taylor, a professional writer, was the grandson of the church president
John Taylor. His father was John W. Taylor, an apostle who not only had been
a polygamist himself but also had continued to marry people into plurality
long after the Manifesto of 1890 announced to the world that the church's
sanction of plural marriage was at an end. In 1905, the church president Joseph F. Smith forced Apostle Taylor and his friend and fellow apostle Mat-
thias W. Cowley to resign from the Council of the Twelve as a part of the cost
required to secure the safety of Apostle Reed Smoot's seat in the U.S. Senate.
Young Sam, born two years after his father's official ostracism, was skeptical
about the validity of virtually everything that occurred in the LDS Church
in the twentieth century.[25] But he also had what D. Michael Quinn once called
Mormon DNA.[26] Born a Saint, he was ordained as a deacon while he was still
a boy and more than half a century later would identify himself as "the oldest deacon" in the church in northern California.

An Adult Aaronic, he was, almost in spite of himself, drawn back into
activity as the members of his ward engaged in the construction of a ward
chapel. He "kept his tools and overalls in his car . . . dropping around every

spare hour" during the final weeks before the dedication of the building. While he gloried in still belonging to a deacon's quorum, he was reminded daily of his Mormon heritage.[27]

This building program did more than bring adult Saints (especially men) back into church activity. It also was the occasion of the physical manifestation of Mormonism all across the American landscape. For nearly a century, the church had maintained missions throughout the nation, but these missions were, for the most part, housed in buildings that had once been large homes. These residential structures were large enough to accommodate small congregations, but they did not look like churches. In the postwar period, the Saints started constructing houses of worship all across the nation that looked like what they were: chapels. They all looked pretty much alike because they were built according to standard plans. From the architectural and aesthetic perspective, they were not particularly distinctive, but from the symbolic standpoint, they were distinctively Mormon. Just as the title of Taylor's chapter implied, by going into one of these newly constructed LDS chapels, Latter-day Saints were symbolically transported to the Wasatch Front. As these structures announced to the outside world that Mormonism was moving beyond the bounds of the traditional Mormon kingdom, they said to scattered Saints that they had come home; Mormon sisters and brothers were there, a bishopric and Relief Society presidency were in place, and the church was fully organized, waiting for them to participate.

And participate they did. With their gymnasiums, chapels, classrooms, libraries, kitchens, Relief Society rooms, and bishop's offices, these new buildings functioned as LDS cultural centers, Mormon enclaves that became, in the mission field, the places of gathering. Since the church's full program involved the Saints in so many meetings that a popular definition of a Mormon in those days was "someone who is planning a meeting, going to a meeting, sitting in a meeting, or coming from a meeting," they were in use day and night, practically seven days a week.[28]

In 1980, the general authorities established a consolidated meeting schedule that changed the situation for Latter-day Saints dramatically by compressing most LDS meetings into three-hour blocks on Sundays. From that point onward, ward members attended Sunday School and sacrament meeting. Men would then attend priesthood meetings, women went to Relief Society, and children and youth would attend age-appropriate meetings. But in the more than three decades before this new way of being Mormon was introduced, the construction and use of all these mission field ward chapels signaled nothing less than the creation of mini-Zions. These were real places in space and time that, because everyone there was participating with other

Saints in LDS activities, operated to re-gather Latter-day Saints into a whole people. In these mission field chapels, Saints who had once lived "in the tops of the mountains" could recover what being Mormon meant.

The years between 1945 and the early 1960s were crucial years for the Church of Jesus Christ of Latter-day Saints. The scattered Saints quite literally built LDS worlds for themselves outside the boundaries of Utah, southern Idaho, and the rest of what had once been the Mormon kingdom. Both insiders and outsiders have probably focused too much on the years since midcentury as a period of unparalleled growth and geographic expansion. Very few, if any, have recognized the extent to which the first ten or fifteen years after World War II constituted a necessary period of consolidation and renewal. In a very real sense, these years form a discrete era in the history of Mormonism, a period in which the Saints prepared themselves for a new effort to carry the gospel to the world. Scattered, spread thin, and often with Mormon identities in a precarious state at the beginning, by the end of the period Saints were ready to assimilate into their Zionic spheres the many new converts sent their way through a local stake missionary program and a revitalized and dynamic program of assigning full-time missionaries to missions all over the United States and across the globe.

Church president David O. McKay's injunction that "every member" should be a missionary stimulated missionary activity throughout the church. By 1960, most of the mission field wards were at least as ready as those at the center to embark on a process of trying to "fellowship" all the world into Mormonism.

In many ways, Mormonism changed as dramatically in the last quarter of the twentieth century as in the last quarter of the nineteenth century. It is no longer a regional faith, much less an American faith. On the one hand, there are more Latter-day Saints outside the United States than inside its borders, and, on the other, the church is no longer a marginal player on the American religious scene. It is one of the largest church bodies in the nation. The LDS community is far too large for any one person or group of persons— whether general authorities or LDS public figures—to have even a nodding acquaintance with Saints from all over the world. The way Saints talk about their faith and themselves has changed or is changing. They are no longer Mormons but Latter-day Saints or, better still, Christians. Efforts are underway to make temple going commonplace for everyone. So many temples are now being built that extended group "driving-all-the-way-through" trips will soon be a thing of the past. The Mormon village is a museum, a tourist attraction rather than a vital place where Saints live out their lives. Even the Historic Tabernacle on Temple Square may soon be relegated to the status of a visitor center as a huge new assembly hall as big or bigger than the Salt Palace will alter general conferences quite as much as the electronic revolution altered them in the second half of the twentieth century.[29]

One indication of how much things have changed is that many Latter-day Saints who have succeeded in the outside world want to revitalize their Mormon identity by retiring to Utah—Provo, Springville, Alpine, St. George, and elsewhere. Having been a part of the scattering, they are now part of a re-gathering as they turn homeward to Zion to recapture a Saintly sense. Sometimes it works, but even Utah is not what it once was. However much the block-meeting plan was developed to make being Mormon easier for Saints who had to travel long distances to attend meetings two or three times a week and twice on Sundays, the plan still exists in areas where ward boundaries extend less than a full square mile. Home teaching is still in place, but structured interaction among ward members is far less a part of LDS life than it once was, while television and the Internet are as ubiquitous in the heart of the LDS kingdom as anywhere else.

Some years ago, I had a long conversation with an LDS mission field bishop whom I know well. I told him what I was learning from the oral interviews with men who had been bishops in California, New York, and elsewhere outside the Mormon culture region. I said that it seemed to me that the Saints lost something when they stopped encouraging or even allowing ward members to build their own chapels. I spoke of how the block-meeting plan seems to have, for good or ill, truly altered the Mormon experience. My friend's obviously heartfelt reply was, "It surely is easier now. . . . We aren't always on our way to a meeting or on our way across country to do temple work. . . ." Hesitating a bit, he added, "But the Saints still love one another."

I responded, quoting Tertullian's jesting words, "See how these Christians love one another." Then I added, "Methodists love one another too." So do Baptists, and Presbyterians, and lots of other Protestants. But like most Protestants, I live in a world where church is for Sundays. During the week, I go away, and, like most Protestant and Catholic Christians, I live my life in a pluralistic culture.

This could have been the fate of the Latter-day Saints who scattered all through the mission field after World War II. Theirs could have become a Sunday religion, too. That it did not was due to the extent to which the LDS Church gathered the scattered Saints into wards, each one of which became both a reflection and embodiment of a Mormon village on alien soil. Working together, ward members built their own chapels, but according to standard plans.

Moreover, without fail, every building story I read had at least one "happening" (a gift of land, payment for materials necessary to keep going, the appearance on the scene of an inactive electrician, and so on) identified by the bishop as a miracle. This means that, regardless of whether the bishop and his flock recognized it, in building a meetinghouse, they were gaining a sense of what building Zion was like. This gave each ward a sense of being an outpost of the Mormon center place, and since all wards—those in the center and those on the periphery—used identical materials and followed the same program, one was very much like all the others. The considerable religious liabilities of the population mobility of the postwar years in the United States was thus undercut, and the very real circulation of the Saints that characterized the second half of the twentieth century was as much an advantage as a disadvantage to the LDS Church.

∾

What will happen as membership growth and geographical expansion change the Mormonism of the twentieth century into the Mormon Christianity of the twenty-first is a question that is crucial to the future of this faith. Exactly what will happen is unclear. But it is obvious that things are changing and that unless the matter of LDS identity is somehow solved in the new multinational situation, the Church of Jesus Christ of Latter-day Saints has little hope of maintaining itself apart from other forms of Christianity. When virtually all the Saints lived in the Intermountain West, acquiring an identity as a Latter-day Saint was almost as natural as breathing. Preserving that identity as the church organized the American mission field was more difficult, but the story told here indicates how it was managed.

In the 1990s, the church separated itself from other Christian bodies by intensifying the emphasis placed on the Book of Mormon as "another testament of Jesus Christ." It also appeared to pay increasing attention to the "Joseph Smith Translation of the Bible."[30] Of equal, if not greater importance, the church perfected an elaborate "correlation program," which ensures that official publications and materials mandated for use in all church programs, including Sunday School, Gospel Doctrine classes, programs for youth, the Relief Society, and so on, are all "on the same page." Just as LDS congregational activities are held in buildings constructed according to standardized plans, the teachings and activities are standardized so that—as far as is feasible—Mormonism is the same wherever it is in the world. Almost a religious franchise, the church remains a constant in a multicultural world.

In the 1990s, the LDS Church also undertook an unprecedented and very costly program of temple construction, with the goal of locating temples in such close proximity to Saints throughout the nation and the world that going to the temple could become a religious activity as routine as attending a sacrament meeting. In doing this, the church undergirded its congregational activities (which take place in the world, as it were) by making it possible for Saints—as individuals and couples—to participate regularly in ritualized temple ordinances, investments of time and emotional ardor that stand apart from the world as they focus on eternity.[31]

Summing up: as the followers of the first Mormon prophet were gathered from among the nations, they internalized their understanding of themselves as Latter-day Saints by being in tension with the culture and by being certain that the literal fulfillment of prophecy was underway. In the time of Brigham Young, the pioneer trek and the rigors of living in the kingdom that concentrated the effects of the gathering functioned as a sort of experiential crucible in which Saints were tested and refined. For two or three decades in the middle of the twentieth century, being gathered into virtually encapsulated LDS communities in the midst of larger cultures also led to LDS identity formation. In all three situations, gathering was critical.

LDS congregations now engage in structured interaction in correlated programs, most of which are held in meetinghouses built according to standard plans, and there is an exponential increase in regular temple attendance among individual Saints and LDS husbands and wives. Whether these two essential elements of modern Mormonism will be sufficient to allow members of the Church of Jesus Christ of Latter-day Saints to internalize their identities remains an open question.[32] Certainly what is happening with Mormon identity as the new century begins is neither as spontaneous as it was when most Mormons lived in the kingdom or as involved as it became after World War II as Saints moved out to join the Gentiles in the mission field. Yet the beliefs and behaviors, activities and experiences that members of the LDS Church continue to share could well be enough to make Latter-day Saint identity formation strong enough to allow Mormonism to withstand the countervailing influences that go with being a diaspora community once again scattered among the nations.

Notes

1: The best treatment of this creation of a Mormon ethnic identity is Dean L. May, "Mormons," in *The Harvard Encyclopedia of American Ethnic Groups,* ed. Stephan Thernstrom (Cambridge, Mass.: Belknap Press of Harvard University, 1980), 720–31. But see also Armand L. Mauss, *The Angel and the Beehive: The Mormon Struggle with Assimilation* (Urbana: University of Illinois Press, 1994), 62–64; and Armand L. Mauss, "In Search of Ephraim: Changing Mormon Conceptions of Lineage, Race, and Ethnicity" (presidential address presented at the annual meeting of the Mormon History Association, Washington, D.C., May 23, 1998). The considerable discussion among sociologists and anthropologists about whether a Mormon ethnicity now exists or ever existed and if so, to what extent was recounted in this address. For a general treatment of the creation of ethnic identity, see Werner Sollors, *Beyond Ethnicity: Consent and Descent in American Culture* (New York: Oxford University Press, 1986).

2. Silvan S. Tompkins, "The Psychology of Commitment: The Constructive Role of Violence and Suffering for the Individual and for His Society," in *The Anti-slavery Vanguard: New Essays on the Abolitionists*, ed. Martin Duberman (Princeton, N.J.: Princeton University Press, 1965), 270–98, describes a series of identifiable stages in an adult's life leading to ever deepening levels of commitment to a cause. Although his work describes reformers' commitment to causes, his theoretical work also applies to the sort of "point of no return" commitment that characterized the lives of Latter-day Saints between 1835 and 1860, in which suffering bound them ever-more firmly to the faith.

3. Jan Shipps, *Mormonism: The Story of a New Religious Tradition* (Urbana: University of Illinois Press, 1985), 41–65, 109–29; Jan Shipps, "Brigham Young and His Times," herein.

4. The extent to which this was not simply a nineteenth-century phenomenon and the extent to which an LDS identity became synonymous with a Mormon and Mormon-American identity are made clear in Jean Wunderlich Oral History, Interviews by James B. Allen, 1972, typescript, Oral History Program, Archives, Historical Department of the Church of Jesus Christ of Latter-day Saints, Salt Lake City. Wunderlich was a German Saint who came to the United States soon after World War I when the "spirit of the 'gathering' was still strong" (8). His transportation was taken care of under a program in which the church "paid the return fare to Utah for all missionaries, whether they had been called from Germany or whether they had been called from the United States" (8–9). Discussing his editorship of the German-language *Beobachter* in the 1920s, Wunderlich said that the church was then moving from "approaching foreign members in their own tongue—I suppose in accordance with the Book of Mormon which says that every person should hear the gospel in their own tongue—to trying to assimilate them into the American life stream." Wunderlich was a protégé of President John A. Widtsoe, who advised him not to "get too closely involved with your country people" (15).

5. This statement is based on a comparison of average yearly increase in the numbers of Saints counted as members in missions as opposed to those in stakes. (Except for one stake in Canada and one in Mexico, all stakes were located in the Mormon culture region during this period.) The *Deseret News Church Almanac* (issued biennially) does not provide yearly statistics that would allow comparison in the 1890s, but between 1901 and 1910 the average yearly increase in numbers of Saints connected in some way to the various LDS missions was 3,625; in stakes, the average yearly increase was 8,885, a number unlikely to be entirely explained by a dramatic difference in natural increase in the Mormon culture region as opposed to that among members in the mission fields outside the Great Basin. For the following decade, the discrepancy was even greater, as the average yearly increase in members in missions was only 3,172, while the number of members reported in stakes increased by 10,172. (This is a rough measurement based on raw numbers, made even less precise by the

existence of the Cardston and Juarez stakes. But this last is offset to a considerable degree by the fact that the Juarez Stake was virtually abandoned when the Saints were forced to flee because of the Mexican Revolution.)

6. The diary of Senator Reed Smoot includes numerous entries about this effort made in 1909 and 1910. Typescript copies of the diary are available in several Utah archives. For a valuable abridged edition of this important diary, see Harvard S. Heath, ed., *In the World: The Diaries of Reed Smoot* (Salt Lake City: Signature Books, in association with Smith Research Associates, 1997).

7. Quoted in Douglas D. Alder, "The German-Speaking Immigration to Utah, 1850–1950" (Master's thesis, University of Utah, 1950), 115.

8. Quoted in ibid., 117.

9. Quoted in ibid., 118. This entire section is adapted from Alder's very fine discussion of the church's decision to suspend the direction to gather in Zion that the Saints had received by revelation. See ibid., 114–18.

10. In the years between World War I and World War II, significant numbers of Saints settled in southern California, which gradually took on some of the characteristics of the Mormon culture region. The church organizations in the Los Angeles area became Mormonism's first "mini-Zion." This story is well told in Chad M. Orton, *More Faith than Fear: The Los Angeles Stake Story* (Salt Lake City: Bookcraft, 1987), chapters 3–5. See also note 12 below.

11. The connection between local Mormons and the missionaries was often more direct than simply having a mission president preside over a branch. Martha Peterson Taysom, *"Glory Is A-Comin' Soon": A History of Mormonism in Indiana* (Kokomo, Ind.: Old Richardville Publications, 1998), chapter 3, describes the situation for Saints in the Hoosier state in the late nineteenth century and early twentieth. She indicates that since Latter-day Saints seldom congregated for services, many of the Saints worshiped in Protestant services on Sundays, and it was their support of and connection to the "Elders" (i.e., the missionaries) that was critical to their Mormon identity in Indiana.

12. The LDS Church operates ecclesiastically on the basis of geographical units. When members are spread across a wide area, their ecclesiastical supervision comes through a mission. But when sufficient numbers of Saints are present in areas contiguous enough to make geographical organization practical, stake and ward boundaries are drawn up, and full-fledged ecclesiastical units are established.

13. Orton, *More Faith than Fear*. Although the subtitle of Orton's study is *The Los Angeles Stake Story*, this work is actually an account of Mormonism in southern California.

14. The exact difference is impossible to determine. Reporting procedures make it necessary to compare the number of convert baptisms with the number of baptisms of children eight years old, the usual age for the baptism of birthright LDS children. See Tim B. Heaton, "Vital Statistics: Sources of Population Change," in *Encyclopedia of Mormonism*, 5 vols., ed. Daniel H. Ludlow (New York: Macmillan, 1992), 4:1518–37.

15. In the 1970s, in addition to getting the James Moyle Oral History Program underway, the LDS Church encouraged local Saints to conduct oral history interviews with those who had served as bishops in wards throughout the church. Many useful oral histories issued from these local efforts, but not all bishops were interviewed. Moreover, because the interviews were conducted by an array of interviewers with

varying levels of skill, the resulting oral histories are by no means equally useful in determining what happened as the new stakes and wards came into being outside the Mormon culture region in the years after World War II. These interviews in the LDS Church Archives are so spotty and so geographically skewed that studying a random selection of available oral histories proved to be impractical. The most revealing interviews form the basis of the following account. The pattern described is clear, even though many of the interviews are best described as amateurish and formulaic.

16. La Farr P. Astle, interview, September 1975, 6, Oral History, LDS Church Archives, Salt Lake City.

17. Ibid.

18. Some of the more revealing of these interviews were with former bishops Giles Leon Vanderhoof, Rex Floyd Ivie, and Floyd Thomas Davidson.

19. Doyle N. Hawkins, who conducted several of these interviews, often made comments about his own experiences as a bishop of a ward in Antioch, California.

20. Wilford Thomas Webb, interview, February 21, 1976, 13, Oral History, LDS Church Archives.

21. George H. Mortimer, interviews by William G. Hartley, 1973–76, typescript, 23, James Moyle Oral History Program, LDS Church Archives, Historical Department of the Church of Jesus Christ of Latter-day Saints, Salt Lake City.

22. Astle, interview, 5.

23. Karl George Jellinghausen, interview, March 1977, 6–7, Oral History, LDS Church Archives.

24. Sam Taylor, *Rocky Mountain Empire: The Latter-day Saints Today* (New York: Macmillan, 1978), 244–48.

25. Taylor's own story and his skepticism about what had happened in the church after the death of his grandfather are in nearly all of his books, but most especially in *Family Kingdom* (New York: McGraw Hill, 1951; reprint, New York: New American Library of World Literature, 1961) and *Rocky Mountain Empire.*

26. Quinn's statement, made to a *Salt Lake Tribune* reporter following his excommunication in 1993, is reported in the news section of *Sunstone* 16 (November 1993): 68.

27. Taylor, *Rocky Mountain Empire,* 248.

28. Jan Shipps, Cheryll L. May, and Dean L. May, "Sugar House Ward: A Latter-day Saint Congregation," in *American Congregations,* vol. 1, *Portraits of Twelve Religious Communities,* ed. James P. Wind and James W. Lewis (Chicago: University of Chicago Press, 1994), 337.

29. Reacting to the electronic revolution, Elder LeGrand Richards is said to have complained bitterly when he learned that the length of the prayer he had been asked to give would be determined not by what he had to say to the Lord but by the appearance of a little red light on the stand.

30. This is not a translation in the literal sense of working to turn a text written in one language into a different language but a particular inspired reading of the King James Version of the Bible that differs from the King James Version in at least 3,410 verses. See Robert J. Matthews, "Joseph Smith Translation of the Bible," in *Encyclopedia of Mormonism,* ed. Ludlow, 2:763–69. An example of an article emphasizing the importance of the JST, as the Joseph Smith Translation is often called, is Richard D.

Draper, "New Light on Paul's Teachings," *Ensign* 29 (September 1999): 22–28. The heading above the text of this article reads "Additional knowledge available through the Joseph Smith Translation helps clarify the Apostle Paul's writings."

31. Although the wording of the temple ordinances was altered substantially enough in 1990 for the alterations to generate the attention of news reporters, the wording is so consistent year in and year out that the ordinances seem impervious to change.

32. Holding a temple recommend, which is mandatory for Saints entering temples, is not a requirement of membership in the church and certainly not for informal admission to the LDS community. But a two-tier system of Sainthood is apparently developing in which members of the church who hold temple recommends are in one category and those who do not are in another.

PART 4

DECIPHERING, EXPLICATING, CLARIFYING: EXERCISING AN INSIDE-OUTSIDER'S INFORMAL CALLING

The Church of Jesus Christ of Latter-day Saints is an ecclesiastical institution that has a clearly defined hierarchy whose priesthood members in its higher reaches are engaged in full-time work for the church. But with no paid clergy to take the lead in ministry in the various wards and stakes, the bulk of the work of the LDS Church gets done as church members exercise the "callings" extended to them by their priesthood leaders.[1] This is an important feature that distinguishes the LDS Church from all Catholic and Orthodox churches and most Protestant churches and from the RLDS Church as well. It is one of the first things I learned about Mormonism, but until I came to know Latter-day Saints as friends and colleagues, this fact of LDS life remained an abstraction, something I read about in books. Not until I watched scholars who were also bishops leave professional meetings early to preside over ward activities on Sundays, and until I observed LDS colleagues leaving themselves time to fulfill their various assignments to perform specific administrative, teaching, or service-oriented church functions, did I confront the reality of a church in which members all have callings.

This reality was far different from the one I have known all my Methodist life. I have been part of one congregation after another in which the lion's share of the work is performed by a small portion of the whole. Yet the idea of a calling proved to be catching, and I soon found myself thinking of the responsibility I was asked to assume at the First United Methodist Church in Bloomington, Indiana, as a calling—even though my assignment was chairing the "Conversation and Coffee" program committee, a pretty un-Mormon assignment.

To some degree, my being tapped for service on the councils of the John Whitmer Historical Association and the Mormon History Association seemed not unlike callings, for they were assignments to positions of responsibility in organizations made up of Latter Day Saints and Latter-day Saints. More-over, although by no means ecclesiastical, these organizations sometimes func-tioned as support groups for Saints whose testimonies were magnified and for those whose testimonies seemed in danger of being undercut by what they learned from their study of the historical record.[2] I recall many instances of Mormon History Association (MHA) members sharing experiences that, they said, increased their faith; the example of LDS and RLDS historians standing in the rain together on the site of the Haun's Mill Massacre while they listened to Alma Blair recount what happened there on October 30, 1838, and after-ward participating in a discussion that revealed how members of both groups had gained an appreciation of their common heritage comes to mind. But I also remember times when faith seemed endangered and help and comfort were needed. The first time I saw evidence of a truly great need for mutual support in one of the Mormon historical organizations was the point at which the historical record and canonized understandings of the past were brought into direct conflict when members of the John Whitmer Historical Associa-tion—most of whom were reared in the Reorganized Church, which taught that the church's founding prophet had never been involved in polygamous relationships—came face-to-face with convincing evidence that Joseph Smith had plural wives.[3] My role in these two organizations in which so many dif-ferent kinds of Saints came together was sometimes simply providing a neu-tral space in which Saints of different persuasions and levels of belief and activity could come together outside formal program venues to talk openly and frankly among themselves. Although I had given up smoking cigarettes before either of these historical associations was formed, Stan Kimball, a lead-ing member of both organizations, once dubbed such a gathering the "Shipps' Smoker." The name stuck, and after-hours gatherings, sometimes described as Shipps' Smokers even if I am not in attendance, are a Mormon History Association tradition to this day.

The responsibility for planning and orchestrating the MHA annual meet-ing programs in 1976 in Kirtland, Ohio (when I was chair of the program com-mittee) and in 1980 in Canandaigua, New York (when I was president of the organization) added to my perception—as absolutely unsanctioned as it might have been—of having been called to fulfill a necessary role. I felt the weight of that informal calling particularly as I oversaw the planning of interfaith wor-ship services, the final event that brings every three-day MHA meeting to a close.[4] These are always held early on a Sunday morning, and in both these instances the gatherings were held in spaces the Saints regard as sacred.

Unlike entrance to LDS temples that have been dedicated, which is restricted to Latter-day Saints who hold temple recommends, entrance to the Kirtland Temple, which is owned by the RLDS Church, is not restricted to members of the Reorganized Church. This being the case, the Mormon History Association sought and received permission from the RLDS First Presidency to hold our worship service in this historic building. As the chair of the program committee, which included members of both Mormon churches, I presided over a planning meeting for a service that would mark the sacredness of the space, without signifying ownership of the history—most especially the dedication of the temple—which had taken place there.

I am not sure exactly how important it was to have a sympathetic but neutral committee chair, but the outcome of the committee's deliberations was a time of worship that, in the presentation of the prayer offered at the temple dedication read antiphonally by Douglas Alder, a member of the LDS Church, and Robert Flanders, a member of the RLDS Church, stressed what all Saints share. At the same time, in its handling of the music, the committee made a real effort to avoid emphasizing how the churches are different.[5]

During the planning meeting, committee members discovered a dramatic difference in tempo and phrasing in the way the hymns sung at the temple dedication—most especially "The Spirit of God like a Fire Is Burning"—are sung in the two churches. So that the spirit of the occasion could be captured without the music somehow seeming all wrong to some of those present, the committee decided against congregational singing and set in motion plans to find a brass choir to play arrangements of hymns from Emma Smith's 1835 hymnal. The committee asked me to invite my son, Stephen, to play the Adagio from Bach's G-minor Sonata for unaccompanied violin as a prelude.[6] The result was an occasion of worship that many who were there recall as one of great beauty and profound meaning.

A service of similar simplicity was held in the Sacred Grove when the association met in New York. Here again, the power of the place was compelling. This time, however, "Brighamites" and "Josephites" sang together, performing a work by Clifford Gates for chorus and tympani, which was commissioned for the occasion.

Although I was "released" from my responsibilities in both professional organizations when my terms of office ended in the early 1980s, the calling motif did not disappear from my consciousness. In fact, the outlines of a new assignment started to take shape before my official duties in the two historical associations were all discharged. This new uncertified calling, which I nevertheless regard as an obligation, is serving as a non-Mormon communicator of information about Mormonism to the general public. The most visible dimension of this position is serving as a source of information and interpretive commentary on news-making events that touch on the Latter-day Saints and the LDS community, especially those that attract the attention of the national media. A less visible dimension is the chore—it might even be described as the drudgery—of crafting the best possible descriptions that can be fitted into the space allotted to Mormonism and its history in general and specialized reference works. In the performance of both these responsibilities, I am called on to disseminate data and provide interpretation that will place information in context. Often correcting misinformation also comes into play.

These tasks fell to me almost by accident or, to be more precise, because I happened to be occupying the right place (a post on the faculty of a university outside Utah, plus official posts in the John Whitmer Historical Association and the Mormon History Association) at a time when media attention was commanded by events occurring in or connected to Mormonism and Utah (the 1978 priesthood revelation, the controversy over the Equal Rights Amendment, Sonia Johnson's excommunication, the International Women's year debacle, the church's sesquicentennial). The publication of things I wrote—especially the Mormon piece in a *Christian Century* series "Churches: Where from Here," edited by Martin Marty, and its subsequent inclusion in a book by that title that Marty edited—added to the general perception that I was a new non-Mormon voice who could serve as an interpreter of the Mormon scene.

In "Surveying the Mormon Image since 1960," I described what it was like to respond to the media's questions during the Hofmann episode. During those hectic weeks of serving as a media resource, I learned that most reporters—even those more familiar with writing about crime than about religion—seemed perfectly willing to delve deeply enough to determine where and how LDS history and the Saints' belief system fit into the story of the "Mormon murders." In the years since then, I have had that same lesson repeatedly drilled into my consciousness by members of the working press who were anxious to learn enough about Mormonism to keep their stories from misrepresenting the actions of members of the Church of Jesus Christ of Latter-day Saints or mischaracterizing their beliefs. Yet many of the non-Mormon reporters who have called me for help have been obviously baffled by what seems to them the enigmatic story of Mormon beginnings as well as by the complexity of the LDS theological and ecclesiastical system.

I remember very well how the voice of one reporter coming across the telephone wire expressed both exasperation and astonishment. "How," he wailed, "can perfectly sane people believe all this crazy stuff?" Because I had spent the first half of the 1980s writing a book designed to answer that very question, I had a ready reply, one I had first devised as a response to students who were likewise bewildered and confused. It usually began with my pointing out that the idea that Joseph Smith found golden plates and had revelations was not any more absurd than the idea that Moses and the Hebrews walked across the Red Sea without getting wet or that Jesus, who was dead, is now alive. But a better and more complete answer is found in *Mormonism: The Story of A New Religious Tradition.*[7]

"Never tell reporters to go read your book" is the first rule the journalist Mark Silk (who is also a Yale-trained historian) put in the pamphlet he was asked to prepare for members of the American Academy of Religion advising them about responding to questions from the press. Professors get similar advice from the staff of Martin Marty's Center for Religion and the Public. These specialists know that, working on deadline, few reporters have time to read an entire scholarly tome. Yet most journalists are not after some superficial account. They call people who are regarded as authorities on the topic on which they happen to be working because they know they need information. They clearly appreciate clarity and brevity. Besides that, notwithstanding their journalistic skill, unless what (so-called) experts tell reporters is couched in terms that are intelligible enough to be communicated to a general audience, being misquoted or, at the very least, quoted out of context is often the result.

When I first started to get calls from the press, I provided the requested information about the Latter-day Saints and located it in the larger story as best I could. But I was often frustrated because I realized that as I added more information, those posing the questions become more bewildered than enlightened. Eventually I became intentional about developing a way of responding to queries that would make Mormonism seem perfectly intelligible rather than bizarre or fantastic. Identifying the critical elements in the story of Mormonism and the fundamentals of LDS theology and doctrine, I donned my historian's hat and listed them in the order they were added to the LDS story. Then, using this time line, I sought ways to get all the basic information across without creating confusion and misunderstanding.

This strategy is one I have also employed in preparing encyclopedia entries. This is a category of scholarly writing whose impact highbrow intellectuals often overlook (and whose worth college and university tenure and promotions committees often disparage). But entries in encyclopedias and other reference works have always seemed to me singularly significant because these classic resources are very often the first ones consulted by middle school, high school, and even college students. They provide basic information that is often as far as students and casual seekers after information are willing to go.

Unless the encyclopedia or other reference work is a specialized one, space constraints are ever present. That brings to the task of preparing reference work entries the same pressing need for brevity as is called for in talking with reporters. These two dimensions of my public communicator calling are therefore interrelated. In fulfilling this responsibility, I wrote the entry on Mormonism in the *Encyclopedia Americana,* the entry on the Church of Jesus Christ of Latter-day Saints for the *Encyclopedia of the West,* and the one that is in the new *Oxford Companion to United States History.*[8] I prepared an entry that the editors entitled "Mormonism: An Independent Interpretation" for the *Encyclopedia of Mormonism* and "Emergence of Mormonism on the American Landscape (1950–1965)" for the *Historical Atlas of Mormonism.* For a very different sort of reference work, I wrote the lengthy essay on the Latter-day Saints in the *Encyclopedia of the American Religious Experience.*[9] Much more substantial than other encyclopedia entries—the manuscript ran fifty double-spaced pages—it is often consulted by undergraduate and graduate students as well as specialists in the field of American religion.

What I have been doing as a public communicator may seem to many Latter-day Saints a duplication of effort. After all, ever since Richard Anderson first put together a system—known as the Anderson Plan—that missionaries could use to explain Mormonism to potential converts, members of the church's missionary department have been working to strip down basic LDS beliefs so that they can be communicated in six easy lessons. In the past quarter-century, officials assigned to the church's Correlation Department have also been working to simplify the gospel message and streamline the story of Mormon beginnings. Much of the material produced by these two departments is clear and brief and surely could assist journalists seeking background information for Mormon stories. But since church publications are, appropriately, faith generating and faith promoting, the information they contain is set in an interpretive framework that does not lend itself to secular eyes and ears. Not only journalists but also academics—professors as well as students—and many ordinary folk are often anxious to learn about Mormonism in a respectful but somewhat less exalted context.

The *Encyclopedia of Mormonism,* published in 1992, has become a much-used and valuable source of information for people investigating Mormonism for some reason other than considering membership in the LDS Church, but its entries are arranged alphabetically. People new to Mormonism still need direction about how everything fits together.

༄

The first of the two essays included in this section is an example of how, in material prepared for reference works, I provide an overview that allows observers to make sense of the Mormon tradition. It was written as a single essay for a great compendium of biography and description of American theologians called *Makers of Christian Theology in America*. As the editors, Mark Toulouse and James O. Duke, put this work together, they decided that my essay should be divided and published in two parts: the first part was simply headed "Joseph Smith," and the other was called "Mormonism since the Death of Joseph Smith."[10] Toulouse and Duke are both professors in divinity schools, and while their work is likely to be consulted by undergraduate and graduate students in the religious studies discipline, it was designed as a resource for students in divinity schools and for working clergy who are often confronted with questions about what other people believe.

The second essay in this section is one of the essays in *Minority Faiths and the American Protestant Mainstream*, which was edited by an eminent scholar of American Judaism, Jonathan Sarna.[11] This work emerged from a project funded by the Pew Charitable Trusts. While not strictly a reference work, it is one of those books with separate essays on a variety of minority traditions, which, quite obviously, is designed as a text for college classes as well as a work for general reading.

In addition to describing the Mormon tradition by using the same explanatory scheme I use in nearly everything I prepare for reference works, I examine here the reaction of the non-Mormon religious and secular community in the United States as the Saints' claims to be the restoration of Israel and the restoration of "all things" are added to the church's foundational claim that it is the restored Church of Jesus Christ. I also address the question of what has been happening as Mormonism has grown and spread across the world. I regard this as extremely important because church growth and geographic expansion seem to be lessening the importance of the LDS tradition's American roots and accelerating the extent to which the truly distinctive elements of Mormonism are the centrality of the Book of Mormon in the Saints' understanding of Christianity and the fact that Saints today are increasingly a "temple-going people."

Notes

1. Callings are often referred to as priesthood callings, but this can be confusing to outsiders who fail to recognize that ordination to the priesthood is a change in status, moving a person from layperson to priest. Brian L. Pitcher, "Callings," in the *Encyclopedia of Mormonism*, 5 vols., ed. Daniel H. Ludlow (New York: Macmillan, 1992), 1:248–50, indicates that the priesthood is a permanent calling that carries with it an "obligation to remain worthy to help build the Kingdom of God on earth, with family responsibilities being central to that call" (249). Specific assignments, which include everything from leading congregations as bishops, serving as counselors in ward bishoprics or as branch presidents, filling administrative posts as stake officers, or serving in positions in the church auxiliaries, are essentially temporary. Members of the church exercise their callings until they are released by priesthood authorities.

2. I did not know at the time but have learned since that a support group aspect often develops in organizations concerned with the study of religion. This is true of the Catholic Historical Society, for example, and even for many of the subgroups within the American Society of Church History and the American Academy of Religion.

3. My sense is that Lawrence (Larry) Foster played a critical, almost pastoral, role in helping members of the RLDS community come to grips with the overwhelming contemporary evidence of the prophet's participation in plural marriage. Foster is the author of *Religion and Sexuality: Three American Communal Experiments of the Nineteenth Century* (New York: Oxford University Press, 1981), which was later published in paperback as *Religion and Sexuality: The Shakers, the Mormons, and the Oneida Community* (Urbana: University of Illinois Press, 1984).

4. Although it might seem odd to call them interfaith gatherings, these meetings have often been extremely meaningful to those participating in them (including me). In the early days, their lopsided interfaith makeup was about 89 percent "Brighamite," 10 percent "Josephite," and 1 percent Catholic (Mario De Pillis) and Protestant (Larry Foster and me) combined. At Canandaigua, Liz Dulany joined the non-LDS contingent of regular attenders.

5. The dedicatory prayer is printed as Section 109 in the Doctrine and Covenants of the Church of Jesus Christ of Latter-day Saints.

6. Stephen, who had been a member of the Cleveland Orchestra, also located a brass choir based in the area and made arrangements for it to play in this service.

7. Jan Shipps, *Mormonism: The Story of a New Religious Tradition* (Urbana: University of Illinois Press, 1985). This question is also answered quite directly in "The Reality of the Restoration in LDS Theology and Mormon Experience," herein.

8. Jan Shipps, "Mormonism," in *The Encyclopedia Americana*, International Edition, 30 vols. (Danbury, Conn.: Grolier, 1997), 19:457–60 (a longer version of this is found in the 1997 compact disc edition); Jan Shipps, "The Church of Jesus Christ of Latter-day Saints," in *Encyclopedia of the American West*, 4 vols., ed. Charles Phillips and Alan Axelrod (New York: Simon and Schuster MacMillan, 1996), 1:320–25; Jan Shipps, "Mormonism," in *Oxford Guide* (Oxford: Oxford University Press, forthcoming). In addition to longer entries, I have prepared many shorter ones.

9. Jan Shipps, "Mormonism: An Independent Interpretation," in *Encyclopedia of*

Mormonism, ed. Ludlow, 2:937–41; Jan Shipps, "Emergence of Mormonism on the American Landscape (1950–1965)," in *Historical Atlas of Mormonism,* ed. S. Kent Brown, Donald Q. Cannon, and Richard H. Jackson (New York: Simon and Schuster, 1994), 152–53; Jan Shipps, "The Latter-day Saints," in *Encyclopedia of the American Religious Experience: Studies of Traditions and Movements,* ed. Charles H. Lippy and Peter W. Williams (New York: Charles Scribner's Sons, 1988), 1:649–65.

10. Jan Shipps, "Joseph Smith" and "Mormonism since the Death of Joseph Smith," in *Makers of Christian Theology in America,* ed. Mark Toulouse and James O. Duke (Nashville, Tenn.: Abingdon, 1997), 210–17, 373–78.

11. Jan Shipps, "Difference and Otherness: Mormonism and the American Religious Mainstream," in *Minority Faiths and the American Protestant Mainstream,* ed. Jonathan D. Sarna (Urbana: University of Illinois Press, 1998), 81–109.

14

Joseph Smith and the Creation of LDS Theology

Joseph Smith Jr., the founder of Mormonism, was born in 1805 into a poor and religiously unconventional Vermont family in which the father was inclined toward deism and the mother was a Christian primitivist.[1] The chief sources of family income were agriculture and trading. Because making a living in New England by these means became increasingly difficult in the early nineteenth century, the Smiths moved to western New York while Joseph Jr. was still a child. There, working at whatever came to hand to earn hard cash while also farming land that was purchased on credit, the parents and their seven children (Joseph was the third son) attempted to build up a family competency in the area around Palmyra. The Smiths lost their farm as a result of chicanery, but they continued to live there and work the property as tenants until 1831. By that time, the younger Joseph had married and established his own household.

From the time they arrived in New York through the 1820s, Joseph Jr. worked with his father and brothers in the fields. They also worked together in other capacities. Since Joseph Smith Sr. had enough interest in the occult to give the family a reputation for scrying, this could well have been a decisive factor in what happened during the younger Joseph's teenage years. Indeed, it seems entirely likely that the father encouraged his namesake in the use of a "seer stone," a sort of psychic Geiger counter that helped him locate lost objects. Surviving historical sources provide hints that the elder Joseph Smith was not displeased when his son's success as an adept led to his being employed in a search for buried treasure. On at least one occasion, the son was engaged as the leader of a company that dug (unsuccessfully, as it turned out) for gold, which the company's organizer believed had been buried in the region by its earlier residents.

That his parents' concern about religion was transmitted to Joseph Jr. is evidenced by the fact that when he was only fourteen, he informed family members that he had learned the true church was not then on the earth. At the time, he seems not to have made it clear to them that this information was imparted in a vision during which God and Jesus appeared to him as he prayed in a grove close to the Smith home. He did say that he gave an account of this experience to a Methodist minister. While the cleric apparently regarded what Joseph told him as little more than a youngster's delusions, events of the next few years would reveal that the adolescent Smith was preternaturally mature.

In an account published in 1838, Joseph Smith described this first vision as a manifestation that distanced him from traditional trinitarian Christianity. The sight of God and Jesus convinced him that the two personages could not be considered part of a single entity. This personal history, which testifies to the rapidity of Smith's move into maturity as a religious figure, then recounted the spiritual events of his early adulthood. Later canonized by believers, it tells of an angel, identified as Moroni, who appeared to the future prophet in a night vision in 1823 and informed him that God had work for him to do. During this same spiritual episode, the angel told Smith that an antique rendering of the history of former inhabitants of the Western Hemisphere was buried in a hill near his family's farm. Moroni said that this historical record was inscribed on thin golden plates and that it not only explained where this archaic assemblage had come from but also disclosed the "fulness of the everlasting Gospel" because it had been "delivered by the Savior to the ancient inhabitants."

Smith said he unearthed the stone box that held the records on the following day. With the plates, he found a device the angel called the Urim and Thummim, an instrument that was to be used in translating the plates. The eighteen-year-old could not undertake this task immediately because he was required to undergo a four-year period of purification before he was allowed to take possession of the plates. By the time he was twenty-five, however, Smith had dictated a full translation of this strange metal document to Oliver Cowdery and other scribes.

Some observers said he translated using the instrument found with the plates; others said he used his seer stone. Although surviving accounts do not always make a distinction between these two vehicles of interpretation, the result was a text that explained itself as an abridgement and redaction of an ancient history recorded by a prophet whose name had been Mormon. When he published it, Smith therefore called the work the Book of Mormon.

Even as Smith was seeing to the coming forth and publication of this extraordinary chronicle, whose content convinced many readers that it was a supplemental work of scripture, he was reestablishing direct communication between divinity and humanity by becoming a prophet. Speaking for God, he announced that the ancient priesthood was restored and that through its offices those who sincerely repented could be baptized into the restored Church of Jesus Christ, the only true church on the face of the earth. As prophet and president of this primitivist body, Smith would go on to lead what his followers understood as the "Restoration," a remarkable religious movement that over the years has developed into a tradition of considerable significance in the overall panoply of world religions.

Deriding his "gold bible," early detractors started calling the prophet's followers "Mormonites," but Smith embraced this derisive term, referring to his adherents as Mormons and to the movement as Mormonism. Revealing their close identification with Christians of the apostolic era who were called Saints and, at the same time, signaling their expectation that the end time was near, members of the restored church also called themselves "latter-day saints." The institution they founded in 1830 was initially called the Church of Christ, but an 1838 revelation established its official name as the Church of Jesus Christ of Latter-day Saints, effectively differentiating this ecclesiastical entity from all other Christian churches.

Joseph Smith, who was known as the Mormon prophet or simply as "the Prophet," led the movement from its beginnings until 1844, when his life was ended by an assassin's bullet. The fact that he became a victim of a paramilitary firing squad whose members regarded him and the movement he headed as a threat to the social and political as well as religious life of the state and nation is often recognized as an unmistakable testimony to the exceptional nature of Joseph Smith's gift as a leader of men and women—a charismatic figure. Although the literary critic Harold Bloom and a few others have also acknowledged his "religious genius," the significance of Smith's theological contribution is rarely credited, even though Mormonism's experiential base is, and always has been, undergirded by a distinctive belief system that rests on a theology of extraordinary complexity.

The reason Smith has been overlooked as a theological figure is obvious. Mormon theology is unlike those versions of Christian theology that gradually came into being as several generations of scholarly clerics worked from scripture, creedal formulations, and historical experience to develop a systematic description of the faith. It is even more unlike those theologies developed by thinkers who used the tools of philosophy, reason, and logic in their efforts to describe and understand Christianity. The theology of the Latter-day Saints was quite literally handed down, delivered through found scripture and the prophetic voice, and it derives almost entirely from the years of Joseph Smith's religious leadership.

Despite the brevity of this period—it lasted only a dozen years or so—the LDS belief system was not revealed whole, complete, as it were, in every detail. As would be expected in the light of the movement's embrace of an open canon and continuing revelation, requisite counterparts to being led by one who has the ability to speak for God, Mormonism's theology was introduced incrementally. While this historical reality does not mandate a chronological description of Joseph Smith's contribution to Christian theology, surveying the sequential introduction of its doctrinal and theological strata opens the structural components of the LDS belief system to view. Such an approach consequently discloses and clarifies much about the unusual and in some instances unique aspects of Joseph Smith's remarkable legacy. For that reason, the following précis emphasizes the concept of layering. At the same time, it stresses the critical importance of Mormonism's first prophet's role in the creation of this certainly distinctive—in fact, unique—Christian tradition.

∽

When Joseph Smith and his followers organized the church that would become known to the world as the Mormon church, they said the true Church of Christ had been removed from the earth at the time of a "Great Apostasy" that occurred at the end of the apostolic era. Under divine authority, which rested on revelation to the prophet, it was now restored. To support the claim that theirs was the only legitimate Christian institution on the face of the earth, its members pointed to three distinctive bona fides: it was led by one who was in regular communication with God and able to speak for him; it had the ancient priesthood, recently restored through the prophetic agency of its leader; and, perhaps its greatest asset, the church had a supplementary scripture, an additional testament of Jesus Christ.

Combined with its strong millennialist bent—the coming forth of the Book of Mormon, in fact, was as significant in the church's early years as a signal of the imminent opening of the millennium as it was as a text—this formidable set of claims had great appeal in the United States in the religiously unsettled situation following the separation of church and state and the demise of established state churches. A sound base for the Mormon movement as a millennialist form of primitivist Christianity was rapidly put into place after the church was established in 1830. Individuals, a few members of a family, and sometimes even whole families became members, and together with their prophet/president and his earliest followers, they turned what is best understood as the apostolic restoration into reality. Mormondom's first theological layer was thus put in place.

In the winter of 1831, the prophet and many members of the Smith family left New York and moved to Kirtland, Ohio, where a branch of the church was prospering under the leadership of a former Campbellite minister. Many of Smith's followers moved there as well. Other Saints moved to Independence in Jackson County, Missouri, the following summer, choosing this area because it had been identified by revelation as the land of Zion, the future site of a temple, and the place where the Second Coming would commence. Although many converts to the new movement did not relocate immediately, two distinct Mormon enclaves were created. This pattern of settlement came in response to several revelations that forecast the congregating of believers in "one place upon the face of this land" in preparation for the great day when heaven and earth would pass away and all things would become new.

The prophet's revelations about what would become known in Mormonism as "the gathering" clearly reflect the Revelation of St. John. But when a literal gathering of Saints took place in the early 1830s, it turned Mormonism toward the Pentateuch as well as the New Testament. While concepts of Zion, Israel, a covenant people, priests, and temples are integral to the Book of Mormon and Smith's pre-1830 revelations, what happened in post-1830 Mormonism constituted a pivotal turn of the movement toward the Old Testament experience. The building of a temple, as distinguished from chapel or church, turned the hearts of these Christian children to their Hebraic fathers in a manner that gave Latter-day Saint communities a singularity that separated them from their Protestant neighbors. In Kirtland, the Saints also started to make a clear distinction between the lesser (Aaronic, i.e., Levitical) and greater (Melchizedek) priesthoods, as the perception of priesthood as a privilege of lineage took hold in Mormon minds and Mormon culture. This was and is important from the standpoint of doctrine and church organization.

Of greater theological moment, Mormons shared with all Christianity the "new covenant" and its figurative conception of Gentiles being adopted into Israel. But as they gathered from the "earth's four corners" during the 1830s, the Saints went through a transformative process that can best be described as turning the symbolic into the literal. The prophet's father was ordained as church patriarch in 1833, and a practice was instituted in which he gave a patriarchal blessing—an essential part of which is a declaration of lineage—to each church member. As Father Smith's ritualistic assertions of membership in the tribe of Ephraim—and, in a very few cases, Mannaseh, Benjamin, and Judah—were bestowed individually, a conception of group kinship through birthright membership in Abraham's family was added to what being Mormon meant. Before much time passed, Saints started to believe that all who were not Mormon were Gentile. Jews and Latter-day Saints were God's only chosen people.

In sum, the literal gathering, the actual building of a temple, the distinction between the two priesthoods, and the institution of patriarchy can be described as the Abrahamic restoration. Constituting a second tier, this Hebraic overlay changed Mormon theology by adding to it, not by taking things away. That was made clear in the religious repercussions of the 1836 dedication of the Kirtland Temple.

This landmark occasion was such a spiritual feast for those in attendance that it is sometimes called Mormonism's Pentecost. From a theological perspective, however, what happened on the Sunday following is of much more enduring importance to the faith. As recorded in Section 110 of the Doctrine and Covenants of the Church of Jesus Christ of Latter-day Saints, on that day the veil was rent, allowing the prophet and the church's "First Elder," Oliver Cowdery, to see Jesus standing in the temple. They heard him say that their sins and the sins of the people were forgiven. He accepted the temple; his name would ever be there; and in the temple's sacred precincts he would manifest himself to his people. When that vision closed, a second opened in which Moses and Elias committed to Smith and Cowdery the keys of the gathering of Israel and the gospel of Abraham. Then, in a final "great and glorious" manifestation, Elijah extended to them the keys to the dispensation of the last days, which he said were even then "at the doors." This extraordinary supernatural event tied together Mormonism's first two theological and doctrinal strata, creating a form of Hebraicized Christianity that held in tension the temple and the church.

Typical accounts of Mormonism during the 1830s are so totally centered on the experience of the Saints living in Mormon enclaves in Ohio and Missouri that the existence of Mormonism in the countryside gets lost. The prevailing picture of this period depicts a group caught up in the exhilaration of living in the presence of a prophet and the excitement of revelation rolling forth, even as members of the group lived through mistreatment and abuse from outsiders. But this experience was not universal because being Mormon in the first few years after the church was organized was not all of a piece. To Saints living in the countryside, membership in this particular Church of Christ differed from membership in other millennialist Christian churches mainly in the security afforded by the church's restorationist truth claims, in the importance accorded the Book of Mormon as a tangible sign of the nearness of the end time, and in preaching that encouraged church members to gather to Zion so they would be there when Christ returned. Apart from emphasis on the impending opening of the millennium, the experience of ungathered members of the church in the early days was curiously prescient of Mormonism at the end of the twentieth century, when residing in enclave communities would no longer be normative for Latter-day Saints. At the same time, an examination of the LDS countryside experience supplies a clear picture of Mormonism in its original formulation by separating from the conventional picture the theological, doctrinal, and organizational enhancement that occurred in the gathering centers.

The transformation of gathered members of the church into a people whose otherness became as manifest as that of Jews or enslaved Ethiopians provides observers of the development of Mormonism with the best evidence of the impact of positioning an overlay of Hebraicism over the earliest form of this movement. For those living through it, their progression toward otherness generated an intense level of hostility against the Saints. Within a year of the temple dedication, the prophet would be driven from Ohio. Many of his adherents followed him, first to Missouri and, when opposition there turned into war, back across the Mississippi River to Illinois. Though initially welcomed to the state, the Saints were soon separated from the surrounding populace by warnings of impending violence. Yet it was in Illinois where what can truly be considered a Mormon kingdom came into being for the first time.

In Missouri, the prophet had been imprisoned and threatened with hanging. He was allowed to escape, however, and he joined his people in Illinois. Although ever menaced by the possibility of being captured and carried back to be reimprisoned in Missouri, Smith spent the final five years of his life in the town on the eastern bank of the Mississippi River that the Saints named Nauvoo. Much of importance occurred in the secular arena between 1839 and 1844, but theological developments in Nauvoo were of greater long-range significance to the tradition. There, within what seemed to him the internally secure environment of an LDS kingdom where his authority was supreme, the prophet added a final layer to the stratified configuration of Mormon theology. Through additional found texts (the books of Moses and Abraham), a sermon preached at the funeral of King Follett, and a crucial new revelation (now Section 132 in the LDS Doctrine and Covenants), the prophet appended a set of esoteric tenets—tiered heavens, proxy baptisms, celestial marriage, eternal progression toward godhood—to LDS theology. As had revelations in Kirtland, these additions would again transform Mormonism.

In particular, this final dogmatic overlay had critical implications for Mormon soteriology and worship practice. They located human life between pre- and post-existence states and placed the ordinances of the temple—most especially the endowment (in and through which power from on high is bestowed on participating Saints) and celestial marriage—at the very core of Mormonism. When unified with the merged gospels of Jesus Christ and Abraham, these tenets set forth a plan of salvation that entails the ceaseless persistence of personality and the eternal endurance of family units. Often called "the fulness of the Gospel," the final additions that Joseph Smith introduced into Mormonism constitute what Latter-day Saints describe as the "Restoration of All Things."

The prophet's revelation concerning the patriarchal order of marriage (i.e., celestial marriage) contained stipulations whereby men living in the dispensation in which the revelation came forth could marry into plurality in the manner of Old Testament patriarchs. Although not publicly promulgated during Smith's lifetime, this revelation was privately revealed to many leading Saints beginning in 1841. When they took the introduction of this new principle and acted on it with the same earnestness as they had acted on earlier revelations announced by the prophet, serious consequences followed. Because some of the Saints were starting to chafe under the palpable political, social, and economic ramifications of living under prophetic leadership in what the city's inhabitants regarded as God's kingdom, incipient internal opposition to Smith was already present in Nauvoo. The practice of plural (or celestial) marriage caused that opposition to break into the open and swell to such proportions that it exposed Nauvoo to external threat that neither the prophet nor the LDS community could avoid. With the apparent complicity of the Illinois governor, Smith was murdered by disguised local militia members in June 1844. To avoid decimation at the hands of an organized mob, the Saints were forced to leave the area less than two years later.

Particular precursors anticipated the developments that, taken together, constitute Mormonism's three distinct layers of theology and doctrine. First, put in place before the organization of the church, the Book of Mormon and restoration of the priesthood had provided a foundation for the movement. Second, a hearty response to revelations calling for the gathering brought believers together to create a Latter-day Saint culture as well as religious organization. This came before and probably stimulated the Hebraicizing of Mormonism, of which the building of the first Mormon temple was a part. Third, a powerful group mystical experience—sometimes described as the Mormon Pentecost—that accompanied the dedication of the Kirtland Temple and the subsequent literal (definitely not merely figurative) organization of the kingdom of God in Nauvoo were antecedent to the introduction of the esoteric doctrines that the Latter-day Saints refer to as the gospel's "fulness."

Taking the preludes to formation of the first layer and the introduction of the second and third into account and considering Mormon theology from a historically stratified perspective are helpful because this illuminates what often appears cryptic and enigmatic. In addition, this approach helps make sense of the high rate of falling away that occurred during the prophet's lifetime and explains the virtual atomization of the movement that occurred after his death. Even as many of the movement's adherents, first in Kirtland and Missouri and later in Nauvoo, welcomed the revelation of new tenets, readily incorporating them into the faith, the addition of each new layer of theology and doctrine changed Mormonism in radical ways. General acceptance of the concept of continuing revelation notwithstanding, each time a new stratum of theology and doctrine was imposed on existing belief and practice, a substantial number of Smith's followers were disturbed enough to leave. Those who rejected new dogma were generally branded as apostate (or worse). Yet persuasive evidence suggests that, in cases too numerous to count, the problem was that the ones who left were so thoroughly committed to the form of Mormonism to which they had been converted that they regarded the new revelations as false prophecy.

Some fell away when it became clear there was more to Mormonism than the truth of the Book of Mormon and the restoration of the priesthood and the church. Others later rejected the form of Mormonism that existed after revelation made it clear the restored church was a family church, one that included membership in the family of Abraham and, in addition, was led by an elect family (the Smiths). In numerical terms, the greatest repudiation of new revelation may have come with the addition of the final theological and doctrinal layer that transformed the movement into what those who were faithful to the end of Joseph Smith's life and beyond believed to be "the restoration of all things." A major reason for defection at this point was the advent of the actual practice of plural marriage.

Despite their having been troubled by the various theological, doctrinal, and organizational additions and perhaps by the lengthening distance between themselves and other Christians, what happened to Joseph Smith's followers after 1844 makes it obvious that many of them had been kept within the fold only by the prophet's charismatic leadership. Following his death, the movement's heterogeneity spawned many Mormonisms. Although most failed, all are significant because the combined histories of groups that trace their origins to Joseph Smith reveal common agreement that the Book of Mormon is ancient scripture. Their histories also indicate an impressive level of acceptance of the legitimacy of the claim that the church organized in 1830 by Smith and his followers was truly the restored Church of Jesus Christ. The issues dividing them can usually be related to acceptance or rejection of restorations subsequent to the initial apostolic restoration. This is especially important in understanding what divided the two largest and best-known of the movement's surviving institutional manifestations.

The Church of Jesus Christ of Latter-day Saints headquartered in Salt Lake City, Utah, has more than ten million members. The Reorganized Church of Jesus Christ of Latter Day Saints (RLDS) headquartered in Independence, Missouri, has far fewer, only a bit over 250,000 at last count. Despite the discrepancy in size, these two institutions are equally important to an adequate understanding of Mormon theology because they reflect the Mormonism that existed at separate stages of the movement's theological, doctrinal, and organizational existence.

Joseph Smith's mother, his brother William, and his first wife, Emma, remained in the Midwest after the prophet's murder. In 1860, as soon as Joseph Smith III was willing to take the lead, a substantial group of the prophet's followers reestablished the church. In doing so, they put forth the original claims of the restored Church of Christ, including the assertion that their leader, the eldest son of the first Mormon prophet, was also a prophet. From that point until 1996, the prophet/president of the "Reorganization," as this group called itself, was always a direct descendent of Joseph Smith. Thus it was a family church in a literal sense. For many years, its members also held onto the concept of birthright membership in the family of Abraham. This situates the RLDS Church precisely at the center of Mormonism as it existed after its first two doctrinal and theological strata were in place. Its location there is affirmed by the fact that from its beginnings, the identity of this Latter Day Saint Church was framed in the light of its downright repudiation of the theological additions that the prophet put in place in Nauvoo. This repudiation disavowed celestial marriage altogether; although Emma Smith knew better, members of the Reorganization believed that the practice had been initiated by Brigham Young. It also rejected the whole complex of dogma deriving from the idea of the restoration of ancient temple ordinances that make possible the immutability of the family unit and eternal progression toward godhood.

The Saints who followed Brigham Young west created the Church of Jesus Christ of Latter-day Saints. After they reached the Valley of the Great Salt Lake, they re-created Nauvoo Mormonism not simply in all its theological, doctrinal, and organizational fullness but also with its various elements on or very near the surface. In view of their geographical isolation, they were able to create a realm "in the tops of the mountains" that was politically and economically organized as the kingdom of God. Plural marriage was not merely accepted there; it was celebrated as evidence of a new patriarchal order of the ages. While they did not repudiate Jackson County, Missouri, as the site of Zion, for all practical purposes the Latter-day Saints turned the Intermountain West into Israel. Whereas its citizens regarded Brigham Young as a prophet, his major theological assertion—that Adam and God were one and the same—has been pushed to the margins as theological speculation. Instead, Young's turning Joseph Smith's prophetic vision into reality is counted his greatest religious achievement.

Young's accomplishment went unappreciated by the nation's political and economic leaders, who regarded it in secular terms. At the same time, the nation's churches, viewing this western Zion in religious terms, condemned Mormons as heretics. What ensued as a consequence is that the U.S. Congress, representing the overwhelmingly non-Mormon portion of the population, moved slowly but deliberately to frustrate the LDS enterprise. The outcome was that, after almost fifty years of its being in the world, the Saints dismantled their earthly kingdom to save their cultural integrity. Then, to save their temples, and hence their distinctive form of Christianity, they relinquished the practice of plural marriage.

Although the implications of surrendering the literal kingdom and giving up plural marriage were not immediately clear, these moves gradually led to a transformation of Utah Mormonism, the most complex form of the faith. The esoterica introduced into the LDS belief system in Nauvoo has not been abandoned, but it is no longer open to view. Bundled into a set of sacred tenets, much as software programs are bundled into packages, this theological layer is now mainly discernible in the concept of the Saints as a "temple-going people." Yet the removal from view of this crowning stratum of LDS belief did not turn Utah Mormonism into a movement somewhat comparable to the Reorganization, even in the eyes of those outside the faith.

The main reason for this is that the Saints held on to the concept of the gathering for a very long time. While church leaders announced in 1921 that Zion is where the people of God are and started discouraging immigration of Saints to the area of the West known as the Mormon culture region, new converts continued to regard Utah and its environs as Zion and continued to settle there. The western Mormon enclave lived on and does so today. Now, however, the membership of the church has expanded so exponentially that gathering all the Latter-day Saints in the West would be impossible. One result of this growth is that living in LDS cultural enclaves is no longer the norm. Members of the church live all across the nation. But that is not all. More Saints now live outside than inside the United States. The practical effect of this shift is colossal, but so are its religious ramifications.

As members of the church flowed into Kirtland from all directions, their response to revelation made way for the creation of such a sense of special-ness that the Saints came to regard themselves as birthright members of Abraham's family. New revelation has not suspended this concept. But as the church itself is moving out to the four corners of the earth with a newly universalized message made possible by a 1978 revelation that extended the privileges of the LDS priesthood to all worthy males, including African Americans, there are indications that figurative membership in Abraham's family may once again be gaining as much importance as literal membership therein. As more Saints are "adopted into Israel," the LDS Church is remind-ing everyone—its own birthright members, new converts, and the world—of the importance of Christ, the Atonement, and its own rootedness in Mor-monism's bedrock, the Church of Christ. It is not renouncing its endowment of idiosyncrasy that being a temple-going people implies, and it is in no way disavowing the peculiarity given to it by the revelations that turned the faith into a form of Hebraicized Christianity. But just as the Reorganization has been doing for generations, the Church of Jesus Christ of Latter-day Saints is presenting itself first and foremost as Christ's restored church.

Lest it appear that the wheel has come full circle, that the Saints are back where they started, neither the Reorganized Church of Jesus Christ of Latter Day Saints nor the Church of Jesus Christ of Latter-day Saints, nor any of the several sectarian Mormon institutions is precisely the same church that was organized by the Mormon prophet and his followers in 1830. The foun-dational elements of Mormonism (the Book of Mormon, priesthood resto-ration, and the restored church) have remained firmly in place across the tradition, but revelation received after 1830 wrought changes throughout. A dramatic example of this is a 1994 revelation to the sitting president of the RLDS Church. By designating as its new president a man who is not a direct descendant of Joseph Smith, this revelation severed the lineage link that his-torically signaled connection between the RLDS Church and Mormonism's founding prophet. The result is likely to be as dramatic in the life of the Re-organization as the 1890 Manifesto was in the life of the LDS Church. But the RLDS Church may well weather the change, for Saints of all stripes share a legacy of continuing revelation. Receipt of new doctrinal tenets and the necessity of assimilating them is a part of being Mormon.

When revelation alters faith, however, the results often generate dissent. In some instances, dissenters' questioning of the legitimacy of new revela-tion leads to schism. Although it does not always do so, schism sometimes leads to the development of new forms of Mormonism. This is a process that started happening in Mormonism in the 1830s. It continues today as groups of Utah Saints refuse to believe that the 1890 Manifesto ending the practice of plural marriage was a revelation and as members of the Reorganization refuse to accept the 1985 revelation that extended priesthood ordination to women. In both instances, the dissenters who refuse to accept the legitimacy of these particular fruits of continuing revelation are creating new forms of Mormonism. Such organizational volatility is eloquent testimony to the health of the tradition and the complexity of the theology that was revealed through the agency of Joseph Smith, the Mormon prophet.

Note

1. The purpose of including this essay in this collection is to outline the explanatory scheme I have worked out to describe Mormon theology to people with little or no knowledge of the LDS belief system. Since it contains no information to which readers would not find easy access in the *Encyclopedia of Mormonism* and standard accounts of Mormon history, I have not included notes here.

15

Difference and Otherness:
Mormonism and the American Religious Mainstream

As he had done nearly every day for over fifty years, Wilford Woodruff, the Mormon church president, made an entry in his journal on September 25, 1890. Writing in a firm hand despite his eighty-three years, the prophet, seer, revelator, and fourth chief administrative officer of the Church of Jesus Christ of Latter-day Saints headquartered in Salt Lake City noted that the U.S. government had "taken a Stand & passed Laws to destroy the Latter day Saints upon the Subjet of poligamy or Patriarchal order of Marriage." As a result, he wrote, he had reached a point in his life that placed him "under the necessity of acting for the Temporal Salvation of the Church."[1] Taken the previous day, the action to which he referred was the promulgation under his hand—and his alone—of a manifesto announcing to the Latter-day Saints and the world interdiction of the practice of plural marriage (technically, polygyny).[2]

While this was a shattering blow to many of the members of the religious institution over which Woodruff presided, it was apparently the only route the Saints could have taken to gain statehood, thereby escaping from what they regarded as the tyranny of federal rule.[3] It is clear, however, that the Saints needed more than political deliverance. They also needed to be delivered from the incessant barrage of denigration and vilification to which they had been subjected by members, both clerical and lay, of churches that made up the American religious mainstream.[4] What follows is an exploration of connections between the federal government's opposition, mainly political and economic, to the western Saints and the antagonism to Mormonism exhibited in the nation's non-Mormon religious communities. This effort to describe and explain the vacillating character of the relationship between those who were Latter-day Saints and those who were not can serve as a lens through which to view the relationship between a minority faith and the

Protestant majority and the developing dynamics of religious life in an increasingly religiously diverse nation.

༄

After having been driven from well-established enclaves in Ohio, Missouri, and Illinois, a sizable portion of the Mormon population left the United States in 1847. They followed Brigham Young west in the aftermath of the murder of the Prophet Joseph Smith, who had founded the movement in the late 1820s and, after 1830, served as the first president of what his adherents believed was a singular restoration of the primitive Christian Church. The Latter-day Saints started to settle in the Great Basin the year before this land stretching between the Rocky Mountains and the High Sierras became U.S. territory.[5] Establishing a city near the Great Salt Lake, which would become the seat of a Mormon kingdom "in the tops of the mountains," the Saints attempted to join the union in 1849. They proposed to call the area—which, among themselves, they were already calling Zion—the State of Deseret.[6] Unfortunately for them, however, the discovery of gold in California and the question of slavery in the territories complicated the issue of statehood so much that, as a part of the Compromise of 1850, Deseret became a U.S. territory. Brigham Young was appointed territorial governor, but Congress refused to accept the name its residents had advanced, calling the area Utah instead.[7]

Disappointed, the Saints nevertheless continued with the creation of Mormon country, a realm that was at once Utah, a U.S. territory where members of a regular religious institution that understood itself as the Church of Jesus Christ carried out the ordinary pursuits of everyday nineteenth-century American life, and Deseret, the kingdom of God populated by Abraham's seed, where "the restoration of all things" proceeded as in days of old. Moving from one to the other, from the secularized modernity of the Utah Territory to the ancient ethos of the State of Deseret, involved migrating from one mode of existence to another.

Less than a decade later, at the end of the so-called Utah War, these two quite separate political and economic dominions were formalized when federal appointees were settled in the territory's executive and judicial offices and the shadow state of Deseret was called into existence. Many Mormons were able to move easily from one dominion to the other, from attendance at a public meeting in a local ward house or a church conference held in a structure on Temple Square (which stood at the center of both Utah and Deseret and was therefore open to all comers) to the sacred precincts of the Endowment House and the temples that would be constructed in Manti, St. George, and Logan, which were reserved exclusively for worthy Saints. Still, even before 1857, all was not tranquil in Zion. Five years before the Utah War, the church had announced to the world at large that divine revelation to the Prophet Joseph Smith had introduced "celestial marriage" into Mormonism.[8] This ceremony (ordinance), a form of wedlock uniting a man and a woman for "time and all eternity," could be performed only in Mormon temples. Although women could be married to only one husband, the revelation said that Mormon men, like patriarchs of old, could be married to more than one wife.[9]

An upshot of the public practice of plural marriage was that while the husbands of plural wives could negotiate the divide between Utah and Deseret with reasonable ease, women who married into plurality were permanent residents of Deseret. Honored in the kingdom, they were regarded, at best, as mistresses—at worst, as prostitutes—in the essentially secularized social and legal systems of the Utah Territory.[10] This helps explain the turmoil that beset the Saints, for when the public realized that many Mormon men were entering "the ancient Patriarchal Order of Matrimony," which involved taking multiple wives, it caused so much outrage that members of the nation's Protestant churches and those who were simply participants in U.S. civil society attacked the Saints, often viciously, from the nation's pulpits and in its press. This made Zion's inhabitants vulnerable to pressure from the federal government, which, by virtue of Utah's territorial status, exercised formal political authority in the area.

The Saints were convinced that the First Amendment protected their unconventional marriage system. But when plural marriage became the boundary that set the Saints apart from all other inhabitants of the nation's religious and secular cultures, the Saints' vulnerability intensified, making them much more easily assailable than they had been as long as outsiders knew only that the kingdom taking shape on the American frontier had different—far less democratic—political and economic institutions.[11] Before the decade was out, the U.S. government started making efforts to curb plural marriage by enacting the Morrill Act, a federal antibigamy statute that outlawed polygamous cohabitation.

The LDS Church responded by challenging the constitutionality of this 1862 statute by setting up a test case and arguing, first in a territorial court and later in the U.S. Supreme Court, that the test case defendant, George Reynolds, practiced plural marriage because he understood it to be a religious obligation.[12] Thus, the church brief argued, his marital actions were protected by the First Amendment.

In the interim between the passage of the Morrill Act and a decision on its constitutionality, Mormons continued to marry into plurality, confident that celestial marriage (often referred to simply as the principle) was a key element in the plan of salvation that God had revealed through the Prophet Joseph Smith. They were able to do this with relative impunity because of two legal realities: jurors empaneled to adjudicate such cases in the Utah Territory were usually Latter-day Saints who decided against the prosecution, and wives could not be forced to testify against their husbands. Subsequent legislation closed these loopholes, but they initially allowed the Saints to get around federal prohibitions against a man's having more than one wife.[13]

The outcome of the Saints' challenge to the Morrill Act's constitutionality was a definitive expression of the government's stand against polygamy, handed down by the U.S. Supreme Court in *Reynolds v. United States* in 1879.[14] In upholding the conviction of Brigham Young's private secretary, who admitted to having more than one wife, the Court said that chaos would ensue if "professed doctrines of religious belief" were allowed to become "superior to the law of the land." It therefore concluded that although the free exercise clause of the First Amendment deprived Congress of power to legislate about "mere opinion," it left it "free to reach actions which were in violation of social duties or subversive of good order."[15] Holding to its distinction between belief and behavior, opinion and action, the Court conceded that polygamous sects might be well ordered but that because polygamy was a corollary of patriarchy whose natural consequence was despotism, the Morrill Act outlawing polygamy was constitutional.

In its description of polygamy as being "odious among the Northern and Western Nations of Europe," the Court neglected to mention southern and eastern Europe, where Catholicism flourished. Was this, as Catharine Cookson argues in "Myths, Morals, and Mormon Panics," an indication that the Court's decision in the *Reynolds* case was intended as a bulwark of Protestantism?[16] Making such a determination is impossible, yet one of the things about how this important decision affected the Saints seems clear. In framing its argument so that patriarchy, a principle that stood at the center of Mormon doctrine, was represented as suspect or even illicit, the Court's decision placed the Latter-day Saints on the horns of a dilemma. If they continued contracting plural marriages and exercising their conjugal rights within those marriages, they would be breaking civil law; if they refused to enter into the "Patriarchal Order" by marrying into plurality, they would be calling the entire Mormon theological program into question. As might have been expected, given the incredible psychic and physical price they had already paid to become a part of the Mormon community, many Saints opted to break the law. In so doing, they set the stage for an inevitable confrontation not only between the Mormons and the American religious mainstream but also between religion and the secular side of society.

The situation for polygamists deteriorated throughout the 1880s. In Washington, Congress had supported the Morrill Act with the Poland Act of 1874. Then the Edmunds Act was passed in 1882, extending the definition of marital plurality—the marriages themselves, not just their consummations, were prohibited—and specifically defining polygamy as action rather than opinion. Its provisions were strengthened five years later by the Edmunds-Tucker Act, a statute stipulating that the government could use virtually any means necessary to stop the practice, including dissolution of the corporation that allowed the LDS Church to function as a legal entity, seizure of church property, and prohibitions against the church's ownership of land, whether improved or unimproved. New federal legislation was subsequently proposed that would have disenfranchised the Saints.

Throughout the decade, federal marshals pursued and arrested known and even rumored polygamists in the Intermountain West. In response, so many Mormon leaders left their wives and families to fend for themselves and hid out in the mountains or fled to Mexico or Canada that all except the most critical business of the church had to be suspended. Despite their efforts to avoid discovery, capture, and prosecution, so many Mormon men were brought to trial and imprisoned that Mormon culture almost collapsed. For all practical purposes, what amounted to a state of war existed in the Great Basin.[17]

Although President Woodruff remained in close consultation with the leaders of the LDS Church in the days and weeks before the Manifesto was released to the press, as Mormon prophet and chief LDS ecclesiastical leader, Woodruff alone assumed responsibility for publicly prohibiting further official countenancing of plural marriage. When, as was perhaps inevitable, the question arose as to whether the Manifesto was merely a decision that had been impelled by the church president's reasoned assessment of the political and legal situation, Woodruff explained that he had been shown "by vision and revelation" that the Saints would lose their temples unless they stopped marrying into plurality. This would mean not only that celestial marriage would be stopped but also that temple ordinances for the living and for the redemption of the dead would have to be discontinued, possibly permanently.[18] Whether for that reason or because so much political pressure was exerted on the Saints, when the text of the Manifesto was subsequently presented to the church assembled in semiannual conference, it was sustained as revelation and, at least officially, accepted as church policy.

∾

The issuing of the Manifesto is one of the most controversial events in Mormon history. Yet whether it is interpreted as the product of revelation or as a human gesture, many historians have failed to point to the significance of the link President Woodruff made between his decision to issue the Manifesto and the preservation of Mormon temples and perpetuation of the distinctive ordinances performed in their sacred precincts.[19] Accounts of what happened almost universally point to the practical effects and political implications of the proclamation that suspended church sanction for further plural unions. Sometimes remarking that the Manifesto terminated the federal raids in Mormon country, histories nearly all allude to the connection between the Saints' suspension of plural marriage and the federal government's subsequent granting of statehood to Utah. They generally also note that the Manifesto signaled other concessions on the part of the Saints; henceforth, in addition to surrendering their peculiar marital practices, the Saints would transform their distinctive political and economic patterns, bringing them into line with those in the rest of the United States. In short, according to most accounts, President Woodruff's declaration announced his intention to preside over the demise of Mormonism as it had existed during the "kingdom period" to make way for the inauguration of Utah Mormonism, a faith lived in the world but not of it.

Interpretations of the Manifesto and the political and economic changes the Saints embraced in the 1890s and beyond fall into three broad categories: the Manifesto as defeat; the Manifesto as pretense; and the Manifesto as visible embodiment of "creative adjustment." The way these interpretative strands differ is interesting because that difference reveals a great deal about the writing of history, religious and otherwise. But what they have in common is not simply interesting. It is critically important to the questions raised in this essay, for they collectively hold to the notion that the American Protestant mainstream was a driving force behind federal antipolygamy legislation and the governmental efforts to force the Saints to dismantle Deseret.

Long before the phrase "the legacy of conquest" was made popular by Patricia Nelson Limerick and the "new western historians," many—perhaps even a majority of those who have written about the American past—explained events in the Great Basin kingdom in the 1880s and 1890s in terms of winners and losers and the power differential that invariably seems to be involved.[20] Zion's defeat, say such historians (who are by no means all non-

Mormon), was followed first by accommodation and afterward by enthusiastic embrace of the patterns and practices, norms and values of the conquerors, that is, the U.S. government and the Protestant cultural center. Accounts written by those in this "defeatist" camp sum up the last two decades of the nineteenth century and the early years of the twentieth century in Gustive Larson's terms, characterizing what happened as the "Americanization" of Mormonism.[21] Some even interpret this galvanizing operation as a process successful enough to turn subversive Saints into super Americans and to transform Mormonism into an idiosyncratic form of Protestantism.[22]

Another interpretation of what occurred is even more dramatic in its acceptance of the metaphor of defeat because it reflects the disillusionment and profound disappointment of its purveyors. A goodly number of those Latter-day Saints who had been converts to Mormonism and suffered for it and their descendants who had been reared in the faith at a time when the kingdom of the Saints existed in its most literal manifestations were initially certain that the Manifesto was a shrewd strategic move to preserve the status quo. Along with many skeptical non-Mormons, they understood the church president's action entirely in terms of pretense—of feigned accession to governmental demands to gain statehood.[23] After that, so they believed, Zion in the tops of the mountains could be reestablished. This time, however, its changed political status vis-à-vis the federal government would make it a kingdom protected by a wall of separation constructed with the material of states' rights rather than physical distance. When this conception of the Manifesto turned out to be fallacious, this group of Saints (who would come to be collectively described as fundamentalists) came to see Woodruff's pronouncement as abject surrender.[24]

A third group, the historians who are practitioners of the "new Mormon history," reject interpretations of President Woodruff's action as defeat or surrender and instead picture the Manifesto as the cornerstone of a period of "creative adjustment."[25] Separating the Mormon past into time spheres that reflect the revelations the Saints received during different periods, this interpretive strategy is used by faithful LDS historians to emphasize the principle of "continuing revelation," a distinctive doctrine resting on the claim that the LDS Church is always led by one who is a "prophet, seer, and revelator," as well as church president, a critical postulate undergirding the assertion that the Church of Jesus Christ of Latter-day Saints is the true church.[26] Since the decision to end the practice of polygamy came from someone designated to receive inspiration (in this case, revelation) for all those over whom he presided, such historians describe the Manifesto as a decree that was—or at least was understood as—the "will and word of the Lord."[27] For those who see Mormonism and LDS history in this mode, the Manifesto served as the dividing line between the distant and the recent past, making way for a voluntary integration of the Saints into American culture even as they maintain Mormon distinctiveness.

As indicated, from the perspective of the history of the relationship between Mormonism and the nation's Protestant mainstream, all three of these interpretive strands agree about the main sources of opposition to Mormonism—and it is likely that Wilford Woodruff himself would also have agreed. Whatever their position regarding the Manifesto, historians contend, almost as a given, that the force mounted against Mormonism was not merely political or even simply political and economic in nature. About this, they are correct. Ample sources certify that in the fight against polygamy, religious pressure was exerted both directly and behind the scenes.[28] They also agree that the religious opposition was led by members of the Presbyterian, Methodist, Baptist, Congregational, and Episcopal churches, which, along with Disciples and Lutherans, made up the nation's Protestant center. Their opposition was tangibly expressed through a process in which signatures supporting opposition to Utah statehood were gathered in Protestant congregations and transmitted to Congress. Most of the petitions were standard expressions of concern intended to alert Congress to the danger that Mormonism posed to the American home and family. Such petitions, whose content was sometimes read into the *Congressional Record,* accorded well with the attitudes expressed by senators, congressmen, and other federal officials in public debate and in the press.

The record of the religious sentiments and church activities of Mormon opponents indicates that politics and religion were so intertwined that the tangled web of religious and political influence is likely never to be unraveled. Because religious figures exercised great political power, political leaders belonged to the higher reaches of the Protestant establishment, and anti-Mormon influence was so pervasive in both arenas, it is often impossible to find enough evidence in the historical record to discern between religious and political influence. In addition, the battle for and against plural marriage conflated religion and politics quite as confidently as do modern historians writing from all three of the principal camps of interpretation of the Manifesto. This means that even the dates of composition and publication of accounts of the battle against polygamy do not settle the issue of whether political or religious antagonism was a more potent weapon against the Saints.[29]

It is nevertheless interesting to note that the 1890s are a fascinating "blip" in what is an otherwise unbroken line of politico-religious pressure against the Saints that lasted from the 1850s well into the 1920s. This is explained by the fact that Utah appeared to be accommodating to the rest of the nation as it moved toward statehood (which was achieved in 1896). Not surprisingly, historical accounts of the period suggest lessened religious opposition to the Saints following promulgation of the Manifesto.[30] In fact, accounts written during the 1890s suggest that for a brief time Protestant opposition to Mormonism diminished dramatically.[31]

But the general conflation of religion and politics reappeared at the end of the century when members and ecclesiastical leaders of the churches in the Protestant mainstream were infuriated by the 1898 election of the polygamist Brigham H. Roberts to the U.S. House of Representatives. He was not allowed to take the seat to which he had been elected, but that did not deter Utah voters from sending another high-profile Latter-day Saint to the nation's capital. The Utah state legislature sent Reed Smoot, a member of the Council of the Twelve, to Washington in 1902. The apostle was allowed to take his seat, but his election engendered enough passionate Protestant resistance to force a four-year investigation of Smoot's right to hold his seat, an investigation that turned out to be a full-scale investigation of Utah Mormonism.

The part played by Salt Lake City's non-Mormon religious leaders in arousing opposition to Smoot and the Mormons is sometimes overlooked, but their hostility to the idea of having an apostle in the Senate was overt and very conspicuous.[32] Just as they had done earlier when they opposed Utah statehood, they began a petition drive. As before, many of the petitions that purportedly contained over four million signatures were gathered in evangelical Protestant congregations throughout the nation. As much as anything else, these petition drives have been used by historians to argue that religious opposition to Mormonism at both the local and national level was a driving force in American politics in the first two decades of the twentieth century.[33]

I am one of those historians of Mormonism whose work fits roughly into the new Mormon history or creative adjustment category of interpretation.[34] But my doctoral dissertation on the Mormons in politics can reasonably be characterized as a work that at least makes me a fellow traveler to those who go the legacy of conquest route. The invitation to prepare an essay on Mormonism for the book *Minority Faiths and the Protestant Mainstream* gave me an opportunity to consider from a fresh perspective the history of the Latter-day Saints and the outside world in the last quarter of the nineteenth century and the first quarter of the twentieth. What became most obvious to me after I revisited the historical record of pioneer Utah and its relationship with the rest of the nation and particularly after I reread the text of the

Reynolds opinion is the extent to which patriarchy forms the nexus between the Supreme Court's opinion in the *Reynolds* case and the Manifesto issued by the president of the church. One provides the basis for the other. While the Court, holding that polygamy was patriarchy's counterpart and that patriarchy led to despotism, forbade Mormons to marry into plurality for religious reasons, no prohibition was put in place to prevent the Saints from freely exercising an outspoken and continuing approbation of the patriarchal order of marriage. Since there was no proscription of temple marriages uniting men and women for time and eternity as long as they were performed for monogamous couples, Saints were permitted to continue establishing patriarchal families. Consequently, even though it is true that President Woodruff relinquished plural marriage, in preserving Mormon temples his action sustained and made possible the perpetuation of patriarchy, which, at bedrock, is one of the cardinal tenets that sets this form of the Christian faith apart from all others.

At one and the same time, then, the Manifesto led to the demise of a marital practice that circumscribed the LDS community and kept it separate from the world, and it opened the way for Mormonism to become a universal faith. In a supremely ironic undertaking, Protestant pressure led to governmental action that begot a Manifesto that paved the way for the current success of Mormonism.

That this is not what the non-Mormon religious community intended is plain. That mainstream Protestantism was unable to work its will altogether as it wished was because the First Amendment remained in place. Even though the Protestant majority functioned as a virtual religious establishment at this point in the nation's history, the First Amendment prevented it from turning into an actual religious establishment. The amendment's prohibition against the establishment of a state religion gave government officials— especially those in the executive branch of government—the independence needed to offset the influence of the religious majority. The amendment's guarantee of the free exercise of religion was equally important. In setting forth the critical distinction between behavior and belief, the *Reynolds* decision left Mormonism's rich store of symbolic resources intact. Moreover, because President Woodruff's foresight in issuing the Manifesto when he did permitted LDS temples to remain in operation, Latter-day Saints continued to have the freedom to exercise their faith even to the extent of creating plural families through proxy ordinances for deceased men and women and allowing widowers to marry second wives for time and eternity.

Searching anew for underlying power issues as they were played out in the political and economic arena might further illuminate the sources of animosity between Mormonism and the American religious mainstream at century's end. As indicated, however, power and the brute force of superior numbers are, at best, only a part of the story of the relationship between Mormonism and the American religious mainstream. Reviewing that relationship with an eye to issues other than power is a fruitful way of unpacking the complicated history of the Protestant mainstream's relationship with not only Mormonism but also other minority faiths.

∽

The focal point of nearly every existing account of early Mormon history (including my own) has been the Mormon prophet. Because this is the case, authors have naturally directed attention to the emergence of the Book of Mormon and Joseph Smith's prophetic career. In following the prophet from western New York to Kirtland, Ohio, historians have been inordinately concerned with the Saints at the heart of the movement. Much attention is thus directed to the story of the Mormons sent by the prophet to establish a Mormon settlement in Independence, Missouri. As a result, regardless of whether the prophet is depicted as a man who spoke for God or one who was a crafty and devious practitioner of the magic arts, existing histories of Joseph Smith and his followers during Mormonism's early years portray an unconventional and iconoclastic movement with two centers, where all of Smith's followers were concentrated.[35]

As it turns out, this is a seriously foreshortened picture, especially of the movement during its first decade.[36] The distortion is not surprising because sources describing the introduction and, at times, subsequent flowering of this new form of Christianity in the hamlets, villages, and small towns of the early republic were for a long time too skimpy and too scattered to allow a worthwhile account of the story of this dimension of the movement to be written. This lacuna was filled by records left by William E. McLellin, an Illinois schoolteacher who became an early LDS apostle. His journals and papers, which surfaced in the historical collections of the LDS Church in 1992 and have now been analyzed and published, give scholars a full and reasonably systematic description of this movement as it emerged connected to, yet apart from, Kirtland and Independence.[37]

Providing convincing evidence that an actual religious marketplace existed in the United States in the middle years of the first half of what has been designated as the "Christian century," these McLellin's journals—one for each year from 1831 to 1836—described a pattern of preaching that verged on debating in the way religious claims were contested and supported. They also characterized the "product" offered by the Saints in the new nation's spiritual emporium. Rehearsing his own sermons and those of other LDS missionaries with surprising fullness, this missionary who became an apostle (but afterward left the church) revealed what the prophet's followers preached about (i.e., subject matter) and often indicated how listeners responded. He also frequently noted the precise biblical texts on which he and his compatriots preached.

This information makes it possible to compare the Saints' message with those preached in the same arena and often from the same pulpit by representatives of other Christian faiths.[38] These accounts also impart a sense of how their understanding that their church was "the Church of Christ" was central to the message being preached by the followers of the prophet. But preachers from many Protestant groups were equally convinced that theirs was Christ's church, and the Disciples of Christ (Campbellites), whose church was also organized in 1830, likewise named their ecclesiastical body the Church of Christ. This meant that the Saints sometimes had difficulty differentiating themselves from other Christians. In particular, they often faced the demanding task of distinguishing themselves from the followers of William and Alexander Campbell, Barton Stone, and others who had managed to take possession of the name Christian.[39]

About midway through these journals, McLellin described an episode that dramatizes the competitive temperament of the U.S. denominations during this period. On April 15, 1833, McLellin and Parley Pratt were at the water's edge with several converts who were ready "to be baptized in the faith of the Church of Christ" when they were interrupted by a representative of a competing denomination who greeted Sophi White, one of those waiting to be baptized, and calling her "Sister . . . urged her to not throw herself away or out of the church of Christ."[40] It is therefore not surprising that by 1834 Smith's followers had started to call themselves Mormons and their church the Church of the Latter Day Saints.[41]

If the Mormons had to share the name of their institution with other denominational groups, their possession of a modern work of scripture made their Christian message unique. The McLellin journals convey the extraordinary importance of the Book of Mormon as support for the gospel set forth in the New Testament; they likewise make clear how Smith's followers used the book in their preaching in those early days. Although the Book of Mormon was almost always mentioned, little or no evidence indicates that it was used as a source of texts for sermons. Instead, LDS preachers pointed to its existence, to the *fact* of the book, as verification for the validity of the Bible and also to its coming forth as the opening event in the last dispensation of the fullness of times. The book was the ultimate sign of the times pointing to a belief that people in the United States in the 1830s were living at the end of time.

Although their author was often in Kirtland, these documents are totally silent about the building of a temple there; they allude neither to the calling of a church patriarch nor to Zion's Camp; and the kingdom of God is mentioned only in the context of a sermon on Mark 1:15, not in connection with the organization of the kingdom of God that accompanied the dedication of the Kirtland Temple.[42] In view of the neglect of these Hebraic elements that were being introduced into Mormonism, McLellin's relative silence about continuing revelation and the prophetic aspect of Mormonism generally, and the stress placed on the Book of Mormon as the herald of the kingdom, these documents suggest that the primary message of early Mormon preaching was millennialist Christianity.[43] Those whose ears were attuned heard that the end was near, a not unfamiliar message. But the sermons Smith's followers preached proclaimed that the coming forth of the Book of Mormon pointed to the imminence of the Second Coming. These Mormon good tidings also emphasized that the Church of Christ had been restored and that in the interval between their delivery of the millennialist message and the end of the world as they knew it, through this institution people could, as promised in the text of the first chapter of the second letter of Peter on which these preachers often spoke, "escape from the corruption that is in the world . . . and become partakers of the divine nature." Both LDS preachers and their listeners read incidences of inexplicable healings and speaking in tongues as testimony to the authenticity of this version of the Christian message.[44] The journals thus show that it was the existence of the Book of Mormon that initially set LDS preaching apart from the exhortations of the "sectarians," as Protestants and Catholics alike were dubbed by the Saints.

When McLellin's description of what was going on outside the gathering centers in the Mormonism of the 1830s is compared with the picture that unfolds when the focus is on the prophet and his followers in Ohio and Missouri, a dramatic contrast materializes. Pouring into Kirtland where their leader was in residence, Smith's followers created the first of a series of gathered communities that obliterated the boundaries between civil society and the sacred, boundaries so clearly drawn elsewhere in the United States as state and church became separate at the state as well as the federal level.

The citizens of this rather ordinary midwestern town were in face-to-face contact with one who could speak for God.[45] If revelations from on high were not announced daily, Kirtland settlers had the medium for receiving such communications in their presence. This separated them from the citizens of nearby Mentor and Painesville. It also separated Saints in Kirtland from the

Saints in such settlements as Amherst, Ohio, not fifty miles away, where the Mormons organized a local church to which the Saints came for meetings but from which they returned to their homes in the vicinity, managing their church membership much as it was managed by Baptists, Methodists, and other Protestants. The difference became increasingly great, not just because the Saints in Kirtland were a part of the Mormon gathering but also because the concept of the patriarchy that connected the Saints in 1830 with the saints in the ancient days was gradually being introduced and made central to the Mormon prophet's teachings. In 1832, Smith announced he had received a revelation explaining that the "restored" Aaronic and Melchizedek priesthoods belonged to the Saints by right since they were "continued through the lineage of your fathers." His own father, Joseph Smith Sr., was called to be church patriarch since "he was the oldest man of the blood of Joseph or of the seed of Abraham" among the Saints. Then, in rapid succession, a School of the Prophets was established, and a rabbi was hired to instruct priesthood members in the Hebrew language. Entwined with the legitimacy conveyed by knowing a smattering of the language of the ancients, priesthood authority over marriage was asserted. As Father Smith, the patriarch, began to give patriarchal blessings to the Saints who were in the center place, confirming their membership into Abraham's bloodline, they ceased thinking of themselves as Gentiles and began declaring themselves literal descendants of the Israelites.[46]

The contrast between the Mormons in the countryside who accepted the millennialist message preached there and the Saints in the gathering places can best be articulated in terms of *difference* and *otherness*. These are concepts whose use in making distinctions within Mormonism can clarify the relationship between this movement and American mainstream Protestantism, not only in the 1830s, when William McLellin was recording his missionary experiences, but also at every point in time since then. Even though difference and otherness are mainly perceptual from within and without, it is important to keep in mind that both are manifested symbolically and literally. Difference is most often manifested in the areas of doctrine and ritual, which means that difference is likely more rhetorical and symbolic than actual. Symbolic otherness is likewise made known in these areas, but actual otherness is nearly always imputed to persons and groups whose beliefs take literal shape visible enough to be recognized by persons outside as well as within a religious community. While Mormonism's original and distinctive beliefs were not unimportant in engendering Protestant antagonism, it is the behavioral aspect of the gathered Mormon community that generated overt and sometimes violent opposition.

It can hardly be said, however, that mainstream Protestantism and Mormonism faced off against each other in the early years of the 1830s, for neither one had then assumed the shape it would later take.[47] The retrospective accounts written by Joseph Smith and some of those who became his followers as Mormonism was coming into being in the western New York "Burned over District" describe an atmosphere of curiosity about and ridicule of the prophet, his followers, and their "gold bible" that generated a fair amount of verbal abuse. Smith remembered this was animated by the hostility of Presbyterians and other local Protestant groups, and he indicated this "persecution" was responsible for the Saints' decision to leave the area.[48] Moreover, non-Mormons in the areas where the prophet and his followers subsequently gathered—in Independence, Missouri, and in the area east of Cleveland, Ohio—were not initially opposed to the coming of the Saints, but they soon started to have reservations about the lack of separation between politics and economics, on one side, and religion in the Mormon community, on the other. When those reservations turned into negative attitudes and hostile action, those attitudes and actions began to function as a boundary between the Saints and the outside world.

This suggests that centrifugal and centripetal forces worked together to bind the prophet and his followers into a gemeinschaft community, within which they moved together toward what would become peculiarity and chosenness in their own eyes and otherness in the eyes of non-Mormons. Accelerating rapidly as new revelations provided a rhetorical and doctrinal basis for their becoming a peculiar/chosen people, the feeling of being a special race in God's sight was undergirded in Kirtland as the structure the Saints described as a temple took shape. When that sanctuary was dedicated, those in attendance said they were united in a rare set of corporate spiritual experiences that ushered them into a sacred realm, and revelation accompanying the dedication led to the organization of the kingdom of God. The sensation of otherness this Mormon "Pentecost" precipitated not only separated the followers of the prophet from non-Mormons but also separated the Saints in the gathering centers from those in the countryside.

As the end of Mormonism's first decade approached, however, two striking factors, one internal and one external, combined to convert the difference of countryside Mormonism to otherness. The first, a factor that served as a significant link connecting the two forms of Mormonism, was the standard invitation Mormon preachers issued to converts to travel to "Zion," a specific place in Jackson County, Missouri, which a revelation given through Joseph Smith had designated as the place where the "winding up scene" would end and the Second Coming would begin. Acceptance of this invitation meant moving to a gathering center. The second factor was external: non-Mormon hostility and violence that first compelled the Saints to leave Independence, Missouri, and afterward led the prophet, his closest associates, and many of the Ohio Saints to flee the Kirtland area. Together, these factors operated to create a congregation categorically separated from the world with which all Latter-day Saints would be identified before 1844, when the prophet was murdered, whether they stayed where they were after conversion or gathered to Zion.

In the course of Mormonism's second decade, the Saints were engaged in a full-scale war in Missouri, fled to Illinois, and built a kingdom of God on the banks of the Mississippi River. They saw their prophet murdered and in the next few years experienced a virtual atomization of the movement, a splitting apart in which the Mormons who would be *other* separated from the Saints who, while holding on to the Book of Mormon and the belief that the true Church of Christ is led by a prophet, were content with *difference*. Although generalizing too quickly is dangerous, it is useful to think of those in the latter category in geographical terms: typically they were the Saints who did not go west.

As many as one-third to a half of the Saints (according to some estimates) understood the prophet's murder and their subsequent sufferings when their Illinois neighbors drove them from Nauvoo as a signal that the patriarchal order had gotten out of hand by introducing such esoteric doctrines as baptism for the dead and, most especially, plural marriage. They therefore retreated to the Mormonism of the countryside. Settling in areas throughout the East and Midwest, they retained their understanding of the Book of Mormon as the signal that the end time was in view. Even though many of them never permanently joined another Mormon community and were branded apostate by the Saints who followed Brigham Young westward, Saints in this group generally went to their graves believing that the Book of Mormon was true and that Joseph Smith was a prophet, even though he might have fallen at the end.[49]

On April 6, 1860, exactly thirty years after the first Church of Jesus Christ was organized by Latter-day Saints, a group of Joseph Smith's former followers "reorganized" the church under the leadership of the prophet's son Joseph Smith III. This reformulation of Mormonism is very important to the story of the Latter-day Saints, particularly to matters being addressed in this essay, for it is the institutional expression of Mormonism as difference, as a form of primitive Christianity set apart from other Christian churches by two major elements: acceptance of the Book of Mormon as scripture and a doctrinal tenet holding that the church would always be led by a prophet-pres-

ident in the Prophet Joseph Smith's direct bloodline. Their history is so unlike the history of the Latter-day Saints who went west that this movement
(known as the Reorganization) can properly be classified as an idiosyncratic form of Protestantism, although a significant portion of its members would
hardly accept this categorization. That they were simply *different* and not
other is a point that has been continually emphasized throughout their history by their negative identification of themselves as the Mormons who did
not practice polygamy, the Mormons who did not go west.

The Saints who went west, however, had no need of negative referents. They
gloried in their otherness, identifying themselves as God's chosen people and
alluding to all who were not Saints as Gentiles. Elsewhere I have argued that
the "trek," the journey across the plains to the Great Basin, was for them crossing the wilderness. Deseret, their kingdom, was promised land.[50] Here it is
important to recognize that the Saints' own understanding of themselves in
Hebraic terms provoked a response among other Christian groups that went
far beyond the sort of competition that made Presbyterians, Methodists, Baptists, and other Protestants maintain their superiority to Roman Catholics and
Jews and even quarrel with or at least be condescending to adherents of forms
of Protestantism that were simply different. Added to LDS doctrinal and theological claims, the Saints' behavior caused the Protestant mainstream to cate-
gorize Mormonism as illegitimate—heretical enough to be dangerous to
Christianity. The Protestant program for dealing with the Mormons was therefore simple and direct: Mormonism must be destroyed root and branch.

The approach the Protestants used in the second half of the nineteenth
century contrasted dramatically with earlier strategies employed in Kirtland
(tarring and feathering the prophet and his counselor and riding them out
of town on a rail), Missouri (conducting a war of extermination), and Illinois (murdering the prophet and driving the Saints from the state). But the
goal, annihilation, was essentially the same. This time, however, the strategy
resembled that being employed with those elsewhere who were regarded as
heathen or pagan, that is, other—particularly the inhabitants of Africa, China,
and other parts of the Far East. The Protestants (and even the Catholics)
called what they were doing "home missions" instead of foreign missions,
but the key to success was converting Saints away from Mormonism, one by
one. Institutionally, this strategy was expressed as Protestant ministers founded missions in rural areas and congregations in the cites and towns. The
Methodists, Baptists, Presbyterians, Congregationalists, Lutherans, and the
Church of Christ all established congregations in Utah during the territorial period. Other missionary efforts included attempts to provide "a true
Christian education for the Mormon youth"; the organization of Loyal

Leagues, Liberty Brigades, Sewing Circles, and other societies for interested LDS women and young people; and even the establishment of a refuge for polygamous wives.[51]

At the same time, Protestants in Utah united in what they regarded as a Christian endeavor to arouse public opinion against the Mormons. Their campaign called for specific changes in Utah: a tax-supported public school system that would be removed from ecclesiastical (i.e., Mormon) control; the abolition of polygamy; the discontinuation of the use of marked ballots in elections; and the separation of church and state in Utah politics. Protestant organizations mounted petition-signing campaigns whenever federal legislation against polygamy was pending, and they lent their support to the anti-Mormon efforts of federal officials both in Utah Territory and at the national level, continuing to do so well into the twentieth century.[52]

The distinction between Mormon otherness and Mormon difference is useful conceptually because it clarifies much about how the Saints were perceived and how they managed to get along in the world at different times in their history. The distinction does not, however, help much in unscrambling the question of the extent to which opposition to the western Saints was a matter of being opposed to their political and economic systems and the extent to which opposition to the Saints was religious, a matter about which historians of nineteenth-century Mormonism have been disagreeing for years.[53] But it helps in interpreting statements of motive since religious and nonreligious incentives for action are often quite at odds with each other.

This seems especially so in the United States. It stands to reason, for instance, that opposition to Smith's followers' taking over Kirtland and making it a Mormon town could have been incited by Protestants in the area. But the accounts of the opposition to the Saints in Ohio, not unlike accounts of the actions of adversaries the Mormons had to confront in Missouri and Illinois, had so many political and economic dimensions that nearly all historians except the Mormons themselves generally explain what happened as political and economic opposition to the Saints. While the Saints experienced the drivings, shootings, beatings, tarrings and feathering, and so on as persecution, historians outside the church as well as some inside usually interpret what happened in political and economic terms.[54] Those who write about the Utah territorial period are particularly prone to use political and economic explanations, perhaps because it is so very difficult to separate the religious and secular elements of opposition to Mormonism from any sort of religious motivation except that which issued from organized Protestant groups—and because the Saints became so adept at moving back and forth between the State of Deseret and the world that was Utah Territory.

Accounting for this is easier if separation of church and state is taken into account. While the Protestants could have as their goal the extirpation of Mormonism, complete destruction of the other, such a goal is not possible within the American constitutional system as long as its prohibition of establishment and free exercise clauses are intact. Recognizing that the Manifesto was one more in an extended series of actions and reactions that resulted in lowering the barriers separating the Saints from "the world," as it is sometimes put, helps clarify the situation since it reveals the limits of federal power.

Keeping in view the way the barriers came down is more important to the story of American religion, however. Because the U.S. legislature can legislate about behavior, not belief, Congress has no power over symbolic otherness. When any group begins to turn symbol into corporeality that appears to threaten social order, as the Saints did when the patriarchal order of marriage became a literal system of plurality that was obvious to all who had eyes to see, the government may step in, but its power is restricted. It can force a group that sees itself or is seen as the other to turn literal practice back into symbol and thereby push and prod the group back across the divide into difference. Yet, and this is the essential matter, the essence of belief that stands at the core of religion is protected.

In summary, then, what this story of Mormonism's relationship to the nation's religious center reveals is that the nation proved itself to be the custodian of such protection. As long as the nation persists in extending such protection to all forms of religion within its borders, the American religious mainstream will continue to be bedeviled and enriched by the presence of a multitude of minority faiths—old and new.

Notes

1. Wilford Woodruff, *Wilford Woodruff's Journal, 1833–1898*, Typescript Edition, 9 vols., ed. Scott G. Kenney (Midvale, Utah: Signature Books, 1983–85), 9:114. An abridgement of this important journal is *Waiting for World's End: The Diaries of Wilford Woodruff*, ed. Susan Staker (Salt Lake City: Signature Books, 1993). The date suggests that Woodruff's reference was to a decision of the U.S. Supreme Court in *The Late Corporation of the Church of Jesus Christ of Latter-day Saints v. United States*, 136 U.S. 1 (1890), which upheld the constitutionality of the provisions of the Edmunds-Tucker Act that threatened dissolution of the church as a legal corporation and seizure of its property unless the practice of plural marriage was immediately abandoned.

2. The text of the Manifesto, headed "Official Declaration," is included as "Official Declaration—1" in the Doctrine and Covenants of the Church of Jesus Christ of Latter-day Saints (291 in the 1981 edition). For circumstances surrounding Woodruff's decision to issue the Manifesto, see Thomas G. Alexander, *Things in Heaven*

and Earth: The Life and Times of Wilford Woodruff, a Mormon Prophet (Salt Lake City: Signature Books, 1991), 261–68. Without exception, historical accounts of the form of Mormonism that took shape in the Intermountain West all assess the importance of the Manifesto to the history of the Latter-day Saints.

3. Evidence that the Mormons regarded themselves as victims of federal tyranny is found in letters, diaries, sermons, and virtually every other form of historical record left by Latter-day Saints who lived in the Utah Territory between 1850 and 1890. Indication of the virulence and intensity of this feeling may be drawn from the sermons and talks of Brigham Young and other leaders of the church between 1854 and 1886 collected in the *Journal of Discourses,* 26 vols. (Liverpool, England: F. D. and S. W. Richards, 1854–86; photo lithographic reprint, Los Angeles: Gartner Printing and Litho, 1956). The following selection, drawn from the index entries under U.S. government, gives a flavor of how this feeling was expressed: "Abuses of against LDS ... ; Anti-Mormon activities of; Blood of prophets upon; Confidence in lacking because of misrule; Corruption by wicked leaders; Dishonest condition of; Evils existing in threaten overthrow of; Graft in probable; LDS injustices of provoke righteous anger; LDS troubles created by; Oppressions by to meet God's retribution; Territorial rights denied by; Wicked men in not opposed by LDS but left to Satan." It is important to note, however, that, in addition to such scornful references, the index contains an equal number of references to Mormon sermons and talks in which the U.S. system of government was venerated. Although some scholars interpret the latter as "window dressing," it is much more likely that the division discloses the Saints' extreme ambivalence toward the nation.

4. The most famous reference to plural marriage as barbaric comes from the 1856 platform of the Republican party. There polygamy is yoked to slavery, and the two practices are described as "twin relics of barbarism." The religious community was more concerned with polygamy as sin than as barbarous practice. Abundant evidence of denigration and vilification of the Latter-day Saints by members of non-Mormon religious groups is found in religious publications. My content analysis of periodical articles indexed under Mormon, Utah, or Latter-day Saints revealed that 30 percent of the total were published in religious periodicals and that of those, only a single article failed to fit into one of my negative categories. At least half of such articles were rated as extremely negative. (See "From Satyr to Saint," herein.)

5. The part of the intermountain region where the Saints settled was in upper California, which became U.S. territory as one of the conditions of the Treaty of Guadalupe Hidalgo that ended the Mexican War.

6. The term *Deseret* came from the Book of Mormon.

7. In view of the importance of naming in religion, which Phyllis Trible pointed out, the refusal of Congress to accept the name proposed by the Latter-day Saints assumes significance as an early indication of suspicion regarding the program the Mormons might be pursuing to create a separate religious culture. See Phyllis Trible, "Eve and Adam: Genesis 2–3 Re-read," *Andover Newton Quarterly* 13 (March 1973); reprinted in *Womanspirit Rising: A Feminist Reader in Religion,* ed. Carol P. Christ and Judith Plaskow, 2d ed. (San Francisco: Harper Collins, 1992), 74–83.

8. Rumors about plural marriage among the Mormons were circulating in the 1830s, and it is quite possible that some covenants of plural marriage were entered into during that decade. Although "the principle," which is how the Saints often

described plural marriage, was not made public until 1852, it was formally introduced into the movement in the 1840s when Joseph Smith revealed the principle to many of his closest associates and dictated to his scribe William Clayton the revelation that would become Section 132 of the church's Doctrine and Covenants. It is important to recognize that this revelation also contained a number of theological innovations that would have made Mormonism unique even without the practice of plural marriage. Although clandestine in the beginning, marriage of Mormon men to more than one wife was generally acknowledged in Utah before the public announcement of it in 1852. For the religious and theological dimension of plural marriage, see Lawrence Foster, *Religion and Sexuality: The Shakers, the Mormons, and the Oneida Community* (1981; reprint, Urbana: University of Illinois Press, 1984), chapter 4. A convenient account of the history of the practice is Richard S. Van Wagoner, *Mormon Polygamy: A History* (Salt Lake City: Signature Books, 1986).

9. Before the completion of LDS temples in the Intermountain West, the Saints established temporary "endowment houses," in which the ordinance of celestial marriage could be performed.

10. This gave first wives an advantage because they were their husbands' legal spouses. But since men entering the patriarchal order to comply with the principle were supposed to have the permission of their first wives, this advantage was typically compromised.

11. Standard works on Mormon political and economic innovations are Klaus J. Hansen, *Quest for Empire: The Political Kingdom of God and the Council of Fifty in Mormon History* (East Lansing: Michigan State University Press, 1967; reprint, Lincoln: University of Nebraska Press, 1974); and Leonard J. Arrington, *Great Basin Kingdom: An Economic History of the Latter-day Saints, 1830–1900* (Cambridge, Mass.: Harvard University Press, 1958; reprint, Salt Lake City: University of Utah Press, 1993).

12. The literature on the Reynolds case is extensive. For accounts devoted to the legal aspects of the case, see Orma Linford, "The Mormons and the Law: The Polygamy Cases" (Ph.D. diss., University of Wisconsin, 1964); and Orma Linford, "The Mormons and the Law: The Polygamy Cases," *Utah Law Review* 9 (Winter 1964 and Summer 1965): 308–70, 543–91. Elwyn A. Smith, *Religious Liberty in the United States: The Development of Church-State Thought since the Revolutionary Era* (Philadelphia: Fortress, 1972), makes an effort to place this case in the context of the history of interpretation of the First Amendment. See also Catharine Cookson, "Myths, Mormons, and Moral Panics: A Critique of Governmental Processes and Attitudes in the Free Exercise Case of *Reynolds v. United States*" (Master's thesis, University of Virginia, 1992), 54–57; and Edwin Brown Firmage and R. Collin Mangrum, *Zion in the Courts: A Legal History of the Church of Jesus Christ of Latter-day Saints, 1830–1900* (Urbana: University of Illinois Press, 1988), 151–53.

13. Accounts of the Saints' refusal to accede to federal legislative prohibitions of the practice of plural marriage are legion, the very stuff of Mormon pioneer history. In addition to the history summarized in Van Wagoner, *Mormon Polygamy,* see Foster, *Religion and Sexuality,* chapter 5. For the story from the point of view of plural wives, consult the selections by plural wives included in Kenneth W. Godfrey, Audrey M. Godfrey, and Jill Mulvay Derr, eds., *Women's Voices: An Untold History of the Latter-day Saints, 1830–1900* (Salt Lake City: Deseret Book, 1982); Annie Clark Tanner, *A Mormon Mother: An Autobiography* (Salt Lake City: University of Utah Press, 1976); Maria S.

Ellsworth, ed., *Mormon Odyssey: The Story of Ida Udall Hunt, Plural Wife* (Urbana: University of Illinois Press, 1992); and the essays in Claudia L. Bushman, ed., *Mormon Sisters: Women in Early Utah* (Cambridge, Mass.: Emmeline, 1976). For a sense of what the experience was like for a Mormon polygamist, see the diary of Charles Ora Card, manuscript, Special Collections, Utah State University Library, Logan, Utah.

14. Holding that religious opinion alone may be held without constitutional inhibition while actions hostile to good civil order are subject to such inhibition, no matter how sincere is the religious opinion undergirding such acts, the Supreme Court set forth "the true distinction between what properly belongs to the Church and what to the State" in this opinion. Since it clarified the meaning of the Jeffersonian concept of a "wall of separation" between church and state, the *Reynolds* decision is important to American religious history, but to Latter-day Saints at the time, it seemed a travesty against religious freedom. See Firmage and Mangrum, *Zion in the Courts*, 151–59.

15. *Reynolds v. United States*, 98 U.S. 167, 164 (1879). The decision of the Court, written by Chief Justice Morrison R. Waite, illustrated the necessity of controlling religiously motivated behavior by referring to human sacrifice and a wife's belief, supported by religion, that it was her duty to burn herself on the funeral pile of her dead husband.

16. Cookson, "Myths, Mormons, and Moral Panics," returns to this argument at many points in this very interesting work.

17. For a standard account of this period, see Gustive O. Larson, *The "Americanization" of Utah for Statehood* (San Marino, Calif.: Huntington Library, 1971).

18. President Woodruff's remarks were made in the Cache Stake Conference held on November 1. They were reported in the November 14, 1891, issue of the *Deseret Weekly* and are printed in the Doctrine and Covenants of the Church of Jesus Christ of Latter-day Saints as "Excerpts from Three Addresses by President Wilford Woodruff regarding the Manifesto," which follow the text of Woodruff's Manifesto. Two monographs describe and analyze from a political perspective the events leading up to President Woodruff's decision that the continued practice of plural marriage would destroy the church over which he presided: Larson's *"Americanization" of Utah for Statehood* concentrates on what happened in Utah, while Leo Lyman, *Political Deliverance: The Mormon Quest for Utah Statehood* (Urbana: University of Illinois Press, 1986), deals with the story from the national point of view.

19. Thomas G. Alexander's 1991 biography of Woodruff, *Things in Heaven and Earth*, is a conspicuous exception to this generalization. But his *Mormonism in Transition: A History of the Latter-day Saints, 1890–1930*, 2d ed. (Urbana: University of Illinois Press, 1986), does not mention the linkage.

20. For an informative study of the writing of western history, including discussion of the work of the "new western historians," see Charles Peterson, "Speaking for the Past," in *Oxford History of the American West*, ed. Clyde A. Milner II, Carol A. O'Connor, and Martha Sandweiss (New York: Oxford University Press, 1994), 743–69. Patricia Nelson Limerick, *Legacy of Conquest: The Unbroken Past of the American West* (New York: W. W. Norton, 1987), was the opening salvo in a notable revisionist movement in western history. See also Patricia Nelson Limerick, Clyde A. Milner II, and Charles E. Rankin, eds., *Trails: Toward a New Western History* (Lawrence: University Press of Kansas, 1991).

21. Larson, *The "Americanization" of Utah for Statehood.* Mark Leone's *Roots of Modern Mormonism* (Cambridge, Mass.: Harvard University Press, 1979) is a Marxist interpretation that goes beyond the argument that Utah was Americanized to suggest Mormon country was reduced to the status of client state.

22. While this characterization may come close to caricature, with its description of Mormonism's being "out of phase" with the rest of the nation, this interpretation is not too far from that found in Klaus J. Hansen, *Mormonism and the American Experience* (Chicago: University of Chicago Press, 1981).

23. On September 27, 1890, the day after the promulgation of the Manifesto, the editor of the non-Mormon *Salt Lake Tribune,* who was extremely suspicious of anything the Saints did, wrote that he believed Woodruff's "manifesto was not intended to be accepted as a command by the President of the Church, but as a little bit of harmless dodging to deceive the people of the east."

24. For interpretations of the Manifesto as submission rather than revelation, see B. Harvey Allred, *A Leaf in Review* (Caldwell, Idaho: Caxton, 1933); and R. C. Newsom, *Is the Manifesto a Revelation* (Salt Lake City: privately printed, n.d.); and Samuel W. Taylor, *Rocky Mountain Empire: The Latter-day Saints Today* (New York: Macmillan, 1978), 12–40.

25. See, for example, Leonard J. Arrington and Davis Bitton, *The Mormon Experience: A History of the Latter-day Saints* (New York: Alfred A. Knopf, 1979); and James B. Allen and Glen M. Leonard, *The Story of the Latter-day Saints* (Salt Lake City: Deseret Book, 1976).

26. James B. Allen, "Line upon Line . . ." *Ensign* 9 (July 1979): 32–39.

27. The addition of the "Excerpts from Three Addresses by President Wilford Woodruff regarding the Manifesto" to the most recent edition of the book of Doctrine and Covenants is evidence that this is the official position of the LDS Church. While not tantamount to a formal statement of doctrine, see also Paul H. Peterson, "Manifesto of 1890," in *Encyclopedia of Mormonism,* 5 vols., ed. Daniel H. Ludlow (New York: Macmillan, 1992), 2:852–53. This work, edited by Daniel H. Ludlow, was overseen by two members of the LDS Council of the Twelve.

28. The generalizations in the following paragraphs are drawn from the research reported in Jo Ann Barnett Shipps, "The Mormons in Politics: The First Hundred Years" (Ph.D. diss., University of Colorado, 1965), especially chapters 6, 7, and 8, which deal with the pioneer period and the first two decades of the twentieth century.

29. This became obvious to me as I was working on my "Satyr to Saint" study. See also Richard O. Cowan, "Mormonism in National Periodicals" (Ph.D. diss., Stanford University, 1961); Dennis L. Lythgoe, "The Changing Image of Mormonism in Periodical Literature" (Ph.D. diss., University of Utah, 1969); and Charles A. Cannon, "The Awesome Power of Sex: The Polemical Campaign against Mormon Polygamy," *Pacific Historical Quarterly* 43 (February 1974): 61–82.

30. See, for example, an article written by the influential western historian Howard R. Lamar, "Statehood for Utah: A Different Path," *Utah Historical Quarterly* 39 (Fall 1971): 307–27.

31. It is quite possible that stories about Protestant opposition were squelched by a Mormon public relations effort that involved securing the services of an influential businessman, Isaac Trumbo, and some of his associates who traveled through the United States subsidizing leading newspapers, thus preventing them from printing

hostile articles about the Mormons during the statehood movement. See Edward Leo Lyman, "Isaac Trumbo and the Politics of Utah Statehood," *Utah Historical Quarterly* 41 (Spring 1973): 131.

32. The challenge to Smoot's occupancy of the Senate seat to which he had been elected was drawn up by the Reverend W. M. Paden, pastor of the First Presbyterian Church in Salt Lake City, and unsubstantiated charges about Smoot's having been a polygamist were added by the Reverend J. M. Lelich, superintendent of the Utah mission of the Methodist Episcopal Church. The entire challenge was orchestrated by the Salt Lake Ministerial Association, which included ministers from all of the city's Protestant churches.

33. Jan Shipps, "The Public Image of Sen. Reed Smoot, 1902–32," *Utah Historical Quarterly* 45 (Fall 1977): 380–400; Jan Shipps, "Beyond the Stereotypes: Mormon and Non-Mormon Communities in Twentieth-Century Mormondom," in *New Views of Mormon History: A Collection of Essays in Honor of Leonard J. Arrington*, ed. Davis Bitton and Maureen Ursenbach Beecher (Salt Lake City: University of Utah Press, 1987), 342–62.

34. My published work speaks most directly to the significance of the Manifesto to the history of the church in two places: *Mormonism: The Story of a New Religious Tradition* (Urbana: University of Illinois Press, 1985), 109–129; and "The Principle Revoked: A Closer Look at the Demise of Plural Marriage," *Journal of Mormon History* 11 (1984): 65–77.

35. This is true for much of the official historiography of the movement, that is, works issued by the various church presses, as well as for noncanonized and even antagonistic accounts of the first years of Mormonism.

36. If the measurement is from the publication of the Book of Mormon and the organization of the church, the first decade extends from 1830 through 1839, but if the starting point is the prophet's first revelations that tie the impending coming forth of the Book of Mormon to the preaching of the gospel that effectively inaugurates this movement, the first decade opens in 1829 and closes in 1838, the year Joseph Smith fled from Ohio to Missouri.

37. Because McLellin withdrew his membership from the church in 1837 and was subsequently branded as an apostate, the church bureaucrat who processed the 1909 acquisition of McLellin's missionary journals (along with a variety of other documents written long after the former apostle left the LDS Church) apparently decided that it would be better to keep them in a safe place since their content might be damaging to the church. In any event, they were never deposited in the church archive, and they were never entered in the catalog that lists and indexes the archive collection. They are, however, not damaging to the church, but quite the contrary. Unusually full and extremely literate, these extraordinary documents describe preaching tours through the midwestern—and on one of the tours, the northeastern—countryside that provide valuable information about Mormonism outside the Kirtland and Missouri settlements. See Jan Shipps and John W. Welch, eds., *The Journals of William McLellin, 1831–1836* (Provo, Utah, and Urbana: *BYU Studies* and University of Illinois Press, 1994).

38. The religious patterns in an area similar to the ones visited by the Mormon missionaries about the same time were described by Alan Taylor, "The Paradox of Popular Religion on the Yankee Frontier: Otsego County, New York, 1785–1820" (pa-

per presented at the annual meeting of the American Historical Association, San Francisco, January 1994). See also Alan Taylor, *William Cooper's Town: Power and Persuasion on the Frontier of the Early American Republic* (New York: Alfred A. Knopf, 1995).

39. I pursued this matter as I edited the McLellin journals and sometimes used the same language in my introduction to the journals and in "'Is Mormonism Christian?' Reflections on a Complicated Question," herein.

40. Note the upper-case *C* in the reference to the Saints' church and the lower-case *c* in the reference to the competing denomination. Throughout these journals the author continues to refer to his church as the "Church of Christ," but on August 1, 1834, he writes of preaching about the "church of the Latter day Saints" for the first time. In making such references afterward he indicated that this was not the church's official name by writing these three words without capitalizing either the *L* or the *S* and by placing single quotes around them. This is significant because the writer was a schoolteacher whose journals make it obvious that he was aware of the rules of grammar and was ordinarily careful to obey them.

41. In these documents, this designation appears first in the fourth journal and again in the 1835 journal. An 1838 revelation confirmed that the Church of Jesus Christ of Latter-day Saints should be the official name of the church, a matter that was so troubling to McLellin that it seems to have figured largely in his leaving the church.

42. Zion's Camp is the name the prophet gave to the 1834 military expedition he mounted from Kirtland to go to the assistance of the beleaguered Saints who were being driven out of Independence. The reference to the kingdom of God is found in the journal entry for August 3, 1835.

43. These journals also reveal an intense biblicism and concern with the spiritual gifts, especially healing and speaking in tongues.

44. Not surprisingly, accounts of the sermons suggest Mormon preachers asserted that the manifestation of spiritual gifts was evidence that the followers of Joseph Smith had the "true" Church of Christ. More interesting to those who read documents closely is the extent to which these are the journals of a literate and gifted writer, whose diary entries are generally composed of correctly punctuated, complete sentences in which words are correctly spelled. But the entries that reflect manifestation of spiritual gifts to McLellin either personally or in the context of a preaching "appointment" are filled with sentence fragments, misspelled words, and misplaced or missing punctuation.

45. This lent to Kirtland an extraordinary character that found expression in the construction of a temple rather than the usual Protestant steepled meetinghouse. The Kirtland "built environment" thus differed from that of nearby settlements.

46. Rex E. Cooper, *Promises Made to the Fathers: Mormon Covenant Organization* (Salt Lake City: University of Utah Press, 1983), 72–78; John L. Brooke, *The Refiner's Fire: The Making of Mormon Cosmology, 1644–1844* (New York: Cambridge University Press, 1994), 211–14. See also Jan Shipps, "Making Saints in the Early Days and the Latter Days," in *Contemporary Mormonism: Social Science Perspectives*, ed. Marie Cornwall, Tim B. Heaton, and Lawrence A. Young (Urbana: University of Illinois Press, 1993), 64–83.

47. Close examination of the revelations canonized by inclusion in the Doctrine and Covenants discloses an unquestionably Christian primitivist character to Mor-

monism in the years before Joseph Smith and his followers settled in Kirtland. See Marvin S. Hill, *Quest for Refuge: The Mormon Flight from American Pluralism* (Salt Lake City: Signature Books, 1989). This aspect of early Mormonism is also in Marvin S. Hill, "The Role of Christian Primitivism in the Origin and Development of the Mormon Kingdom, 1830–1844" (Ph.D. diss., University of Chicago, 1968).

48. Larry C. Porter and Jan Shipps, eds., "The Colesville, New York 'Exodus' Seen from Two Documentary Perspectives," *New York History* 62 (April 1981): 201–11. A June 18, 1830, letter from the Reverend Diedrich Willers to the Reverend L. Mayer and the Reverend D. Young that clearly expresses a Protestant minister's skepticism about Smith's "translation" of the Book of Mormon was published in *New York History.* See D. Michael Quinn, "The First Months of Mormonism: A Contemporary View by Rev. Diedrich Willers," *New York History* 54 (July 1973): 317–31.

49. For the various groups of Mormons who refused to go west but formed small congregations in the East and Midwest, see Stephen Shields, *Divergent Paths of the Restoration: A History of the Latter Day Saint Movement,* 3d rev. ed. (Bountiful, Utah: Restoration Research, 1982).

50. Shipps, *Mormonism,* 41–65; Jan Shipps, "Brigham Young and His Times: A Continuing Force in Mormonism," herein.

51. T. Edgar Lyon, "Religious Activities and Development in Utah, 1847–1910," *Utah Historical Quarterly* 35 (Fall 1967): 292–306; Gustive O. Larson, "An Industrial Home for Polygamous Wives," *Utah Historical Quarterly* 38 (Summer 1970): 263–75.

52. Examples are the story of Thomas C. Iliff, the Methodist superintendent for Utah, who traveled throughout the nation urging Christians to protest the seating of the polygamist B. H. Roberts in the House of Representatives, and a Baptist circular entitled the *Mormon Octopus,* which had a picture of an octopus that was superimposed on a map of the United States but had its tentacles reaching into all the western states. On another page, it had a drawing that purported to be the Great Seal of Utah, whose outer edge was encircled with the phrase "Utah for Mormons only" and whose motto was "In polygamy we trust."

53. Klaus Hansen, for example, has long argued that it was its seemingly un-American character, particularly its political system, that incited the greatest antagonism to Mormonism. This argument, which was initially made in Frank J. Cannon and Harvey J. O'Higgins, *Under the Prophet in Utah: The National Menace of a Political Priestcraft* (Boston, Mass.: C. M. Clark, 1911), is restated and expanded in Lyman, *Political Deliverance,* and in Firmage and Mangrum, *Zion in the Courts.* Analysis of what was written about the Mormons in the periodical press and elsewhere suggests, however, that plural marriage cannot be sufficiently disentangled from the political and economic elements of Mormon practice to make a strong argument one way or the other. Most members of the non-Mormon religious community probably regarded plural marriage as equally un-Christian and un-American.

54. A particularly forceful example of this interpretation of what happened is Kenneth H. Winn, *Exiles in a Land of Liberty: Mormons in America, 1830–1846* (Chapel Hill: University of North Carolina Press, 1989).

PART 5

HOW MY MIND WAS CHANGED AND
MY UNDERSTANDING AMPLIFIED

From time to time, the editors of the *Christian Century* invite well-known (and typically venerable) theologians and churchpeople to write retrospective descriptions explaining how time might have seen alterations in their understandings of humanity, divinity, and the workings of the world. In responding to these invitations, writers ordinarily compose meditations on how their own philosophies and convictions have been affected by expanding knowledge and their life experiences. The resulting personal essays are published in a long-running "How I Changed My Mind" series. Regardless of whether I am acquainted with the writers or know their work well, these occasional essays have always been fascinating to me because they provide glimpses into the intellect and judgment of sagacious, well-respected individuals. In revealing changes in ideas and attitudes, they also point to how thinking itself is a dynamic process.

When I wrote "Is Mormonism Christian? Reflections on a Complicated Question," the first of two essays in this, the most personal section of this book, it was not intended to be something that would fit into the "How I Changed My Mind" series.[1] But there is much in this essay that hints at a clear modulation, in the course of my career, in the way I have approached what Mormonism is and whether it is Christian. These are separate issues, and, as it happened, I addressed the question of how Mormonism ought to be classified before I dealt with the question of whether it is Christian. When this essay (considerably rewritten for publication here) appeared in *BYU Studies* in 1993, it was the first time I had written anything directed squarely at the question of whether Mormonism is Christian.

But I did change my mind about a closely related issue, one that also pertains to where to place Mormonism in the various categories (church, denomination, sect, cult) sociologists use to classify religious bodies. This is the

matter of what underlay Joseph Smith's ability to attract followers to a religious movement as unconventional as this one, something about which many
observers of early Mormonism commented. From the beginning of the twentieth century when this movement became a subject of interest to such serious non-Mormon scholars as I. Woodbridge Riley and William Alexander
Linn, this was a critical question, one central to every significant interpretation of Mormonism.[2] In academia after 1948, when Alfred A. Knopf, one of
the most respected trade publishers in the country, published Fawn McKay
Brodie's No Man Knows My History, a seemingly well-documented biography of the first Mormon prophet, her description of Joseph Smith as a ne'er-
do-well with such a vivid imagination that he came to accept his own inven-
tions as truth appeared to be carrying everything before it.[3]

Her interpretation of Smith's magical pursuits and his production of an
"invented History" cast in pseudo-Elizabethan language and published as a
scripturelike work was treated as fact by many non-Mormon scholars. But
it seemed intuitively wrong to me, not because I mistrusted Brodie's scholarship but because her account failed to explain how so many followers,
among them educated people and members of the clergy of existing religious
institutions, were attracted to the movement he founded. As I said in my
dissertation, any effort to explain the Mormon prophet as a conjurer of tall
tales and Mormonism in terms of a "gigantic hoax" is bound to result in
distortion:

> Official church literature proclaims Joseph Smith as translator, prophet, and
> martyr, and is forced thereupon into an endless justification of the many
> events in his life which fail to fit that pattern. Even so, the religious movement
> he started is probably more understandable in these terms than it will ever
> be in terms of unmitigated villainy or mental derangement. For if Joseph
> Smith were a knave, then those who joined him were dupes; if he were a
> madman, those who joined him were fools. In either case, all subsequent
> Mormon history must be explained with reference to Smith's personal mag-
> netism, the exploitation of his martyr-like death, and the use of the various
> psychological devices which are associated with persecution and peculiarity.[4]

Consequently, in spite of my lack of training in and inadequate knowledge of the phenomenology of religious experience, I embarked on a two-
pronged reading project, with one prong focused on Joseph Smith and the
other on religious experience. Since my mentor in the University of Colorado history department at that point was Hal Bridges, a professor preparing a book about American mysticism, it is not surprising that I read a great
deal about mysticism. Nor should it be surprising, I suppose, that when I

wrote the first chapter of my dissertation in 1964, I would describe the Mormon prophet as a mystic.

A decade later, when I revised that chapter, making numerous additions and deletions to turn it into "The Prophet Puzzle: Suggestions Leading toward a More Comprehensive Interpretation of Joseph Smith,"[5] my description of Joseph Smith as a mystic was a part of the material I deleted. I had changed my mind or, more accurately, I had gained enough additional knowledge to recognize the distinction between a mystic, whose encounter with the divine can be communicated only indirectly and metaphorically, and a prophet, whose encounter with the divine is communicated directly and forcefully. Those who heard Joseph Smith's utterances were convinced that God spoke *through* him. He therefore fits precisely the classic definition of a prophet as "one who speaks for God." His authority was not the amorphous charismatic aura that is so often said to surround mystics. The prophet's charisma was more compelling because it was more focused. Each time he made a "thus saith the Lord" statement that his followers accepted as having come from God, Smith's authority was enhanced. So augmented, his authority led from peak to peak, moving his followers ever further away from the evangelical ground on which their fellow Americans stood.

This deepened appreciation of Joseph Smith's role as prophet was crucial to my realization that Mormonism, instead of fitting in one of the standard sociological categories, is a religious tradition; it departed from existing Christian tradition as Christianity departed from Judaism. A key deviation from what existed in 1830 was this new movement's prophetic leadership and the principle of continuing revelation that accompanies prophetic leadership. In clarifying this different approach to defining Mormonism, I developed many parallels between Mormonism and other new traditions, especially early Christianity. In so doing, I described at length the many points at which this new tradition abandoned both Catholic and Protestant beliefs and practices. I also described the manner in which Mormonism rooted itself in the Hebraic as well as the Christian tradition.

At no point did I intend to argue that Mormonism had stopped being Christian. But what I argued contrasted sufficiently with the Saints' claim that, as a restoration, the Church of Jesus Christ of Latter-day Saints is *the* truly legitimate form of Christianity that my argument was sometimes read as trying to distance Mormonism from Christianity. Hence, the essay reprinted here is not an instance of my mind being changed. In the final analysis, it simply more clearly articulates a position I have held for a very long time: Mormonism is a legitimate way to be Christian; it is just not my way of being Christian.

∽

To this point, the parts of this book that contain personal narrative describe how, as I studied the story of the Latter-day Saints, I came to comprehend the essence of history and its complex interactions with religion. Although hints of things transcendental are found here and there, my narrative thus far relates a story that is essentially rational, a hardheaded account of cerebral workings that led to abstract analysis and logical conclusions. For that reason, what I have written here is best characterized as intellectual autobiography. There is practically no spiritual autobiography in it. But that is not true of the second piece in this section, for I have selected a brief meditation that I published in *Sunstone* in 1993 in the wake of Lavina Fielding Anderson's excommunication from the LDS Church.[6] More than anything else I have ever written for publication, these reflections on a tragic event move beyond my effort to observe as objectively as is reasonably possible and to describe what happened in the past and what is currently happening in the LDS community. As a result, my lament for Lavina (as I sometimes think of it) reveals as much about me as it does about this seventh-generation LDS sister and the others in the group of Saints who were disciplined in the fall of 1993.[7]

As I poured out my feelings of sympathy for my friend, I suddenly realized that when an institution cuts off one of its members, especially one whose religious heritage is entirely tied up in the tradition the institution represents, that is not merely a form of punishment. No matter how an indicted Saint reacts to an edict of excommunication, such a judgment is a kind of death. Even though shunning is not a Mormon practice, excommunication demands from friends and family mourning not unlike the Jewish practice of reciting kaddish after the death of a relative.

As what I wrote makes clear, I was likewise able to comprehend for the first time the significance and power of the performance of proxy ordinances that are so central to Mormon ritual observance. When, on the Sunday following Lavina Anderson's excommunication, I took the sacrament in my own Methodist church, which signified my understanding that Christ's death on the cross promised remission of my sins, it became a ritual performed not for myself alone. In this instance, a more or less ordinary ritual experience overrode religious boundaries, permitting a spiritual connection between my longtime Mormon friend and me.

For years, I had realized that my contemplation of Mormonism was driving me deeper into my own Methodist tradition, as comparison and contrast bestowed on me a deeper level of understanding and a greater appreciation of what John Wesley wrought in the wake of Aldersgate.[8] Skeptics and conservative Protestants alike will conclude that what I was doing as I became an ever more active Methodist was girding myself with Protestant armor that would help me withstand the Mormon message. But I am quite sure that something far more profound was happening. The ground was being prepared so that in an exhilarating moment, the occasion for which was distressing, a spiritual connection was opened to me that I had theretofore carefully kept closed. This hallowed conduit, operating outside the ecclesiastical framework of both the LDS Church and United Methodism, connected me to Latter-day Saints in an entirely new way, enriching my intellectual understanding with a religious sensibility that had not previously been evident.

Notes

1. "Is Mormonism Christian? Reflections on a Complicated Question," was first published in *BYU Studies* 33, no. 3 (1993): 439–65.

2. I. Woodbridge Riley's 1902 Yale University Ph.D. dissertation was published as *The Founder of Mormonism: A Psychological Study of Joseph Smith, Jr.* (New York: Dodd, Mead, 1903); William Alexander Linn, *The Story of the Mormons* (New York: Macmillan, 1902).

3. I have placed the adjective "seemingly" before "well-documented" in this description of Fawn McKay Brodie's *No Man Knows My History: The Life of Joseph Smith, the Mormon Prophet* (1945; 2d ed., rev. and enl., New York: Alfred A. Knopf, 1976) because, during a private conversation, Brodie told me that while she had done a great deal of research in the records available in the 1940s, especially those outside the LDS Church Archives, she had made no attempt to gain access to Joseph Smith's unpublished writings. In fact, she was probably unaware of the existence of the sort of introspective documents that are included in Joseph Smith Jr, *The Personal Writings of Joseph Smith*, comp. and ed. Dean C. Jessee (Salt Lake City: Deseret Book, 1984). She said also she did not consult the holograph record that includes accounts of spiritual experiences written by many of the prophet's closest associates. It is impossible to say that having had access to these records would have altered her interpretation of the prophet, but it is true that the data on which she based her biography were one-sided and incomplete. (See "Remembering, Recovering, and Inventing What Being a People of God Means," herein.)

4. Jo Ann Barnett Shipps, "The Mormons in Politics: The First Hundred Years" (Ph.D. diss., University of Colorado, 1965), 29–30.

5. Jan Shipps, "The Prophet Puzzle: Suggestions Leading toward a More Comprehensive Interpretation of Joseph Smith," *Journal of Mormon History* 1 (1974): 3–20.

6. Jan Shipps, "Knowledge and Understanding," *Sunstone* 16 (November 1993): 11–12.

7. This group is known collectively as the September Six. One was disfellowshipped (which means that she could return to activity after proper repentance); all the others were excommunicated.

8. *Aldersgate* is the expression Methodists use to refer to the powerful spiritual experience in which, in Wesley's own words, his "heart was strangely warmed." Although he was already an ordained Anglican cleric, it was this experience, which took place in a chapel at Aldersgate, that led the founder of Methodism to initiate field preaching and organizing Methodist classes that would eventually lead to the formation of Methodism as a denomination separate from the Anglican church.

16

Is Mormonism Christian?:
Reflections on a Complicated Question

Since I, a staunch member of the First United Methodist Church in Bloomington, Indiana, have been studying the Latter-day Saints for close to forty years, it is perhaps not surprising that I am frequently asked whether Mormons are Christians and whether Mormonism is Christian. Put to me by journalists, academics, denominational bureaucrats, participants in adult forums in various local Protestant and Catholic churches, active Latter-day Saints, bona fide anti-Mormons, my students, and a variety of other interested people, the query comes in both forms. Whatever the form, a forthright yes or no seems to be expected.

Because many people think the two questions are one and the same, inquirers are often startled when I respond by asking if they wish to know whether Mormons are Christians or whether Mormonism is Christian. Moreover, since their question, whatever its form, seems so straightforward to so many, inquirers are surprised—and sometimes impatient—when I attempt to determine the framework within which the question is being asked. Yet before I can formulate a response, I must know both the substance of the question and its context.

The two queries are essentially the same if the inquirer's main concern is analogical (Is the LDS Church like the Presbyterian church, for example, or are Mormons similar to Catholics?), analytical (How is Mormonism related to other forms of Christianity?), or historiographical (What have historians said about the connection between Mormonism and Christianity?). If the framework for the inquiry is more theological and religious than theoretical and academic, these are not simply two versions of the same question. While they are obviously related, quite different theological propositions inhere in them. Inquirers who want to know whether Mormons are Christians signal their assumption that a divine determination is made about individuals on a case-by-case basis. The more usual query—"Is Mormonism Christian?"—presumes a divine economy in which redemption depends on an individual's membership in a true or authentic "body of Christ."

To discover whether an inquiry is more theological and religious than theoretical and academic or vice versa, I respond to all inquiries about this issue with a series of counterqueries whose answers will allow me to determine what sort of question I have been asked. Does the inquirer wish to know, for example, whether some particular Mormon—say Marie Osmond, Orrin Hatch, Hugh Nibley, or Paul Edwards—is a Christian? Or is it a matter of whether some particular group of Mormons is Christian—say the members of the Reorganized Church of Jesus Christ of Latter Day Saints or the Mormon fundamentalists in Colorado City? Alternatively, is the question a normative one? Am I being asked whether Mormon theology is congruent with some particular form of Christian theology; whether the institutional structure of the LDS (or RLDS) Church is sufficiently similar to the institutional structure of the Christian church in New Testament times to make it Christian; whether Mormon doctrine is compatible with traditional Christian doctrine; or whether Mormon rituals and worship forms are comparable to Christian rituals and worship forms?

If the inquirer answers yes to any of these questions, I ask for more information about presuppositions that underlie the query: by what standard does the inquirer believe that individuals, organized groups of persons, or institutions are accorded status as Christians? Does one proceed in the Protestant fashion and look to the Bible, assuming that words speak for themselves? Or does one look to authority and tradition, as Catholics do, asking someone who, like the pope, can speak ex cathedra? If not, how about asking a prophet who can add "thus saith the Lord" to his or her words?

By responding to these queries with such counterqueries, I point to my conviction that definitive answers to normative questions assume the reality of discoverable norms (rules or sets of standards that can be authoritatively established). Within human communities, however, authority always rests on a base of cultural support. In the absence of a single source of authority whose nature is universally respected, humanity has to struggle along with provisional rules and standards. Thus, I conclude that definitive answers to normative questions are not forthcoming in the sort of pluralistic situation in which the contemporary world finds itself. All my years of study notwithstanding, if the question of whether Mormonism is Christian is a normative one, I do not presume to provide a normative answer.

It is nevertheless obvious that my continuing—even strengthened—Methodist commitment over the many years in which I have had an opportunity to learn more about Mormonism is a negative answer to the question of whether I believe that the Church of Jesus Christ of Latter-day Saints or one of the other institutional forms of this tradition is *the only* legitimate Christianity now present on the earth. This negation has proved frustrating to some of my Mormon friends, something I first learned when the late Richard Poll asked somewhat sorrowfully, "How can you know so much and not believe?" But many Saints have apparently recognized that my own religious commitment has allowed me to develop a deeper appreciation of their tradition as I have become more familiar with it. I believe they are right.

Because I was doing research during the "Arrington Spring," soon after Leonard Arrington was first installed as church historian and when access to the LDS documentary record was as open as it had ever been and is ever likely to be again, I had access to the central texts related to the founding of the faith. My closeness to those early Saints—as I have become acquainted with them and their church through the historical record—and those who live in the present has made me equally unwilling to say that Mormonism is not *a* legitimate form of Christianity. Actually, even in my earliest writing about the Saints, I never said that Mormonism is not Christian. But up to now, in addition to writing Mormon history, I have mainly addressed historiographical and analytical issues connected to it.

Those I have addressed at length. For example, the essay I wrote for the *Encyclopedia of Mormonism* surveyed the historiographical situation.[1] It describes what historians have said about this matter from the middle of the nineteenth century, when Robert Baird erroneously classified Mormonism as a liturgical form of Protestantism—presumably something like Lutheranism—up to the recent renewal of old charges that Mormonism is a non-Christian cult. I also investigated and commented at great length on the early recording of the Mormon prophet's story in a careful consideration of the account based on what Joseph Smith's mother said about what occurred.[2] Much more recently, during the 1999 Sunstone Symposium I served as the respondent in a session in which Klaus Hansen presented an overview of the writing of those historians whose work is a part of the "new Mormon history." My commentary surveyed the writing of Mormon history from the 1830s onward, showing how historians have been making arguments for and against the legitimacy of this as a Christian movement from the time its history was first recorded.[3]

I also provided my own classification of the movement in *Mormonism: The Story of a New Religious Tradition*. This book begins and ends with analogy. It opens with an observation that just as the early Christians believed they had found the only proper way to be Jewish, so the early followers of the Mormon prophet believed they had found the only proper way to be Christian. It closes with my conclusion that the Mormonism of the Church of Jesus Christ of Latter-day Saints is best understood as a form of corporate Christianity that is related to traditional Christianity—in other words, the forms of Protestantism, Catholicism, and Eastern Orthodoxy that existed in the first third of the nineteenth century—in much the same way that early Christianity was related to Judaism. I did not say the same about the Mormonism of the Reorganized Church of Jesus Christ of Latter Day Saints, since it appears to me that it can be classified as an idiosyncratic form of Protestantism. This "Josephite" body never accepted "the restoration of all things," and in the years since my book was written, RLDS emphasis on the importance of patriarchy, which is central to the notion of "the restoration of Israel," has been dramatically attenuated by the selection of someone not in the direct Joseph Smith family line as its prophet-president.[4]

In saying I am unwilling to provide normative answers when the framework of an inquirer's question is theological or religious, however, I do not mean to say I am unwilling to confront this issue in a religious setting. From time to time, I am invited by various church groups to talk about the Mormons. (Since most Protestants have not caught up with recent changes in nomenclature, they nearly always speak of "the Mormons" rather than the Latter-day Saints.) When I accept such invitations, I am confronted with a real challenge—even if the members of the group that extended the invitation have not seen one of the *God Makers* videos. While those who invite me to talk usually tell me that the Mormons are "really nice people" who "take care of their own" and "have a great choir," most of the members of these groups know very little about the Saints' history (except that they practiced polygamy), and they know even less about Mormon doctrine and LDS theology.

The task I set for myself in such situations is not merely connecting Mormonism to Christianity—after all, I am talking about a church of Jesus Christ. The task also involves showing how this connection "plays out" in the Mormonism of the Church of Jesus Christ of Latter-day Saints and in the Reorganized Church. As I do so, I sometimes try to clarify the distinction with a speculative comparison. In view of Mountain Mormonism's historic emphasis on the restoration of Israel, it could well be the sort of Christianity that might have developed if the outcome of the Jerusalem conference (Acts 15:1–30; Gal. 2:1–10) had favored St. Peter rather than St. Paul, that is, if potential converts to Christianity had been required to first become a part of the "chosen people."[5] "Missouri Mormonism" may well signal what Christianity might have been without the conversion of Constantine and the subsequent integration of religious and political authority. With this comparison, I make the point that both of these churches in the Mormon tradition are forms of Christianity, yet both differed from the Christianities that existed in 1830—and they still do.

As is well known, the extent of the difference was first manifested in a dramatic manner when the followers of the Mormon prophet responded to the revelations to "gather" by establishing settlements in Kirtland, Ohio; in Independence, Far West, and elsewhere in Missouri; and in Nauvoo, Illinois. The very existence of these Mormon "kingdoms" set the Saints apart. This contrast was spectacularly intensified when a large body of Joseph Smith's followers fled to the Intermountain West after the prophet's murder and introduced the public practice of plural marriage.

Acceptance of the plural marriage principle, regardless of whether one adhered to it, became the most obvious testimony that the Saints who followed Brigham Young gave assent to a truly distinctive set of beliefs. It bound the Saints who went west together and provided them with a means of identification that kept them from being confused with members of the many other innovative Christian movements that originated in the United States in the nineteenth century. For the "Josephites" and many of the other Saints who did not go west, plural marriage became a standard against which they could define themselves. Proving that the practice was not part of Mormonism became important to them as a means of identification, as significant a negative marker for them as it was a positive marker for the "Brighamites."

If plural marriage told LDS people, whose church prescribed its practice, who they were and if it told RLDS people, whose church proscribed its practice, who they were, plural marriage told everyone else in Victorian America who the Mormons were not. If they practiced polygamy or even believed in its practice, they could not possibly be Christian.

The Mormon fundamentalists, who refuse to relinquish polygamous practice, believe that the LDS Church jeopardized its birthright—its exclusive claim, its very Mormonness—when it surrendered the practice of plural marriage in response to pressures from the U.S. government. I think they are wrong if they believe that the LDS Church renounced the essence of Mormonism by giving up plural marriage. However, it is possible that this renunciation could prove to have been an early signal pointing to an eventual relinquishing of enough of the LDS Church's distinctiveness to bring it into what some might call the traditional Christian fold. If something like that proves to be the case, I will obviously need to reexamine my interpretation of this movement as one that cannot be fully comprehended in Troeltschian categories.[6] But that is a matter that will have to be dealt with in my next book on Mormonism, not in this one.

ᕰᕍ

What I do here is confront directly the question of whether Mormonism is Christian by examining the situation from a different and fairly complicated angle that calls for looking at the significance and implications (and even the pluses and minuses) of labeling and naming in culture and religion. Doing so requires me to associate this matter of labeling and naming with the zero-sum game that results when exclusive claims are set forth so that they create situations in which churches claiming that theirs is the only legitimate form of Christianity are forced to hold that all other forms of Christianity are illegitimate. After noting the active and ongoing naming and labeling shift occurring within the Church of Jesus Christ of Latter-day Saints as it moves away from the Mormon moniker, I consider two possible connections central to the way the Mormonism Christian question is being worked out: (1) the connection between the growth and geographical expansion of the LDS Church and its move from Mormon and Latter-day Saint to Christian definitions of the church and its members; and (2) the connection between the growth and increasing social and political significance of conservative Christianity and its need to have something to define itself over and against, a need that defining Mormonism as not-Christian helps satisfy. Finally, in a more personal vein, I return to the main question of the essay. After pointing to the obvious yet usually overlooked reality that the "Is Mormonism Christian" question is in some sense a generic question, I suggest the following: if the members of one group of people gathered into a community that calls itself Christian are permitted to decide that a person or everyone gathered into a different community that likewise calls itself Christian is not Christian, then some pretty un-Christian defining is going on.

ᕰᕍ

Teeming with an almost incredible variety of European immigrants superimposed on a much older Anglo-Dutch Yankee culture, New York City's Lower East Side in the early decades of the twentieth century produced a childhood archetype known as the "Dead End Kid." A youngster of this ilk, familiar to aficionados of gangster movies of the 1930s and 1940s, survived in the bewildering metropolitan milieu by becoming cocky, impudent, resourceful, and extremely suspicious.

No logical connection exists between those B-movie urban urchins and the matter of whether Mormonism is Christian. Yet every time I try to organize my reflections on how the question of whether Mormonism is Christian has been answered, I remember snatches of dialogue from the films in which the Dead End Kids appeared:

Adult to scruffy looking pre-adolescent: "What's your name, kid?"
Kid: "Who wants ta know?" Or "What's it to ya?"

Despite such questions, the Dead End Kids themselves were always asking for the "monikers" of newcomers, which is not surprising since names were extremely important in their polyglot neighborhood. Names established identities, determined boundaries, and sent encoded messages about how the members of one of these clusters of preadolescent first-generation Americans ought to treat the "new kids on the block" who came from different immigrant stocks.

The same principle holds for religion. Names matter. They matter a lot. For that reason, whenever people I do not know ask me if Mormonism is Christian, a little computer inside my head starts sorting out possibilities. Who wants to know? What's it to 'em? Or to put it another way, is there a hidden agenda?

In the past thirty years, certain conservative Christians, charging that Mormonism is not Christian, have established a sometimes bitter adversarial relationship with Mormons. During the same period, one finds everywhere within Mormonism—in the *Church News* and the *Ensign,* in the public statements of LDS officials, in Sunday School lessons, and in talks the Saints give in ward sacrament meetings, as well as in private conversations—an escalating emphasis on the suffering of the Savior, the atonement of Christ, personal salvation, and so on. In view of these conflicting convictions about whether Mormonism is Christian, I often get the feeling that I am being asked for my opinion so that the inquirer can use what I say to score points for either the Latter-day Saints or those who oppose them.

And why not? If one looks at LDS history from the perspective of the Saints' perception of themselves and others' perceptions of them, it has always been thus. An agenda has always existed, and it has never been hidden.

When the Prophet Joseph Smith and his followers first appeared on the American religious scene, the new nation was becoming as religiously diverse as the Lower East Side would later be ethnically varied. In this case, however, the newcomers spoke a very familiar language. They came preaching repentance, calling on their hearers to listen to the words of Jesus Christ, and reminding those who had ears to hear that the "Lord your Redeemer suffered death in the flesh" and afterward rose "from the dead that he might bring all men unto him."[7] The prophet's followers said that by the spirit of prophecy and revelation, Jesus had directed them to establish an ecclesiastical organization headed by Joseph Smith Jr., who was "called of God and ordained an apostle of Jesus Christ."[8] They named their new fellowship the Church of Jesus Christ.

Its name and straightforward proclamation of the uniquely salvific significance of the suffering of Christ notwithstanding, this new ecclesiastical association never became a party to the informal denominational compact that, in the eyes of a majority of American citizens, turned the Christian church in this new nation into a pan-Protestant body. But this was not an instance of membership tacitly sought and implicitly denied. Sufficient reason on both sides kept the Church of Jesus Christ that Joseph Smith led from becoming a member of this larger body of Christ. For one perhaps unfamiliar example of the lack of ecumenical feeling on the prophet's part, listen to how Apostle William E. McLellin described a sermon preached on December 14, 1834: "President Smith preached . . . three hours in Kirt[land] during which he exposed the Methodist Dicipline in its black deformity and called upon the Elders in the power of the spirit of God to expose the creeds & confessions of men—His discourse was animated and Pointed, against all Creeds of men—."[9]

Such total refutation of the doctrines of every other Christian body reflects the extent to which the claims of this particular church of Jesus Christ were exclusive. Its members asserted that their church was set apart from all other churches that were called Christian because theirs was the only restored church of Jesus Christ that had been on the earth since the days of the "Great Apostasy." They maintained that their way of being Christian was the only legitimate way to be Christian. They also believed that in becoming members of this restored church, they had become as Christian as Christians had been in New Testament times.

These "New Testament Christians" or latter-day Saints, as they soon called themselves, believed that theirs had to be the only authentic church of Jesus Christ because it was the only church in which men who held the restored Aaronic and Melchizedek priesthoods presided. It quickly became a tenet of their faith that men who were not ordained members of these priesthood orders could not legitimately act for God in space and time.

Still, Smith's followers were by no means the only ones whose preaching of the crucified Christ was coupled with exclusive institutional claims. In the same year that Smith's followers established their church of Jesus Christ, another new Christian church was also established in the United States. This church was organized by the adherents of Thomas Campbell and Alexander

Campbell, who called themselves Disciples of Christ. Like the members of the church headed by the Mormon prophet, the members of this newly "restored" church were committed to the doctrines and practices found in the New Testament. Members of both churches expected an imminent millennium, and in each case, the members believed that through their church—and only through their church—a "restoration of the ancient order of things" would be accomplished.

Exclusivity, then, was not the claim forming the barrier that kept the Saints outside the denominational compact. The Book of Mormon was a much more serious stumbling block. By accepting this found text as testimony to the truth of gospel claims, the Saints rejected *sola scriptorum,* the Protestant principle of vesting final authority in the Word only as it was manifested in the Old and New Testaments. Moreover, the Saints' church was the only Christian church of substantial size that was headed by a prophet, one who also assumed the role of church president and high priest. Theirs was a church that—in terms whose meaning was specified in the work of the sociologist Max Weber—made neither office nor tradition definitive, settling ultimate authority instead on charisma adhering in a single individual. This practice was anathema to Protestants in the United States.

The Saints' obedience to the revelations directing them to "gather" to Zion moved the Saints away from the prevailing Protestant congregational pattern and toward the creation of independent LDS enclaves that could (and sometimes did) function as virtually autonomous political, economic, and cultural units powerful enough to challenge the separation of church and state in the United States. But the movement's true distinctiveness was not always recognized in the early years, and many observers failed to realize that this new church of Jesus Christ would withstand the centrifugal pull of Protestant hegemony long enough to become something other than an idiosyncratic Protestant denomination. That it did so is surely related to the Saints' possession of the Book of Mormon, the gathering, the leadership of the prophet, and all of Mormonism's other singular factors, including, after 1852, the publicly acknowledged practice of plural marriage.

But another reason—one that might be called "product labeling" in contemporary parlance—probably helped Mormonism escape the fate that awaited the Campbellites. The original aim of the Disciples of Christ was to be the church to end all churches, the ecclesiastical institution that, by the force of its theological claims, would attract all other Protestant churches to merge with it, bringing an end to denominationalism.[10] In claiming the name Christian, the Campbellites found themselves drawn into the Protestant compact and could only watch as their "true" church—the one supposed to end all churches—gradually lost so much of its distinctiveness that it turned into yet one more Protestant denomination—or into two if the Christian/Disciple schism is taken into account.

A close reading of Apostle McLellin's journals prompted me to reconsider this labeling matter as Joseph Smith's followers had to work through it in the 1830s. These valuable documents provide firsthand evidence that historians who write about a religious marketplace in the early republic are not simply using an effective metaphor. In the 1830s, an actual religious marketplace existed in towns, villages, and hamlets all across the nation. Preachers of every stripe proclaimed the Christian gospel in the schoolhouses, courthouses, meetinghouses, and even barns that formed the public square of that day. This competition for converts meant that Baptist preachers had to find a way to distinguish themselves from Congregationalist and Presbyterian ministers, Disciples, and similar groups; Methodist circuit riders had to find a way to distinguish themselves from all the other evangelists; and so forth. Since the texts for their sermons were drawn from the same scriptures (the Bible) that all the other preachers used, what to call themselves and their message posed a real problem for Saints on the religious hustings.

It was not simply a question of using common scriptural texts. Although Mormon missionaries usually told their listeners about the Book of Mormon and generally directed those who responded to their gospel presentations to "gather to Zion," the basic LDS message was, at many points, virtually the same message that Protestant ministers were preaching. Most particularly, according to Richard Bushman, the Mormon message often coincided with what members of the new Disciples of Christ were preaching.[11]

But Bushman, in his delineation in *Joseph Smith and the Beginnings of Mormonism* of the difference between the Mormon prophet's followers and this group whose members were confiscating the Christian label by calling their church "the Christian Church," did not explore the implications of the Disciples' rapid appropriation of this label for either the Disciples or the Saints. Yet the fact that another group challenged the Saints' appropriation of the name Christian appears to have been important in the formation of Mormon distinctiveness and possibly even a factor in Mormonism's survival as a movement whose adherents became a "peculiar people."

Scholars usually report that Smith's followers shortened to "Mormon" the derisive "Mormonite" appellation their opponents had given them. Not so often mentioned, but equally consequential, is their taking Eber D. Howe's scornful naming of the movement in his anti-Mormon work *Mormonism Unvailed* and turning it inside out so that, by 1839, in an epistle from Liberty prison, Joseph Smith himself could proclaim that "truth is 'Mormonism.'"[12]

Adopted by his followers, this distinctive label sent a signal to potential converts that this church was not a Christian church in the usual sense of the term, even if the Mormons who were licensed to preach the gospel contended on reasonably equal terms with all the other preachers who were proclaiming the gospel of Christ.

Today, members of the Church of Jesus Christ of Latter-day Saints may be sorry that the need to distinguish themselves from the Campbellites forced the early Saints to forego calling themselves Christians, thereby relinquishing the only name that could have provided Mormonism with an unambiguous Christian identity. But from the standpoint of the identity construction critical to the preservation of distinctiveness, the adoption of an alternative label in their early formative stage worked to the Saints' advantage.

While the Mormon gospel was Christian, it was not the same gospel being preached by Methodists, Baptists, Presbyterians, and representatives of all other existing forms of Christianity. Those who accepted the gospel, repented, and were baptized under the hands of Mormon missionaries did not simply become Christians. They were convinced they were the Saints that God promised (through revelation to Joseph Smith) to gather out from "among the Gentiles."[13] As such, they understood themselves to have become members of a chosen lineage, a peculiar people. It is therefore not surprising that the prophet's followers erected a sturdy rhetorical fence between themselves and those who were not part of the group. Naming the *other*, they denominated as "Gentile" all those who had not yet heard the Mormon gospel and especially those who had heard it and refused to accept it. This naming became a primary means of establishing the distinctiveness of the LDS Church.

In the light of a contemporary rhetorical shift that seems to be turning Mormon into an adjectival modifier used to signify a particular kind of Christian, I may seem to be making too much of the fact that at a critical juncture in the establishment of their church, the Saints accepted and came to relish Mormon and Mormonism as alternative labels. But there can be little doubt that their embracing the label Mormon in lieu of being called Christian contributed to a perception that Mormonism is not Christian.

The Saints' naming of those who would not hear the LDS message also figured in the conception of Mormons as non-Christian. Writings about Mormonism penned in the nineteenth century by Catholics as well as Protestants reveal that Christians in both those camps were stung by the "Gentile" label. Their understanding was (and is) that the primary purpose of Christ's life and ministry was to extend the gospel to the Gentiles. It therefore seemed to them both strange and ironic that these upstart Saints would use this particular term to imply that Christians who were not Mormons remained outside the gospel bounds, especially since the negative naming was being done by the members of an institution that bore the name of Jesus Christ.

Distinguishing so plainly between themselves and those outside the community was nevertheless useful and perhaps even necessary during the decades of fortress mentality that characterized the kingdom period of Mountain Mormonism. While opposition to this flourishing movement was not entirely—or even primarily—grounded in religion, between 1850 and 1890 the Saints had to face intense political and legal harassment that was nearly always explained in religious terms. That they believed all their opponents were Gentiles must have helped them slough off charges that Mormonism was the very antithesis of Christianity. Considering the source as Gentile surely helped them ignore indictments that the Saints were not only un-Christian because some of them engaged in the practice of plural marriage but also un-American because they were all helpless pawns in the hands of tyrants who had turned a U.S. territory into a theocratic state. In view of such negation of all they held dear, the Saints' confidence that they were a chosen people and that, as such, they were the only true Christians must have sustained and comforted the LDS community.

The LDS political kingdom and the practice of plural marriage were the most public and hence visible evidences of that part of the "restoration of all things" that rooted Mormonism in the Old Testament as well as the New. When coerced to give up both at the end of the nineteenth century, the LDS Church started what was at first an almost imperceptible transfiguration that would ultimately lift once again to public view the Christianity that had always been at the base of Mormonism. Following the publication of the 1890 Manifesto that renounced the church's sanction of plural marriage, the Saints started to move away from—or at least to deemphasize—the Hebraicism appended to Mormon Christianity in Kirtland, Missouri, and Nauvoo, Illinois. Not, however, until after the mid-twentieth century did the Saints start to give up labeling outsiders—whether Christian or not—as Gentiles.

This turn away from labeling outsiders as other has coincided with the dramatic turn to which I referred earlier, a turn toward Christian rhetoric and Christian themes, not only in Mormonism's official presentation of itself to the world but also in Mormon life generally. I located these shifts by closely analyzing the LDS missionary lessons since the 1960s and the contents of the *Ensign* since 1971, but all sorts of other church publications provide evidence of the commanding presence of Christian rhetoric in modern Mormonism. I regard the casual manner in which Mormons are increasingly referring to themselves as Christians as even more convincing evidence that

Mormons are coming to think of theirs as the Church of Jesus Christ more than they are thinking of it as the Mormon or LDS Church.

I keep a notebook of examples of linguistic signals that show how rapidly this shift is taking place. One of the items recounts a three-way conversation among a graduate student who was a true-blue birthright Latter-day Saint, the chancellor of our university, and me in the early 1990s. I am sensitive to the shift and often anticipate altered LDS rhetoric, but I must admit that I was somewhat surprised to hear my young friend explain that her husband had learned Japanese when he was "serving a Christian mission" in Japan.

This change in how the Saints think of and talk about themselves and how they think of and talk about those who are not Saints suggests to me that having attained a firm LDS identity during 125 years or so of creating and living in a separate and distinct Mormon culture, the Saints no longer have a sociological need for Gentiles. They do not need an *other* to set themselves apart either rhetorically or categorically. If this reading of what is happening is correct, it calls into question the somewhat cynical notion that is sometimes articulated, even by Latter-day Saints, that the paramount reason for the increasing level of the Saints' collaboration in ecumenical efforts to relieve distress, hunger, and suffering in the world is that the LDS Church wants to improve its public image as a Christian organization. The interreligious activities reported in the *Church News* and described nearly every week on the *News from the Church of Jesus Christ of Latter-day Saints* audiotape, which the church distributes to media outlets, signal instead the self-confidence of a people whose identity is now fixed and steadfast enough that they no longer need to be segregated from other denominations.

Saints, however, are not being universally welcomed into the Judeo-Christian fold. Several reasons may account for this. While such ecumenical bodies as the National Conference of Christians and Jews and various interchurch relief organizations are pleased to have a new cooperative partner, some mainstream Protestant denominational bodies seem reluctant to accept a newcomer on equal terms, perhaps because they have been, in the sociologist Wade Clark Roof's words, "hemorrhaging members."[14] Some mainline churches are clearly worried about the impact of the success of the LDS missionary program on the size of their congregations. But this pragmatic consideration, at least among the Methodists, is of less importance than the LDS Church's doctrinal insistence that all Christian baptisms are null and void except those performed by properly ordained holders of the LDS priesthood.

I expect this negative reaction exists in most of mainstream Protestantism for this subject seems to have become a matter of particular touchiness since Vatican II, when the Roman Catholic church accepted Protestant baptisms as legitimate.

Notwithstanding the refusal of the Presbyterians to accredit Mormonism as Christian, many members of the old Protestant "establishment" seem willing to make a place for the Saints in the American religious mosaic. Furthermore, if the signals from Salt Lake City—where the Tabernacle Choir gave a concert to celebrate the renovation and rededication of the Cathedral of the Madeleine—are at all indicative of a larger pattern, the same may be said of the nation's Roman Catholic community. But the same cannot be said for most of the neo-evangelicals and Protestant fundamentalists who form the conservative Christian coalition. For them, the matter of "sheep stealing" is extremely important, as are various doctrinal issues. But, to return to my main theme, I believe that neither of these matters is as potent as labeling. This time, however, the issue is turned on its head. As the Saints' need for an *other* has been steadily diminishing during the past quarter of a century, such a need has been escalating in conservative Christianity. That need is being satisfied by the Latter-day Saints, although they are by no means the only ones serving as negative markers of conservative Christian identity.

For the most part, Christians in this fundamentalist-evangelical-Pentecostal coalition share an emphasis on the critical need for an experiential encounter with Jesus Christ (being "born again"), and they likewise share acceptance of the Bible as both "inerrant" and the only source containing the revealed Word. Moreover, many of the members of the independent congregations belong to such ecumenical organizations as Youth for Christ. In the National Association of Evangelicals, the coalition has its own ecumenical organization. Yet the various constituencies in this conservative Christian coalition differ so much among themselves over significant points of doctrine and ritual, as well as the proper form of church organization, that finding a unifying descriptor (one that at once includes and excludes) has turned out to be a formidable task.

To the dismay of members of the mainstream Protestant denominations that have always regarded themselves as evangelical, the neo-evangelicals have practically succeeded in taking possession of the evangelical designation. (Some Methodists are also bothered because many of these new evangelicals have also been trying to take exclusive possession of John Wesley.) Since not all fundamentalists describe themselves as evangelicals and not all evangelicals are fundamentalists, capturing this label has not proved sufficient. As a result, at least some conservative Christians have been engaging, with some success, in a two-pronged effort to take exclusive possession of the Christian label.

In their most wide-ranging and sustained attempt to de-Christianize those who do not agree with their position on the inerrancy of the scriptures and other "fundamentals," many Christians in the conservative coalition condemn the liberal stance of the National Council of Churches (successor to the Federal Council of Churches of Christ in America), making it obvious that they question the "real" or "true" Christianity of members of the historic Protestant denominations that maintain membership in a body concerned with inclusiveness and the social gospel. More important, conservative fundamentalists, neo-evangelicals, and Pentecostals characterize as potentially apostate any Christian willing to surrender one whit of Christianity's exclusive claim. They often place beyond the pale Christians who affirm the existence of other legitimate ways to be religious.

According to many conservative Christians, however, the ultimate heresy of liberal Protestantism is not its inclusiveness. Its greatest heresy is its tendency to acknowledge the validity of modern scholarship, especially the work of the scholars in the so-called Jesus Seminar who question the historicity of the virgin birth and all the others who place early Christianity in cultural context and study it as a social movement, as well as those who question the historicity of the Bible's Old Testament books—the Book of Daniel in particular. No matter what the intensity of such people's commitment to the cause of the gospel of Jesus Christ, the right wing of the neo-evangelical/fundamentalist coalition describes such Christians as secular humanists and reads them right out of Christianity.

A somewhat different, but equally exclusivist, approach may be seen in modern evangelicalism's renewed embrace of old charges that America's indigenous religions (Seventh-day Adventism, Mormonism, Christian Science, and Jehovah's Witnesses) are non-Christian cults. Such charges were a staple of Protestant journalism in the nineteenth century, when Protestants and Catholics believed that the responsibility to carry the gospel to the heathens and pagans included an obligation to carry the gospel to "benighted" Mormons, Adventists, Christian Scientists, and Jehovah's Witnesses. The home missionaries, as they were called, who undertook such assignments assumed it was also their place to warn the members of traditional Christian bodies— and anyone else who would listen—against these new movements.

Even after the Saints renounced the practice of plural marriage and gave up their political kingdom, some efforts were still made to warn Americans about the danger Mormonism posed to the nation. Yet for almost half a century, there was a clear break in Protestant efforts to convert Latter-day Saints away from Mormonism. Soon after the end of World War II, however, certain conservative groups renewed the attempt to take the Protestant version of the gospel to participants in all sorts of "new religious movements," including those that would increasingly be described by evangelicals and fundamentalists as the four "major American cults," the largest of which was Mormonism.[15] Significantly, however, this "mission ministry" began not as a campaign to warn potential converts away from these "new" movements but as an effort by conservative Christians, who were convinced that they were the only ones with access to "true truth," to share the gospel with those in darkness.

Although those who have succeeded the Southern Baptist minister John L. Smith, the first publisher of the *Utah Evangel,* are now trying to keep people from becoming Mormon as much as seeking to induce Latter-day Saints to leave their faith, Smith's early ministry seems to have been primarily directed to converting members of the Utah Mormon church away from Mormonism and into evangelical Protestantism. To a lesser extent, this was true of the ministry of the Reverend Wesley Walters, a Presbyterian clergyman whose reporting of research into the early life of Joseph Smith was aimed as much at convincing LDS believers that Smith was not a prophet as at warning Presbyterians away from Mormonism. Early efforts of Ex-Mormons for Jesus and several other groups of dissident Saints were also directed to Saints whose faith appeared to be wavering. Convincing Saints that they have been deceived seems to have been the primary objective animating Jerald Tanner and Sandra Tanner, Mormon converts to Protestant fundamentalism who publish the *Salt Lake City Messenger* and have produced a mass of exposé material designed to prove that Joseph Smith, Brigham Young, and LDS leaders from the 1830s onward all had or have clay feet. But because there were other evangelists who mounted similar ministries to Adventists, Christian Scientists, and Jehovah's Witnesses at about the same time, it is clear that the Mormons were by no means the only—or even always the principal—domestic target of conservative Protestantism.

As I read it, this mission started to change in the 1970s for two quite different reasons. First is the set of interrelated elements that propelled post–World War II Mormonism out of its intermountain sanctuary, away from the sidelines, and onto the nation's cultural and religious main stage, where it challenged conservative Protestantism on its home turf. A second and more complex reason is related to the creation of the Moral Majority and the sense of danger conservative Christians felt when they realized they shared with the Saints a common social and political agenda. This very closeness caused evangelicals and fundamentalists to pull back and led many of those who had theretofore eschewed the anti-Mormon crusade to take strenuous measures to define Mormonism as beyond the Christian pale.

So far as their distinctiveness in the mainstream white American culture is concerned, the Saints started to lose their status as peculiar people sometime between 1950 and 1970. Evidence of this shift includes the ubiquitous presence of the Tabernacle Choir on radio and television and in almost every American home equipped at that time with a sound system and roundtable for playing the "new" LP records; the gradual ascent into the nation's consciousness of an array of attractive, distinctly Mormon personalities from the political, sports, and entertainment scenes (Ezra Taft Benson, George Romney, Johnny Miller, the Osmonds); integration of "those amazing Mormons" into the idealistic representation of American culture found in middlebrow print media (*Coronet, Reader's Digest*); and the depiction of Mormons—although not always so identified—in a series of low-key radio and television spots that espoused and connected the Saints to American family values. Both because the church worked at its image so hard and because the media's purposes were served by pointing to real-life Leave-It-to-Beaver families (at least in the 1950s and 1960s), the LDS image was transformed during these middle decades from exotic outsider to inordinately wholesome, "squeaky clean" insider.

On the religious scene, the remarkable success of the LDS missionary program in the 1950s, 1960s, and 1970s was news, but so was the success of Adventist missionaries and Jehovah's Witnesses. Because the exceptional rate of growth of conservative Christian congregations was also newsworthy, it was perhaps inevitable that the heralds of the several movements would seek out the same audiences. Evangelical and fundamentalist missionaries from the United States were challenged by Adventists and Witnesses as often as by Latter-day Saints in overseas mission fields, but the Mormons were the ones who appeared to be making the most headway at home. Mormon proselyting was especially successful in suburbia, the field whitest to the harvest, where LDS missionaries contended most directly with conservative Protestantism and where the Saints often seemed to be winning.

Yet neither Mormonism's increasing visibility and acceptability in the culture nor the news about its fantastic rate of growth was the main source of the perception that Mormonism might really be a threat to American Protestantism. That came with the growing realization that Mormonism was no longer "out there" somewhere. The appearance—apparently sudden and seemingly everywhere—of new LDS meetinghouses, easily identified as Mormon because they were all built according to standard architectural plans, signaled that Latter-day Saint success was not likely to be temporary.

This emergence of the Saints on the American religious landscape was actually not as precipitous as it looked, for the Saints had long been present in many areas of the nation. But before World War II, local Mormon organizations outside the Intermountain West and California were nearly all associated with the geographical headquarters of regional LDS missions, which, for the most part, were housed in Victorian mansions or other substantial dwellings in residential areas. Although signs identified them as LDS mission headquarters, these structures did not resemble churches and therefore did not advertise the existence of LDS congregations outside Utah. While a number of LDS ward houses had been built in southern California and all along the West coast before 1941 and while several substantial meetinghouses were located in the larger urban areas of the nation, these buildings also did not effectively advertise the presence of LDS congregations, for the structures' architecture was not peculiarly Mormon.

This situation changed dramatically between 1945 and 1965 as LDS men from the Intermountain West, most of whom were members of the church's lay priesthood, settled with their families in many different areas of the United States. Joining branches of longtime relocated "Mountain Saints" and the rapidly expanding cadre of LDS converts who had never "gathered to Zion," these "Utah Mormons" provided the lay leadership critical to the organization of LDS stakes and wards all across the country. The formation of these basic congregational units of the church called for building meetinghouses on an unprecedented scale.

In what turned out to be a brilliant decision from the standpoint of the maintenance of LDS identity in an altered situation, leaders of the church decreed that the church's standard building plans would be used for all these LDS structures. Their edict, which appears to have been made on practical and economic grounds, has been much maligned on aesthetic grounds. But in view of the significance of place to the Saints, the sagacity of the decision that led the Saints to build structures giving the appearance of a new religious "franchise" is evident in retrospect.

The reason this is the case is fairly obvious. Members of virtually all of these newly formed "mission field" stakes and wards included western Saints who had been born in the church. They had been reared in a Mormon culture rooted as firmly in a sense of place (Zion in the tops of the mountains) as in the sense of unity and order implicit in a world whose structure rests on a coherent "plan of salvation" and a clearly defined system of ecclesiastical hierarchy. In many of these newly organized units, there were also members who were lifelong Saints or longtime converts who had never moved west but whose religious imagination and institutional life revolved around Salt Lake City, Mormonism's center place.

The new LDS congregations also included substantial and sometimes overwhelming proportions of recent converts; they needed a special place where the "Mormonizing" process could go forward. No matter what their physical location, the neat, utilitarian, multifunctional structures built according to the church's standard plan were distinctively Mormon places. The very fact that these clearly identifiable LDS structures could be found in town after town and suburb after suburb cultivated among the Saints what might be called a Zionic sense, making the LDS meetinghouses themselves agents of assimilation and signals that wherever the Saints gather, there Zion is.

The Saints were not the only ones able to read this signal, however. It was also read by evangelicals and fundamentalists—and by some members of churches in the Protestant mainstream—who surmised that the growth of Mormonism, which they regarded as non-Christian, was endangering Christianity itself. As suggested, their worry was strengthened in the early 1980s after the television evangelist Jerry Falwell moved from the religious to the political arena and created the Moral Majority, into which he welcomed the Latter-day Saints, whose social and political agenda was correctly perceived to coincide almost precisely with that of conservative (evangelical and fundamentalist) Protestantism.

In recent years, students of culture as well as religion have identified and started intensive study of a cross-cultural phenomenon they describe as "fundamentalism." Fundamentalist movements are characteristic of those cultures in which change, rather than stability, has become the normal condition. Specialists in the study of these movements say that in whatever culture they appear, the people who are attracted to them are threatened by the blurring of gender, race, and all the other apparently inborn status distinctions emblematic of traditional cultures. As indicated by Martin Marty and Scott Appleby, directors of the massive Fundamentalism Project at the University of Chicago, a critical identifying element of such a fundamentalist movement is not merely its construction of an *other*, over and against which it can stand. An *other* must be constructed whose properties and attributes are very close to, but not exactly the same as, the properties and attributes of those in the movement. Because the primary function of the *other* is creating clarity where confusion might reign, it cannot be truly foreign.[16]

The Reverend Jerry Falwell was not wrong when he concluded that many of the Latter-day Saints and the members of the conservative Christian coalition shared similar values, lifestyles, and political preferences. They are for traditional family values, and they stood firmly against the Equal Rights Amendment. They define homosexuality as aberrant and homosexual practices as sinful, they are against abortion—although the LDS position is less rigid and more nuanced—and they oppose the ordination of women. They express their distaste for long hair (on men), short skirts (on women), and rock music. They even share a strong preference for the King James Version of the Bible.

What they do not share is a theology and a plan of salvation. This difference is, at base, the reason for the activities of Concerned Christians, Inc., an organization that seeks to accomplish its goals by propagating the messages in the *God Makers* books and films prepared and distributed by Ed Decker and Dave Hunt. It also explains the accelerated rekindling of anti-Mormonism by all the other groups who oppose the Mormons by arguing they are a non-Christian cult. Mainly composed of evangelicals and fundamentalists, these groups are sometimes joined by ex-Mormons, but their ministry is not aimed primarily at the Saints. It is directed first and foremost to those who are not Mormon. As various advertisements of their films and publications explain, these groups believe that they serve the Christian community by "exposing and bringing to full knowledge the real doctrines of false prophets and teachers of the Mormon Church." Their purpose is providing conservative Christians with information that will allow them to discriminate effectively between "false truth" and "true truth."

Decker and Hunt's rabid book and appalling films, which feature cartoonlike renderings of temple ceremonies, have been widely shown and appreciatively received in hundreds, perhaps thousands, of evangelical and fundamentalist congregations. These groups seem grateful to have the *other* named and classified. Although no means of precisely determining the source of most of the support of these and other anti-Mormon efforts exists, and while there is no way to identify the purchasers of the books and pamphlets that purport to reveal the secrets of the "temple cult," the appeal of works in this genre, including *Secret Ceremonies,* a best-selling book by Deborah Laake, is certainly not their artistic merit or reportorial excellence.[17] Rather it is that they touch on the point where Mormonism diverges most dramatically from traditional Christianity, thereby providing evangelical and fundamentalist readers and viewers of video presentations with negative confirmation of their own conservative Christian faith.

❧

I am certain the charge that Mormons are members of a non-Christian "temple cult" must be as distressing to Latter-day Saints as the charge that liberal

Protestants are secular humanists is disturbing to Methodists like me. But my study of Mormon history has helped me put these charges in perspective: there was a time not long ago when the label "Mormon" was not always enclosed in parentheses when it was used by members of the Church of Jesus Christ of Latter-day Saints. By reminding the members of the LDS Church that they were God's chosen people, that label enclosed the Saints within communal bounds and signaled that those who remained outside were Gentile. As an identifying label, "Christian" (even "conservative Christian") cannot do the work of including only those who ought to be included within the boundaries of the neo-evangelical/fundamentalist/Pentecostal coalition nearly so well as the label "Mormon" once worked to include Saints and only Saints in the LDS community.

The designations conservative Christians use to exclude those who are not adjudged worthy to be drawn inside their particular Christian circle are less parsimonious than the Saints' designation of outsiders. They are likewise less charitable and more offensive. Yet it seems to me that when I am described as a secular humanist and members of the Church of Jesus Christ of Latter-day Saints and the Reorganized Church of Jesus Christ of Latter Day Saints are described collectively as non-Christian, what is really being said to us all ultimately has less to do with our Christian faith or lack of it than with the fact that, to those who make such charges, we are Gentile.

A final personal observation: even though I suppose I can understand why people keep indicting liberal Christianity for its openness, its social activism, and its failure to accept the principle of inerrancy; even though I think I am able to comprehend why the same people or others like them keep trying to tear Mormon Christianity down by endeavoring to prove it not true; and even though I appreciate the positive function of negation and refutation, I regret that such things have come to pass because I am certain that winners and losers alike will be drawn within the circle of God's love someday. I am convinced that the time will come when Christians will no longer need to choose up sides and come out fighting. Meanwhile, when I am asked by one set of Christians whether I think they ought to be warning people away from another set of Christians, I refer to Matthew 13 and the parable of the wheat and the tares: "So when the plants came up and bore grain, then the weeds appeared also. . . . And the servants . . . came and said to [the Lord], '. . . do you want us to go and gather them?' But he said 'No, lest in gathering the weeds you root up the wheat along with them.'"[18]

In the fullness of time, a decision will be made in a higher court as to whether the Holy Catholic church that evolved from the apostolic church described in the New Testament managed to stay Christian; whether the

Protestants, including the Anglicans, who separated from the Roman church maintained their status as Christians; whether the Methodists who separated from the Anglicans continued to be Christian; and whether the new Christian movements that evolved in the United States in the nineteenth century—Mormonism, Seventh-day Adventism, Christian Science—are authentically Christian. Till then, as one who sees "through a glass darkly," I withhold judgment, counting within the definition of Christian any church, sectarian movement, liberal or conservative coalition, or new religious tradition that gathers persons together in the name of Christ and, in so doing, creates genuine community wherein women and men may—to use Methodist phraseology—take up the cross and follow him.

Notes

1. Jan Shipps, "Mormonism: An Independent Interpretation," in *Encyclopedia of Mormonism,* 5 vols., ed. Daniel H. Ludlow (New York: Macmillan, 1992), 1:248–50.

2. Jan Shipps, *Mormonism: The Story of a New Religious Tradition* (Urbana: University of Illinois Press, 1985), 87–107.

3. The title of the session was "Mormon History and the Conundrum of Culture." While not available as a printed text, both Hansen's paper and my remarks are conveniently accessible from Sunstone in an audiotape format.

4. In its selection of Grant McMurray as church president in 1993, the RLDS Church cut the line, up to that point unbroken, of having as prophet-president a direct descendant of Joseph Smith.

5. Whether this historic emphasis will continue is an open question.

6. Ernst Troeltsch, one of the earliest and most influential sociologists of religion, characterized Christian institutions as either churches or sects. The way this classification relates to Mormonism is discussed in Lawrence A. Young, "Sect," in *Encyclopedia of Mormonism,* ed. Ludlow, 3:1291–92.

7. Doctrine and Covenants, 18:11–12.

8. Ibid., 20:2.

9. Jan Shipps and John W. Welch, eds., *The Journals of William E. McLellin, 1831–1836* (Provo, Utah, and Urbana: *BYU Studies* and University of Illinois Press, 1994), 152.

10. William A. Clebsch, "Each Sect the Sect to End All Sects," *Dialogue* 1 (Summer 1966): 84–89, speaks of the "morphology" of American religion and points to his belief that the exclusivist tendency in American religion has made every group hope, at some time or other, to be "the sect to end all sects." Certainly this was the initial goal of the Campbellite organization.

11. Richard L. Bushman, *Joseph Smith and the Beginnings of Mormonism* (Urbana: University of Illinois Press, 1984).

12. Eber D. Howe, *Mormonism Unvailed* (Painesville, Ohio: By the author, 1834); Joseph Smith Jr., *Teachings of the Prophet Joseph Smith,* comp. Joseph Fielding Smith (1938; reprint, Salt Lake City: Deseret Book, 1976), 139.

13. Doctrine and Covenants, 133:12.

14. Wade Clark Roof, "Mainline Protestantism," in *Taking Stock and Charting Change: Religious Reconfigurations in America since the Sixties,* ed. Jan Shipps and David Smith (Indianapolis: Privately printed on the occasion of the retirement of Robert W. Lynn from the head of the Religion Division of Lilly Endowment, Inc., 1990), 6–12. Roof used the phrase "hemorrhaging members" in a public presentation of the material in this chapter.

15. Anthony A. Hoekema, *The Four Major Cults* (Grand Rapids, Mich.: Erdmans, 1963).

16. Martin Marty and Scott Appleby, "Conclusion: An Interim Report on a Hypothetical Family," in *Fundamentalisms Observed,* ed. Martin Marty and Scott Appleby (Chicago: University of Chicago Press, 1991), 842.

17. Deborah Laake, *Secret Ceremonies: A Mormon Woman's Intimate Diary of Marriage and Beyond* (New York: W. Morrow, 1993).

18. Matt. 13:27–29 RSV.

17

Knowledge and Understanding

Back in the days when non-Mormons were called Gentiles, the editors of *Dialogue* invited me to write an essay about what it was like to be a token "Gentile" in the heterogeneous gathering of scholars who do research on Mormonism and write about it. They asked me to include some description of my being a frequent participant in discussions and institute programs with LDS students and faculty in Bloomington, Indiana. This invitation challenged me to reflect on what it meant to be located metaphorically in a place where I could stand with one foot in the Mormon community and the other in a complicated world where I was a wife, daughter, mother, grandmother, Methodist, and member of a university faculty holding appointments in religious studies, history, and American studies. By the time I finished the essay I had given a name to my marginal position. I called myself an "inside-outsider in Zion." By this, I meant to indicate both my location and status and to signify my awareness that I was accepting the task of continuing enough research in the historical sources and maintaining enough contact with Mormonism as both religion and culture to be able to speak responsibly, when asked, as I so often am, about how it is with the Saints.

In the intervening years, some things have changed. Since my mother, father, mother-in-law, and father-in-law are now all dead (making *us* "the old folks," as my husband says), I am no longer called on to fill a daughter's role. Also, I am no longer the director of the IUPUI Center for American Studies, so I do not have to deal with administrative tasks. I helped organize and am one of the two leaders—the other is a nuclear physicist—of an adult forum called the Wesley Conventicle at the First United Methodist Church in Bloomington. The focus of my research shifted as I started to work in earnest on a book about Mormonism since World War II. But some things seem to stay the same. When something of consequence occurs in Mormondom, the telephones at my home and office begin to ring, and I am asked to provide context and commentary from outside the LDS community.

In the course of conducting research on modern Mormonism and in talking at length with LDS friends about their faith (and mine) and their experience of being Mormon and my experience of being Methodist, I have come to know that the temple and its rituals are critical elements in the symbolic construction of chosenness that makes it possible for Saints to retain a sense of themselves as a peculiar people. Moreover, in the process of learning as much as it is appropriate for me to learn about the temple ordinances and ceremonies, I have amassed a fair amount of information about temple rituals in which one person participates for another; this is to say that I have gained knowledge about proxy baptisms and other ceremonies in which one person stands in for another. Frankly, although I was able to obtain knowledge in this arena of Mormon studies, with my Protestant background and hardheaded show-me-the-data attitude, I had not gained understanding. I could appreciate the significance of the temple and even comprehend the importance of the endowment and marriage for time and eternity in the lives of Latter-day Saints. But this proxy business was beyond me; I just did not understand it.

That is, until the first Sunday after my friend Lavina Fielding Anderson was excommunicated from the Church of Jesus Christ of Latter-day Saints. Since the 1993 semiannual general conference of the church was in session that day, probably not many Saints were aware that October 3, 1993, was worldwide communion Sunday, the day on which Christians all over the world—no matter how divided in other ways—all become one, ritually reconstituting the body of Christ in space and time. Ordinarily this is not one of the more meaningful ceremonies of the church to me. But since it is about the only ritual occasion that brings Orthodox Christians, Catholics, and evangelical, conservative, fundamentalist, and liberal Protestants from throughout the world together as the church universal, I generally try not to miss the worship service on that day.

This year, however, I had another reason for being sure to attend. As spelled out in our Book of Discipline, the doctrine of the United Methodist church provides for open communion. The opening words of the liturgy for this part of the worship service are that "Christ our Lord invites to his table all who love him, earnestly repent their sin and seek to live in peace with one another." Everyone is welcome regardless of religious affiliation (or lack of same). Moreover, since our doctrine is silent on the matter of who may be called to assist the ordained minister(s) in serving the ritual bread and wine (we use grape juice), members of the laity in our congregation are regularly asked to help serve the sacramental elements at the Lord's table. It so happened that I was, for the first time ever, one of five lay members invited to serve in this capacity on this particular Sunday.

I was assigned the tasks of assisting with the removal of the linen cloth that covers the sacraments during other parts of the service and then offering the elements to all who came to the altar to kneel and commune with the Lord and one another. I was directed to return to the table when all had been served to help with the ritual recovering of the elements, thus interring the symbols of Christ's body and blood to await their being brought again to the people of God in the next serving of the sacrament.

How simple, how routine, thought I as we were receiving our instructions. About this I was mistaken, truly mistaken. That this would be neither a simple nor routine worship hour for me was foreshadowed even before the service opened, for at the conclusion of our little instruction session our senior minister placed his hand on my shoulder and said, "I was so sorry to hear about your friend."

Nothing, I think, is so heartrending as shared grief. Or so heartwarming. All the previous week I had been trying to stand outside the circle of the accused to see the situation, as best I could, from both sides. Only then could I answer journalists' questions about the significance of the church's move to discipline six members of its own intellectual community. While I always alluded to the personal tragedy in separate cases, I also asserted that such actions shore up boundaries and clarify what being Mormon means. In a cool interpretative mode, I pointed to the hemorrhaging—the metaphor is Wade Clark Roof's—going on in various denominations in the Protestant mainstream (including my own), suggesting that the LDS Church might be learning what happens when boundaries become so fuzzy and so permeable that they no longer give members a sense of who they are and what being Christian truly means.

Yet the "fall housecleaning" had been tugging at my heart all week. I did not know Maxine Hanks, Paul Toscano, or Avraham Gileadi, but my friends Lynne Knavel Whitesides, Michael Quinn, and Lavina Anderson had been in my consciousness and in my prayers. Somehow most especially Lavina, for she is a sister whose life has touched mine at many different points since we first met in the mid-1970s. The evidence that my sorrow was reverberating in my own congregation made it doubly hard for me to be sanguine about the fact that on this Sunday, likely for the first time in more than four decades, Lavina would be unable to take the sacrament.

Our congregation sang hymns, heard the reading of the scriptures and special choral music, and listened to what I have no doubt was a fine sermon.

But I sat there unable to participate. All my attention was concentrated on those words about all who love the Lord being invited to Christ's table.

Then the prolegomenon was over, and the invitation to the Lord's table was extended to the congregation. I moved to the front and even though increasingly exercised, I at first performed my assigned duties without incident. Yet the lump in my throat made intoning the liturgical "This is Christ's body and blood, shed for you and all humanity" more difficult than I had expected. Still, I managed pretty well until everyone who came had been served. I even held the cup for the minister to partake of the bread and wine.

At that point, the two of us laywomen who had been assigned to replace the white linen cover moved to do so, signifying the ritual's conclusion. But as I picked up the cloth, Lavina came so forcefully to my mind that I was unable to stem a torrent of tears. I almost dropped my end of the cloth, and as I moved quickly to keep it from touching the floor, I missed a step and almost fell.

There I stood in front of the congregation, as spiritually distraught as I had been in a very long time. But then I remembered: I may be Methodist, but Lavina is a Mormon through and through. We may have no conception of rituals "by proxy," but the Saints do. When death—or excommunication, which is a kind of death—makes it impossible for people to participate in needed ritual acts, the Saints know that a brother or sister in Christ can perform that act for them. Knowing that, I remembered my taking of the bread and wine and understood the concept of participation in rituals by proxy. It comforted me. And I am certain that Lavina was comforted, too.

Included in this work are any number of essays that may be read as milestones on the path along which I have traveled as I grappled with various ways of writing about an extraordinary religious tradition. This final essay was written specifically as a summing up.[1] It begins as a memoir. After a look back to where I started and an assessment of how far I have traveled, it then does two very different but not contradictory things. The first provides, very briefly, some theoretical explanation for what has been happening to Mormonism during my extended sojourn in its promised land. The other suggests what I regard as a more cogent and compelling answer to the question of how a non-Mormon could attain the status of inside-outsider, a question that I addressed in this book's first essay.

Obviously, what happened to me personally is important in these two projects, hence the narrative account of the trip that carried me to Cache Valley in 1960 and the description of what I encountered there. But the answer that becomes clear at the turn of the century is that the passage changing my position from auslander to inside-outsider is much more directly related to the dramatic alterations in Mormon culture and radical change in the Church of Jesus Christ of Latter-day Saints that have occurred in the past forty years. My encounter with Mormon culture during the year in which I completed my undergraduate degree was critically important, as were my years of graduate training, my assignment to teach both history and religious studies at IUPUI, my participation in the Mormon History Association, my writing *Mormonism: The Story of a New Religious Tradition,* my having the opportunity to work so closely with the McLellin journals, and so on. But the astonishing happenstance that put me in the right place at the right time is also vitally important.

In Logan, in 1960, I encountered a religious institution ensconced in a culture shaped by LDS belief and practice and immersed in Mormon history. I stayed close enough long enough to learn the language, a more critical competence than is often acknowledged. And I stayed long enough to become familiar with the tradition's story and to appreciate what it means to Mormonism. As I did all this, I moved along with it as the tradition moved away from being a provincial faith embedded in a particular culture to being a believing, practicing, and worshiping community present in a great variety of cultures. Observing that transformation has been both a privilege and an extraordinary adventure.

In 1860, after a woman journeyed across the plains and mountains, sometimes having walked all the way pulling a handcart behind her, the coming of yet another female convert to Zion was an occasion often marked by the pathos of recognizing that others in her party failed to make it all the way. Poignancy always marked her arrival because her entry into the "kingdom in the tops of the mountains" signaled departure from the life she had known before she became a Latter-day Saint.

A hundred years later, my entrance into Zion was not compelled by conversion. Neither did it come after months of alternately walking and being jostled and bounced about in a wickedly uncomfortable vehicle. I was accompanied by my husband, Tony, and our eight-year-old son, Stephen, as our small family moved to Utah so that Tony could pursue a new career as a librarian. We reached the Mormon state in a small Hudson Rambler station wagon after only a few days on the trail. Yet as I reconstructed my entry into Mormon land in preparation for a talk on what it has been like to be a "fellow traveler with the Saints for nearly forty years," I realized there was a certain dramatic structure to my arrival as well.

Tony and I were both children of the Great Depression. We reached adolescence during World War II, when automobiles were in such extremely short supply that many families were unwilling to risk the "fender-benders" (hitting unexpected obstacles, minor collisions) that seem to accompany allowing teenagers to learn to drive. When the two of us met, we discovered that we were both accustomed to walking a lot and making use of public transportation. We continued to do so from that day to the day we eloped in the spring of 1949 till the spring of 1960. By that time, Tony had earned his Ph.D. in English; he had six years of experience teaching in an English department; and he was about to get a master's degree in library science. I had a well-burnished "PHT" (putting hubby through), and we were both ready for something new.

Invited to Utah State to be interviewed for a position in the library, Tony traveled to Logan, which appeared to him to be a nice college town and the home of what was advertised as the world's largest cheese factory. While in Logan, he was offered the post, and, upon his return home, we talked of living in a small town after years of residing in the environs of Chicago and in midtown Detroit. Since Tony liked the people he met at Utah State and thought he could do the job, we concluded that we should go. After we made that decision, Tony wired off an affirmative response. Then he said, "Oh, by the way, there is no public transportation. We will need a car."

We therefore did the following as part of our preparations for departure, in this order: first, we read *Consumer Reports* to tell us which one, and then we bought a car. Next, we joined "Triple A." Then we learned to drive. This last we did on busy Detroit streets with an instructor we found listed in the Yellow Pages who, we came to suspect, had an "in" with license bureau personnel that permitted his students to receive driver's licenses regardless of whether they really passed the test. Whether we were correct about that is unimportant. Both of us were novice drivers when we left Detroit.

That did not seem to matter much once we got outside the metropolitan area, for we had asked AAA for an itinerary that would take us first to Georgia and then to Utah by the easiest possible route, avoiding high mountains and the four-lane roads we called "super highways" in those days. Following our "trip-tik" to the letter, we made a quick trip south to bid our families farewell. Then we started to wend our way west. We drove north till we reached Iowa, turned west, and drove across that state and then across the high plains of Nebraska and Wyoming.

By the time we made it to the Wyoming-Utah border, we had started to think of ourselves as experienced travelers and to think of Tony, who had driven all the way, as an experienced driver. Having ascended gradually, we hardly realized we were much above sea level. The West seemed to be endless flatland, and this had made us cocky about what a snap driving to Utah had been.

During the trip, Stephen had become expert in reading AAA strip maps. As we reached Bear Lake, he examined the last page of the trip-tik and called our attention to the short section of highway between where we were and our destination. With the enthusiasm of a weary child who has been imprisoned in the backseat of a car for many days, he exclaimed, "Oh boy! We're nearly there!"

He was right, of course. But that final leg of the journey to Logan made it clear to us that we were still inexperienced in traveling by automobile. At the same time, the drive from Bear Lake to Logan generated in all three of us a wonder that is hard to describe. Leaving the little lakeside town, we started the precipitous climb to the summit, from which one can view a sight that is glorious: a lake so blue that it gives new meaning to very concept of blue as a color surrounded by snowcapped mountains when you look in one direction and by a desertlike area when you look in another. The beauty is breathtaking. On this day, it almost took our breath away to travel along a road—not so wide as it is now—complete with switchbacks, hairpin turns, and stretches that seemed to us to be nothing more than narrow shelves carved into the mountainside.

Having never seen elevations of this magnitude before and having never viewed a natural spectacle of such magnificence, I was awestruck. I was also as fearful for our safety as I had ever been. Yet almost before I had time to appreciate this close proximity of awe and terror, we had managed the heights and were descending past mountain meadows into a canyon from which, in places, the mountains stand virtually perpendicular to the road and the Logan River that, for many miles, runs alongside. In the years since, I have been to and through more impressive canyons (Zion's Canyon, for example, and the Grand Canyon). But at the time, this one was sufficient to make it seem that we were negotiating a passage through a chasm that was separating us from everywhere we had been and everything we had done before we entered it.

As it turned out, that was true only for me, not for Tony and Stephen. But when we reached the mouth of the canyon and the narrow passage through which we had traveled opened out onto an amazing vista, I gazed transfixed. The scene revealed a valley dappled in light and shadow, with the sun's rays reflecting off the stone of Utah State's Old Main Tower and the pristine whiteness of the Logan Temple. It was enclosed by mountains standing afar, and it seemed to be another world.

Soon afterward, a longtime Logan resident told me that if you stand on the bench at the mouth of the canyon and look to the left, you can "see all the way to Paradise." Surely that appeared to be true. I also quickly learned that if you look to the right, you see places with far less evocative names (like North Logan and Smithfield). Yet I continue to cling to the idea that what I saw as I first encountered Cache Valley after that simultaneously exhilarating and fearsome passage is as astonishing and as welcoming a sight as any nineteenth-century Saint could have seen upon entering Zion.

Still, reality set in all too rapidly when we located the six-room, ranch-type dwelling an agent had rented for us. Unloading our belongings into the bare rooms of this modest house standing on the edge of a typical housing development cul de sac, I again took up my ordinary life as wife and mother, although this time with the occupation of college student rather than salesperson or housemother. Yet things would never be quite the same.

Elsewhere I have described my encounter with Mormon culture and how it seemed to me both unexpectedly familiar and altogether strange. What I intend here is to be more analytical than I have been in writing about my experiences up to now. Before assuming an academic posture, I will add that I am certain I was made more attentive to what I would see in Logan and more sensitive to the changes I would observe in the succeeding decades by that striking experience of passage, of moving out of a space and time that was familiar into one in which both space and time were measured with instruments alien to me. The impact of that experience and its aftermath also permitted me to recognize the underlying as well as the superficial differences between Mormon culture and the cultures I had encountered in the South and Midwest.

The texture of a culture is always better captured in stories than in analytic language. This is particularly true in a situation in which religion and culture are dyadic, each intimately involved and interacting with the other, as was true in Mormonism in the late nineteenth century and first half of the twentieth. Cultural texture, however, can be deceiving at a point in history when radical change is underway. Then an examination of the underlying structure is more revealing because it facilitates not only "before and after" description but also (after-the-fact) identification of what survived and what was lost.

From the perspective of these observations, analysis is likewise critical because the very fact that transition was occurring made possible the genuine sharing of experience that characterizes "fellow traveling." As long as the LDS Church–Mormon culture dyad was as tightly bonded as it had been for nigh onto a century, both by religious practice and by the Saints' perception of the blood of Israel being universally present in LDS veins, someone not Mormon could be a friendly outsider or an unfriendly outsider, but that person would always be an outsider unless and until he or she converted to Mormonism. Even then, becoming an insider often took years, sometimes a generation or more.

That Mormonism would soon start the dramatic move away from what it had been toward what it would become is critically important to my story because the precise timing and particular place of my entry into Zion, on the cusp of change in a place where that change was proceeding slowly, permitted me to observe the before as well as the after and to experience the passage from one reasonably settled state to the other. This passage, the transition from one to the other, is perhaps best described as a time of flux. Its unsettled character provided both an avenue of ingress and a grounding for me to stand on while I traveled along, permitting me to become an "inside-outsider" in the process.

∽

Clearly the timing was right. Of those who became new Saints each year after World War II, converts were an ever-greater proportion of the total. But the main business of the LDS Church in the 1950s was not—as some suppose—managing exponential church growth occasioned by conversion.[2] This was a decade in which nine new overseas missions were established and also in which, under the leadership of church president David O. McKay, the church's international aspect moved to the forefront of the leaders' attention.[3] But even more urgently than establishing new missions and sending out proselyting forces, the church leaders during that tumultuous decade were kept busy dividing and reorganizing wards and stakes, calling new priesthood leaders, and scrambling to meet demands occasioned by population growth in the traditional Mormon culture region.[4] They also had to see the gathering into new branches, wards, and stakes of Saints who had settled either outside the Intermountain West or in regions inside it where members of the church had not previously settled. At the local level, LDS priesthood leaders baptized the fruits of the LDS baby boom, reactivated "Adult Aaronics," built buildings, and oversaw everything else necessary to create "mini-Zions" all across the United States and Canada, as well as in Europe and a few other parts of the world.

Not until 1960, and then for the first time since the early decades of Mormonism's existence, were more people added to the LDS Church membership roll through conversion than as a consequence of natural increase. This persisted, initiating a new state of affairs for the church in which exponential growth fueled by conversion would become the normal condition. Although it was not obvious at the time, it so happened that my arrival in Zion in 1960 occurred during a pivotal year.

Logan was likewise the right place. Cache County had not escaped the reorganizing and adding of new stakes and wards entirely, going between the end of the war and 1960 from two stakes to four, plus a student stake organized at Utah State in 1958. By no means did this expansion in northern Utah reflect the same explosive growth of the church occurring in Salt Lake, Utah, and Weber counties. Logan remained provincial.[5] With a population that was more than 90 percent LDS, it was still so very Mormon that it was a perfect arena in which to behold Latter-day Saint culture and observe the workings of the LDS Church before the transformation that would carry this religious movement from peoplehood to church membership.[6]

Two main characteristics suffice to limn out a picture of the church-culture dyad in Logan in 1960. One of these was primarily an earmark of Mormon culture and the other a sometimes overlooked feature of the LDS Church. Both were characteristics of the Mormonism that was rapidly passing away, characteristics that in symbiosis accounted for much that had been distinctive in Mormonism for well over half a century.

The most notable attribute of the Mormon culture I first observed was that it was *tribal*. The population was overwhelmingly composed of peculiar (i.e., chosen) people; the size of Logan's Gentile community was only ample enough to reveal how truly Mormon the culture was. As was true of American Jews in this same period, however, by no means were all Logan Latter-day Saints *observant*. It would have been hard to settle on categories signifying observance or, to use the LDS concept, activity levels among Logan Mormons. I suspect (since the parking lot was so visible) that the geographical proximity of a temple where temple work could conveniently—and obviously if not publicly—be done meant that however important compliance with the Word of Wisdom was (and it was very important indeed), levels of activity among the Saints were not entirely determined by whether one abstained from smoking and consuming coffee and alcohol. Neither was activity level calculated mainly on the basis of the bustle that accompanied the fulfilling of ward and stake assignments. Having pioneer ancestors made up for lots of missed meetings.

Surely there were times that suggested the expression "as busy as a four-ward chapel" originated in Logan, as active members of the Church of Jesus Christ of Latter-day Saints scrambled to keep up with what was required of them in those days. But almost equally visible among the town's Saints were "Jack-Mormons," who advertised their position in the culture by smoking and drinking coffee in public and consuming alcohol in their own homes and the homes of their friends. Perhaps the mold that would produce "cookie-cutter" Mormons was in the process of being forged elsewhere, but it was not yet in widespread use. In Logan, LDS culture was still being produced by Mormon folk of every stripe.

One often reads or hears about the authoritarian character of the LDS Church, about the way in which it demanded obedience above all else. I am convinced, however, that the critical characteristic of the LDS institutional structure at this time was the extent to which the church was, to coin a word, "auxiliarized." The institution's auxiliaries (the Sunday School, the Mutual

Improvement organizations, the Primary organization, the Women's Relief Society) and its departments (missionary, genealogy, and so on) initially came into being as aids to the priesthood. Even as the hierarchical structure of the priesthood had remained intact during the early 1900s, the church's auxiliaries gained so much strength—in some cases virtual sovereignty—that they seemed almost as strong as the priesthood itself.

The church today appears to function as a well-tuned machine, whose parts mesh so perfectly that it is difficult to tell where one auxiliary or department ends and another begins. But between 1900 and 1950, the auxiliaries essentially stood on their own. Each one had its own authority hierarchy that started at the ward level and moved up through the stake level to the Council of the Twelve, where a specific apostle was assigned to preside over it. Specified members of the Twelve were also responsible for the several church departments. The various auxiliaries raised their own money, produced their own materials, and even stood physically apart. The Relief Society Building housed the Relief Society; the Primary offices were somewhere else; the Sunday School had separate offices; and so on. By the 1940s, the church was renting offices all over Salt Lake City for its auxiliaries.

Back then, there was no church bureaucracy to speak of, and with no e-mail or other form of instant communication besides the telephone, auxiliary officers and their minimal staffs developed a high degree of independence. Their general presidencies would often consult with one another, but the real negotiating and jockeying for resources took place in the Council of the Twelve. The First Presidency and the Twelve presided over the whole church, of course. But the Twelve operated as a sort of federation in which each member represented an auxiliary or department.[7]

This was, to say the least, a convoluted system, especially when two departments were responsible for different parts of a single task (like acquiring the land for a ward chapel and constructing it) or if several auxiliaries needed or wanted to cooperate at the local level. But this system was not a particular problem for Logan in the 1950s and 1960s because telephone communication provided instant access to church headquarters and because so many LDS leaders in Logan were personal friends of general authorities. Moreover, the fact that the church was auxiliarized had certain advantages for some, shall we say, idiosyncratic Saints who were uncomfortable with (or simply did not like) their bishops or stake presidents. Without formally rejecting priesthood authority and becoming inactive, such Saints could seek out and develop relationships with authority figures whose claim to spiritual jurisdiction rested on their being auxiliary "file leaders." This could, and sometimes did, provide needed emotional "space" while allowing Saints to maintain their connection to the institution.

I should note that my knowledge of gross gradations in the culture, the difference between superactive Saints and Jack Mormons, was immediate and direct. But my understanding of how the church worked in those days became clear to me only after I read oral histories from the period and did considerable informal interviewing on my own. In hindsight, it is easy to appreciate the extent to which the culture's tribalism and the church's being auxiliarized coalesced to create the distinctive culture described in Thomas F. O'Dea's *Mormons,* Samuel Woolley Taylor's *Rocky Mountain Empire,* and Mark Leone's *Roots of Modern Mormonism.*[8]

From observing and interacting with the Latter-day Saint intellectual community across the years, I have become convinced that, more than any other, it is Leone's unappreciated work that gets far enough below the surface to illuminate the crucial differences in the Mormonism I confronted in Logan and today's Mormonism. In his *Roots of Modern Mormonism* (which was published in 1979 but based on fieldwork done earlier in the St. George area), Leone, an anthropologist, describes a community that shared symbols whose content was still open enough to permit Saints to fill them with meaning and figure out how the whole fit together.[9] Although few church members probably realized it, many of them were doing theological work. As Leone pointed out, in sacrament meeting talks and gospel doctrine classes, and I should add study groups, Saints constructed their own theologies.[10] This gave midcentury Mormonism a flexibility and resilience that would become impractical—even exceedingly risky—when the LDS community began being composed of as many converts as persons who were born Mormon, and sometimes even more.

In point of fact, LDS doctrine and theology were never as much of a do-it-yourself affair as Leone and the anthropologist Janet Dolgin argued.[11] Nevertheless, it is true that as long as being born Mormon was analogous to being born Jewish and LDS communities were primarily composed of what Michael Quinn called "DNA Mormons," there was a sort of malleability to the belief system undergirding LDS culture that in today's Mormonism would likely lead to fragmentation and possibly schism.[12]

As a student at Utah State, I had little opportunity for anything other than student-professor interaction with my instructors and most other members of the faculty. I was not privy to much of the candid discourse centering on the issue of blacks and the priesthood that surely must have been going on in Logan's intellectual community during the 1960–61 academic year.[13] But as the wife of "Dr. Shipps, librarian," I had the opportunity at various social events to engage in conversation with librarians and their spouses, some of whom were on the faculty.

Even though we were newcomers, Tony and I quickly learned that the people on the guest lists of most of the dinner parties to which we were invited did not fit into the "active Mormon" category. The signals were pretty blatant: after greeting us on the first such occasion we attended, the host gave us a choice of scotch, bourbon, or something he called "sasparillo." Except for Tony and me, everyone there was LDS, but nobody asked for sasparillo.[14]

I soon discovered what at the time seemed a curious thing about these events: the pattern of the conversation was practically always the same. People would begin by talking about news of the day; then the conversation would turn to university politics and the latest faculty gossip; and perhaps there would be some discussion of a recent book or article. About the time the second round of drinks was being poured, however, the latest Mormon joke would turn the talk to Mormonism, where it would stay for the rest of the evening. That we were new to Utah and I had an intense curiosity may explain this, but I think not. Although these dinners and other social occasions had different configurations of people each time, I heard stories of the same general genre again and again, and it now appears manifestly obvious that these were ritual occasions during which Mormons were bearing testimony to their experiences as Latter-day Saints. Moreover, just as the bearing of testimony in sacrament meeting builds faith, so in telling their stories to each other as much as to Tony and me, these Saints were reassuring themselves that their skepticism and their strained relationships with the institutional church were justified.

As I recall, we never attended a sacrament meeting—the Presbyterian church was the only Protestant church in town so, when we went, we went there—but Mormonism's orthodox side was presented to us by our neighbors, by LDS friends I made in classes at the university, and by the stake missionaries (we called them home teachers) who visited periodically. Because the Mormon story was engrossing and LDS religious and cultural practice was fascinating to me, I asked lots of questions and listened intently to the answers. But if, at first, I found it somewhat bizarre to be bombarded with information about the church and the culture from these almost diametrically opposed directions, the upshot was that after nine months I not only left Logan with a baccalaureate degree in history but also carried with me firsthand knowledge that the story of Mormonism (its church and its culture) was far more complicated than it appeared on the surface. This consciousness of complexity would become the reason for an idea that is in practically everything I write about the Latter-day Saints, one that may be simply stated as follows: there are many truths about Mormonism, not just one.

∽

Although my direct interaction with LDS scholars (and Latter-day Saints in general) was virtually suspended for almost a decade after we left Logan, entering graduate school at the University of Colorado and doing an M.A. thesis and doctoral dissertation on Mormonism meant that I continued scrutinizing the Saints. I beheld a continuation of the bifurcated vision of Mormonism I had met head on in Logan. As I set about trying to make sense of the LDS story, I found that historical accounts diametrically opposed to each other existed for practically every occurrence in the Mormon past and that these opposing accounts were based on two quite separate bodies of data arising from two different sets of historical sources.[15]

That I managed to avoid being pulled one way or the other is, in large part, because I did most of the archival work on my dissertation in the collections of the Utah State Historical Society and the Utah State Archives and Everett L. Cooley presided over both.[16] A man of wide knowledge and irreproachable historical integrity, he took an interest in my work, and as we discussed what I was finding, he posed such penetrating questions about my dependence on this or that historical source that I started to realize how even contemporary documents carry interpretation along with information. There can be no doubt that my dissertation was and my work ever since has been the better for his mentoring. It was critical in bringing balance to the sources I examined and the meaning I imputed to them, thereby keeping my options open for greater understanding.

But if those options remained open, it seemed for a time after I completed my degree that avenues that would allow me to follow a career as a working historian might be closed. Available posts for history teachers at both the high school and college levels were few and far between in the area around Bloomington, Indiana (where we had moved from Colorado so that Tony could accept what seemed a perfect position for him, librarian for English at Indiana University, and where Stephen, a promising musician, could pursue training as a violinist in a music school that was ranked one of the very best in the nation).

As recounted in the introduction to part 1, for two years I worked on the fringes of sociology and psychology at the [Kinsey] Institute for Sex Research, a turn of events that first appeared to be a detour, if not a dead end. But the opportunity to gain new skills in an area that required familiarity with statistical analysis and computer modeling and the introduction to survey research that I received led me to undertake a research project on American perceptions of the Saints between 1860 and 1960. Since the skills I had acquired during my stint at the Institute for Sex Research were in very short supply in university history departments at this juncture, my work at the Kinsey Institute and the historical research I started while still there led directly to an appointment on a university faculty tenure track. To earn tenure, however, I was required to develop a research agenda that would carry my work far beyond my dissertation. In so doing, I undertook a program of research that called for so much back and forth commuting to Utah that Tony started calling himself a "latchkey husband."

For years I had mainly been an observer of the passing Mormon cavalcade. Now I again found myself in a real Mormon community. This time, however, the LDS community I entered was the community of Mormon intellectuals then gathering around *Dialogue: A Journal of Mormon Thought* and taking shape in the Mormon History Association, both of which were founded in the mid-1960s.[17] The great majority of this community's members were born under the "new and everlasting covenant." With believing blood in their veins and the LDS tradition bred into their sinews, they were Mormons ethnically as well as religiously. Most were Utah residents, but a significant number were scattered throughout the nation. Many subgroups stayed in close touch by mail and telephone. LDS intellectuals also gathered in annual and regional conferences that periodically reaffirmed the reality of the community's existence to its far-flung membership.[18]

In the 1970s, this loosely organized community stood in sharp contrast to the ever more rigidly organized and strictly regulated religious body to which the great majority of LDS intellectuals belonged and in which many were active participants. The church in which they had been reared was in the process of being changed as missions were established all around the world and huge numbers of converts flowed into the institution. The church was not merely filling up with converts; an increasing proportion of the eight-year-old LDS cohort being baptized every year was made up of children of converts with no family tradition of being Mormon.[19]

Although these developments were cause for great celebration, they meant that the LDS Church was rapidly losing its provincial character. The church's general authorities faced the herculean task of presiding over an organization in which (1) congregations in some parts of the world were made up almost completely of converts; (2) congregations in other areas were composed of variable admixtures of converts and those who had been born into LDS families and reared in the church; and (3) congregational (ward) populations in Utah and elsewhere in the Great Basin and along the Pacific coast were composed almost entirely of "birthright" Saints. The First Presidency and the Twelve had to make sure that, as it welcomed people of every race, social class, and ethnic background as members, the church itself would not be reduced, as some Protestant denominations had been, to little more than an institutional umbrella under which a family of congregations gather, each one different from all the others.

This had not been particularly difficult for the LDS Church when the numbers of Saints had been reasonably finite and distance had not prevented the exercise of close oversight of the church by the leaders.[20] By the 1970s, however, church growth and geographical dispersion were making it difficult for them to safeguard the tradition by seeing to it that Mormonism would be the same in whatever locale it was found, especially since the problem of doing this was compounded by two idiosyncratic features of LDS institutional structure. One of these is that congregations are led by local members of the lay priesthood, a feature that complicated the management of the congregations made up almost entirely of converts. The other complicating feature was that many vital elements of the church's life were being handled by the several church auxiliaries, each with its own hierarchy and reporting procedures extending from the ward level up to the Council of the Twelve.

This arrangement worked very well in Great Basin congregations, where virtually the entire surrounding neighborhoods were Mormon, but it posed great hardship in small mission field congregations.[21] All this meant that older patterns of church governance were stretched to the limit in an effort to keep lines of communication open and to keep the institution's central organization from being so overwhelmed with details, particulars, and technicalities that it would be unable to deal with larger issues facing the church.

During the turbulent 1960s, many LDS intellectuals were convinced that the denial of the priesthood to black men was the most critical issue the church faced. In point of fact, however, so many other issues occupied the time and energy of those who stood at the head of the church then that the placement of the priesthood question in the church's problem priority order is by no means clear. Other issues looming large were (1) the need to maintain doctrinal consistency; (2) the need to establish unambiguous reporting lines; (3) the need to establish an activity program that could be followed by wards, stakes, and branches throughout the church; (4) the need to reduce the number of meetings and activities in which individual Saints

were expected to participate so that they could fulfill their family duties; and
(5) the need to stop the drain on church resources and church order occasioned by duplication of effort in departments and church auxiliaries. To deal
with these and other matters occasioned by the growing institutional and
ecclesiastical complexity that accompanied church growth and geographical expansion, the First Presidency revived an oversight and coordination
program that had existed in one form or another since 1907. Originally called
the Committee of Correlation and Adjustments, in one of its several earlier
incarnations it had been called and functioned as the Union Board of the
Auxiliaries.

By 1960, the necessity of some form of correlation became evident to the
First Presidency and the Twelve, which then included men who, before being called as general authorities, had been successful leaders of large business enterprises. Consequently, a broad effort at correlation was undertak-
en. It started with a review by a committee of general authorities of the
purposes and courses of study of the priesthood and the various auxiliaries.
Following up on the outcome of this review, the First Presidency organized
the church's instructional and activity efforts into three divisions. One of
them included everything that dealt in one way or another with children; the
other two were the youth and adult divisions. Three coordinating committees, each headed by a member of the Twelve, were then formed and charged
with overseeing these divisions. The oversight extended to all the church's
many departments and auxiliaries serving the children, youth, and adults of
the church.

By the beginning of the 1970s, correlation had extended to the planning,
preparation, translation, printing, and distribution of church materials. In
a related development, the First Presidency established the Correlation Department, composed of all the members of the Council of the Twelve, with
a three-man executive committee made up of the president of the Twelve and
the next two senior apostles. This brought under the direct control of the
priesthood hierarchy all church curricula, all periodicals published with the
imprimatur of the church, and all church organizations, including those that
had formerly operated with quasi-independence, producing and publishing
their own periodicals and instructional materials.[22] This was not a new system reflecting some newly revealed doctrinal principle; priesthood authority over the whole church had been there in principle from the days when
the Prophet Joseph Smith presided. In the past, every arm of the church—
every department, auxiliary organization (the Sunday School, Primary, the
soon-to-be-renamed Mutual Improvement Association for the youth, and
the Relief Society), educational activity (the Church Educational System,

Brigham Young University, Ricks College), and all departments (missionary, genealogy, building, and so on)—had been ultimately responsible to the priesthood and the general authorities presiding over it. The move to place correlation in the vanguard was essentially a much-needed systemic renovation. It foreshadowed, however, the demise of the quasi-independence of any part of the church (especially its auxiliaries and its institutions of higher learning) that had grown when the reporting structure in the church was much less straightforward than it would become after 1970.

In the next two decades, along with the development of an elaborate church bureaucracy that also answers directly to the priesthood, the authority of the Correlation Committee was gradually extended to a point in the 1990s at which all "communications are transmitted through a single priesthood line from the First Presidency and Council of the Twelve to stakes and wards and thereby to families and individuals."[23] Although that reclaiming of direct priesthood ascendancy over the whole did not occur all at once, a striking alteration in the church that did have a one-fell-swoop feel to it came about in 1980, when a consolidated meeting schedule dramatically decreased the time Latter-day Saints spent in meetings, formerly spread throughout the week, to a three-hour block on Sundays. Coming at what from this turn-of-the-century perspective can be seen as the midpoint in a reorganization that concentrated LDS religious authority in a single priesthood line, the consolidated meeting schedule sounded the death knell of the auxiliarized church and announced its successor, the correlated church.

Notwithstanding its worthy goal of creating a worldwide church in which doctrinal and institutional integrity can be maintained, the standardizing, simplifying, "cookie-cutter" effect of correlation seems to be bearing more heavily on some parts of the Mormon community than on others. Not surprisingly, its workings have stirred more reaction and controversy among members of the LDS intellectual community than in other parts of the church. As it did when Laurel Thatcher Ulrich was not approved as a speaker at an official women's conference held at BYU, this reaction nearly always surfaces whenever the church's need to maintain control over its pulpits—in LDS nomenclature, stands—to ensure that dependable information will be dispensed appears to undercut the prophetic dictum that "the glory of God is intelligence." Few people seem to have questioned whether LDS seminary and institute classrooms should be places in which correlation rules supreme. But a virtual fire-storm that escaped the bounds of the ordinarily enclosed LDS intellectual universe was created when it became clear to all, both inside and outside the community, that BYU classrooms were being defined as such pulpits.[24]

Dialogue, the *Journal of Mormon History, Sunstone,* and Signature Books are all organs of the LDS intellectual community (although Signature Books, which publishes some regional material not connected to Mormonism, is rarely recognized as such).[25] They are independent voices and are therefore not put through correlation.[26] This independence from correlation extends to the content of papers presented at annual meetings of the Mormon History Association and in the various Sunstone symposia.[27]

This does not mean the Church of Jesus Christ of Latter-day Saints has absolutely no control over what is published in the pages of these periodicals, the books Signature publishes, and the papers given at the Mormon History Association and Sunstone symposia. As a matter of policy, since they are not correlated, no reference to articles published in these independent organs may appear in church magazines, but church authorities do not have the same total control over the actions of those members of the LDS intellectual community who depend on the church for their livelihoods as they have over church magazines. As far as can be determined, a written policy directing staff members of the Church Educational System, the faculties of Brigham Young University and Ricks College, and those employed at the church's museum, libraries, archives, and Historical Department not to submit articles to *Dialogue* and *Sunstone* has never been put in place. Yet a clear understanding exists that this is contrary to church policy.[28]

Of greater moment, since many (maybe most) of those who write for these periodicals and make public presentations at symposia and conferences are Latter-day Saints who wish to maintain their standing in the church, they are subject to priesthood authority. Their bishops or stake presidents may call in members to caution them that in making public their differences with what church authorities have written or said, they could be "flirting with apostasy."[29] This has happened to a number of Saints I know quite well, and several of them have described these interviews to me. Most report that the warnings about how what they have published in the pages of one or another of these independent publications or said in public symposium sessions could place their membership in jeopardy came in civil (and, in most cases, caring) conversations in which fairly gentle admonitions were delivered. But as has been made clear in the spate of disfellowships and excommunications that made news in the early 1990s, those who ignore such admonition may be severely disciplined.

There is also the matter of the warning against "alternative voices." In the church's annual conference in 1989, Dallin Oaks, speaking for the leadership, said that while many of the opinions put forward in independent forums were well-motivated, others were assertions of "lost souls who cannot hear the voice of the Shepherd and trot about trying to find their way without his guidance." Then referring quite clearly to correlation, he said that the church had "procedures to ensure approved content" that "provide a spiritual quality control that allows members to rely on the truth of what is said." In the absence of this "quality control," Saints would have no way of knowing that ideas depending entirely on "the interpretation and sponsorship of scholars who lack . . . authority" have not corrupted "Gospel truths." Saints were thus warned against such "alternate voices" as "are heard in magazines, journals, and newspapers and at lectures, symposia, and conferences."[30]

It is therefore no surprise that in a talk on the importance of correlation given to the All-Church Coordinating Council in 1993 by Boyd K. Packer, one of the apostles who sits on the executive committee of the Correlation Committee, scholars/intellectuals—the terms were used as synonyms in this address—were identified as one of three groups that had "made major invasions into the membership of the Church."[31] Of greater long-term significance, however, the apostle who now is acting president of the Council of the Twelve and might well become president of the church, recognized the immense importance of the principle of correlation and of the Correlation Committee's work. He said, "Except for its having been established, we could not now possibly administer an ever-growing multi-national and multi-lingual church."[32] However much traditional Mormons might look back with nostalgia to a time before correlation—and this includes many Saints who do not think of themselves as intellectuals—he is probably correct about this.

The simplest and most parsimonious theoretical explanation for what has occurred in the past forty years, as Mormonism has moved away from being a tribalized and auxiliarized church to being a correlated one, is movement from gemeinschaft to gesellschaft. These terms, which describe contrasting ideal types, were introduced into the sociological literature by Ferdinand Tönnies as he sought to describe the changes in social relations accompanying the shift from the direct and very personal patterns of a rural, almost feudal system to the far less personal and more structured patterns of a modern urbanized culture.[33] *Gemeinschaft,* which is sometimes inadequately translated as community, refers to a set of social relations characterized by face-to-face contact in which "people essentially remain united in spite of all separating factors."[34] The clearest example of gemeinschaft is the kinship network (in Mormon terms, the patriarchal family whose members are sealed for time and eternity). Although not precisely opposite, *gesellschaft* (sometimes translated as society) depicts a more impersonal set of social relations in which people are "essentially separated in spite of all uniting factors." A system that is more legal than familial is substituted for a social order in which personhood is elemental, where the critical thing is who people are, not what they say or do. Justice is critical. Individuals are isolates; whether they are "of the folk" or where they stand in the circle of family and community is less important than what they say and do. Merit matters, and so does conformity. Rules (and laws) are not made to be broken. People belong when, measured against an acceptable standard, their words and actions are sufficiently congruent for them to be within the pale.

The eminent sociologist Talcott Parsons would go on to derive from Tönnies's typology a well-known set of "pattern variables" in which are embedded evolutionary assumptions that movement from gemeinschaft to gesellschaft, from traditional to modern culture, is inevitable. My use of Tönnies's typology to characterize the change that has occurred is not intended to suggest Mormonism moved from being a tradition that represented some sort of ontological perfection to being a modern manifestation of that tradition in which that perfection gets lost among a standard set of carefully designed programs and rationalized procedures. Instead, I am suggesting the usefulness of the gemeinschaft-gesellschaft typology as a means of capturing the difference between the Mormonism that survived in Logan, St. George, and other areas away from the Mormon center in the 1960s and the Mormonism that is everywhere present at the turn into the twenty-first century.

The sheer size of the community means that the face-to-face intimacy present in former decades is no longer practical—or even possible. In stakes throughout the church, conferences that bring together all the members of all the wards in the stake are held twice a year, and as late as the early 1960s, a major responsibility of members of the Council of the Twelve and members of the Quorum of Seventy was attendance at stake conferences throughout the church. This meant that ordinary members came into direct contact with church leaders and, collectively, the church's general authorities came into direct contact with ordinary members, not just with their representatives. The longevity principle that elevated to the church presidency the apostle who had served longest in the Council of the Twelve meant that there was a good chance that every adult Latter-day Saint had, at one time or another, been in the same room with the man who occupied this exalted office. With a membership still small enough that the church could gather its priesthood leadership from every LDS stake into annual and semiannual conferences held in the Tabernacle on Temple Square, the leaders were more than images on a television screen. In the evocative words of the political scientist Benedict Anderson, whose work on origins of nationalism is both pertinent and suggestive here, this was no "imagined community."[35] It was intimate, face-to-face.

While the virtually revolutionary move from being a religion embedded in a particular culture to one present in many cultures needs to be analyzed more fully so that the case of the Latter-day Saints, which may be documented precisely, will help historians of religion understand how the same sort of shift occurred in other traditions, that is a not a task for this work. Instead, I conclude this summary essay by returning to the autobiographical mode, describing what I saw from the 1970s onward, and indicating what I made of what was happening.

∽

Armand L. Mauss, in an introduction to an essay collection called *Neither White nor Black: Mormon Scholars Confront the Race Issue in a Universal Church,* said that the generative force that led to *Dialogue*'s founding in the mid-1960s was the issue of blacks and the priesthood. Surely he is correct insofar as it was the presenting issue, to put the matter in medical terms. But as important as the question was of whether priesthood denial to blacks was doctrinal (as John J. Stewart argued on practically every page of his slim volume *Mormonism and the Negro*) or mainly a legacy of practice (as Lester E. Bush argued so cogently), considerable evidence suggests that in the case of *Dialogue*'s founding, this particular issue was a part of a larger exploration of Mormon history that also gave rise to the organization of the Mormon History Association at about the same time.[36]

In any event, there can be no doubt that the LDS intellectuals at the forefront in publishing *Dialogue* and those involved in forming the Mormon History Association (in many instances they were the same people) regarded the history of the Saints as vitally important to their understanding of their faith. I heard the assertion that "Mormonism does not have a theology; it has a history" so often it seemed to be the mantra of the LDS intellectual community. Despite the warning issued by one of their own, the Mormon iconoclast (and classically trained philosopher) Sterling McMurrin, that a full and open reconstruction of the Mormon past was impossible, the prevailing general agreement was that that was just what was needed.[37]

The community of Mormon intellectuals I met when I became active in the John Whitmer Historical Society and the Mormon History Association in the early 1970s seemed certain that history would clarify what Joseph Smith was about, how the First Vision came to occupy such a central place in the prophet's story, where plural marriage became part of the Mormon experience, and so on. If a convincing narrative that would illuminate Smith's prophetic claims and locate Mormonism vis-à-vis American culture was their priority, however, filling in the details of the history of the Great Basin kingdom, clarifying the role of Mormon leaders (especially Brigham Young), and recovering the history of those not in leadership roles, especially Mormon women, were also seen as mandatory tasks.

Dialogue's founders and the organizers of the Mormon History Association not only agreed about the importance of history but also shared another characteristic: almost all were active Latter-day Saints.[38] Many of them assumed heavy new responsibilities in addition to their often substantial church assignments. But neither *Dialogue* nor the Mormon History Association was in any way officially connected to the LDS Church, and had they been led by others—and in this instance the role of Leonard Arrington cannot be overstated—their independence might well have moved the journal and the organization in the direction of the Godbeite movement and their wonderfully titled periodical, the *Keep-a-pitchin-in*.[39] Church leaders, however, did not push these Saints in the direction of apostasy. Instead, the First Presidency and the Council of the Twelve appointed Arrington to be the church historian after these independent efforts were well underway, and his appointment may have figured in the extent to which the interest of the intellectuals who had became a true scholarly community by the early 1970s was directed to Mormon history more than to religious and theological issues.[40]

Before the decade of the 1970s was half over, two more independent publishing ventures were underway. One, *Exponent II,* was designed to appeal to LDS women, and the other, *Sunstone,* started out as a journal produced by young Latter-day Saints who were either still in school (in some cases graduate school) or not long past receiving their baccalaureate degrees. These two publications also turned attention toward the LDS past, although not so directly as *Dialogue* and the *Journal of Mormon History,* which started publication in 1973.

Searching for "models who combined a dedication to the faith with a spirit of individual action," a group of Mormon women in Boston published *Mormon Sisters,* a book of historical sketches that were developed from lectures they prepared for a Cambridge Latter-day Saint Institute class.[41] In *Exponent II,* the periodical established by essentially the same LDS women, they also looked to the past for inspiration. Recalling a time when feminist and Latter-day Saint did not seem such a contradiction in terms, they elected to reprint selections from the first *Woman's Exponent* instead of publishing things that could be regarded as revisionist history. *Woman's Exponent* had flourished at a time when it served the church's purposes to advertise to the world that LDS women could be self-reliant women, even feminists, and polygamous wives at the same time.[42]

In contrast, *Sunstone* apparently turned to history because that is what people interested in Mormonism seemed to be writing. Although camouflaged to some degree by the magazine format, a content analysis of the substantive articles in *Sunstone*'s early issues underscores the LDS intellectual community's interest in history, no matter what the age of the editor/publishers. Moreover, that "theological" was soon dropped from the name of the symposia organized as an adjunct to the magazine reveals the extent to which those proposing papers for symposium programs in the 1980s were more interested in history and contemporary social issues than in theology.

∽

In the "brave new world" emerging as this is being written, e-mail, the Internet, and the more elaborate connecting mechanisms of the electronic milieu in which we now exist are turning into reality the virtual communities that were once science-fiction fantasies. In all the palaver, the constant talk about the positive possibilities for connection these communities generate and the dangers they pose, I have heard surprisingly little mention of the virtual communities that existed earlier, the ones held together by cords connected to those little black instruments called telephones. Neither is there much recognition that virtual communities once rode on the ether of postal systems with twice daily deliveries in cities and towns and rural free delivery in the countryside.

I knew historians of Mormonism had long been gathered into such communities, for I had been corresponding with some of them. But I had no idea of their extent until I looked through the *Dialogue* records deposited in the Special Collections of the Marriott Library at the University of Utah some years ago, and until, also at the University of Utah, I examined letters to Fawn Brodie from Dale Morgan, Wallace Stegner, and many other historians, plus the incredibly extensive web of correspondence in the papers of Sterling McMurrin, Obert C. Tanner, and other "swearing elders."[43] I was struck by the far-reaching dimensions of the LDS intellectual community and the extent to which these Mormon historians, although far more diverse than some realize (including as it did Saints of practically all activity levels), were gathered into a community not entirely unlike an extended LDS ward.

For all that, I have news for those McLuhan-types who extol virtual communities as superior to the real thing. Encountering the members of the Mormon historical community on paper, in letters written directly to me, and in their published writings did not hold a clichéd candle to encountering that community in the flesh in the early 1970s. In the wake of Leonard Arrington's death, much has been and will continue to be said and written about the "Arrington Spring." Instead of adding yet another account from a different perspective, however, I finish this book by focusing on two sometimes overlooked components of this well-known story.

The first is that those who were brought into the community of scholars writing Mormon history were by no means all Mormon historians. This new community embraced an entire contingent of RLDS historians, historians who were not and had never been Saints, and historians without graduate training if their work demonstrated their willingness to abide by the canons of professional history. (This last category included such Mormon women as Linda King Newell, Valeen Tippetts Avery, and Susan Arrington Madsen.) This new diversity may account for some of the exhilaration that characterized the milieu in which we were doing Mormon history in the 1970s and early 1980s, and it certainly accounts for much of the probity and candor that marked the history written by the community's members.

Even though the lion's share of the research for it was done in the archives of the LDS and RLDS churches and was often written by historians in the employ of one or the other of these churches, the very porosity of the historical community from the late 1960s onward meant that the new Mormon history would be as independent of the LDS Church as were many of the venues in which it would be published.

LDS apostle Boyd C. Packer's well-known talk about what the church's history ought to contain was an explicit warning to historians that LDS history was escaping the informal monitoring that had made possible the classification of LDS history into clearly defined Mormon and anti-Mormon categories. This development did not sit well with many church authorities (perhaps some in the RLDS Church as well as the LDS Church). The subsequent transformation of the staff of historians Arrington had assembled to create the Joseph Fielding Smith Institute, the restrictions placed on the use of materials in the LDS Church Archives, the move to discourage Church Educational System staff members from participating in the Mormon History Association, and the prohibition against references to articles in *Dialogue* and *Sunstone* in church publications were all obvious efforts to assuage this dis-ease about what was happening to LDS history.

Another crucial yet often overlooked component to the Camelot and post-Camelot story is the larger setting in which it was taking place. Even though it was not the prelude to returning to Jackson County, this was as surely the winding-up scene in the second act of the Mormon drama as the murder of the prophet and the final years in Nauvoo had been the winding-up scene of the first act. Moreover, just as leaving the kingdom on the Mississippi and the pioneer trek occasioned passage from what had been to what would be, the 1970s and 1980s were years of passage in which a community that was tribal and an institution that was auxiliarized bade farewell to the kingdom it had known in the tops of the mountains. In Mormonism's third act—whose opening was perhaps most clearly announced by the change in the church's logo and the disappearance of "the Mormons" from materials produced by the church's Public Affairs Department for distribution to the print and electronic media—the LDS community is composed of members calling themselves Christians or Latter-day Saints rather than Mormons. They belong to a correlated church.

The great irony in the story of the past (and passing) generation of Mormon historians (my generation—or perhaps I should say—our generation) is that as the business of reconstructing what happened in the Mormon past moved forward, the truism that *Mormonism doesn't have a theology so much as it has a history* has been supplanted by one of the most important products of correlation, an ever more clearly defined theology in which the content of the tradition's symbol system is being filled up, clarified, and systematized. This is an ongoing process that is likely to take another generation or two. I am nevertheless convinced that, in time, the Book of Mormon will, as it was in the beginning, be more significant for the faith than the Joseph Smith story and that what goes on in the temple will be far more meaningful to future generations of church members than anything they could learn from either correlated or uncorrelated versions of their tradition's history.

Finally, I will say a word about writing about the Saints from a Gentile/non-Mormon perspective. When I wrote my first article about the denial of the priesthood to blacks, my master's thesis, my dissertation, and even "The Prophet Puzzle," which was the lead article in the first issue of the *Journal of Mormon History,* I was an outsider. As an observer, I was able to see some things more clearly from the outside than would have been possible from the inside. But there was much that I missed. In addition, if those who argue that only women can write women's history, only African Americans can write African American history, and only Mormons can write Mormon history are correct about outsiders being engaged in acts of appropriating other people's stories, I stand convicted.

But when I reentered the community of scholars doing Mormon history in the 1970s, the boundaries of their community had become so porous that as a non-Mormon I could enter it without reassuming my former status as an outsider. I never became a Mormon writing Mormon history. I was and continue to be a Methodist who has spent forty years sojourning in the promised land and describing what there is to see. During this extraordinary tradition's passage from what it was to what it is becoming, Mormonism made a place for me.

Will there be places for people like me in the future? Who can say? Only time will tell.

Notes

1. Under the title "Observations of a Gentile/Non-Mormon," I read this final essay in a Sunstone Symposium plenary session, July 15, 1999, in Salt Lake City. The title of the session was "Fellow Travelers along the Way."

2. For information about the missionary efforts during this decade that would lead to the tremendous growth of the church in the second half of the twentieth century, see Bruce A. Van Orden, "Preparing for a Worldwide Ministry," *Ensign* 29 (October 1999): 32–51. The two pages devoted to the decade of the 1950s concentrate on the leadership of David O. McKay, president of the Church of Jesus Christ of Latter-day Saints, and his "inspired counsel" that every church member should be a missionary. See "The Scattering of the Gathering and the Gathering of the Scattered," herein.

3. During the 1950s, new missions were organized in Central America, South Australia, the northern and southern Far East (Japan, Taiwan, and Hong Kong), northern Mexico, New Zealand, Brazil, Germany, and the Andes (Uruguay, Argentina, Peru, and Ecuador).

4. New stakes formed in the United States during this decade numbered 118.

5. For the best history of Logan, see F. Ross Peterson, *History of Cache County* (Salt Lake City: Utah State Historical Society, 1997). This volume is part of the state's Centennial History Series. Logan's provincial character obtained in all of Cache Valley, the northernmost part of Utah.

Washington County in southern Utah also remained provincial far longer than the settled areas along the Wasatch Front. In Washington County, St. George was the center place. The great interpreters of southern Utah are the Peterson brothers, Charles (Chas) and Levi. Charles Peterson's major work on the area, *Take Up Your Mission: Mormon Colonizing along the Little Colorado River, 1870–1900* (Tucson: University of Arizona Press, 1973), did not carry the story past the turn of the century, but its final sentence reveals the twentieth-century history of the region. Written by a man who had lived there most of his life, it read, "Shaped by the determination of its settlers and the paucity of its natural resources, its character would yield only slowly to the greater society of which it was a part" (272). Just how slowly is clearly disclosed in Levi Peterson's magisterial biography of a woman whose career exemplifies the area, *Juanita Brooks: Mormon Woman Historian* (Salt Lake City: University of Utah Press, 1988).

6. This is the title of the initial chapter of the book I am writing that deals with the Latter-day Saints since World War II.

7. This characteristic of the inner-workings of the Council of the Twelve was gleaned from extensive diaries of Apostle Reed Smoot, which I studied intensively at one point, and the oral histories of several general authorities describing what went on during the first half of the century and even in the 1950s, many of which I read before they were closed to researchers.

8. Thomas F. O'Dea, *The Mormons* (Chicago: University of Chicago Press, 1957); Samuel Woolley Taylor, *Rocky Mountain Empire: The Latter-day Saints Today* (New York: Macmillan, 1978); Mark Leone, *Roots of Modern Mormonism* (Cambridge, Mass.: Harvard University Press, 1979).

9. Leone's work reveals how slowly change came to southern Utah.

10. Ibid., especially 170–72.

11. Janet L. Dolgin, "Latter-day Sense and Substance," in *Religious Movements in Contemporary America,* ed. Irving I. Zaretsky and Mark P. Leone (Princeton, N.J.: Princeton University Press, 1974), 519–46.

12. Quinn's description of himself as a DNA Mormon was initially made in response to a question from a reporter from the *Salt Lake Tribune.* It is repeated in the report on the excommunication of five intellectuals and the disfellowshipping of another that Lavina Fielding Anderson described as the "Fall Housecleaning." See "Disciplinary Actions Generate More Heat," *Sunstone* 16 (November 1993): 68.

13. This was the year of publication in Logan of John J. Stewart's *Mormonism and the Negro: An Explanation and Defense of the Doctrine of the Church of Jesus Christ of Latter-day Saints in regard to Negroes and Others of Negroid Blood* (Logan, Utah: n.p., 1960). That same year, second and third editions of this work were issued in Orem, Utah, by Bookmark, a division of Community Press. At Utah State, this work generated heated discussion even among the students. But in the student body, this theological and doctrinal issue was soon entangled with discussions of and gossip about black members of the USU football team dating white girls.

For the significance of this issue to Mormon intellectuals, see Lester E. Bush Jr. and Armand L. Mauss, eds., *Neither White nor Black: Mormon Scholars Confront the Race Issue in a Universal Church* (Midvale, Utah: Signature Books, 1984). According to the introduction, the denial of priesthood to blacks was "the single most crucial issue in Mormon relationships with others during that entire decade [the 1960s]" (4).

14. As far as I can determine, none of the people with whom we socialized during our year in Logan had been excommunicated from the church. All were still, at least nominally, LDS.

15. One of these bodies of data is composed of the accounts left behind by those who, from the first, were convinced that the Book of Mormon was precisely what it claims to be, that Joseph Smith was a prophet, and that the church restored through his agency was the true church. The other includes the writings and various other records left behind by those who were convinced that Smith was a fraud and that the church he organized was a human creation. Versions of the past canonized by the LDS Church are based on the former and rarely acknowledge the existence of the latter, while the opposite is true of the reconstructions of the LDS story that receive the anti-Mormon imprimatur of being advertised in the *Salt Lake City Messenger,* published by the Mormon apostates Jerald Tanner and Sandra Tanner.

16. In the early 1960s, A. Will Lund presided over the LDS Church Archives. He was so suspicious about why a non-Mormon was interested in materials held by the

church that I concluded it would be better to pursue information elsewhere. As many graduate students do as they begin research, when I started doing serious research in Utah, I was engaging in the proverbial "fishing expedition," casting about to see what I could hook on to that would lead me into what I suspected was a more complicated history than the opposing accounts provided, on one side, by Frank J. Cannon and muckraking journalists and, on the other, by B. H. Roberts. Lund would always ask me to specify exactly what I wanted to see, and when I was unable to be specific, he as much as suggested that I should be doing my research elsewhere.

17. My association with local Latter-day Saints in Bloomington came a bit later. It was mediated by Douglas D. Alder, who spent a sabbatical year at Indiana University. After he introduced me to local Saints connected with the university, I started to participate in the activities of the LDS Institute (then located in a house on the edge of the campus). Afterward, I found my way to the local ward, where I came to know Saints who had no university connection.

18. In addition to the annual meetings of the Mormon History Association and, after 1979, annual Sunstone symposia in Salt Lake City, members of this community came together in sessions held in connection with the meetings of professional historical associations (the American Historical Association, the Organization of American Historians, and, most especially, the Western History Association) and in regional Sunstone symposia.

19. The difficulty of rendering exact statistics that would reveal the extent to which the church was increasingly becoming a convert as opposed to a "birthright" church is described in Tim B. Heaton's excellent article "Vital Statistics: Sources of Population Change," in *Encyclopedia of Mormonism*, 5 vols., ed. Daniel H. Ludlow (New York: Macmillan, 1992), 4:1518–37.

20. Before dividing the church into areas and calling local leaders as area presidents were instituted, one critical way this oversight was exercised was that when local stake conferences were held—no matter what the location—one of the church's general authorities presided.

21. In his 1978 presidential address to the Mormon History Association, Douglas D. Alder suggested a five-category typology of Mormon wards that described the emerging variety in types of wards present in the church.

22. In 1971, the various publications of the auxiliaries were suspended, and three new magazines to serve the children, youth, and adults of the church were established: the *Friend*, the *New Era*, and the *Ensign*.

23. See Frank O. May Jr., "Correlation of the Church, Administration," in *Encyclopedia of Mormonism*, ed. Ludlow, 1:323–25.

24. This "fire-storm" centered on the university's decision not to grant continuing status to assistant professors in the English department, but it broke out in other areas at other times as well. Eventually, the university would be placed on the list of censured institutions maintained by the American Association of University Professors.

25. *Exponent II* is not included in this list because its intended audience (Mormon women) extends far beyond the boundaries of the LDS intellectual community. It was, however, established by members of that community and continues to be edited by women who are, in every sense of the word, Mormon intellectuals.

26. Whether the works that issued from the Historical Department during the years it was headed by Leonard Arrington should be submitted to the Correlation Depart-

ment for review was one of the bones of contention that led to the reduction of the size of the staff Arrington assembled and its eventual transfer to BYU, where it was organized as the Joseph Fielding Smith Institute of Church History. See Leonard Arrington, *Adventures of a Church Historian* (Urbana: University of Illinois Press, 1998), especially chapter 10.

27. If the presenters give permission, their Sunstone symposia presentations are a form of publication since audiotapes are made of all symposia sessions and are available for purchase from the Sunstone Foundation.

28. This policy does not extend to publishing in the *Journal of Mormon History* and presenting papers at Mormon History Association meetings. It was not immediately put in place when *Dialogue* and *Sunstone* were first published. The early issues of these periodicals include many things that were written by the members of the BYU faculty as well as by CES staff members and Saints who work in the church museum, libraries, archives, and so on.

29. Disagreement itself is not apostasy. But Saints who make public their disagreement with church doctrine and the propriety of the actions of church authorities, thereby, presumably, seeking to convince others that their opinion is the correct one, are placing their church membership in jeopardy.

30. Dallin H. Oaks, "Alternate Voices," *Ensign* 19 (May 1989): 27–30. A version of this warning against alternative voices has been incorporated in the church's *General Handbook of Instructions: Book 2, Priesthood and Auxiliary Leaders* (Salt Lake City: Church of Jesus Christ of Latter-day Saints, 1998), 326–27.

31. The other two groups identified in this address were the feminists and the gays and lesbians. The All-Church Coordinating Council is made up of department heads and senior personnel in the LDS Church Office Building in Salt Lake City, the structure that, when this address was given, housed the church bureaucracy. The copy of this May 18, 1993, address is in the stacks of the LDS Church Library. Extensive quotes from this address (perhaps from a pirated copy) were reported in "Elder Packer Names Gays/Lesbians, Feminists, and 'So-called' Scholars Three Main Dangers," in the News section of *Sunstone* 16 (November 1993): 74–75 (quotation on 74).

32. Ibid., 74.

33. I am much indebted in this description of Tönnies's influential theoretical insights to Thomas Bender, *Community and Social Change in America* (1978; reprint, Baltimore: Johns Hopkins University Press, 1982), 17–28.

34. Ferdinand Tönnies, *Community and Society,* trans. Charles P. Loomis (New York: Harper, 1963), 33, as quoted in Bender, *Community and Social Change in America,* 17.

35. Benedict Richard O'Gorman Anderson, *Imagined Communities: Reflections on the Origin and Spread of Nationalism,* rev. and enl. ed. (London and New York: Verso, 1991). Verso is the imprint of New Left Books, which first published this work in 1983.

36. Armand L. Mauss, "Twins of the Times: *Dialogue* and the Race Issue for Mormons," in *Neither White nor Black,* ed. Mauss and Bush, 1–6; Stewart, *Mormonism and the Negro;* Lester E. Bush, "Mormonism's Negro Doctrine: An Historical Overview," in *Neither White nor Black,* ed. Mauss and Bush, 53–97. The evidence to support my assertion comes from an examination of the *Dialogue* archival record in the Special Collections Division of the Marriott Library at the University of Utah and

from an analysis of the content of the issues from the first decade of this periodical's existence.

37. McMurrin repeated his warning many times, but it was perhaps most clearly and precisely stated in an interview with Blake Ostler, which was first published in the January 11, 1983, issue of the *Seventh East Press*, an independent student newspaper at BYU, and afterward reprinted as "An Interview with Sterling McMurrin," *Dialogue* 17 (Spring 1984): 18–43. McMurrin's work, *The Theological Foundations of the Mormon Religion* (Salt Lake City: University of Utah Press, 1965), is still regarded by many as the standard work on this topic.

38. The founders of the John Whitmer Historical Association were nearly all active members of the RLDS Church.

39. See Ronald W. Walker, *Wayward Saints: The Godbeites and Brigham Young* (Urbana: University of Illinois Press, 1998).

40. The intellectual community's interest in history may also be explained by the absence among them of a large number of philosophers and theologians. The University of Utah's Sterling McMurrin, whose book on Mormon theology is the one most non-Mormon scholars turn to, and Truman Madsen, who was named to the prestigious Evans chair in theology at BYU, joined their putative ranks. But as this community was becoming a self-conscious enclave within Mormonism in the 1960s, the LDS Church could count few classically trained theologians among its active members. Paul Edwards, one of the leaders of the RLDS intellectual community, was trained in philosophy at Edinburgh University, but if his interest is measured by his major publications, history appears to have been the matter of greatest concern to him.

41. The editor of this collection, which carries the subtitle *Women in Early Utah*, was Claudia L. Bushman. It was initially published in 1976 in Cambridge by Emmeline Press Limited, whose name evoked the memory of Emmeline B. Wells, who for thirty-five years was editor of the *Woman's Exponent*, a publication owned and published by Latter-day Saint women. This work is currently available in a new edition from the Utah State University Press.

42. I tried to assess the implications of publishing histories that are interpretations of the past and reprinting historical documents in "*Exponent II*: Mormonism's Stealth Alternative," *Exponent II*, 25th Anniversary Issue (Summer 1999): 29–33.

43. Brigham Madsen, "The Education of a BYU Professor," *Dialogue* 28 (Spring 1995): 36. In this article, Madsen explained, "During my years at BYU I became a member of the 'Swearing Elders,' an informal organization founded by Sterling McMurrin and William Mulder, both on the faculty of the University of Utah. The purpose of the group of about forty men was to meet monthly to listen to speakers who had something of interest to say about Mormonism or the Mormon church. Several other BYU faculty were participants and traveled each month to the University of Utah where the meetings were held." See also Thomas A. Blakely, "The Swearing Elders: The First Generation of Modern Mormon Intellectuals," *Sunstone* 10 (January 1986): 8–13; and Richard Poll, "The Swearing Elders: Some Reflections," *Sunstone* 10 (January 1986): 14–16.

INDEX

Jan Shipps is professor emeritus of religious studies and history at Indiana University–Purdue University, Indianapolis. She also holds the title of senior research associate at the university's Polis Center and is a columnist for Beliefnet.com. She has a B.S. from Utah State University and an M.A. and Ph.D. from the University of Colorado. She is coeditor of *The Journals of William E. McLellin* and the author of *Mormonism: The Story of a New Religious Tradition* and some fifty articles and reviews on topics related to the Latter-day Saints, their religion, and their history.

Typeset in 10.5/13 Minion
with Minion display
Designed by Paula Newcomb
Composed by Jim Proefrock
at the University of Illinois Press
Manufactured by Thomson-Shore, Inc.

University of Illinois Press
1325 South Oak Street
Champaign, IL 61820-6903
www.press.uillinois.edu